THE TELEWORK HANDBOOK

New ways of working in the information society

Sponsored by:

Hewlett Packard

Part funded by Compris Adapt, a European Social Fund initiative

You bought the book... now join the club

Simply ring 0800 616008 or check out **www.tca.org.uk** to arrange payment details and we will send you membership information about the Telecottage Association – you are entitled to six months free membership through your purchase of this book.

the workers to the central workplace just as was done on the farms three centuries ago. We talk about the benefits of 'location-independent' work yet we struggle with massive traffic problems and sprawling suburbs. And we continue to be faced with the scepticism (at best) or entrenched resistance (at worst) of mid-level managers.

Of all those points, the most perplexing for me these days is that we face problems like tight labour markets yet many organisations limit their ability to solve those problems because they remain steadfast in their resistance to or outright rejection of telework. All I can say is that the split we are starting to see between the organisations that 'get it' – that is, understand the business benefits of well-planned, well-managed telework programs – and those that don't will only become larger. Instead of seeing a fairly uniform telework uptake rate across all organisations, as was once presumed to be the likely future, we will see a widening gulf between the organizational haves and have-nots.

That observation gives me the perfect opportunity to emphasise the role of a book like this one. This third edition does the near-impossible: it improves on the second edition, which I had thought was rather outstanding. Not content to leave well enough alone, Alan and his colleagues have updated and upgraded it – and unlike software updates and upgrades, this 'new and improved' edition actually is. Organisations that want to be on the forward-thinking side of that telework divide will be well served to rely on this book.

Having been involved in this field since 1982, and having seen dozens and dozens of telework/telecommuting manuals, books and guides, I think I am qualified to separate the substance from the hot air. The book you are holding is as substantial, practical, and useful as they come. It is not only thorough and comprehensive, but it is also highly readable and a source of the occasional chuckle due to the excellent cartoons.

More important, it is balanced: it is not a sales pitch for telework in its various forms, but a resource that helps you understand the pros and cons in depth and then enables you to decide on the appropriate course of action. As such, it is a refreshing departure from many of the similar guides on the market these days.

Among the countless tips and checklists to guide you to success, be sure you don't miss Alan's 'seven survival tips for stress-free teleworking' that appear on page 106. Anyone who starts his list of tips with an admonition about software installation on Mondays is tops in my book – and this book is tops in the field of telework.

We move into this decade and century with the energy and enthusiasm to create a world and workplaces that are better, more efficient, more humane, and able to take advantage of the plethora of technology we have without being victims of all those wonderful tools. Telework is a big part of this process, and an increasingly central one at that. I continue to be enthusiastic about telework and, perhaps oddly, increasingly concerned that we have created our own monster. The good news about today's mobile-office technologies is that we can work just about anytime and anywhere – and the bad news is the same.

That's why as I move ahead with telework I also move in new directions dealing with our need to re-establish the boundaries that used to clearly exist between work and the rest of our lives. This is an imperative not only for teleworkers but for almost anyone who does or can do 'office work' away from the 'office'. My book *TURN IT OFF: Controlling the Anytime–Anywhere Office* (to be published in March 2001) will touch on these issues, as will my new website **www.turnitoff.com**. Alan Denbigh and I often trade barbs about how much we both need to read that book as we exchange emails at odd hours and on weekends and holidays. Such is the fate of telework advocates, but in Alan's case at least, his long hours have paid off handsomely with this book.

Gil Gordon
Email: gilgordon99@cs.com

Contents

Introduction i
Acknowledgements. ii
Chapter 1: Overview 1
Chapter 2: Company teleworking 39
Chapter 3: Survival guide 80
Chapter 4: Getting work 117
Chapter 5: Ideas for telebusinesses 148
Chapter 6: Centres for teleworking 164
Chapter 7: Staying safe and legal. 195
Chapter 8: Quality for teleworkers 231
Chapter 9: Disability and teleworking. 251
Chapter 10: Email and the Internet 266
Chapter 11: Teleworking equipment 287
Chapter 12: Training for teleworkers 317
Sponsors. 341
Index: 345

Disclaimer

While every effort is taken to ensure the accuracy of the information given in this book, no liability can be accepted by the author or publishers for any loss, damage or injury caused by errors in, or omissions from, the information given. Readers are expected to check all essential information and to seek professional or expert advice as appropriate to specific circumstances.

Introduction

by Alan Denbigh, Executive Director of the TCA

Every year the TCA receives thousands of enquiries about the subject of telework, remote working or (inevitably!) e-work. We provide answers at several levels of detail and in researching these issues enhance our own knowledge which we can then share with you in this book. We do it simply because we believe that telework has so much to offer individuals, business and even the planet that we want to see more of it happening!

We started out from a belief that people who are excluded from the workforce either by distance, caring responsibilities or a disability could be re-enfranchised by using the new technology the world is rapidly absorbing. And we believe that what is good for the individual in this case is also good for the corporate.

On a personal note I believe that work should not be impeded by convention – we are there to do a job of work, not to be somewhere filling up the hours. We should work to our strengths and not have to fight a system in order to have a life and support our families. The rest of your life is too important!

So to help you put more balance into your life or business, use our guide. It is a reference guide so we never thought that you would read it from cover to cover, although some have and have been complimentary about the experience.

Lastly, thanks to all who have contributed to this book. It was written entirely through teleworking collaboration and relies on research carried out by telephone or over the Internet. My co-author Imogen Bertin carried out all her work from Ireland, and her enthusiasm, knowledge and writing skills have greatly enhanced the book.

More information about the TCA can be found at **www.tca.org.uk**.

Acknowledgements

We are very grateful to our sponsors – you can read more about them in the sponsorship pages at the end of the book.

Information and assistance in preparing this handbook has been received from many different sources and in many cases from information available over the Internet. The TCA wishes to thank all those who have contributed their time and knowledge, in particular:

Joanna Slevin, Lloyds TSB Bank plc
Andrew Bibby, journalist
Kitty de Bruin, Netherlands Telework Association
Stephen Cawley, Assistant Editor, PC Live, Dublin
Patrick Cotter, Waterstones Bookshop, Cork
Ashley Dobbs, former Chair of the TCA
Mark Dyer, accountant
Denise Cox, email marketing consultant
Michael Gaffney, Nortel
Brian Goggin, Wordwrights
Gil Gordon, Gil Gordon Associates
Paul Healy, Small Planet, Dublin
Brian Higton, Cygnet Solutions
Chris Hudson, Communications Workers' Union of Ireland
Ursula Huws, Analytica
Ian Jackson, BT Workstyles
Stephen Jupp
Malcolm Lake, Effective Quality Management
Deborah Lowe, co-editor of *Teleworker* – the journal of the TCA
Sheila McCaffrey, KITE Telecottage and chairperson, TCA
Neil Mclocklin, BT Workstyles
Bill and Cathy Murray, Small World Connections
Patrizio di Nicola, Italian Telework Association
Brian O'Kane, Oaktree Press
Barnaby Page, former co-editor of *Teleworker*, the journal of the TCA
Stephen Simmons, Cornix
Peter Skyte, MSF Union
Rhys Taylor, ACRE
Peter Thomson and Chris Ridgewell, VIP Consultants
Nicole Turbe-Suetens, French Telework Association
Richard Warren, SteppingStones
Colin Wheeler, cartoonist
The staff of the WREN Telecottage
Louis Wustemann, editor, *Flexible Working* magazine.

Overview

What is teleworking?

Teleworking is working at a distance from the people who pay you, either at home, on the road, or at a locally-based centre. Teleworkers use email, phone and fax to keep in touch with their employers or customers.

Teleworking is part of a range of flexible work practices which are becoming widespread and also include flexitime, part-time working, job sharing and career breaks.

Various terms are used to describe the new forms of work, including teleworking (the catch-all term for workers who use tele-technology), telecommuting (often used to describe those who work for one employer and spend only part of their time working from home), distance working, flexible working, flexiplace working and remote working. The terms 'telecommuting' and 'teleworking' are attributed to US academic and consultant Jack Nilles, who in 1973 worked on the first documented pilot telecommuting project with an insurance company.

Computerworld, the American computer magazine, publishes an annual "100 best places to work in IT" survey. In June 1999 the survey found that of the 100, 97% offer flexitime, 89% offer telecommuting and 69% offer a fitness centre. During the same month, as US telecommuting consultant Gil Gordon points out on his website (**www.gilgordon.com**), the HR consultants Hewitt Associates published their annual survey of 1,020 general employers and found that 79% are offering flexitime, 66% part-time employment, 40% job sharing and 35% telecommuting.

The old saying is that when America sneezes, Europe catches a cold. The best European employers, particularly in the high-tech and IT sectors, are looking seriously at the teleworking option as we move into the new millennium and a predicted IT skills shortage. The European Foundation for the Improvement of Living and Working Conditions sponsored a 1998 survey of 30,000 Europeans about their preferred working conditions. They found that:

- Nine percent of people work mainly at home. A further 23% do some of their paid work at home. But to meet people's preferences these figures would nearly need to double;
- One in four people (25%) would like to be self-employed but in reality only 13% are;
- Nearly one-third (30%) of people would like to work part-time (less than 30 hours a week) but in reality only one in five (20%) work part-time;
- Most people would prefer a working week of 34 hours but in reality the average working week is 39 hours.

Europeans are looking for less hours spent at work, autonomy, self employment and the flexibility to work from home. In Britain the government has set up a website to look at work-life balance issues (**www.dfee.gov.uk/work-lifebalance**), and a £1.5m Challenge Fund to help employers explore work-life balance policies.

At the same time, a report by IDC for Microsoft, *Europe's growing IT skills crisis,* estimates that the skills shortage in Western Europe will reach 1.7 million IT professionals by 2003, amounting to about 13% of the total demand. Datamonitor estimate that this will cost the European economies over €100 billion a year for the foreseeable future. The IDC report is based on 12,000 interviews with IS managers, surveys of recruitment agencies and factors in reskilling of workers for IT from other sectors such as manufacturing. IDC predicts that the shortage will be worst in 2000 and 2001 but will ease slightly from 2001 to 2003 as companies address the skills gaps by adopting the Application Service Provider (ASP) model where computer software is accessed from centrally managed resources over the web, cutting down to some extent the need for companies to maintain their own IT support staff. IDC points out that the UK is particularly affected due to its dependence on distributed IT environments demanding greater IT resources and skills.

Teleworking is one possible way for companies and self-employed people to manage the stressful changes in traffic congestion, property costs, skill shortages, and family duties affecting working life.

Background and history

In the 1970s era of oil crises, the concept of moving the work instead of the gas-guzzling commuter made sense. But the idea took time to catch on because a number of factors had to be in place for it to work – a good reason to do it, cheap and reliable data communications and organisations that were willing to change the way they worked.

What UK managers want

A June 1998 *Management Today* survey identified the following top 10 desires among 5,000 of its readers, who were asked "if you could change just one thing to improve the balance between your work and personal life what would it be?"

1. Work fewer hours
2. Change company culture
3. Work flexible hours
4. Reduce commuting or avoid it
5. Work from home
6. Change jobs or relocate
7. More staff
8. Earn more
9. Retire
10. Reduce stress

The accompanying article noted that the average UK worker puts in 46 hours a week compared to 40 hours for French and German workers, yet GDP per hour, regarded as the best measure of labour productivity overall is about 25-30% higher in France and Germany than in the UK.

Teleworkers help AA and Prudential provide flexible response

The AA takes calls from motorists requiring service assistance. Details of the calls and motorists' locations have to be entered into computers by call centre workers. Since 1997, some of this work has been done from people's homes.

The staff working from home have ISDN lines and PC workstations provided by the AA, connected to the central automated call distribution system which routes incoming calls to teleworkers. All standard call centre functions are available, including the facility for supervisors to listen in on calls and check performance.

The AA's interest in teleworking began with a recruitment problem. Its Leeds call centre was suffering competition from neighbouring centres for a limited number of workers in the "call centre capital" of Europe. They also wanted to make their shift times more flexible because most calls happen in two peaks – 7.30 am to 11 am and 4.30 pm to 8.30 pm – corresponding to the rush hours. Split shifts are a lot easier to manage for staff who don't have to travel to work. The teleworkers can also provide backup staff temporarily available to manage peaks in demand.

A pilot of nine people, which included four registered disabled teleworkers, was so successful that the AA decided to close its Leeds call centre and move the staff entirely to teleworking. However this expansion has been delayed by a recent takeover and management changes at the AA. In the interim, sixty home-based teleworkers are currently "long-lined" into a centre in Edinburgh.

A trial of five distributed call centre agents by the Prudential insurance company has shown substantial productivity increases of around 20%. Call centre communications manager Shaun Martin said the increase was immediately visible: "Agents are not disturbed because they are away from the main call centre". The trial involves direct sales of PEPs and pension products. Technology has been provided by Special Telephone Systems, and includes either ISDN or Kilostream connections for all agents utilising a satellite working feature on its Supercall 2000 ACD device.

The Pru has found flexibility in summoning up extra capacity using teleworkers to be particularly valuable. Over Christmas they were able to get an extra teleworker online in a few minutes, instead of the more normal four-hour delay during which customers would have otherwise heard a recorded announcement. Shaun Martin believes his project is unusual because it is set up as an external extension of the office rather than a remote operation. Agents visit the office regularly to keep in close touch with colleagues.

The recessions of the late 1980s and early 1990s dampened economic activity and removed one of the main drivers for teleworking – the need to expand organisations without crippling increases in overheads. In the UK and the US unrealised predictions were made for the potential of telework.

In 1985, the Institute for the Future forecasted that 40% of US employees would be teleworkers by the year 2000. In fact the figure is about 9% according to a recent survey of 1000 adult US workers by the John J Heidrich Centre for Workforce Development.

In 1994 the European Union placed the adoption of telework at the top of the Bangemann Report list of actions to make Europe more competitive. The EU set a target of 10 million teleworkers in Europe by the year 2000. Last year, against the background of an explosion in Internet use, the European Commission's *Telework 99* report estimated there are over 8 million teleworkers in Europe. The Commission's ECaTT project separately estimated the figure at 9 million in autumn 1999 (**www.ecatt.com**).

Reasons for implementing telework

There are a variety of drivers for adopting teleworking that fall into four main categories:

- **improved competitiveness** – large companies can keep down costs and overheads (particularly premises) and increase productivity in comparison to non-teleworking competitors. Small companies that are growing fast can expand without major capital investments;
- **better lifestyles for workers** – more flexibility, less commuting stress, and better balance between home and work lives, especially for those with caring responsibilities or disabilities, leading to less absenteeism and greater staff retention;
- **environmental considerations** – reduced commuting may mean less pollution, less energy usage, better use of office space and less traffic congestion;
- **improved, cheaper technologies** – developments in the use of ADSL, ISDN, and the Internet as well as the development of hotdesking systems for mobile workers are making teleworking a practical alternative.

The Small World Connections/*Flexible Working* magazine 1997 corporate teleworking survey found that 35% of companies say they introduced teleworking at the request of staff. Around 30% do so to reduce office costs, and another 30% to ease travel or commuting problems. Maternity, illness, office relocation and overcrowding are all cited by about 10% of companies. Very few companies reported productivity or efficiency as the initial reason for adopting teleworking, although 56% listed productivity increases as a benefit. Office cost reductions were identified by 46% of respondents as a major advantage while 45% (rising to 60% of respondents already using teleworking) felt that staff effectiveness was a major advantage.

What jobs can be teleworked?

Teleworkers work in a wide range of fields. As a general guide, all jobs that do not involve physical production, extensive face-to-face customer contact

BT sends 7,500 workers home

BT had an ambitious project to get 7,500 of its 119,000 staff working from home by March 2000. The project, Options 2000, was introduced to staff in a series of roadshows. BT offered a one-off grant of £650 to staff taking part to cover extra furniture and equipment.

Senior executives believe that as well as saving money on premises costs, Options 2000 makes workers more productive, and helps the environment by cutting down on car journeys. The initiative followed a six-month trial involving 36 workers at BT Cellnet. The trial results showed 91% of staff were satisfied with teleworking and 77% felt it had increased their productivity. Car usage dropped by a total of 86,000 miles.

It will be at least five years before the impact of the larger Options 2000 project can be fully assessed. The scheme is voluntary, aimed at administrative staff and there is a guarantee that teleworkers will be treated equally with office-based staff. Neil Mclocklin, head of BT's Workstyles consultancy group, says that the change reflects a move from supporting buildings to supporting people, and points to developments like a system to order company cars over the BT intranet as further evidence of this shift in emphasis.

or expensive specialist equipment can be teleworked. Other tasks suitable for teleworkers include those where the work can be easily measured, those that involve mental rather than physical effort, and those that do not require extensive hands-on management or a large degree of team work.

Typical teleworker categories listed in John and Celia Stanworth's *Telework: The Human Resource Implications* and by the Gee Publishing/Small World Connections 1999 survey include:

- **professionals and management specialists:** architects, accountants, management, marketing, public relations, human resources, project managers, account managers, finance, financial analysts and brokers;
- **professional support workers:** bookkeepers, translators, quality managers, proofreaders, indexers, researchers, senior administrative staff, trainers, web designers;
- **'itinerant' field workers:** company representatives, surveyors, quantity surveyors, engineers, inspectors, property negotiators, auditors, journalists, insurance brokers, landscape architects;
- **information technology specialists:** systems analysts, software programmers, technical support, software localisation engineers and engineers;
- **clerical support workers:** data entry staff, word processor operators, directory enquiry staff, telesales staff.

What managers think of teleworkers

The Department of Employment's 1994 *Teleworking in Britain* survey asked managers to compare teleworkers and office-based staff over a range of variables:

Attribute	Productivity	Reliability	Loyalty	Quality	Staff Turnover	Absent-eeism
Better	47.3%	25.7%	21.6%	29.7%	25.7%	31.1%
Same	20.3%	41.9%	33.8%	36.5%	23.0%	24.3%
Worse	5.4%	4.1%	6.8%	4.1%	9.5%	1.4%
Don't know	16.2%	16.2%	17.6%	16.2%	16.2%	20.3%
No answer	4.1%	2.7%	4.1%	6.8%	5.4%	5.4%

Additionally many call centre tasks can be carried out by teleworkers operating at a distance from the main call centre, such as telesales, sales support, technical support, telemarketing and telereservations.

Teleworking advantages

(Adapted from *A Manager's Guide to Teleworking* and *TeleFutures*)

Employer teleworking advantages

■ **greater productivity**

Productivity gains quoted in published research due to teleworking range from 10–60%. The improvements can be attributed to:

– **reduction of distractions**: office gossip, interruptions of colleagues, noise in open-plan offices or call centres, *etc.*;

– **reduced commuting**: staff can be available for work at a given time irrespective of traffic conditions, breakdowns, *etc.*;

– better coverage during **severe weather**: BT's 1994 Inverness Directory Enquiries experiment which included 12 people working from home found that the teleworkers were able to provide a service even when their office-based colleagues were unable to come to the office in bad weather;

– **reduced sickness**: studies have shown that teleworkers have lower absenteeism. Lombard North Central Bank found their average sick leave halved from six days to three days per annum. Travelling to work puts up a barrier which may encourage the decision to stay away, anticipating a worsening condition. Removing the effort of strain and commuting means teleworkers may consider themselves fit to work. An improvement in their condition during the day may also mean they put in half a day's telework, but would not have turned up for work if commuting was involved. Fewer people to mingle with means fewer bugs to spread, and no central office means no sick building syndrome;

- **reduced absenteeism**: research by Joanne Pratt for the Telework America Association in 1999 suggests that when teleworkers have to take time off for family or personal obligations (health, banking, legal, car repairs, family events or emergencies), most go back to work once the event has been dealt with (which typically takes two to four hours), whereas office workers tend to take an entire day off;

- **increased flexibility:** staff working from home show greater flexibility. Teleworking may assist a company to provide a service out of hours – a rota of teleworkers could more easily provide this than getting people into a centre at times when travel might be considered unsociable or even dangerous.

■ **retaining valued staff**

Individual staff training costs can amount to tens of thousands of pounds per annum, and skills updates are estimated to take up 10–20% of managerial time, so losing valued and skilled staff is a drain on resources. If staff need to move in order to fit in with a partner's career, teleworking may provide a solution whereby the employee could continue to work for the company. Introducing teleworking may also give a company access to the skills of former staff members who have left due to early retirement, family reasons, travel difficulties and so on, thereby increasing the available skill pool and helping companies to maintain the "corporate memory".

■ **accessing a wider pool of skills, or skills only needed on occasion**

A teleworking policy allowed Helensburgh-based publishers Crossaig to trawl more widely for staff – the number of people with medical and specific technical knowledge that they need does not live within commuting distance of their office. Without a teleworking policy the company might have had to relocate, be restricted in its growth or provide extensive and costly staff training. Employees live up to 80 miles away and may visit the office only once or twice per year.

Brian Goggin of Wordwrights, based near Limerick, designs and develops courses for large organisations ranging from Aer Lingus to IMI – mostly Dublin-based – from a spare bedroom in his home. "If you are good at what you do, most companies don't care how or where you do it," he says. Goggin believes companies will streamline their organisations further and make more use of services like his. "Companies know they can hire us for a particular project without having to commit to taking us on forever."

■ **reducing office overheads or avoiding moves to larger premises**

In 1997, Hewlett Packard's Irish operation began to run out of space. General Manager Elma Murphy explains: "We looked around and found half the desks were empty half of the time – so desk sharing seemed like the way to go". Now half of the 160 staff have no dedicated deskspace, and although the major business benefit has been increased employee satisfaction, desk sharing has also allowed HP to fit 120 people into one office block which three years ago was tight for space for 60 staff. "Reasonable office space in Dublin is £20–£30 per square foot so you can do your own calculations on the savings", comments Murphy.

- **reducing the time that mobile workers spend "in the office"**
Salespeople working for IBM in the US have cut out trips to the office between calls. Using laptops and wireless modems they interrogate stock and price databases from the customer's office and print out quotations immediately. (BBC Radio 4 *In Business*, October 1995).

- **maintaining competitiveness – faster services and lower costs**
At Instant Search, a small teleworking business based in Lancashire, customers phone in their requests for information on companies held at Britain's Companies House. Staff take down details and credit card numbers and then perform expert online searches of the Companies House databases. The information is swiftly faxed or emailed to the customer, providing savings in time and money over paper or in-person searches made directly by the customer.

- **facilitating the management of a locally-based service**
Barclays has equipped its corporate managers with laptop computers and access to an intranet to improve speed of lending decisions and ensure that more decisions are taken on a local basis. Paul Harrison, head of mid-corporate banking, says the aim is to make managers more accessible to their customers and other professionals such as accountants. The scheme, known as "Barclays in a briefcase", has put 1,200 corporate and agricultural managers, who typically serve customers with turnovers exceeding £500,000, out where they should be – with customers. To support the managers Barclays has introduced a leading-edge intranet including a new Lending Advisor® knowledge-based package which helps the managers to make lending decisions. The package provides an up-to-date picture of the customer's financial performance enabling managers to agree financial support on the spot at customer premises. Lending Advisor® has reduced decision times by increasing the percentage of decisions taken locally from 30% three years ago to 60% today.

- **taking advantage of labour in a different locality or timezone**
Cigna Benefits Processing, based in Loughrea, Co. Galway, handles health insurance claims for the American market. The claims are posted to a PO box at JFK Airport in New York and sent by courier to Loughrea, where the Irish workforce is in constant contact with Cigna computers in the US via a leased line telephone link. The results of the claims are logged on the American computers for printout and dispatch of cheques by mail. The Loughrea location allows the US company to operate extra processing

"overnight" and has the advantage of far lower staff turnover and training overheads compared to the American operation.

In Silicon Valley, the computer workers nod off after a hard day's work as the day is dawning at the KITE telecottage near Enniskillen, Northern Ireland, run by Sheila McCaffrey. Handwritten CVs for that day's Silicon Valley job vacancies arrive by fax from San Francisco, are formatted neatly and sent back ready for immediate dispatch to clients of a job placement agency. Another recent KITE contract involves filing and preparing medical reports for a hospital in Boston. "They sometimes need us to do reports when it is the middle of the night over there and it would be hard to get anybody to do the job. We get a spoken report, put it into the computer and send it back down the line," explains Sheila.

- **facilitating relocation or disaster recovery**

When Digital's office in Basingstoke, UK, burned down, the company decided to restructure the 110 workers based there. All except 11 now telework. The remaining 11 are the core staff operating a virtual office with "hotdesking" facilities for the other workers when they need to use the office. When in the office, teleworkers pick an empty "hotdesk", plug in their laptops and notify the receptionist which telephone extension they are using. The company, since bought out by Compaq, has said it saved around £330,000 a year on premises costs.

Employee teleworking advantages

- **job satisfaction**

Teleworkers are more satisfied with their work than non-teleworkers. In 1990 Ursula Huws and others surveyed 118 teleworkers and found that they were rarely dissatisfied with their tasks, their place of work, or life as a whole. They were mildly dissatisfied with their financial situation, relations with friends and neighbours, equipment and leisure time available.

A European research study (PATRA, 1993 **www.swan.ac.uk/psychology/patra**) suggested that teleworkers can in fact suffer more stress than office-based workers, but they are happier with their lot, and the stress symptoms decline the longer a person has been teleworking. The PATRA report also noted that teleworkers suffer fewer problems, such as repetitive strain injury, probably due to their freedom to take breaks and move around when they wish. Teleworking can allow time spent in traffic jams and on crowded suburban trains to be exchanged for more leisure, greater involvement in the local community, and a better family life. Teleworking can also satisfy the desire for autonomy and escape from office politics that a number of workers express (40% cited this as a major reason for wanting to telework in Mitel's 1998 Teleworking Britain survey).

- **freeing up commuting time and expense related to office work**

According to figures the Department of Environment, Transport and the Regions issued to the TCA in April 2000, commuters take an average of 23 minutes to complete their journey to work (in London this rises to 34

minutes). The average weekly journey time therefore accounts for around five hours per week – over half a working day simply to get to work and back. The time and the cost is usually borne by the employee.

A 1998 report by the RAC, *Motors or Modems?* predicts that one in ten car journeys could be replaced by "virtual travel". The RAC believes 40% of the people who want to work from home will do so by 2007, that shopping and banking trips will be partially replaced by services delivered over the Internet, replacing 6% of trips, and that the use of videoconferencing will expand to replace 25% of business travel by 2007.

Aside from transport costs for cars or public transport season tickets, there are a number of costs which, taken together, mount up for the employee. These include: clothing (the need to maintain a business outfit including several changes of suits, shirts and shoes and the associated cleaning bills), lunch and drink costs. Those who commute often do not realise that for perhaps a 13-hour day out of the house, they are being paid for a little over half of their hours.

■ **retaining work after relocation**

Nicola Sheridan teleworks for Ireland's semi-state Voluntary Health Insurance (VHI) company from her home in Castlebar, Co. Mayo on the west coast. Nicola had 11 years' experience as a systems analyst with VHI in Dublin when she married and moved to the west. "I was lucky to have a progressive boss, who figured I could still do the job from home, put forward the idea of an "Electronic Cottage", as he called it, and arranged the whole set-up." Nicola converted some space over her garage and VHI supplied the office equipment. She visits Head Office on average once per month and her boss visits her at least once a year.

■ **balancing work and caring for families**

Pauline Knight has worked for IBM Ireland in Dublin for over 20 years and is currently involved with the company's community relations programme with schools. "I had been thinking about retiring because my husband, who is already retired, had been complaining he never saw me – but I didn't feel ready to quit despite the stresses of the job such as having to be on the road by 6.30 to be sure of getting a parking space in central Dublin. My boss suggested I try working from home and, although my first reaction was one of panic, I've spent two or three days at home since last summer. You certainly need to be self-disciplined but I do a lot of work with teams in the US and the flexibility is very useful to take account of the time difference."

Although some jobs require the teleworker's presence during a core of hours in order to communicate with colleagues, many tasks may not require this core presence, giving the teleworker the opportunity to work at times convenient to them – which can sometimes be early in the morning or late at night. Teleworking does not solve the issues of child care, but the additional flexibility and lack of wasted commuting time make it easier to deal with the problems raised. In emergencies it is possible to work with children around, particularly very young children who spend a lot of time asleep. Teleworking can help women returners to combine work with child-rearing, and allow fathers greater involvement with their children.

■ **providing jobs in remote areas**

The former Grampian Regional joined forces with IT experts Hoskyns to create a telework centre in the remote Forres region near Aberdeen in Scotland. Initially 80 jobs were created processing council tax forms and parking tickets quickly and economically. The Forres centre worked not only for local councils but also for a number of councils based in the south-east of England where wage rates are substantially higher than in Scotland. Cap Gemini (now owners of Hoskyns) has subsequently opened three further centres in the Moray Firth area of Scotland providing over 500 jobs and covering a range of services for major clients in sectors including ebusiness, financial, business administration and web-enabled call centres.

■ **providing jobs for staff with disabilities**

Cathy Cumberbeach is a trilingual PA with 20 years experience. Seven years ago a car crash and subsequent stroke left her with reduced use of one arm and a number of other health problems that preclude full-time office work. Through a scheme organised by the Disabled Drivers Association as part of an EU-funded project, Cathy has worked processing claims from her home office for an insurance company based in Dublin, which leaves her some time free to freelance her secretarial skills to other local businesses. Even if she were able to work full-time, insurance rules in Ireland which impose heavy premiums to cover workers with impaired mobility, might discourage an employer from taking her on for a conventional office job.

Teleworking disadvantages

Employer teleworking disadvantages

■ **management resistance to the change**

Many surveys have indicated the main barrier to teleworking is management attitudes. The Small World Connections/*Flexible Working* magazine 1997 corporate teleworking survey indicated that the attitude of senior managers was considered a negative factor in 60% of teleworking schemes. Other drawbacks to teleworking noted by the same survey were loss of feedback (60%), isolation (53%) and loss of control (47%). On the isolation issue, there was a split between those who were using teleworkers and those who were not. A majority of non-teleworking companies (56%) cited isolation as a problem, while only 35% of those actually using home-based teleworkers felt that it was a problem. Similarly, over half of non-teleworking companies were worried about loss of control, compared to a quarter of those using home-based teleworkers. The authors noted: "Have the attitudes of managers changed in the light of their experience of teleworking, or have organisations with favourable managers implemented teleworking earlier [than others]?"

BT, when it experimented with its teleworking directory enquiries operators in Inverness in 1994, found that middle-management resistance to change was a far greater obstacle than the technical issues which had to be overcome. Mitel's 1998 survey carried out by MORI interviewed 465 "knowledge workers" of whom 65% said teleworking was held back by a lack of company policy. Mitel also interviewed employers and found about 36% of small companies and 59% of the top 1,000 companies had some teleworking arrangements but only 4% and 9% respectively said that most or many of the workers were teleworking. Two-thirds of employers said that they do not encourage staff to telework.

The Gee Publications/Small World Connections 1999 survey found that 75% of organisations felt that managers needed educating about the potential of flexible working. Less than 30% said that flexible working strategies were actively promoted to staff. Although over 70% agreed that flexible working initiatives were an effective means of improving staff retention, less than half said that flexible working strategies would be available even on an ad-hoc basis to retain specific staff.

The same 1999 survey also found a split between the attitude to teleworking for managers and for administrative and clerical employees. The two main groups of people within organisations who were teleworking on an ad-hoc basis were managers and professional/technical staff who were perceived to be in a position of trust – their superiors were confident they would not slack when working at home. But over 80% of respondents did not offer teleworking even on an occasional basis to administrative or clerical staff, who were viewed as needing support from colleagues and essential to the effective running of the main office.

■ monitoring teleworkers' productivity

Some work tasks, such as answering directory enquiries calls, are very easily measured and unlikely to create much of an issue. Others, where work measurement is less easy, need to be piloted on a longer-term basis until comparative statistics reveal whether value for money is being achieved. In all approaches a degree of trust is involved, and managers need to bear in mind that even in the existing office-based situation where they can "see" if someone is working, there is actually no guarantee that the work is being done, or being done efficiently. Conversely, not being able to see the employee does not alter this reality. This involves a change from "eyeball" management to management by results to see whether the work done represents good value to the employer, is completed to the correct quality and is delivered on time.

■ motivation of teleworkers

Contrary to expectations, most research shows that motivation may not be a major issue. However, the results need to be treated with caution because many teleworking pilot studies have involved volunteers, anxious to make the system work, who may well have regarded working from home as a privilege that they were keen to retain. Implementing teleworking on a trial basis is advised (see Chapter 2, *Company Teleworking*). In the case of long-term teleworking employees, research by ICL/CPS found motivation and loyalty to be important corporate benefits of their teleworking scheme since staff appreciate the flexibility afforded by teleworking.

> **Nortel Networks: 15% of worldwide workforce to telework**
>
> Canadian telecoms company Nortel Networks has been running a telecommuting programme for over five years. By September 1998 the company had 4,000 teleworking employees, of whom about 1,600 are full time teleworkers who no longer have traditional offices. The company even paid workers in Richardson, Texas $200 a month for six months to switch so that office space equivalent to a four-storey building could be recovered.
>
> In Britain and Ireland about 600 staff telework. Nortel says "telecommuters have reported 10% higher employee satisfaction ratings and 20% higher productivity than the general Nortel Networks population". The company has estimated that about 20% of its employees are suitable to telework but Christoph Haas, marketing manager for 'Alternative Workspace Programmes' believes that a realistic target may be 15% by the year 2002. Nortel sells a home office solution which it also uses for its own staff, consisting of an ISDN router connecting phone, fax and PC securely.
>
> (adapted from an article in *Flexible Working*, 03/2000 by Andrew Bibby
> www.eclipse.co.uk/pens/bibby/telework.html)

- **isolation and consequent damage to corporate culture**

The BT directory enquiries project found that, although they had designed voluntary opportunities for team members to socialise, some preferred to use the time for their own hobbies or home activities. Some of the distractions that make up "normal" office life also provide an important informal communications system which is not available to teleworkers. However, where teleworkers are linked by the corporate email system, it is often used for social contact and informal communication as well as to send and deliver work. The necessity for a team to be in the same place in order to work effectively may also be overstated, as many group projects are in effect broken up into different modules carried out by individual team members. Software tools such as Microsoft Netmeeting and custom developments of Lotus Notes can enable a design team to remotely input alterations to one object viewed by all the group at their own locations.

- **security**

Security is often perceived as a risk because it is assumed that the existing arrangement is automatically more secure than a distributed working method. While there may indeed be security risks, usually the process of trialling telework will allow risks to be identified, and appropriate measures taken depending on the value and sensitivity of the information concerned (see Chapter 2, *Company Teleworking*). Since companies with a strong security culture such as Motorola and IBM can set up secure systems that allow their staff to log in from locations around the world, it's clear that security technology is not a severe obstacle. An increasing number of companies are adopting teleworking but believe that trust and confidentiality are key issues in maintaining security. Therefore teleworking trials often involve existing company employees of long standing, rather than new recruits.

Employee/self-employed teleworker disadvantages

■ **keeping 'office' and family separate**

The opposite side of the coin from management concerns about motivation is the need for teleworkers to be able to "switch off". Despite the rosy picture, working from home can cause family stress, particularly if the teleworker does not have a separate room or office for work. Typical strategies include ensuring there is a separate "home office", use of voicemail on the work telephone line to buffer after-hours calls, and clear understandings about work duties between the teleworker and their family on issues such as interruptions and working hours.

Children often find it difficult to understand that a parent can be physically present in the home, but inaccessible to them while teleworking. Partners may find irregular working hours in the evening and weekends difficult to cope with, and computers don't take kindly to pet fur.

Teleworkers sometimes find that their work is not taken seriously by family, neighbours and colleagues when they first start working at home. However, the initial scepticism usually wears off. Fletcher (1992) found that 27% of teleworkers thought that others perceived them not to be working when at home, but the same report noted that 57% of teleworkers thought that friends and neigbours looked upon their work situation favourably.

■ **reduced career prospects**

"Out of sight, out of mind" is a real fear for many teleworkers. Employed teleworkers may worry that they will receive less pay than office employees for the same work, or that they will not get the same opportunities for promotion because they may not be informed when vacancies occur (Murray, NCC, 1992). They may feel that they have continually to remind their employer that they are there, what work they are performing, that they are serious about their career and that teleworking is not a soft option. In particular, teleworkers need to ensure that their skills are kept up-to-date and that they are not left out of training opportunities. Some managers interpret a desire to work from home as a lack of commitment to corporate culture.

■ **isolation**

The disadvantage most frequently reported by teleworkers is isolation from the companionship of the workplace. The 1992 survey by Bill Murray for the National Computing Centre found that 75% of respondents cited loss of face-to-face contact as a significant problem. Solutions include ensuring regular managerial contact, supplemented with face-to-face meetings for the work team on a regular basis, and the use of available communications technologies such as Lotus Notes, email, videoconferencing and audioconferencing, involving the teleworkers in decisions and developments.

Isolation worries have been a major issue in the attitude of the trade union movement to teleworking. Telecentres (see Chapter 6) can also help to overcome isolation by providing a place for teleworkers to meet and discuss common problems. Some telecottages operate a jobs or skills agency and act as a source of work.

- **personal security**

Nomadic teleworkers (such as salesmen operating from car and home) can be vulnerable to attack, burglary and car crime due to the high value of the IT equipment and samples which they may carry with them.

- **moving to self-employment**

Sometimes a move to teleworking is accompanied by a move to self-employment. These teleworkers take on the usual risks of self-employment – they need to earn adequate income for their needs, insure themselves against sickness and incapacity, contribute to a pension fund, and buy new equipment periodically. A teleworking 'veneer' will not prop up a business idea that is fundamentally unsound, and those moving to self employment must through market research satisfy themselves on the viability of their service. Potential self-employed teleworkers should seriously consider the risks involved in giving up a conventional job, such as loss of social welfare benefits, as well as examining the many opportunities that teleworking can offer.

How many teleworkers are there?

Researchers differ regarding what constitutes teleworking, which explains much of the disparity between different estimates. However, existing estimates are still useful in sketching out trends and giving some guidance on how differing legal and social conditions affect teleworker numbers.

The LFS figures

Telework research typically involves small, unrandomised sample surveys which are often funded by organizations that wish to promote equipment or service sales and may seem open to bias. Britain is the only country in Europe which keeps large-sample figures on teleworking collected through the official Labour Force Survey (LFS). Until the introduction of the LFS survey questions there was very little "hard" data on who was teleworking where, and doing what. The LFS survey identifies people working from home, people working using home as a base, and those who spent one day working at home in the reference week of the survey question (occasional homeworkers). It then checks whether these people need both a computer and a telephone to do their work. Those who do are identified as teleworkers.

Year	1997	1998	1999
Teleworker homeworkers	225,000	256,000	255,000
Teleworkers using home as base	504,000	589,000	693,000
Occasional teleworkers	285,000	301,000	357,000

The LFS survey questions were designed by Ursula Huws and define the different categories as follows. **Teleworker homeworkers** are those who in their main job work mostly in their own home and must use a computer and a telephone to complete their work tasks. **Teleworkers using home as a base** usually work in a number of different locations, and while they are on the move. **Occasional teleworkers** are those who do not usually fall into the other two categories, but who spent at least one day doing so in the reference week when the survey was taken. In 1999, 5% of the workforce in Britain was teleworking for at least one day a week, of whom 69% were men and 31% women. Over half (55%) of the teleworkers have no dependent children (Institute of Employment Studies analysis of Labour Force Survey quoted in the Mitel report *Virtually There: the evolution of call centres*).

Huws, Jagger and O'Regan in the 1999 Institute of Employment Studies (IES) publication *Teleworking and Globalisation* use the LFS figures to identify further trends. "There are major gender differences between those who work at home, and those who work from their homes... 41% of female teleworkers work at home, compared with only 15% of their male counterparts, whilst 59% of male teleworkers compared to 33% of female teleworkers use their homes as a base but work at a variety of different locations." Female teleworkers are more likely to work part-time (47%) compared to men (12%).

They go on to show that only 2% of teleworkers are in the 16–24 age group, compared to 14% of the whole workforce. About 22% of teleworkers are in the agegroup 25–34 compared to 26% of all workers. Nearly a third (32%) are aged 35–44 compared with 25% of all workers. A further 29% are aged 45–54, compared with 22% of all workers. And 73% of teleworkers are married or living with their partners. "In each case these proportions are slightly higher than in the general population.... Given the fact that teleworkers are more likely to be married and in their thirties and forties than non-teleworkers... the difference is slight and it would be difficult to use these statistics to support an argument that teleworking results from a lifestyle choice to put family before work."

Just over half (52%) of teleworkers are employees, with 47% self-employed and 1% paid family workers. A total of 9% of teleworkers are disabled. There are high numbers of teleworkers in banking, finance, insurance and business services, and teleworkers are more likely to be in professional occupations such as managers or associate professional or technical staff. Business services accounts for 34% of teleworkers compared with 15% of the total workforce. The public sector is underrepresented with 14% of teleworkers but nearly a quarter of the total workforce.

Overall, the IES analysis concludes: "Taken together, these results suggest the propensity to be a teleworker is not associated strongly with any unusual demographic features or type of work... the occupations in which the teleworkers are over-represented appear on the whole to correlate quite logically with those with the greatest propensity to make extensive use of ICTs in combination with a certain minimal level of autonomy."

Other survey results

The European Commission's ECATT survey interviewed 7,500 people in the EU member states and 4,000 businesses in early 1999 and confirmed many of the trends in the British LFS figures.

- One-third of teleworkers are described as "occasional", working from home less than one day a week.
- Of the regular teleworkers, over half spend hours equivalent to just one day a week teleworking. Less than 7% work at home full time.
- 81% of regular (more than one day a week) teleworkers are men.
- 68% of teleworkers are in the 30–49 age group.
- Most teleworkers have high levels of education or are qualified professionals (60%), twice the figure for the labour force as a whole (30%).
- The larger the company, the more likely it is to have teleworkers. More than half of all European teleworkers are employed in companies with over 250 employees.
- Teleworking is most prevalent in the financial/business services sector (8.5%) and the distribution, transport and communications sector (5.5%).
- The differences between teleworking and non-teleworking households are small, indicating that the media stereotype of women teleworking to combine family and work duties is inaccurate.

There are considerable differences in the prevalence of teleworking in different European countries ranging from 2.8% in Spain to 16.8% in Finland.

Very occasional, or *ad hoc* teleworking is much more common than planned schemes. The 1999 Small World Connections/Gee Publishing survey of 122 organisations found that up to 85% of British financial sector companies use *ad hoc* teleworking, ranging down through 60% of IT and professional services companies and 45% of government sector organisations to a mere 29% of manufacturing companies. As with formal schemes, there is a general trend that the larger the organisation, the more likely they are to have *ad hoc* teleworking. Four main reasons are given for using *ad hoc* teleworking:

Country	ECATT Total 000s	ECATT % workforce	ECATT % supplementary	ETD '98/'99 000s	ETD % workforce	Eurostat 1998 % Internet/hh
Finland	355,000	16.77%	5.96%	220,000	10.0%	17%
Sweden	594,000	15.17%	7.19%	300,000	9.0%	40%
Netherlands	1,044,000	14.53%	6.27%	1,200,000	18.2%	20%
Denmark	280,000	10.48%	3.90%	300,000	11.6%	25%
UK	2,027,000	7.62%	2.83%	1,455,000	5.5%	11%
Germany	2,132,000	6.04%	1.61%	1,800,000	5.1%	7%
Ireland	61,000	4.44%	2.56%	58,000	7.1%	8%
Italy	720,000	3.59%	0.67%	350,000	1.7%	6%
France	635,000	2.87%	0.61%	420,000	1.8%	4%
Spain	357,000	2.81%	0.77%	120,000	0.9%	5%
Portugal	–	–	–	100,000	2.2%	3%
Luxembourg	–	–	–	–	–	14%
Belgium	–	–	–	250,000	6.2%	8%
Greece	–	–	–	50,000	1.3%	3%
Austria	–	–	–	67,000	2.0	7%
Total EU	9,009,000	6%	1.97%	6,690,000	4.5%	8%
US	–	–	–	15,700,000	12.9%	–
Japan	–	–	–	2,090,000	7.9%	–

Source: Status Report on European Telework, European Commission, 1999. Note that the definitions of "teleworker" used may vary from country to country and thus make comparisons difficult. The ECATT figures are based on telephone surveys of 7,700 people. – supplementary teleworkers are those who work less than one full day a week at home. The ETD figures are based on estimates made by national co-ordinators in each member state. The US figures come from CyberDialogue, mid-1998 telecommuter figures. The Japanese figures are estimated by Wendy Spink based on a 1996 survey. The abbreviation hh stands for household.

- To work on a particular project/deadline (98%);
- a domestic crisis (78%);
- severe weather, strikes etc. (75%);
- illness (52%)

In early 1998, BT surveyed 500 large organisations employing over 50 people in Britain and found that three-quarters of those with over 1,000 employees had some sort of flexible working arrangements in place, including work from home, on the move or based at various locations. Overall, 16% had employees teleworking on a regular basis, and this was expected to increase to 37% in five years' time. The Small World Connections/Gee Publishing survey found that 61% offered flexitime but only 14% offered home-based teleworking, although 25% expected to be offering or expanding teleworking options within three years.

Teleworking still remains a minority work practice in most companies. A survey for Ireland's Information Society Commission of 830 companies by MRBI found that although 39% reported providing remote access to their computer networks, less than 5% of companies have more than 10% of their workforce doing any teleworking at all.

Ursula Huws in her 1993 survey found companies with between 20 and 200 employees had very few teleworkers – the phenomenon was limited to very large or very small companies. A 1999 survey by Amárach Consultants in Ireland for AIB bank looked at the prevalence of teleworking in SMEs with less than 50 employees and found the same blip of increased teleworking in very small companies – those in business for less than two years and with less than five employees were most likely to be using teleworking (50% as opposed to 26–30%).

Social and economic factors

Gender

Research has been carried out to look at gender differences and teleworking. Some studies had compared high-level professional male teleworkers against low-level clerical female workers, leading to the predictable conclusion that the women fare worse than the men. To examine whether this problem was widespread, the Social Affairs directorate of the EU commissioned Ursula Huws of Analytica to carry out a survey using a properly controlled sample across Europe (*Teleworking and Gender*, 1996). Female teleworkers have tended to be concentrated in areas such as data entry, telesales or routine computer programming, whereas male teleworkers have tended to be professionals or executives involved in systems design, sales management or engineering. To avoid this distortion Huws selected her sample of 188 freelancers through a translation agency with workers in all European countries and discovered that gender differences in conditions, problems experienced and other factors were much smaller than had been previously reported.

County Council telecentre leads to major Workstyles change

Surrey County Council opened its Epsom neighbourhood telecentre in September 1997. The telecentre facilities included: free car park, open plan area for nine people (seven desks with PCs, two desks free for laptop use), a quiet room for two people (two desks with PCs), a very quiet room for one person (one desk with PC), telephones on all desks, meeting/interview room, conference room for ten people, reception/ waiting area, kitchen facilities, telecentre support officers to help and suport users, photocopier, printer, virus checker, fax machine.

An evaluation six months later showed that two-thirds of those using the £88,000 centre felt that it improved their productivity and motivation. The other third felt positively about the centre but had not used it enough to comment further. The evaluation report states: "flexible working and property rationalisation are mutually compatible and together can produce substantial benefits in increased productivity, improved service delivery and substantial cost savings."

Telecentre manager Kathryn Hitchings explains that Epsom has provided an oasis of non-interruption where staff can get work completed and make it home at a reasonable hour. In addition, the telecentre provides neutral space not "owned" by one department where communication between different departments takes off. "Recently the deputy director of social services and a bus inspector were chatting in the kitchen area about disabled access on buses – that would never have happened outside the telecentre environment". Kathryn also notes that Epsom provides unstigmatised space where staff can meet clients: "we don't have a big notice saying 'mental health' over the door, for example". There has also been an emphasis on stress reduction, with days where aromatherapy and reflexology have been available for staff from the fire and rescue centre, a project which was evaluated and found to reduce stress, improve morale and improve absenteeism.

As a result Surrey embarked on a major "Workstyles" reorganisation programme in 1998 affecting 3,400 staff in 83 buildings which will see the council instigate a single corporate headquarters, four major area offices with telecentres similar to Epsom, and 20 local offices which will provide "touchdown" space allowing staff to work closer to home for at least part of the week. Over 80% of access to council services is already made by telephone. Kathryn says "There is apprehension among staff because we will be introducing desksharing, but on the whole the change is going well." **www.surreycc.gov.uk**

In fact, although previously women teleworkers had been reported to have greater difficulty with interruptions from family, Huws found that they tended to opt for clearer boundaries and working hours than their male counterparts, suggesting that they prefer and instigate a more rigid work structure. Huws also found quite a few of the male teleworkers were "new men" who had chosen to telework in order to be with their children or partners, and to adopt a less stressful rural lifestyle. Men who made these choices were "feminised" in labour market terms, often adopting less secure and lower-paid work in exchange for their lifestyle choice. Overall, both men and women suffered from high levels of stress and insecurity. Twenty per cent worked more than 50 hours a week; 12% worked over 60 hours and 9% over 70. Huws comments: "Although the most common reason given for preferring to work from home was the desire for autonomy or 'to be my own boss', these self-employed teleworkers had little or no control over the flow of work… Periods without work could not be enjoyed as 'leisure' but were times of hardship and anxiety about where the next job might come from."

The Mitel 1998 Teleworking Britain survey indicated a significant gender split with fewer female respondents (30%) inclined to telework compared to male counterparts (40%), though other surveys have indicated that women have a more favourable attitude to teleworking than men.

Self-employment

In her 1996 study on telework and gender, Huws also found that the main reason for choosing teleworking was a desire for personal autonomy. About half of the teleworkers in Britain are self-employed compared to around 14% of the labour force as a whole (the self-employment figures for Europe are around 13% of the labour force, though much of this is made up of small farmers in southern Europe, and up to 16% in the US). The increasing proportion of self-employed teleworkers in part reflects the move for small businesses to go online, rather than any change in workplace for the self-employed, but working from home can also provide a low-overheads way to start up self-employment.

Work by the Institute of Employment Studies on the British LFS figures indicates that while the percentage of self-employed people has remained relatively stable for the past twenty years, there is a trend towards decreased incomes, with an increasing percentage of self-employed women and a reduced amount of private pension coverage. In the US, a move towards self-employed teleworking for professionals has been charted by journalist Dan Pink as the move to a "free agent nation". Pink believes skilled staff look at the collapse of the old equation where they gave their loyalty to a company in exchange for job security and vote with their feet for autonomy, believing that having five or six clients is more secure than having one employer. His articles can be found at **www.fastcompany.com**.

Overall, current changes in patterns of employment seem likely to lead to more teleworking, with trends towards more part-time workers, more service and IT-based jobs, and more women at work who require flexible employment patterns.

Labour rights

There is a general European consensus that those who work from home need protection from what Bill Walsh of MSF union describes as the "long and discreditable history of exploitation of home workers". In 1996, the International Labour Organisation issued an international convention on homeworking, providing minimum levels of protection. The convention covers employees and the "pseudo self-employed", but not the genuinely self-employed, whom the convention describes as those with "the degree of autonomy and of economic independence to be considered an independent worker under national laws, regulations or court decisions". The convention specifies the following rights:

- the homeworkers' right to establish or join organisations of their own choosing and to participate in the activities of such organisations
- protection against discrimination in employment and occupation
- protection in the field of occupational safety and health
- remuneration
- statutory social security protection
- access to training
- maternity protection

The ILO convention has already been adopted in Ireland and Finland.

The introduction of the EU's Working Time Directive, limiting weekly working hours to 48, may also increase teleworking, both through growth in the outsourcing of peak-flow work to self-employed teleworkers, and to companies introducing telework to enable their employees to carry out their duties within the 48-hour limit. However, it may have a negative effect on some teleworker's conditions because, like the ILO homeworking convention, it does not apply to the genuinely self-employed. Therefore more and more peak-flow work requiring intermittent long working hours may go to self-employed teleworkers because they fall outside the scope of the directive.

In addition, the burden of labour legislation makes it difficult for the self-employed to become employers themselves – if they employ others, as opposed to networking or subcontracting other self-employed people, then they make themselves extremely vulnerable since their employees have more rights over them than they can exert over their customers to get paid. EU legislation giving part-time workers the same employment rights as full-time workers may exacerbate this problem as the self-employed previously often started to employ by taking on part-time staff. Therefore the overall effect may be an increase in the number of self-employed people with fewer employment rights and unfavourable working conditions, leading eventually to a two-tier employment rights structure.

The 1998 second European survey on working conditions by the European Foundation for the Improvement of Living and Working Conditions shows that less than one-fifth of Europeans who are employed on a permanent, fixed-term, or temporary contract work more than 45 hours a week. The figures are much higher for self-employed people (nearly 50% working over 45 hours) and for small employers (over 70% working more than 45 hours).

Other difficulties faced by self-employed teleworkers include getting training to maintain their skills, and anomalies of social welfare systems that disadvantage those who become ill or otherwise unemployed, when compared to traditional, office-based PAYE employees. In general welfare systems have not moved with the changes in work patterns. In the UK and Ireland, if you have been self-employed for more than a year, you are only entitled to minimal, means-tested welfare benefits (unemployment assistance) should you become unemployed or suffer disability or illness. Although self-employed people in Britain pay national insurance, their contributions only cover the National Health Service and Old Age Pension, not the wider range of benefits available to PAYE employees.

The IR35 regulation recently introduced in Britain may also affect self-employment figures. Its intention is to close the taxation loophole whereby companies, particularly in the IT and engineering sectors, retain "contractors" who are actually employed by their own personal limited company. The contractor is often working onsite for one company for many months, and to all intents and purposes behaves like an employee, but the set-up allows the contractor to reduce their tax bills through paying a low salary but high dividends. At the same time the client company can access labour without the duties imposed by conventional labour legislation. The likely effect of IR35 is to make companies much more careful about buying contracted services in case the situation in retrospect is deemed an employment. It may also "export" work from Britain since, if the work is carried out by someone in another country not under direct control of the company, the engagement is very unlikely to be deemed an employment.

There has been some movement by employment agencies towards sourcing work for the self-employed and providing support services such as training and discounts on items like insurance and stationery through "affinity groups" but provision of such services remains patchy.

The "pensions gap" is a major issue for self-employed teleworkers. On the one hand, ageing populations in many countries are putting severe stress on state-run pension schemes. On the other, in Britain and Ireland particularly, many people are being encouraged to become self-employed, thus moving outside company pension systems. Few of the new self-employed workers take out suitable personal pensions, exacerbating the pensions "time bomb". Pension contributions may well have to become compulsory for the self-employed in a number of European countries.

Some trade unions have opposed the introduction of teleworking and flexible work on the grounds that it leads to casualisation, low pay and loss of employment rights, while others see it as a way forward and an opportunity to increase their membership and provide services to the new breed of workers. The CWU in Ireland and the HK Union in Denmark, have moved to organise teleworkers, including the self-employed.

Study helps Cambridgeshire Council defeat gridlock

A 1997 study funded by the Department of Transport and Cambridgeshire County Council indicated that the council could reduce time and distance travelled by its 4,000 staff by between 4 and 8% through adopting flexible working methods.

The study, carried out by HOP (Home Office Partnership), used a systematic analysis of which jobs could be affected by transport/telework substitution, and considered a range of different flexible work options for different types of job. The report estimated:

- *Commuting distances reduced by up to 1.25 million miles*
- *Commuting time to work reduced by up to 70,000 hours*
- *In-work travel reduced by up to 900,000 miles.*

Edna Murphy of HOP points out many of the changes suggested are self-financing through savings in running costs, as well as having environmental benefits in a gridlocked city like Cambridge.
www.hop.co.uk and **www.flexibility.co.uk**

The rural urban divide

In rural areas, where the decline of agriculture continues to cause growing unemployment, teleworking may support job creation without sacrificing greenfield sites to manufacturing industry. Geographically isolated areas which suffer disadvantages through increased transport costs can also benefit from teleworking jobs. However, Internet and e-commerce may also prove a threat to rural economies leading to scenarios where vans deliver books ordered from Amazon.com while local bookshops close down through lack of trade. Rural dwellers also find it harder to select, buy, maintain and get support for computers because they have fewer computer shops and are less likely to have contact with people who have good IT skills and can act as mentors for new computer users.

So, although telework undoubtedly offers opportunities to rural dwellers, it is city and suburban dwellers who are currently benefiting because of their greater skills and the higher levels of telecoms infrastructure and physical communications available in urban areas. Teleworking is clustered around the south-east of Britain, or in areas with large service-sector employment, according to Ursula Huws in her 1993 survey.

The Rural Development Commission's study on *Teleworking and Rural Development* (1996) found that current statistics were unreliable, but that, in the main, professional teleworking was concentrated in London and south-east England, while home-based work for a single employer tended to be carried out by low-paid women in peripheral areas. The report was also pessimistic about back-office functions being relocated to rural areas, suggesting that these tend to locate in industrial urban areas with large labour pools. Areas of opportunity for teleworking identified included Internet marketing of specialist rural products, tourism teleworking, information services and services aimed at rural communities.

Globalisation

The global village is still some way away for many teleworkers despite the handful of high-profile examples of rural dwellers working for European and American clients featured in newspaper articles. The 1996 *TeleFutures* survey in Ireland confirmed that although 26% of the sampled companies allow their employees to telework, and 28% want to outsource certain tasks to teleworkers within a year, 81% would prefer to use a teleworker within a radius of 25 miles who would be available for face-to-face meetings.

However, it is very much here for call centres and the software development industry. Ursula Huws is currently director of a major three-year EU-funded project looking at how the technical ability to move work around the world at the click of a mouse is affecting where work is going, when and why. The Emergence study will try to track how the changes will affect employment in Europe. Huws comments: "Incoming calls can be rerouted from an overflowing call centre in Bradford to Barbados or Brisbane. Software might be developed in Manchester, Minsk or Madras. You can get your routine typing done anywhere nimble fingers can be found pounding a keyboard linked to a modem, whether in a Kettering home, or a multi-storey block in Kuala Lumpur". Huws' team from the Institute of Employment studies will collaborate with researchers in 22 countries to look at which areas of the world are favoured, and which at risk of losing employment, what criteria control location choices, and the trends in home-based and mobile teleworking. (**www.emergence.nu**).

Environmental considerations

Teleworking is theoretically good for the environment because it reduces traffic pollution, uses less energy than conventional office work and encourages rural development. In the US, clean-air legislation, particularly in California, has led a number of large companies to introduce telecommuting programmes in order to reduce environmental damage caused by their employees commuting to work. In Holland, action by the transport ministry, concerned at the negative effect of congestion on the economy has led to over a third of companies adopting traffic demand management plans, including telework options such as staying at home and using email to avoid the morning peak.

Conventional employees with company cars and petrol benefits often use them mainly to get to work and back and may also have their parking costs paid for. While a teleworker may still need the company car, the use and associated costs are usually greatly reduced. In some cases the need for the company car may disappear and an alternative arrangement may be to the benefit of employer, employee and environment. In two-income

WWF practises what it preaches

The environmental charity World Wide Fund for Nature (WWF) has used teleworking, email and videoconferencing to save thousands of pounds on airfares while preparing its submission to CITES, the convention on endangered species.

WWF activist Stuart White explains that the organisation has 15 regional organisers covering four or five countries each. "Part of the job is providing PR, managing volunteers and creating a local profile. All the regional officers are home-based teleworkers and have been for at least 10–12 years", says Stuart, who also says the organisation has an "email culture".

"Being an environmental organisation we use telephone conferencing a lot and have videoconferencing facilities which are mainly used to link to our other offices. I even interviewed someone for a job over the video link – they were in Switzerland so they came into the Swiss WWF office and used the link." (**www.wwf.org**)

households, where one person works from home, it is likely that the need for a second car will be reduced.

A 1993 study of transport/telecommunications substitution by Horace Mitchell and Eric Trodd states that more miles on the data highway as opposed to the physical road results in:

- fossil fuels being conserved;
- emissions reduced and thus damage to the ozone layer reduced;
- revitalisation of rural areas.

Figures from the Department of Transport, Environment and the Regions give an average journey to work time in Britain of 23 minutes, rising to 34 minutes in London – which amounts to about five hours per week, but the figures do not include the 5% of the workforce who already work from home. For those who use rail or tube to get to work the figures rise to about ten hours a week spent travelling to and from work.

A methodical approach has been taken by the Norwegian Institute for Transport Economics, which assessed the possible impact of teleworking on the cities of Oslo and Bergen. Two scenarios were developed: the "supplement", where little is done to stimulate teleworking and the "substitute", where teleworking is actively promoted. The former is predicted to lead to 10% of the population homeworking for more than one day a week, while the latter will lead to around a 20% takeup. The report also analyses the potential of teleworking on the reduction of travel and of travel-based pollution and estimates a 3–6% reduction in car travel (both cities already have good public transport systems). This reduction is considered to be significant for peak-hour traffic.

In 1997 the RAC commissioned the report *Motors or Modems* and stated "the RAC believes IT will play a major and so far under-rated role in solving the congestion problem. A revolution in the way businesses use information technology is happening. 'Virtual' travel, is, in many areas of business, about to become a reality". The report predicted an optimistic scenario in which commuting travel was reduced below the levels of car traffic that would otherwise be expected by 18% in 2007, while business travel reduced by 20% and shopping travel dropped by 6% during the same period.

The 1998 report "Teleworking: the shortest route to work?" sponsored by Telecom Éireann, Telework Ireland and the Dublin Transportation Office interviewed 503 Dubliners and found that 7.6% occasionally worked from home using a computer though more than half of these spent less than a day a week at home. The report used benchmarking and data from the DTO to estimate the transport substitution effect of teleworking on the morning peak traffic and found it to be small using the DTO's "most likely" scenario: if 17% of employed people telecommuted in 2016, the peak reduction would be 5.3%. However in the shorter term (next five years), the reduction in total trip numbers predicted from telecommuting is only slightly less than that of the Luas adapted-tram system planned for Dublin.

However, Gil Gordon points out in his July 1999 edition of Telecommuting Review (**www.gilgordon.com**) that transportation trends remain stubbornly static in California, despite heavy state incentives towards telecommuting and public transport. Between 1990 and 1998, the proportion of people driving to work alone dropped by a marginal amount from 78.2% to 77.3%. Gordon quotes a presentation by Anthony Downs of the Brooking Institution who believes that traffic congestion will continue to increase because it is a result of our pursuit of objectives such as flexibility and speed which we don't want to give up. John Adams, a University College London geography professor, agrees and has predicted that the new technologies will encourage us to move more rather than less, leading to a polarised, car-dependent Britain suffering urban sprawl, increased crime, and less time spent in local communities or with neighbours and friends due to increased time spent interacting with colleagues on the Internet.

The effect that Internet home shopping may have on traffic congestion is currently uncertain. A recent RAC survey (*Report on Motoring* 2000) interviewed 1583 British motorists and found that 36% would support the growth of home shopping even if it increased the number of vans and lorries on their roads. Equal numbers (46%) thought that increased home shopping would lead to less pollution, and to more pollution.

A shift of emphasis in the travel industry may impact on telework/traffic substitution. Large companies are now awarding their travel contracts to companies like Rosenbluth who manage not just ticket purchase, but the company's travel avoidance, by checking with staff whether their trip is necessary. Rosenbluth offers alternative videoconferencing links to its corporate customers such as British Aerospace – a change brought about partly by the slashing of commission rates on air tickets and the shift towards Internet purchase which cuts out the travel agent. American Express reports that the number of companies paying a management fee to their travel agents for travel avoidance has increased from 50% to 65% in fifteen months.

The EU SAVE project, operated by EA Technology in Sheffield, estimated that working at home consumes up to 80% less energy than working in an office. Similar reductions in carbon dioxide emissions are also achieved. The project surveyed 106 Sheffield office workers and 22 homeworkers. Andrew Wright of EA Technology comments: "The average energy consumption for offices is much greater than for domestic use because it's a lot less controlled – corridors need heating, lights are left on for cleaners, PCs are left on in the evening and so on. A shift to teleworking would also create a much flatter electricity load profile – currently domestic and office supplies impose peaks on the system in their different areas, requiring additional system capacity and the starting-up of less efficient generators at peak times." Home offices are also occupied full-time, in contrast to wasted office space. Cornell University estimated that over 40% of all desks are unoccupied on any given work day, the equivalent of 3 million empty desks in the UK.

Technology trends and telework

As this book goes to press in Spring 2000 the big imponderable for the spread of teleworking is whether recent technology improvements to ACD computers will allow "virtual" or distributed call centres, using agents based at home, to take off. A survey by the TCA and the Institute of Employment Studies sponsored by Mitel and published in 1999 found that only 4% of call centres currently employ homeworkers, but 42% expect to do so in future and 44% are cautiously positive about the idea, believing that it is a good idea to use homeworkers in some cases. Most major financial services operations in Britain are believed to be considering offering this option to staff.

The call centre industry is growing rapidly. Figures vary but there are probably around 10,000 UK call centres though most are small with 10-24 agent positions. The Mitel survey found that recruitment difficulties were a major challenge for 18% of centres, with 22% reporting staff retention as a major challenge, and 19% saying the same about absenteeism. Matching workflow to the number of agents is a big problem (serious for 19%, and significant for a further 40%). Nearly one-third of call centres surveyed offer stress counselling or psychological counselling to their staff due to the stressful nature of the job.

However, the call centre managers surveyed saw barriers to homeworking due to the strong hands-on management tradition in the sector, worries about data security and fraud and about how to deliver training and team-building exercises to teleworkers. Informal training and consultation with other staff on unusual calls were also seen as being restricted for homeworkers.

The shift of call centre work towards higher skill areas in Europe, such as the establishment of shared services centres where additional administrative, distribution and accountancy work is carried out, may also lead to more jobs offering telework as an option, due to requirements to recruit and retain skilled staff. Many call centres now use "skills based routing" to automatically send calls to the available agent with the most appropriate language and technical skills to answer a call, irrespective of the location of that agent.

The other area of technology change likely to strongly affect teleworking is the rapid spread of ecommerce which is predicted to have major effects on the size, structure and location of many companies, as well as providing many unexpected opportunities for business startup that are often suited to teleworking, such as answering customer service or technical support queries originating from ecommerce websites.

PCs get mobile and march through the home

Market Research group Romtec (**www.romtec.co.uk**) reported in its March 2000 review that the market value of retail notebook computers has increased by 160% in a year – notebooks now account for 11% of retail PCs sold and 28% of machines sold through business channels. Romtec also noted the widening of the mobile market, with an increasing mix of sub-notebooks, handheld and palmtop devices available. The spread of mobile working, desksharing and hotdesking in companies is also leading IT managers to consider replacing desktop PCs with notebooks for many applications. Prices for desktop PCs have now been declining for over two years, making home PCs considerably more affordable.

Irish consultancy Amárach (**www.amarach.com**) reported at the end of 1999 that 47% of British adults now have a PC in their home, compared to 36% in Ireland, but lagging considerably behind the US (66%) with Canada even further behind (68%). Amárach points out that home PC usage has a crucial effect on usage of the Internet. In the US and Canada, home Internet users make up well over 90% of Internet users. The equivalent figures for the UK are 72%, and for Ireland 53%, though these figures are rapidly increasing. Home Internet access via TV set top boxes is also being introduced though the success of PC/TV convergence is currently uncertain – as Apple's Steve Job points out "You go to your TV when you want to turn your brain off. You got to your computer when you want to turn your brain on." The introduction of "free" Internet service providers is also continuing to have a strong effect on the spread of Internet usage.

Computer magazines are currently featuring articles predicting that multiple computers, perhaps connected on wireless networks, will become a feature of the home, and that the new Bluetooth protocol to allow a variety of computerised devices to communicate at a distance will lead to heavily "wired" homes. Such developments are bound to increase the amount of computer-based work done at home. Developments in the business market, such as the growth in application service providers who will "rent" up-to-date software to clients over the Internet, are also likely to reduce the current support costs for companies of setting up home-based teleworkers.

High-speed Internet access and VOIP

Europe is gradually following in the steps of the US and moving towards broadband communications (broadband is the term for data communications where speeds exceed 2 Mbit/s). ISDN, which is a narrowband technology providing speeds of 128 kbs, is already widely available and used by teleworkers, but new technologies such as cable modems and ADSL are just starting to roll out. ADSL offers the possibility of speeds up to 1000 times faster than current standard modems, but it is likely to be quite highly priced and, as with ISDN, is only available within about 4 km of the nearest ADSL-capable exchange, so a re-run of the recent sagas which teleworkers have encountered in obtaining ISDN service in rural areas seems all too likely.

In urban areas of the UK and Ireland true competition to the home is beginning to be available with the roll-out of cable Internet access. Average cable modem speeds are around 512 kbs but speeds slow when network usage is high. Access to low-cost, high-speed Internet access from homes will lower cost barriers to teleworking and provide new opportunities for work applications in the ecommerce sector. In addition, there is considerable interest in the spread of Internet telephony (aka voice over IP or VOIP) as this could also reduce telephony costs considerably, although quality is still not as good as for standard telephone lines.

Next generation mobiles

The area of greatest change for teleworkers over the next few years is likely to be mobile data services. It is already possible to use small palmtop or handheld computers with GSM modems to send and receive email or browse the web, and every teenager now knows how to send SMS text messages over mobiles. The current fad is wireless access protocol (WAP) phones which provide access to "cut-down" Internet content including entertainment information services, bank balance enquiries, and even cheap airline tickets. However, just around the corner is GPRS, a faster mobile data technology (115 kbs), closely followed by the third generation of mobile data services, UMTS (384 kbs), which should be able to provide mobile devices with high-quality sound and miniature videophones.

The proliferation of mobile devices is likely to prompt a move towards personal "follow me" numbers which can reach a teleworker in the office, at a hotdesk, at home or on the move. Already **www.yac.com** is offering a "free" service where your personal number can also be used to send voicemails and faxes to your email address when you are out of contact.

As more and more companies move beyond occasional homeworking to to desksharing schemes, technology solutions for highly mobile workers will continue to improve. Already many PABX manufacturers offer products where all extension numbers are "programmable" – you just pick up the nearest phone, key in your PIN number and your calls come through to you. Company intranets are increasingly used to provide facilities such as information on teleworking schemes, and booking systems for facilities like workstations or meeting rooms.

Getting the right support – an unsolved problem

Many teleworkers, experienced and novice alike, require remote technical support for their equipment. The plethora of add-on devices which now accompany the basic PC multiplies the likelihood of problems. Most people either rely on their company IT department or whoever they bought their computer from – very frustrating when your system has crashed and a deadline is imminent or when the software company and the hardware company blame each other as you tear out your hair in front of a dead machine. Although some computer manufacturers offer good post-sales technical support, and some specialist companies are now offering premium rate telephone helplines, there has been no major progress in providing adequate technical support over the past three years and it remains a major issue. Whether a move towards application service provision (ASP) over the web will plug the gap remains to be seen.

Training: reducing the overheads

Methods of training delivery are changing rapidly. Many companies are moving towards providing much of their IT-related training through Internet-delivered open-learning. Major companies are developing their own online "universities", while the widely-recognised Microsoft training qualifications are also available in self-learning formats for individuals. Both Microsoft and the groups behind the European Computer Driving Licence IT literacy qualification have also pioneered online exams which provide immediate pass/fail results and where the questions asked can be varied to focus on areas where the candidate appears weak.

As telework practices spread, and the need for constant updating of software and other work skills increases, the days of conventional courses involving travel to a training centre may be numbered, on cost and convenience grounds alone. However, instructor-led courses are still vital for some subjects and remain popular with students – the best courses combine different methods of delivery as appropriate.

The changes in training also provide two direct opportunities for telework. Firstly, the preparation and conversion of materials for open and distance learning is a sector that is reasonably open to teleworking in order to source the skills needed. Secondly, the widespread introduction of videoconferencing into colleges and training organisations offers opportunities for specialists in many areas to be paid for imparting their knowledge without having to travel unnecessarily. Interactivity and quality in videoconferencing have shown marked improvements in recent years.

So what's the conclusion?

While there are many gaps in the data and research available on teleworking, enough progress has been made in recent years for three things to be certain:

- teleworking continues to spread as a trend, driven by technology improvements, skill shortages, office property costs, desires for work-life balance and commuting pressures;
- most people who telework like it;
- almost all pieces of research into telework should be treated with suspicion unless you have access to details of the questions asked and survey samples used.

Much of the research to date has been funded, designed or driven by companies which sell teleworking technology or have a vested interest in presenting teleworking in a positive light. Base your actions on your own research, trials and experiences – it's your life, your family and your money.

Bibliography

Each chapter has a separate bibliography and contacts list. Because of the fast-changing nature of teleworking, the bibliographies are arranged in reverse date order, and subordered by alphabetical title. Prices are omitted due to the difficulty of maintaining accurate price information updates.

Periodicals

Flexibility
Editors: Edna Murphy, Andy Lake
Source: Home Office Partnership (HOP), Jeffreys Building, St John's Innovation Park, Cambridge
Comment: Periodical available on website www.hop.co.uk

Flexible Working
Source: The Eclipse Group, 18-20 Highbury Place, London, N5 1QP
Tel: 020 7354 5858 Ref: ISSN 1360-9505.
Comment: Periodical covering teleworking with other flexible working issues. Web-based subscription to online version available at www.irseclipse.co.uk/publications/flexi.html

European Journal of Teleworking
Source: Addico Cornix Publications, 64 Morrab Road, Penzance, TR18 2QT
Tel and fax: 01736 334702.

Telecommuting Review
Editor: Gil Gordon
Source: Gil Gordon Associates, 11 Donner Crt, Monmouth Jn, New Jersey, USA
www.gilgordon.com
Comment: US web-based publication covering a wide range of related topics

Telecommuting Magazine
Editor: Melissa Murphy
Source: www.telecommutemagazine.com

Telewerken
Source: Overkleeft Uitgeverij BV, Brinkpoortstraat 38, 7411 HS Deventer, Netherlands
Tel: +31 570 611044 Fax: +31 570 612042 Email: kene@wxs.nl
Comment: Dutch teleworking magazine

Teleworker Magazine
Editor: Alan Denbigh Tel: 01453 834874 Fax: 01453 836174
Email: teleworker@compuserve.com
Source: TCA Tel: 0800 616008 or 01203 696986 Fax: 01203 696538
Web: www.tca.org.uk
Comment: Bi-monthly magazine for TCA members

Publications

Europe's Growing IT Skills Crisis *Date:* 2000
Authors: Andrew Milroy and Puni Rajah of IDC for Microsoft
Source: Microsoft or IDC websites.

Business 2010 *Date:* 2000
Authors: Amarach Consultants for Allied Irish Bank
Source: www.aib.ie/roi/business/businessbanking.asp

**Nothing but Net: American Workers
and the Information Economy** *Date:* 2000
Authors: John J. Heidrich Centre for Workforce Development,
Rutgers University and Centre for Survey Research and Analysis,
University of Connecticut

The Social Implications of Hypermobility *Date:* 2000
Author: Professor John Adams, University College London
Source: Prospect Magazine
www.prospect-magazine.co.uk/highlights/hypermobility/index.html – or full
research at www.oecd.org/env/docs/epocppct993.pdf

Teleworking and Globalisation *Date:* 1999
Authors: Ursula Huws, Nick Jagger and Siobhan O'Regan
Source: Institute of Employment Studies, Mantell Building, Falmer, Brighton BN1 9RF
Tel: 01273 686751 Web: www.employment-studies.co.uk

Teleworking Directory *Date:* 1999
Authors: Monica Blake et al
Source: Turpin Distribution Services Ltd Tel: 01462 672555 Email: turpin@rsc.org
Comment: Subdivided into books, journals, other publications, electronic resources
and organisations. Brief details on content. ISBN 07123 08512

Teleworking Survey *Date:* 1999
By Small World Connections for Gee Publishing Customer Services, 100 Avenue
Road, Swiss Cottage, London NW3 3PG Tel: 020 7393 7666

Virtually There: The Evolution of Call Centres *Date:* 1999
Authors: Institute for Employment Studies and the TCA for Mitel
Source: Firefly Communications Ltd, 25/4 The Coda Centre, 189 Munster
Road, London SW6 6AW.

Motors or modems? *Date:* 1998
Authors: National Economic Research Association
Source: RAC Web: www.rac.co.uk

Teleworking Britain *Date:* 1998
Authors: Mitel/MORI Tel: 0870 909 888 or 020 7381 4505
www.mitel.com or www.firefly.co.uk

**Working Anywhere –
exploring telework for individuals and organisations** *Date:* 1998
Authors: Department of Trade and Industry www.dti.gov.uk and
Department of Environment, Transport and the Regions

Corporate Telework Survey *Date:* 1997
Authors: Small World Connections
Source: PO Box 162, South District Office, Manchester M20 3BB Tel: 0161 445 0630
Fax: 0161 445 1403 Web: www.smallworldconnections.com
Email: small_world@compuserve.com

Motors and Modems *Date:* 1997
Author: NERA
Source: RAC

Teleworking: Guidelines for Good Practice *Date:* 1997
Author: Ursula Huws
Source: Institute for Employment Studies, Mantell Building, University of Sussex,
Brighton BN1 9RF Tel: 01273 686751 Fax: 01273 690430
Web: www.employment-studies.co.uk

Teleworking and Potential Reduction in Work Travel *Date:* 1997
Authors: Institute for Transport Economics, Norway
Source: Tel: +47 22 573800

IT for All *Date:* 1996
Author: H.M. Government
Source: Department of Trade and Industry
Tel: ISI Info line 0345 15 2000 Email: info@isi.gov.uk

Prepared for the future? The British and Technology *Date:* 1996
Author: Motorola
Source: Tel: 01753 575555
Web: www.mot.com/General/Reports/British-Tech/future.html

TeleFutures – a study on teleworking in Ireland *Date:* 1996
Authors: Imogen Bertin and Gerard O'Neill
Source: Enterprise Ireland
Web: www.forbairt.ie/about/publications/telefutu

Teleworking – A Director's Guide *Date:* 1996
Authors: Various
Source: BT, IoD, Tel: Director Publications, 020 7730 6060

Teleworking and Gender *Date:* 1996
Author: Ursula Huws Web: http://dialspace.dial.pipex.com/town/parade/hg54
Source: Institute for Employment Studies, Mantell Building, University of Sussex,
Brighton BN1 9RF Tel: 01273 686751 Fax: 01273 690430.

Teleworking and Rural Development (report 27) *Date:* 1996
Author: Rural Development Commission
Source: RDC, 141 Castle Street, Salisbury, Wilts SP1 3TP Fax: 01722 432773
ISBN 1 869964 53 5

Teleworking: an overview of the research *Date:* 1996
Author: Ursula Huws
Source: Analytica, 46 Ferntower Road, London N5 2JH
Tel: 020 7226 8411 Fax: 020 7226 0813

Teleworking: Thirteen Journeys to the Future of Work *Date:* 1996
Author: Andrew Bibby

Contact: Turnaround Distribution, 27 Horsell Road, London N5 1X2
Tel: 020 8829 3000

The Social Implications of Teleworking *Date:* 1996
Source: The European Foundation for the Improvement of Living and Working Conditions, Loughlinstown House, Shankill, Co. Dublin Tel: +353 1 282 6888
Web: www.eurofound.ie
Comment: A series of three informative papers covering the legal situation in a number of European countries: 1) The legal and contractual situation of teleworkers 2) The social security position of teleworkers 3) Teleworking health and safety issues

A Manager's Guide to Teleworking *Date:* 1995
Author: Ursula Huws on behalf of the Department of Employment
Source: Dept of Employment, Cambertown Ltd, Unit 8, Goldthorpe Ind. Estate, Rotherham, S. Yorks Tel: 0171 273 6969.

Being Digital *Date:* 1995
Author: Nicholas Negroponte
Source: Coronet Books ISBN 0–340–64930–5
Comment: Negroponte works at MIT; this book is thoughtful and widely read futurology about the Internet age.

How Vehicle Pollution Affects our Health *Date:* 1995
Source: Ashden Trust, 9 Red Lion Court, London EC4A 3EB

Teleworking in Ireland conference proceedings *Date:* 1995
Authors: Imogen Bertin and Brian Goggin
Source: Imogen Bertin, Reagrove, Minane Bridge, Co. Cork
Tel: +353 21 887300 Web: www.cork-teleworking.com

Transport Statistics Report *Date:* 1995
Source: Department of Transport,
HMSO, Publications Centre, PO Box 276, London, SW8 5DT

Working at a Distance – UK Teleworking and its Implications *Date: 1995*
Source: Parliamentary Office of Science & Technology, Houses of Parliament, Millbank, London Ref: ISBN 1 897941 85 4

Work at Home: Estimates from the 1991 Census *Date:* 1995
Authors: Alan Felstead and Nick Jewson
Source: Employment Gazette, Department of Employment

Teleworking: Right for your Business, Right for your People *Date: 1994*
Author: BT
Source: BT, Tel: 0800 800 060 Web: www.wfh.co.uk

DTI Teleworking Study 1992–1993 *Date: 1993*
Author: Horace Mitchell
Source: Brameur Ltd, 237 High Street, Aldershot, Hants GU11 1TJ

Psychological Aspects of Teleworking in Rural Areas *Date: 1993*
Author: PATRA deliverable report
Source: Available from Professor David Oborne, Psychology Department, University of Swansea.
Comment: This report is a literature review. Other reports from the PATRA project may also be available from Professor Oborne.

**Self-Employment and Labour Market Restructuring –
The Case of Freelance Teleworkers in Book Publishing** *Date: 1993*
Authors: Celia Stanworth, John Stanworth, David Purdy
Source: Future of Work Research Group, University of Westminster, 35 Marylebone Road, London NW1 5LS Tel: 0171 911 5000

Teleworking – BT's Inverness Experience *Date: 1993*
Author: BT
Source: BT, Tel: 0800 800 060
Comment: Much of the information from all pre-1994 BT booklets is summarised in the Teleworking Explained book, listed below.

Teleworking Explained *Date: 1993*
Authors: Mike Gray, Noel Hodson, Gil Gordon
Source: John Wiley & Sons, Baffins Lane, Chichester Ref: ISBN 0 471 93975 7
Comment: Extremely comprehensive though dated teleworking guide.

Teleworking in Britain – A report to the Employment Dept *Date: 1993*
Author: Ursula Huws
Source: Research Strategy Branch, Employment Dept, Moorfoot, Sheffield, S1 4PQ, or Tel: 020 7273 6969 ISBN PP51 16304 494 52
Comment: Thorough national survey. Ref: Research Series No. 18

Transport/Telecommunications Substitution *Date: 1993*
Authors: Horace Mitchell and Eric Trodd, Brameur Consultancy
Source: Horace Mitchell Email: 100142.31@compuserve.com

Analysis of a Major (UK) Teleworking Survey *Date: 1992*
Author: W. Murray
Source: The National Computing Centre, Oxford Road, Manchester M1 7ED

Telework – The Human Resource Implications *Date: 1992*
Author: John and Celia Stanworth
Source: Institute of Personnel Management, IPM House, Camp Rd, Wimbledon, London, SW19 4UX ISBN 085292 465 8
Comment: Very clear and comprehensive guide to issues affecting employed teleworkers and personnel management

The Economics of Teleworking *Date: 1992*
Author: Noel Hodson, SW 2000, for BT
Source: BT, Tel: 0800 800 600
Comment: A shorter version of this report is available free as part of the BT Teleworking Programme

Contacts and URLs

DTI Information Society Initiative Tel: ISI info line 0845 715 2000
Email: info@isi.gov.uk Web: **www.isi.gov.uk**

Labour Market enquiry line, Office for National Statistics, 1 Drummond Gate, London SW1V 2QQ Tel: 020 7533 6176

The Analysis website has information on trends and statistics relating to telecoms infrastructure **www.analysis.com**

BT Working from Home website **www.wfh.co.uk**

Government website on work-life balance issues:
www.dfee.gov.uk/work-lifebalance

EA Technology (EU SAVE programme). Contact Andrew Wright, tel 0151 347 2364

www.telecommute.org is Telework America, the American teleworking association.

www.crew.umich.edu is a "Collaboratory" on electronic work methods.

www.dnai.com/~isdw – the Institute for the Study of Distributed Work has a number of academic resources available.

www.eclipse.co.uk/pens/bibby/telework.html is journalist **Andrew Bibby's** home pages which contain a number of articles on telework.

The Telefutures report is available online at **www.forbairt.ie/about/publications/telefutu**

Teleworking – the Shortest Route to Work? by Amárach consultants for Dublin Transportation Office, Telecom Éireann and Telework Ireland is available at **www.amarach.com/future/telew.htm**.. This site also holds links to AIB's survey of teleworking in SMEs (2000).

www.isc.ie is the Irish government's Information Society Commission which has included questions on teleworking in some of its survey work.

Gil Gordon's website is a mine of useful information – probably the best telework website in the world – **www.gilgordon.com**

The Emergence EU project tracking movement of work, and trends in telework and mobile work in 22 countries, is at **www.emergence.nu**

The ECATT project tracking telework and ecommerce changes through surveys is at **www.ecatt.com**.

European Telework Development project, which maintains the European Telework Online (ETO) pages at **www.eto.org.uk**.

www.tca.org.uk is the location for the TCA web pages.

Ursula Huws website: **http://dialspace.dial.pipex.com/town/parade/hg54**.

Company teleworking

This chapter covers introducing teleworking to companies (for PAYE workers). The next chapter (*Getting work*) deals with starting up and maintaining a teleworking business as a self-employed person. Please note the disclaimer in the preface to this book – we have done our best to collate information on issues like company teleworking policies and agreements, but it is up to individuals and organisations to check documents with their professional advisors where appropriate.

There are four main routes by which teleworking is implemented. Some organisations are "hybrids" with more than one route occurring simultaneously.

1. In conventional organisations, **planned introduction** of teleworking involves three identifiable stages – the idea, the trial and the "contagion" by which the practice spreads into widespread usage within the organisation. In this scenario, teleworking is no different from other changes that are introduced within organisations – it has to be justified, planned, and carried out with the consent of the people it will affect.

2. **Tacit** teleworking describes the silent spread of teleworking in most conventional organisations, usually through the practices of a management elite who often insist on being given laptops and modems so they can telework after hours or on the road.

3. In some practices of professionals and academic organisations, teleworking is often **endemic**. For example, at the Open University, which as its core business deals with remotely located students using teletechnology, there is an established tradition of email use and flexible work arrangements. Small virtual organisations sometimes begin from a distributed, flexible working basis. In these organisations, a review of issues such as software standardisation, security and training can be very productive.

4. For some, the introduction of teleworking may accompany a **move to self-employment,** or be a method of reducing overheads and improving productivity for an existing small business.

As with all change processes, a planned implementation is preferable and employers are advised to draw up a written policy specifying how the teleworking arrangements will operate, in consultation with employees and unions or employee representatives as appropriate. The usual procedure is to:

- Carry out a feasibility study looking at existing telework (if any), plus costs and benefits to the organisation of implementing teleworking;
- Research existing sample telework policies and individual employee agreements (see page 49);

- Consult with employees, unions and employee representatives to draw up draft policies and agreements;
- Carry out a pilot project to assess a change to teleworking using a small group (see box);
- Monitor and evaluate the pilot project and decide whether a larger roll-out will be beneficial to the organisation.

Stages of implementation

Feasibility studies

It is worthwhile to begin by assessing the existing level of tacit teleworking at the beginning of any attempt to trial teleworking. Many personnel and human resource departments have no idea of the extent of teleworking going on in their organisations – a celebrated exercise at the World Bank indicated that there were no teleworkers according to the human resources department, but a different story was told by the IT department – over 1,000 telecoms links being used for around 240,000 man days per year. If you don't have the time or resources for a formal staff survey, do your own simple research – check the date and time stamps on emails you receive from colleagues. How many of these are happening outside working hours? How do you know if they were sending the emails from the office or from home?

The feasibility study should outline the business case – including the operational, strategic, cost or employee advantages to be gained. The study should give a draft implementation plan with timescales and draft budgets. The feasibility study should recommend whether to set up a formal or informal introduction of telework. Experimentation on a small scale is a good way to get a feel for whether it will suit you company without making

---

Setting up a pilot teleworking project

- set up a steering group or project team
- identify the planned costs and benefits to the company
- identify suitable jobs for teleworking
- select suitable staff members
- draft and agree changes to contracts and agreements
- arrange training for teleworkers **and their managers**
- install equipment for the home office, mobile office or hotdesking system
- provide continuing support to teleworkers
- monitor and evaluate the pilot

major investments of time or money. It also allows different styles of telework to evolve for different situations. It is overkill to do a formal trial or develop a complete personnel policy for one person who occasionally takes a laptop home to complete a report, or for someone who occasionally accesses the company network to pick up messages while travelling abroad. If you do opt for an informal approach, some simple precautions will avoid the more predictable types of failure:

- Select teleworkers who are experienced, trusted members of staff with good skills in IT, time management and communication;
- Ensure that the teleworkers' line managers are supportive of the experiment, and check that the line managers have adequate IT skills;
- The teleworkers must be satisfied that they have suitable equipment and skills. Employers are still responsible for employee health and safety outside the office, and have a duty to provide adequate training for all work tasks;
- Have some system for reporting back what went right and wrong;
- Monitor costs, however informally;
- Communicate the experiment clearly to colleagues, supervisors and employee representatives such as unions so that they know that it's happening and don't think that it's a suspicious secret or a perk available to a privileged few;
- Make sure that the teleworkers know how to indicate if they want to give up the experiment. Reassure them there will be no repercussions if they do give up.

If the informal approach works, you will need to think about whether to expand teleworking, and if any formal trials or procedures are required.

Estimating costs and benefits

A textual description of various advantages and disadvantages of teleworking for companies can be found in Chapter 1 – *Overview*. This section focuses on establishing a rough estimate and methodology for financial costs and benefits which is likely to be needed before a company will agree to run a pilot teleworking programme. It draws on some material from the dated but valuable book *Teleworking Explained* (1993) by Mike Gray, Gil Gordon and Noel Hodson, as well as on material available on the websites of Gil Gordon and Jack Nilles (see references).

A straightforward monetary cost/benefit is given in the box overleaf. However, the calculation will depend on individual company circumstances. For example, some organisations will see a quantifiable benefit in providing family-friendly policies leading to improved staff retention. Others may be concerned to show a contribution towards environmental factors such as savings in energy, or reductions in commuter traffic. In an organisation where introduction of teleworking results in savings on office space (though desksharing or hotdesking), there will be a direct financial benefit which will not apply to an organisation where the teleworkers retain their previous workspaces onsite.

Because the main payback for most companies is either increased productive hours per week for a staff member, or increased productivity, the calculations look more favourable for high-level staff members with high pay or chargeout rate per hour than for staff with more basic skills. Many of the published case studies of teleworking are for pilots carried out in IT departments where ability to use teleworking equipment starts from a high base level, and hourly rates are often high. The payback for basic clerical staff with lower pay rates, who will also need more training, may not look so advantageous from a purely cost-based point of view. Paybacks for part-time homebased teleworkers will obviously take longer if a home equipment setup duplicates office equipment but both equipment sets are only used part-time.

First, estimate the one-off costs of change such as:

- Equipment for the home office (PCs, phone lines, chairs, desks, filing)
- Training for the teleworkers (consultants or in-house)
- Training for their managers
- Lost productive time during the setup period for teleworkers and their managers
- Time spent by HR department designing telework policy, establishing new agreements and procedures and monitoring the trial.
- Time spent by IT department specifying, installing, testing and supporting the teleworker equipment
- Health and safety inspections of home offices.

Next, look for costs that you will be able to measure both before and after the teleworking pilot and work out how to obtain these figures. The topics to be examined will include measurements of:

- Output and deliverables of the teleworker – quality and quantity, hours worked, targets and deadlines met, satisfaction with their working life, stress levels
- Changes in employment costs – salary, expenses, support staff, office space and overheads, training costs, recruitment and retention, sick leave
- Travel costs – company car expenses, season tickets, time spent travelling, communications costs while travelling, air tickets, hotel bills (some of these costs are borne by the employer and some by the employee – so the costs and benefits to each need to be distinguished).
- Environmental issues – energy consumption, waste production, traffic reduction – if these are important to the company's objectives.

This should enable an estimation of annual running costs to add to the one-off setup costs. The payback periods for those telework programmes which have been published are in the region of 18–24 months but will vary widely.

Teleworking implementation costs

These costs, based on a trial in Lloyds TSB Bank's information systems department were presented at the TCA's 1996 conference. The costs are per annum with most costs averaged over three years.

PC hardware and software support	£1,400
Office dial-in facilities (LAN access)	£126
ISDN telephone installation	£133
ISDN telephone line rental and usage	£937
Furniture	£110
Sundry setup and support expenses	£2,901
TOTAL	**£5,607**
Payback	
Two additional hours per week	£4,000
Two sick days a year saved	£700
10% productivity improvement	£2,800
Staff recruitment and training savings	£1,000
Two days a year travel disruption saved	£700
TOTAL	**£9,200**

The 1997 SWC/*Flexible Working* magazine corporate teleworking survey reported average setup costs for a home based teleworker of £3,500 with annual running costs of about £1,500. Average setup costs for a nomadic teleworker were £3,700, with maintenance costs of £2,250.

Nortel provides two offerings for its employees who wish to telework – part-time and full-time – and supplies a cost-benefit justification adapted to each country where it offers teleworking. The figures for Ireland are given here. Conventional office space charge assumption (against which cost avoidance is measured) is US$32,000 per employee per year – **monthly cost $2666.67**. Call costs assume 800 mins/month remote access part-time and 1600 mins/month full-time using eircom lines.

Setup charges	Part time	Full time
ISDN installation	$441	$441
HOMEbase equipment	$995	$995
HP 65 combined printer/fax copier		$600
Furniture		$1,500
Subtotal	**$1,436**	**$3,536**
Monthly charges	**Part time**	**Full time**
Office space (cost of central office facilities)	$1600	$533
Technical support	$125	$125
ISDN line rental	$37	$37
Call charges	$84	$167
Subtotal	**$1,845**	**$862**
Cost avoidance year/teleworker	**$9,856**	**$21,653**
Payback period (years)	**1.7**	**2.0**

Identifying suitable teleworking jobs

In order to select appropriate areas for pilot projects, consideration needs to be given to the job descriptions. Some categories were listed in the previous chapter on page 5.

Jobs suitable for teleworking include those with:

- a high degree of information processing
- clearly defined areas of individual work
- clear objectives and measurable outputs
- minimal requirements for supervision.

Setting up a pilot project

The first step is to establish a team or steering group for the teleworking pilot. You will need a project manager, clear responsibilities and reporting arrangements, and links to a sponsoring board member. The person driving the pilot project should have a neutral outlook on teleworking – neither a champion for teleworking nor a total sceptic – to ensure a measured and reasoned approach to the study. A number of organisations offer consultancy in telework trials and feasibility studies and are described at the end of this chapter. You may not need to use a consultancy at all, but it is worthwhile talking to consultants to get an idea of the areas they cover – you may find that you go back to them at a later stage for specialist help with a particular area of the project.

One important reason for ensuring that there is a steering group is "corporate amnesia". If the telework programme is the territory of one individual, and that person moves job or company, there is a strong likelihood that the programme will die when they leave. There are many examples of good programmes which have withered without their champion; so try to set up a structure that will be resilient to this problem.

The second step is to identify the parameters that will be used to assess the success of the pilot – without a clear measure of success or failure it will be hard to spread teleworking beyond the pilot study to other areas. Often a more detailed working of the initial cost-benefits case using the specific examples of the prospective pilot teleworkers will reveal what measurements will be feasible and should be collected. In looking at how to evaluate the pilot project, the team should consider whether the function chosen for the project is limited to that unit, or whether it is representative of the wider activities of the company.

A common error is to attempt the pilot project too quickly – a realistic timetable allows time for problems to develop and be resolved without constant "firefighting", and anxieties among those involved. The project should build in opportunities for individual and group meetings to review progress in order to identify quickly and resolve teething problems.

The problem most widely encountered in teleworking trials is "middle-management syndrome", which describes the difficulties encountered in

Financial services sector saves on training and recruiting costs

The Nationwide Building Society has joined a growing group of financial services companies taking advantage of teleworking to retain skilled staff. Employee Relations manager Denise Walker explains: "We employ teleworkers because we want to try and access people with experience who prefer to work from home – such as mothers with small children."

Nationwide has had a policy of allowing employees to request the option of homeworking from their managers for several years. There are about 85 fulltime employees on formal homeworking conditions contracts, made up of 40 staff in three regional mortgage lending control teams, and additional staff in the technology division. The Nationwide staff union have agreed a homeworking allowance of £104 pa and provided input to the teleworking resources pack.

Walker stresses "Teleworking needs a different type of manager who can manage people they can't see, remembering, for instance, to include all teleworking employees in messages which are automatically circulated." The company is actively looking for opportunities to develop the teleworking option further. (adapted from articles in *Teleworker* and *Flexible Working* magazines)

At the Prudential insurance company a pilot scheme for telesales consultants began in summer 1998 with five "guinea pigs" selling home insurance. Teleworking allowed one of the five, Kamini Govindasamy, to double her hours and wages "Before I worked in a big office with 60–80 other people... Now I can give a hundred percent to the customer because it is quiet and I can have a one-to-one relationship with them without asking them to repeat things because I can't hear.

The Prudential teleworkers have monthly meetings with their line manager to discuss progress. Jean Tomlin, director of sales and operations, says the telesales consultants have reduced unprodcutive time and in some cases this has lead to increased hours. The teleworkers were supplied with PCs and ISDN or Kilostream links to the Pru's main database at the call centre in Essex.

management cultures where status depends on the number of people reporting to a manager. These managers prefer to see staff sitting at their desks or attending constant face-to-face meetings and find it hard to make the change from eyeball management to managing by results. Another source of resistance can be managers who themselves are not happy using tele-technology such as PCs and the Internet. They can become a major obstacle to an effective trial.

Staff selection

There are four qualifying factors which must be in place before an employee should be selected for teleworking:

Some organisations using teleworkers in Britain (April 2000)

This table is intended to show the breadth of business areas now covered. It is not intended to be a comprehensive guide, or as a work-finding guide for prospective teleworkers.

Company	Type of work	Numbers
Local Authorities		
Aberdeen City Council	IT, Economic Development, Legal and Corporate	12
Birmingham City Council	Housing Department	2 f/t, 1 pt/t
Cambridgeshire County Council	Social services, registration of Old People's homes	10+
Dorset County Council	Various	20
Gloucestershire County Council	Trading standards	10
Horsham District Council	Councillors' pilot scheme	12
Kent County Council	Social services, occupational therapists, educational psychologists, consultants	100
Leicester City Council	Computing and telecoms	3
London Borough of Enfield	Various	47
London Borough of Lewisham	Social services	12
London Borough of Sutton	Environmental services, planners, architects	15
North Wiltshire District Council	Councillors and IT staff	50
Oxfordshire County Council	Social Services	350
South Hams District Council	All departments	50 p/t
Stoke-on-Trent City Council	Various	12
Suffolk County Council	Social services, trading standards, technical and professional workers	30+
Surrey County Council	Telecentre-based teachers, personnel officers, social services, environmental health, planners and business support	236
Wakefield Metropolitan Council	Various	30
Wiltshire County Council	Education welfare officers	15
Financial Services		
Barclays Bank	Branch managers	600
Britannia Building Society	Word processing	5
Co-operative Bank	Debt collection and others	40
Ellis and Buckle Claims Mgt	Telephone researchers	n/a
Lloyds TSB	Systems developers Also "work options" scheme open to all staff	160
Nationwide Building Society	Recruitment consultants, buildings administration	300
Royal Bank of Scotland	Various	29
Sedgwicks	Claims processing, policy documents	13
Skandia Life	Managers	3+

Company	Type of work	Numbers
Publishing and media		
BBC News	Journalists	17
Classic FM	Presenter	1
Crossaig Ltd	Editors and indexers	14
Surrey Advertiser	Various	2
Computers and IT		
BT	Various	7000
Cable & Wireless	Telesales, fault handling, 999 Business Sales and others	3,000
Canon UK	Sales, training, engineers, support	252
Cisco	Sales	360
Hewlett Packard	Sales, training, engineers, professionals	100
ICL	Various	300
Nortel	Various	600
Unisys	Various	10
Others		
Action Aid	Canvassing work	77
Asda	Admin/surveyors	n/a
Automobile Association	Call centre operators	150
British Airways	Various	n/a
British Gas	Field service engineers, managers	7,000
Cleveland Police	Police officers	120+
Davis & Co. Solicitors	Solicitors	20
Design for Learning	Training, research, distance learning	57
GlaxoWellcome	Research	2+
Glenigan (business info)	Field researchers	12-15
Intrinsic	Consultants, PR, admin	95
Jupiter International Group PLC	Sales and Marketing	3
Lily Industries	Sales Force	n/a
Marsh Insurance Brokers	Insurance technical processing	14
Manchester TEC	Business advisers	9
Multiple Sclerosis Society	Helpline staff	35
Open University	Sales force and academics	75
Post Office Consulting	1 secretary, 1 disabled worker	2
Prudential	Call centre agents, direct sales	5
Rank Xerox	Sales team	300
Sema Group UK Business Systems	Various	n/a
SmithKline Beecham	Legal, IT, HR, f/t and p/t	n/a
Styal Prison Project	Admin, market research, data inputting, billing	12-15
The Virtual Office Group	Executive coordinators, secretaries, "pop-up PAs"	30
WWF	Regional organisers	15

- suitable job description (or tasks within job description which can be "clumped" together to be carried out on teleworking days)
- suitable personality and experience of employee
- suitable personality and supportive attitude of their line manager
- suitable space and facilities for home office or mobile working.

It may be that teleworking is being offered to staff with caring responsibilities or with a particular reason to want to work from home – in which case the staff will be self-selecting. Where the pilot project can choose the prospective teleworkers, it is important to select people suited to the demands that teleworking may place on them. In particular, introverted people who are poor communicators are unlikely to adapt easily but may be attracted by the solitary workstyle. Some companies have used psychometric tests and counselling to ensure that applicants are likely to make a success of the change. The key personality traits are:

- self-disciplined
- good decision-making and problem-solving skills
- good self-management and time-management abilities
- good communication skills
- ablity to cope with reduced social contact.

Some employers consider that established, mature staff are more likely to want to telework and to be successful at it. Kevin Curran and Geoff Williams in their *Manual of Remote Working* (1997) emphasise that, although there are no personality inventories on the market which specifically measure suitability for working at home, several provide

Letting the train take the strain for mobile workers

A summer 1998 survey by BT shows that of 500 business train travellers, over two-thirds work on the train. About half of those who work forty hours a week do so, and over 80% of those working more than 55 hours a week.

Companies come in for some stick with 14% of "journeyworkers" frustrated that they do not have the right technology. Nearly one in five believe they could reduce their working hours and improve efficiency if they had the right equipment.

Almost half wanted carriages dedicated to executives who want to work, and 40% want power supplies for laptop computers installed on trains. Only 12% would like to see trains with mobile meeting rooms, and would be prepared to pay for these.

---

information about traits essential for remote working such as level of need for contact with others, self-discipline and preference for certain kinds of work. These inventories include the Work Environment Scale, the Myers-Briggs Type Indicator and the Work Style Reference Inventory. However, use of psychometric testing is considered controversial and unfair by some HR professionals and many trade unions. Problems might arise if someone who is keen on teleworking is denied the chance to participate in a trial due to unfavourable personality traits. Clear and open policies on teleworker selection can help to overcome such difficulties.

Policies, agreements and unions

A survey carried out for *Flexible Working* magazine in 1997 by Cathy Murray of the Small World Connections consultancy showed that only 25% of home-based teleworkers have special employment contracts covering the arrangement, making both employers and employees vulnerable to misunderstanding and often failing to provide any outlet on either side for the expression of contentment or dissatisfaction with teleworking.

At the pilot project stage it is advisable to draft a company telework policy for discussion with employees, employee representatives and unions, which can also be revised to take account of the findings of the pilot project. Guidelines and examples to assist in preparing telework policies and individual telework agreements are given later in this chapter.

Setting up a home office

The pilot project team must establish what equipment will be needed by teleworkers to carry out their work tasks at home. The IT department will probably want to establish a standard "home office" or "mobile worker" kit. However, bear in mind that needs vary with the job description. At the Irish airports authority Aer Rianta, the pilot teleworking trial quickly discovered that their standard equipment specification, although high-level and including ISDN lines and a combined printer/fax/scanner/copier, was not suitable for two buyers who frequently needed to be logged into the company's retail management system whilst sending a fax *and* talking on the phone simultaneously. The kit would only allow two of these three operations at any one time.

The team will need to establish that the prospective teleworker has a suitable home office available – ideally in a separate room. If the teleworking arrangement is planned as a regular one, employers should check that the teleworker has a computer workstation and adjustable chair that comply with health and safety legislation – regardless of whether the equipment belongs to the employer or employee. A visit is recommended by a manager or health and safety specialist prior to beginning a telework trial to assess any problems such as inadequate supply of power points, as well as to investigate the local telecoms infrastructure. Some areas may have old-fashioned exchanges which are unsuitable for high-speed modem traffic. Line quality to a teleworker's home can be poor due to long runs of overhead poles. Availability of ISDN services should also be checked if they will be needed. (See p. 99 and Chapter 11, *Teleworking equipment*).

Any disruption to the home caused by installation of equipment should be kept to a minimum and negotiated with the staff member and their family in advance. Some issues which need to be borne in mind in designing the home office are covered in Chapter 7, *Staying safe and legal*. There is a checklist of home office equipment on page 315 in that chapter.

Funding the setup of the home office can happen via different mechanisms. The employer may provide equipment, or supply a budget and allow the employee to make the purchases. In some situations employees may provide their own equipment. Whatever the arrangement, a risk assessment, which may be carried out by the employer, or through a checklist procedure by the employee, is advisable to comply with health and safety legislation.

Training

Both management and prospective teleworkers will need training in order to adapt to the new circumstances. Much of this will focus on effective communication. Management in particular may need to adapt to a new culture – managing by results – which requires skills in the areas of delegation, co-ordination and orchestration. The common thread to the new management skills is improving interpersonal skills for a work environment involving less authority and more trust.

The general consensus among teleworking consultants is that an initial induction or information session is needed first to cover what teleworking is, the business case for introducing it, and the likely advantages and pitfalls. This induction will usually take place at an early stage of the pilot project and is often part of the selection process – it allows those interested in taking part to get enough information to make a decision on whether to pursue their interest, and offers opportunities for discussion with their line

Equal access to a fair process at Lloyds TSB

Lloyds TSB bank offers flexible working options including teleworking to its 71,000 staff. Joanna Slevin of Lloyds TSB drafted this policy of access to the new work options, published in the company's *Work Options* pack.

Meeting business goals will remain our priority
Requests will be evaluated on their impact for the business and the needs of customers and colleagues will be considered first. The impact of the scheme will be expected to have a neutral or positive effect on the business.

Flexibility is not an entitlement
Flexibility is a different way of working which is not an entitlement or a way of conferring preferential treatment. Managers will approve requests that are consistent with business needs. If the arrangement does not work for the business it will not be approved.

Equity means equal access to a fair process
There are standard request forms to help you think through the proposed arrangements, how it will affect you, our customers and your colleagues. Your manager has to make a sound business decision and the aim of the policy is to ensure it is done fairly. The same process is available to everyone but it does not promise the same outcome for all.

Working in partnership
You and your manager should work together to get the best from any proposed work option. You should understand how well it will affect the business. The process will be monitored centrally to ensure it is consistently and fairly applied.

Job performance is relevant
Managers will consider job performance when evaluating a request. For example, staff who have shown that they are able to work well without supervision are more likely to adjust successfully to working off-site. For those who have weak time management or communication skills, this option may not be appropriate.

---

manager – this is important as a supportive line manager is one of the most important predictors of success. It can also double as a training session for members of the steering group or project team, and bring forward issues for their consideration.

Once staff selection for the final project has taken place, a second training session is needed. Opinions are divided on whether the second session should take teleworkers and managers as separate groups, or combine them – practical issues such as availability and size of training room will probably decide this. The second session should:

- indicate top level support for the trial and spell out the business benefits to the company;

Teleworking and public administration

A report by teleworking expert Ursula Huws for the Local Government Management Board sums up the pros and cons of teleworking for public sector organisations:

- Savings and costs on office space could be up to 50% but there may be hidden costs of refurbishment, infrastructure and staff retraining;
- Initial setup costs will probably be around £1500 per worker but will vary on telecommunications in place and the availability of competing providers;
- Continuing costs will include telecoms, maintenance and technical support, insurance and health and safety checks;
- Management and training costs will be incurred but are an investment in staff development which should lead to productivity increases;
- The impact of teleworking on productivity varies considerably and is likely to be between 10 and 30% for local authority workers;
- Work-life balance for employees – often a major motivator – will be improved;
- Staff retention may improve – teleworking increases staff commitment, important during a time of skill shortage when public administration is competing against higher private sector wages.

Huws concludes local authorities need to recognise the diversity of teleworking forms and use them appropriately, and that they must take a cross-departmental strategic overview approach.

Other possible advantages include attracting more applicants to job adverts in a time of skill shortage (London Borough of Enfield got over 1,000 replies the first time they advertised posts with a teleworking option) and reductions in traffic congestion (Cambridgeshire County Council estimated a 4–8% reduction in time and distances travelled if teleworking were available to all managers and admnistrative staff).

- ■ introduce any documentation such as survey forms, or communication agreements, or the company telework policy;
- ■ discuss the changes needed for management by results/at a distance;
- ■ look at any practical issues such as how to forward calls to the home office, how to schedule meetings which need the teleworker's presence and how to ensure that computer files are appropriately updated (synchronising data between the home office and the company office);
- ■ look at HR issues such as insurance cover in the home office, security policies and what to do if the trial is not working out;

- explain to the teleworkers and their managers the plan for monitoring the trial and the criteria for success;
- encourage manager/teleworker pairs to complete a communications agreement covering issues like how often email and voicemail should be checked, what should happen in the event of the teleworker being needed urgently in the company office, what core hours the teleworker must be available for, and so on. More information on communications is given in Chapter 3, *Survival Guide*;
- provide plenty of opportunities for discussion.

Further management training material may also be needed to cover:

- specifying aims and criteria clearly;
- agreeing and negotiating work tasks;
- relating pay to performance (where appropriate);
- conflict resolution skills for remotely based teams.

Colleagues will also need to be informed of the teleworking initiative, including the company's reasons for introducing it, who is managing the project and what the outcomes are likely to be, as well as how they will be measured. Open information should dampen speculation about the long-term teleworking intentions of the company and also assist the teleworkers in their communications with non-teleworking colleagues.

Other training strategies may include a programme of workshops for new teleworkers, allowing new teleworkers to shadow more experienced teleworkers, and allocating mentors to the teleworkers. Specific IT training modules will probably be required, such as the use of dial-up email via a modem.

It is important not to assume that prospective teleworkers are competent IT users – check and assess that they are happy using the software and hardware needed in their job and remedy skills gaps before beginning a trial – otherwise you will be measuring IT training deficits, not the effects of teleworking. Look at the context of any other organisational changes which may be occurring at the same time. Often teleworking is introduced as part of a series of changes, and may occasionally be seen as taking things a step too far – one corporate which has pioneered teleworking reported that during its introduction of teleworking, there were 14 different change programmes going on within the company, and the teleworking trial suffered from the level of confusion caused by the number of simultaneous changes occurring.

IT issues and support

Early involvement of the company's IT department in the teleworking pilot is very important, and an IT staff member should be included in the steering group. IT staff are likely to be involved in specifying home office equipment, enabling remote access to company networks, installing and checking equipment at the home office, providing training in use of remote dial-up connections, and providing continued technical support.

Most IT staff already provide some support via a telephone helpdesk, but they may not be used to the problems that arise when you can't just nip up the stairs and directly check out the offending screen. Therefore clear guidance on provision of support to the teleworkers, and conditions under which a home visit might be appropriate, or where the teleworker may have to return their equipment for repair or upgrade need to be set out. The IT department staff may themselves require further training in telephone helpdesk operation.

Telework trials sometimes require revision of company information – security policies, and issues such as procedures for data backups, keyboard locking and passwords for home-based PCs may also need checking.

Monitoring and evaluation

Although both managers and teleworkers may find the monitoring process a chore, without information to indicate any changes in levels of productivity or job satisfaction, it will be hard to make the case for widespread introduction of teleworking. The level of monitoring will vary according to business needs, but could include:

- Running costs: *eg* stationery, telecommunications
- Productivity: deadlines and work targets met and unmet, ability to deal with multiple priorities
- Effect on colleagues, customers and levels of service (*eg* extended hours of customer service, reduced telephone hold-time for customers)
- Changes in work activity (for example a reduction in breadth of tasks due to only a proportion being suitable to teleworking)
- Working hours, sick leave and absence, staff turnover
- Satisfaction and stress levels in working life
- Changes in motivations for teleworking (*eg* childcare, reduced distractions, *etc.*)
- Relationship between teleworker and manager
- Changes in communication patterns
- Technical support and IT issues
- Issues of isolation or demotivation.

Case study: Lombard North Central

Lombard undertook a two-year teleworking trial for ten professionals. All changes in working conditions were drafted into existing employment contracts. Managers visited worker's homes to advise on health, safety and security issues. The final results initially showed 20% productivity gains, which settled down to 10% above normal, but the quality of work also improved. Sick leave reduced by 50%, from the company's average of six days a year to three days.

In measuring productivity, remember that hours worked may not be an appropriate measure for knowledge workers since overwork can often lead to reduced productivity – people are not machines. Measuring the costs is usually much easier than assessing the benefits.

Staff-management ratios is an area which needs to be monitored. Existing evidence on whether teleworking leads to changes in staff-management ratios is contradictory according to a review of teleworking carried out by Ursula Huws for the Local Government Management Board in Britain. She notes that the FI group, a software company using home-based workers employed one manager for every five programmers, one for every eight systems designers and one for every ten systems analysts which was more than twice the industry standard at the time. In contrast Noel Hodson gives a case study, in his publication *The Economics of Teleworking* (BT, 1994), of teleworking trials in the Prudential Insurance Company which apparently led to a large saving in management time because it was associated with the closure of 200 branch offices each employing two managers.

Providing continuing support

Those who have been teleworking for some years report that lack of positive feedback becomes an increasing problem. Often teleworkers only receive feedback when there is a problem to be solved or a deadline to be met – they can get left out of team back-slapping when a contract is won, or a customer's letter of satisfaction is posted on the office noticeboard. Rank Xerox, veteran of long-term widescale use of teleworkers, ensures that teleworkers are kept on circulation lists, listed in the company directory, invited to departmental meetings and to social functions.

The teleworking organisation can lack much of the informal communication that comes from people working in close proximity and needs to find a way of replacing the useful parts of this. However, the introduction of teleworking for part of a department can lead to a "them and us" situation. Management may need to think of measures to discourage this split (one employer encouraged a lottery syndicate to encompass all team members rather than just those "in the office").

Experienced telework managers have also reported the need to develop a "sixth sense" about detecting during telephone conversations when teleworkers have a personal problem. Don't forget that teleworking does not necessarily mean working at home in isolation 5 days per week, 20 days per month. A sensible teleworking programme should include regular face-to-face management meetings as well as opportunities for colleagues to mix at the office.

The pilot project team needs to create a support function which will deal with both technical and managerial issues arising from the project. In the main, these issues will be provision of technical support for computer and other equipment usage, and continuing management contact covering the following areas:

- reviewing performance
- determining pay and bonuses
- agreeing goals and improvements in performance
- individual development – counselling and training
- training (both giving and receiving)
- general gossip and banter that forms part of all working life
- providing space for brainstorming, feedback and general discussion on the operation of the department.

The pilot team should specify the arrangements both for monitoring of telework arrangements, and for review of the telework policy itself.

Drafting policies and agreements

This section extracts some common issues which need to be addressed, drawing in part on work carried out by Cathy Murray of the Small World Connections consultancy, published in *Flexible Working* magazine in January 1997, and in part on the Irish government's *Code of Practice* for teleworking which contains a policy template (**www.entemp.ie/e-work**).

General issues

Teleworking can be required as part of an employee's job description, or it can be introduced as a voluntary arrangement. Where the arrangement is voluntary, the policy should set out the provisions for suspending or terminating the arrangement and returning to conventional office working. Usually this involves specifying a period of notice by either side, which is often one month. Other issues such as the return of company-owned home office equipment will also need to be specified.

It is usual for teleworking agreements to specify a number of core hours when the teleworker is available for telephone contact by colleagues. Outside these hours, it is up to the teleworker to decide their pattern of work in order to achieve the tasks they have been set. Otherwise working hours are not altered by teleworking, although there may need to be variations to the procedure by which overtime and sick pay are agreed, claimed and monitored by the employer. A procedure for the teleworker to report for meetings at the office as required should also be included.

Suitable jobs and teleworker selection

The effect of teleworking on colleagues remaining in the office, and on customers should be considered alongside issues of employee and job description suitability. Oxfordshire County Council stipulates that there should be no adverse effects on the level and quality of service, or increases in the workload of non-teleworking colleagues. It is important to avoid any unfair extra workload, either on those who are teleworking or on those who are "back at the office".

Sometimes teleworking is introduced as part of a company disability policy or equal opportunities policy. In relation to disability, consideration should be given to appropriate support mechanisms such as specialised equipment which may be required by individual employees. It is possible that excluding certain workers from teleworking could have equality and industrial relations implications, so laying out clear criteria on selection in the company teleworking policy is important.

The home office

The company policy should list a procedure for establishing whether a suitable home office or other teleworking workplace is available.

Employers normally provide all relevant IT equipment (computers, faxes, scanners, photocopiers, modems *etc*) and supply and pay for a separate telephone line, often with an answerphone or voicemail to buffer "after hours" calls without disturbing the employee. Whether the equipment belongs to the employee or the employer, the policy should spell out the situation on:

Confessions of a teleworking convert

Like many managers, Ian Jones thought teleworking was great – especially as the company he directed sold home office insurance policies – but not for him, just for independent small businesses. That was until he was forced to try it after his baby daughter was diagnosed with a potentially fatal illness.

"I thought that the office wouldn't cope without me for two or three days a week, that staff would run riot, clients would wonder who was in charge, colleagues would believe I had lost touch.

"Then after my daughter's diagnosis what was, I suppose, a normal family life became one interrupted by a series of hospital visits building up to a bone-marrow transplant operation. Thankfully my fellow directors were very understanding and for most of two months I commuted to and from the hospital and, with the assistance of ISDN and a laptop, continued with some work and kept in touch with the office.

"I was surprised at how easy it was to overcome the possible disadvantages of teleworking – distractions, lack of motivation, feelings of isolation, and how quickly I realised the personal advantages – reduced commuting, increased leisure and family time. From a business point of view I find my time is better managed and the split between home and office is an advantage rather than a hindrance.

"As a result I believe I have been more productive as an individual and working from home has not undermined me as an individual, or undermined the effective management of the company. Quite simply, teleworking has worked – and I am now in the fortunate position of honestly being able to claim I understand my clients because for two days a week, I'm one of them." **www.tolsonmessenger.com**

BBC trial makes monitoring sense

The BBC completed a six-month trial of teleworking for 17 staff in 1999. Project manager Geoff Adams-Spink set clear objectives:

- To establish the potential for savings in accommodation and other costs;
- To determine which areas of the production process would lend themselves to teleworking;
- To establish whether there are "soft" benefits such as improving sickness rates and staff retention;
- To test the effect on the creative process of some staff working remotely.

Monitoring took place through a combination of surveys and interviews. The teleworkers returned a weekly survey to the project and both teleworker and their line manager completed surveys halfway through and at the end of the pilot.

Benefits included improved morale and staff retention. The vast majority (82%) said that they would be attracted to a post or would consider staying in a post if teleworking were part of the package. Staff were also more willing to work anti-social hours such as early mornings or Christmas Day because it didn't involve a long commute to the office.

Downsides included technical support, with only 54% of teleworkers saying that the IT support they received at home was as good or better than the service in the office. One teleworker said that they felt invisible while working from home but others overcame problems by regular visits to the office. The teleworkers involved in daily radio programmes were least successful. Geoff comments that for teleworking to succeed in the daily radio sector will require substantial re-education for peers and managers.

Of the 17, 14 will now continue teleworking. Geoff believes the issue of accommodation and cost saving is open to question. "In order to release space, most departments would need to offer the teleworking option to a substantial number of staff, and very careful planning would be necessary to avoid undue congestion in the office when staff are required back at base." On the soft issues, he's quite convinced: teleworking delivers improved morale, enhanced productivity, reduced sickness rates, greater loyalty and better retention.

- provision and ownership of equipment and furniture
- maintenance and technical support arrangements
- insurance
- personal use
- provisions against misuse (this may already be covered in the company's IT security policy)

- arrangements for returning items if the teleworker changes jobs or returns to office-based work.

In large organisations it is usual for there to be an inventory system for the equipment provided to the home office, including labelling, a procedure for returning the equipment if the teleworking arrangement is ended, procedures for replacement if the equipment is lost, stolen or damaged, and for repair when necessary. If an arrangement is made for the teleworker to use their own equipment rather than the company's, then it is important that the teleworker checks their home insurance policy to ensure the equipment is covered for such usage and that they inform their insurer of their plans.

With regard to furniture, some employers (such as GlaxoWellcome) expect the teleworker to supply their own furniture whereas others, particularly those whose employees may be involved in long hours at the computer, choose to supply suitable ergonomic office furniture so that they are certain that they are carrying out their health and safety responsibilities. Another solution is to provide an allowance for the purchase of suitable furniture (Shell UK provides this as an option for teleworking employees – the amount granted is £300).

Stationery and other office consumables will also be needed in the home office. In some companies these are provided from central stores, in others a stationery/postage allowance is paid, or expenses are reclaimed.

Privacy for employees working at home is another issue which should be clarified in a company policy. The privacy clause should indicate procedures regarding any home visits for health and safety inspections (see page 60 below). Mechanisms for telephone and mail redirection to protect privacy should also be provided if required. Oxfordshire County Council recognises the right of its employees to keep their home telephone numbers and addresses confidential – something which is not difficult if a separate telephone line paid for by the employer is used, and if the postal address remains the main office. For reasons of personal security Surrey County Council advises its teleworkers not to hold meetings with clients in their homes but to use council premises instead.

The area of childcare can be problematic to cover in a teleworking policy. Some agreements specify that the teleworker must have adequate childcare during working hours – teleworking is no substitute for childcare, despite the usual media stereotypes of the toddler cuddled on mummy's knee while she taps at the keyboard. But all parents will be familiar with the problems of the suddenly sick or distressed child, and since one of the aims of a teleworking agreement is to provide flexible work practices which allow better balance between home and working life, agreements which are draconian in this area may be self-negating. A statement to the effect that employees must complete their assignments on time, and that the company expects children to be cared for while the employee is working, particularly during school holidays, is probably sufficient. It should also be noted that a strong statement in this area combined with a teleworker group that is all female might conceivably lead to equal opportunities disputes.

Some agreements also specify the duty of the teleworker to maintain their home office area safely for themselves, and for others, including family members or work colleagues who may enter it.

With regard to insurance, the company is normally responsible for the worker while they are using the home office. Some employers, such as AT&T, specify that they are not liable for accidents involving third parties or family members, and that the teleworker should take out their own insurance to cover such eventualities. There are many examples of insurers providing cover for employees working at home, but in the case of Stoke City Council, it has been necessary to agree with the insurance company a "cordon" around the working area which is clearly specified. For employer liability purposes, the insurer/employer is responsible for this work area and so should take steps to check that, for instance, the electrical wiring is safe in the home office room. Outside this area the employer is not liable (*eg* if the worker falls down the stairs and suffers injury).

Health and safety

Because of the employer's health and safety responsibilities, some companies insist on initial and periodic inspection visits to the home office. This is an issue which must be handled with some sensitivity due to the difficult border between home and work – family members may resent being "on parade" for the boss's visit, while workers may feel stressed by the need to present in as good a light as possible their entire home and family, not just the home office, to their employer. Usually a period of notice before a home visit is specified in writing.

Shell UK provides its teleworkers with detailed guidance on teleworker health and safety, covering the following issues:

- Equipment layout
- Positioning of cables
- Lighting
- Ventilation
- Handling and carrying equipment
- Suitable chairs
- Lighting levels
- Noise levels
- Ventilation and humidity
- Fire safety issues such as the fitting of smoke detectors and access to an extinguisher.
- Inadvisability of allowing children to play with company PC.

This level of detail may not be required in some situations. It is important

Telecommuting myths

The state of Arizona in the US has run a largescale telecommuting programme which was evaluated by a team from Arizona State University. The evaluation team came up with a list of common "myths" brought up by people in focus groups as initial barriers which were not born out by the actual experience of telecommuting:

- *I won't know they're working at home;*
- *I won't get promoted if I telecommute;*
- *Telecommuters must work at home five days a week;*
- *Telecommuters are not available when you need them;*
- *Telecommuting isn't for everyone so it's not fair;*
- *Everyone will want to telecommute;*
- *Equipment will be expensive;*
- *Telecommuters cause more work for supervisors;*
- *Telecommuters cause more work for co-workers;*
- *Our type of jobs aren't compatible to telecommuting;*
- *The public would not support state employees working from home;*
- *Our employees deal with confidential information so they can't telecommute,*

The actual experience refuting these issues can be found at **www.telecommuting.state.az.us/evaluation/common.html**

that employers specify how they will check and monitor the health and safety of the employee's working environment. Oxfordshire County Council issues a health and safety checklist to employees for completion, while Glaxo Group Research includes in its teleworking contract that "the individual must provide a working environment which satisfies Company security and health and safety requirements". Health and safety issues are covered in more detail in Chapter 7, *Staying Safe and Legal,* pages 195–9.

Communication procedures

Effective communication is the key factor for successful teleworking. The change to teleworking requires replacement of many of the informal communications methods of the traditional workplace, so it can be useful to clarify how the teleworker is expected to use different methods (phone, fax, email) to avoid misunderstandings and communication difficulties. If the company already has detailed reporting procedures or communications guidelines between colleagues or between managers and subordinates, these may need some revision to incorporate teleworking. It is more usual to find that there are no communications guidelines in place, in which case it is probably worthwhile to ask teleworkers and their managers to sit down with a draft communications agreement and come up with a structure which suits them.

The issues which should be addressed in the communications agreement include:

- location of the home office or other remote workplace and contact details

- use of fax, phone, email, collection of voicemail (this should also include common-sense guidelines such as not carrying on commercially sensitive conversations using mobile phones in public places where they can be overheard).

- agreed core contact times – reporting-in arrangements, arrangements for teleworker to receive work instructions, arrangements for informing manager of task completion, and arrangements to keep the office informed of the whereabouts of a remote employee

- arrangements for access to technical support for equipment or software problems

- arrangements for scheduling meetings with colleagues and managers

- delivery of internal communications (memos, newsletters) to the teleworker

- access as appropriate to groupware technology such as intranets, computerised diaries, or "Netmeeting"-type software

- arrangements for monitoring work performance (note that where keystroke or call-listening methods are used, the employee must be informed of their use)

- procedures for reporting problems such as harrassment via email or other abuse of company communications systems
- any arrangements for non-teleworking colleagues to act as "office buddy" or mentor for the teleworker
- arrangements for reviewing the teleworking arrangement and dealing with any training needs.

Career development and training

A training assessment should be carried out for teleworkers. Likely topics will include:

- computer/IT skills *eg* remote access/Internet usage
- self-management skills *eg* priority setting, time management
- ability to recognise and deal with symptoms of isolation and demotivation
- training needs of the teleworker's manager – *eg* management by results, goal setting, progress monitoring, giving feedback
- health and safety training (this may already be covered in standard company induction training) – the responsibility of the employer for health and safety of employees, and the responsibility of employees to take reasonable care of their health and safety, and to report defects in equipment or working conditions leading to risks.

Some potential teleworkers worry that they may miss out on opportunities for promotion or training, and become isolated from the company. Many agreements or policies contain a clause stipulating that entitlements and arrangements for career development, training and performance appraisals will be unchanged by a teleworking arrangement.

Security

Security procedures are usually similar to the Company's existing security procedures, but may require adjustment. For example, if secure-document waste is normally shredded, but the teleworker has no access to a shredder, it may be necessary for documents to be returned to the office for shredding. Issues to consider include:

- dealing with secure document waste
- locking the home office/password protecting the home computer
- checking for computer viruses
- ensuring software installed complies with licences (non-duplication)
- keeping data backups (it is advisable for one set of backups to be held at the central office site in case of damage or theft at the home office)
- confidentiality and non-disclosure agreements.

See Chapter 8, *Staying safe and legal* (pages 222–6) for further security guidelines, and Chapter 12, *Teleworking equipment* (pages 307–12).

Terms and conditions

An employee who teleworks has the same employment rights, and is protected by the same employment legislation as all other employees. However, some clarification of elements of terms and conditions may be needed such as:

- What core hours must be worked (if any)?
- Which hours or days are to be worked in the office and which teleworked?
- What is the procedure for agreeing and monitoring working time, overtime, sickness and holiday arrangements?
- Is there any change to the application of bonus systems?
- Is there any element of piecework – if so how is this applied?
- Reimbursement of expenses (see below) for heat, light, cleaning of the home office, stationery, postage, telecommunications, travel
- Benefit-in-kind: taxation implications of any personal use of equipment such as PCs
- Fringe benefits – will there be any change in their application?

Expenses. The introduction of teleworking may involve readjustment in pay and conditions which can have financial implications for both sides. Most companies pay allowances to teleworkers to cover their home office costs. This might cover paying for office cleaning, taking post, getting office supplies, *etc*. Review arrangements for petty cash expenses. For smaller organisations, a system of reimbursing receipted expenses, plus payments covering any increased costs are the norm. For larger organisations with many teleworkers, the administrative burden of handling individual receipts may be uneconomic, in which case an annual or monthly agreed allowance will be preferable.

A fixed amount payable to the employee revisable on a yearly basis is perhaps the neatest way of proceeding. The sums involved may be based on before and after usage or on an apportionment in relation to space used for work within the home. In the latter case, the basis of the allowance should be an analysis of the running costs of the house (heat, light, cleaning repairs, insurance, council tax) divided by the proportion of the house used for business. These amounts should be declared on the annual P11D form returned by the employer. Alternatively, dispensation for the amounts should be agreed with both the Inspector of Taxes and the Contributions Agency. Employees could be liable for tax if the employer pays more than can be shown to be a justifiable amount.

Shell UK pays an allowance to its teleworkers of between £1,040 and £1,860 depending on the number of days spent working at home. Oxfordshire County Council pays £50/month for wear and tear on the home office plus increased energy usage. At the other end of the scale, GlaxoWellcome Research Group believes that added expenses for teleworkers are balanced out by savings on travel and does not make any payment. This was also the position of Britannia Building Society when it trialled teleworking – heating costs would be balanced out by travel savings.

The payment of allowances has tax implications. All non-cash benefits and expenses provided to employees in the course of their employment are taxed. However, for this reason many employers include statements in teleworking agreements forbidding personal use of equipment, or advising the teleworker that it is their responsibility to seek advice on the tax implications of personal use. The 1999 British budget included a measure to exempt PCs provided by employers from being treated as a perk or "benefit in kind". This exemption covers equipment worth up to £2000 but there is a catch – it will only apply to companies which do not restrict the provision of equipment just to senior staff and directors. The tax charge on mobile phones was also abolished in the 1999 budget.

Advice should be sought before making any one-off payment to compensate for a change in working practices since these can also be deemed a taxable benefit. More information about taxation isues is given in Chapter 7, *Staying safe and legal*.

It is difficult to be definitive about types of expenses in isolation so it is wise to verify with the Inspector of Taxes and the Contributions Agency the detail of compensation arrangements before paying the expense. One of our advisers said: "You could line up ten tax inspectors and get ten different answers" – and suggested agreement should be sought in writing. The problem is not confined to inspectors as different tax advisers also give conflicting advice, reflecting the complexity of interpreting tax law and its changing nature as new ways of working develop.

According to some sources recompense can be made for proportions of heat, light, cleaning and council tax. Small World Connections, in its 1997 corporate teleworking survey for *Flexible Working* magazine reports that 85% of companies using teleworkers pay for business calls, while 75% supply office stationery. Around 25% pay for insurance, while 5% pay for heating, lighting and a contribution towards rent.

Travel. An employee working at home can argue that the home is the real place of work and hence travel to the office is business travel and reimbursable tax-free. Maurice Parry-Wingfield of Touche Ross however advises caution in this area: "It is essential that the employee is formally instructed by the employer to work at home rather than at the employer's workplace and to use the equipment at home. If teleworking is purely a matter of personal choice the employee will not be able to claim deductions for domestic or travel expenses provided."

The situation is clearer for mobile teleworkers such as salesforce staff who use home as a base – in most situations, all their travel costs will be reimbursable.

Oxfordshire County Council's Flexiplace scheme

Oxfordshire County Council employs 16,000 people, 80% of them female, and over 60% part-timers, many of whom work flexitime. In 1992 the Council introduced a flexiplace scheme, as part of a bottom-up, grassroots initiative to allow working from home where appropriate. Now flexiplace is mainstream for Oxfordshire, and the council is moving towards introducing desksharing. The prime consideration has been that there should be no effects on the level and quality of the service provided. To date the scheme has been largely "budget neutral" – costs have to be met from the normal operating budget of the relevant department, and there have been no major workspace savings. However, there have been reductions in journeys and their associated costs which are important because Oxfordshire suffers from traffic congestion and the council wants to reduce any unnecessary journeys.

Personnel officer Hilary Simpson says the introduction and development of the scheme was "pleasingly non-eventful", but that by now everyone who was going to volunteer probably has done so. "We let it grow and when we started, the technology probably wasn't sufficient to support what we were doing. Now the first point of contact for most councils is by phone and everyone has email so during this year we will be raising the profile of our Flexiplace and Travelwise schemes to match the technology advances". Hilary stresses that giving employees flexibility about where they work is "an efficiency issue, an environmental issue and an equal opportunities issue" and that people design their own work patterns. The Council pays to employees who regularly work a substantial proportion of their time at home a £50-a-month allowance to cover increased energy costs and household wear and tear.

Example 1

An animal health inspector can now drive straight from home to markets in North Oxfordshire without reporting to the head office in South Oxfordshire first. The Council is making major savings on the cost of journeys back to base, freeing the inspectors to devote more of their time to looking after animal welfare.

Example 2

A management accountant in the department of leisure and arts works a 30-hour week contract, of which ten hours are now home-based. "I tend to work in the office between the hours when my children are at school. Then at home I usually work in the evenings when I can really get my head down."

Example 3

The head of the trading standards information unit works 25 hours a week. Normally she spends mornings in the Oxford office, and then does the rest of her work from home.

Self-employed teleworking contractors

Once companies begin to allow their own employees to telework, it is often the case that they become happier with the idea of using contractors who work at a distance as well, because they are more familiar with managing at a distance. The number of self-employed teleworkers, part-time arrangements, and flexible agreements is continually increasing. Employers need to ensure that they do not, through the nature of their arrangement with the contractor, establish an employee-employer relationship without intending to. Simply creating an agreement which absolves the employer of any responsibility for the contractor's tax and national insurance payments is unlikely to be valid if the conditions are not agreed by the relevant authorities. Further guidance is given in Chapter 8, *Staying safe and legal* (pages 205–10).

Draft teleworking agreement

While a company telework policy will answer most issues which could arise between a teleworker and the company, a specific agreement signed by the teleworker is also advisable. This can refer to the company policy in places, or specify exactly the arrangements for that teleworker. It will usually be drafted as a variation to the employee's existing contract of employment. The draft given below can be varied to take account of individual circumstances, and likely topics for inclusion are italicised.

Name: _____
Address at which the telework/distance work will mostly be performed:
_____

Telephone number: _____
Mobile telephone number: _____
Details of position/nature of work _____
_____

Hours of work *(office-based hours, home-based hours, core hours, flexible hours, recording of working time, overtime, etc.)*
_____

Communications structures *(core contact times, arrangements for meetings, feedback, mentoring, etc.)* _____
Reporting-in procedures _____
Home Office arrangements *(technical requirements, provision of equipment and furniture, maintenance arrangements, prevention of misuse, personal use of equipment, health and safety, insurance)*
_____

Training *(induction training, technology training, self-management skills etc.)* _____
Security and confidentiality arrangements *(any differences from standard company policies)*

Terms and conditions *(any differences from standard company arrangements)*

Arrangements for suspension/termination of teleworking

Monitoring and review process

- I have read and understood the company policy on teleworking and agree to a teleworking arrangement as set out above.
- I have agreed that a health and safety risk assessment will be required on the proposed workplace for teleworking.
- I will operate in accordance with the company safety statement.
- I have informed my mortgage/insurance company that I intend to use my home for business purposes.
- I understand that teleworking is not a substitute for childcare.
- I understand that the teleworking arrangement does not affect my status as an employee.
- I understand the arrangement for termination of the teleworking agreement by myself or by the company.

Signed (employee) _____
Signed (company) _____
Date: _____

Trade unions and consultation

For a teleworking agreement to be successful, it must be widely supported and agreed by both management and workers. This is likely to depend on three factors:

- **Consultation** – often happens through a trade union.
- **Voluntary** nature of the agreement – anyone who becomes dissatisfied with the arrangement must have available to them a clear route back to the main office.
- **Timescale** – all involved will need time to consider the issues and for discussion before any decisions are made or agreements signed.

The 1997 TUC report *New Information and Communications Technologies at Work* highlights trade union concern that: "Teleworking can lead to the development of a two-tier employment structure, with full-time, permanent, office-based workers at the core and part-time, temporary, home-based workers at the periphery." These concerns are also tied to a more general phenomenon of "pseudo self-employment" where companies encourage workers to become self-employed in order to reduce their

Shell UK: culture changes and premises savings

Shell's retail arm has swapped a prime Central London office for a mixture of homeworking and sharing space at satellite offices located near the company's filling stations around the M25. Lydia Ney of scheme architects and designers BDG McColl comments "If you work next to a petrol station and there is no sandwich bar nearby, you have to eat whatever the station sells. If those are the products you are responsible for promoting, it will certainly make you conscious of product quality."

The scheme has moved over 100 staff from Shell Mex House into buildings around the M25 refurbished as telecentres. Property costs have been cut by 45%, while reorganising the company into a flatter management structure based around products rather than regional operations.

Most of the financial and operations staff have been relocated to a core office near Ealing, with another 30 staff working from a Crawley core office, but most of the senior finance, property and network-planning staff work at home and use drop-in facilities at the filling stations. There is also a group of trading and marketing staff who have always been mobile workers.

Although the buildings differ in shape, each satellite office has the same layout. By reception there is a break-out zone for ad-hoc meetings and drop-in working with data points built in to the furniture. Next there is a services hub with stationery storage, printing, scanning and fax facilities. Further back from the reception bustle are meeting spaces of varying sizes and a larger area of workstations with PCs. At the back of the space lie quite enclosed spaces for concentrated work.

The centres are open 24 hours and staffed by receptionists from 9 am to 5 pm. Outside that time staff can gain access through a swipe card. All instructions for facilities and equipment are set out both on labels attached to the machines and in a handbook issued to all staff.

Technical support is provided through a helpline run by Shell's IT department and backed up by another helpline dealing with facilities problems and run by Honeywell. Hotdesks and meeting spaces can be booked from anywhere on the Shell Intranet using Microsoft's Schedule software. Senior staff are not allowed to pull rank in booking space, and anyone who does not show up for their meeting can be bumped from the booked space after one-and-a-half hours.

Staff who opted for home offices have been given a laptop with docking station and combined fax/printer/scanner plus a budget of £600 to buy homeworking furniture. Full training and instructional handbooks formed a vital part of the project.

(Adapted with permission from an article by Louis Wustemann in Flexible Working Magazine www.irseclipse.co.uk/publications/flexi.html)

responsibilities (the example is often given of Rank Xerox consultants in Britain who were given the option to become self-employed rather than being made redundant in the 1980s).

The document states: "It is clear that while teleworking suits some workers well, for others it creates problems. These may vary from person to person and will also vary in different workplaces, depending on the particular teleworking arrangements. Trade unions need to be able to respond to the issues affecting a particular worker or group of workers in different situations".

The TUC report highlights the equal opportunities issues which may be raised by teleworking. "25% of telework managers in Ursula Huws' 1993 survey listed 'maturity' as a criteria for recruiting teleworkers and over 45% listed self-sufficiency. There is a danger of bias if managers make largely subjective judgements over [such] factors… as with all recruitment situations, selection of teleworkers should be based on criteria that can be objectively measured… some may be barred from teleworking because they do not have access to a quiet space which could be used for work during the day… it would be highly discriminatory for such factors to militate against employment and this creates a strong equal opportunities argument for not designating certain jobs as teleworking jobs."

One of the case studies listed in Small World Connection's 1997 corporate teleworking survey (published in connection with *Flexible Working* magazine), an NHS trust, specifically mentioned that in future they will be assessing staff suitability for teleworking as part of a pre-recruitment exercise using a structured questionnaire format.

Another case study in the same document, on Skandia Life, gives details of the reasons why three out of seven teleworkers dropped out of a teleworking trial instigated to cover a skills shortage by utilising women returners over a period of years. One of the teleworkers is described as "playing games" and not putting in the time and effort to get the work done. Another had "a short history of domestic crises interfering with work which eventually resulted in the individual leaving of her own accord". The third showed "no apparent problem for some time and it seemed that the individual concerned was enjoying the work and getting on well, until out of the blue it seemed that she was no longer able to carry on teleworking. It seems likely that pressure from the family contributed in this case."

Skandia Life had discussed the special demands of teleworking with all the teleworkers before the project began, and suggests that other companies might like to learn from their experience and in future get feedback from other family members before recruiting teleworkers. This sentiment is understandable, but again shows the "territorial" and borderline difficulties which can arise between equal opportunities, business objectives and employment rights when home and work overlap.

The isolation from co-workers inherent in teleworking can restrict negotiations for appropriate rates of pay, as shown in the University of

Virtual company design proves Intrinsic worth

Intrinsic is a company providing software to manage databases for advertising campaigns. Set up in 1993 by Dr Steve Treadwell and Shaun Doyle, the company is based in Faringdon, Oxfordshire but 93 of the 95 employees work from home in locations ranging from Glasgow to the Isle of Wight. The company had a turnover of £1.5 million in 1998 and recently received a £4 million injection of growth capital from GE Equity. Clients include Thames Water, Sainsbury's, Orange and Norwich Union.

Dr Treadwell believes the company's success is due to the way it began life on a virtual basis. "We tend to attract certain types of people – mature self-confident people who feel they can work independently and whose family commitments make working from home a more realistic option". Employees are supplied with office equipment, computers and ISDN lines but Dr Treadwell believes there is no substitute for face to face contact between staff. "We usually bring the whole company together at a country house somewhere. We do have some presentations but the main purpose of the day will be for people to socialise and chat, to put a face to the voice they speak to on the phone."

Work times are flexible, and Dr Treadwell says the biggest problem is persuading people not to work too hard. "We had to threaten to switch off the email server because people were going into their offices for hours on a Sunday evening and we don't want that. They would burn out." (**www.intrinsic.co.uk**)

Westminster's 1993 Work Research Group survey of self-employed teleworkers in the UK publishing industry. Over 100 respondents indicated that loneliness, isolation and lack of contact with clients and colleagues caused problems. Over half of the interviewees did not receive a "living income" due to insufficient workload and low rates of pay. The report noted that "neither the National Union of Journalists nor the Society of Freelance Editors and Proofreaders has been able to foster sufficient solidarity amongst freelancers to maintain any generally observed rates of pay." Many unions are concerned that teleworking can mask an attempt by employers to push employees towards self-employed status.

However, the Manufacturing, Science and Finance union is campaigning to see a wide range of employment opportunities being made available to the home-based worker.and has produced guidelines, and a code of practice for employees:

- Teleworkers should be employees of an enterprise and not deemed self-employed;
- To avoid isolation, contracts of employment should require home workers to periodically attend the office;
- There should be a separate room available at home for teleworking, a separate telephone and payment for additional costs such as heating and lighting;

ACAS telebuddies pair up for professionalism

ACAS, the Advisory, Conciliation and Arbitration Service, has about 600 employees. Staff are involved in resolving disputes between individuals and their employers and in resolving large-scale industrial disputes, covering a wide geographical area and travelling between ACAS offices as well as to client sites. A considerable level of informal homeworking had developed, so ACAS decided to run a pilot project in a region to gauge effects on staff and service levels. ACAS also commissioned research from the Institute of Employment Studies on the best method of developing good practice in homeworking.

A case study based on the IES work has been published which emphasises telebuddies as one of the most successful features of the ACAS scheme. Everyone is paired with a buddy who is kept in touch with current work. Because they are fully briefed on each others' caseload, buddies can stand in for each other in case of sickness or if their buddy is on holiday or over-booked. The buddy is also first port of call if someone needs information or advice, or just wants to talk through a difficult problem.

IES report author Ursula Huws comments: "If you have a lot of people essentially doing the same job for an organisation it's fairly easy to pair people in this way, but it can also work for freelancers". Huws has paired herself with a friend who is also a long-established teleworker although her friend's work is more focussed on writing and editing than research. "We share all sorts of trumphs and frustrations. Over the years we have developed a pattern of ringing each other up whenever we've got something to share. If you need to blow your top, it's much better to do it to a trusted buddy than a client. And sometimes you need a pat on the back from someone – the sort of feedback you'd get from a colleague at the next desk if you were in an office.

www.acas.org.uk

- There should be regular meetings between teleworkers and the provision of electronic mail and telephone links with other teleworkers, all to be provided at the employer's expense;
- There should be regular weekly liaison discussions between a teleworker and his or her supervisor/manager;
- Teleworkers should enjoy the same rates of pay and employment benefits as office-based workers including childcare provision and family leave. There should be a defined number of working hours. They should be included in career development and appraisal schemes including training opportunities;
- All computer equipment should be provided, paid for and serviced by the employer who will be responsible for the installation, maintenance, insurance and compliance with health and safety requirements. The

employer should also accept legal responsibility for any accident or injury;
- Teleworkers should have access to trade union representation and be able to attend meetings within working hours. Health and safety advisors and trade union representatives should be able to visit teleworkers;
- Teleworking should be voluntary with a right to return to working from the office.

Source: Peter Skyte, MSF Union **www.msf.org.uk**

In addition, the banking trade union BIFU notes the following points for negotiators:
- desk, chair, paper, pens to be supplied by the company;
- no 'spy in the home' cameras or key depression monitoring to be fitted to a homeworker's VDU;
- management should ensure that each homeworker has the opportunity to meet and discuss issues appertaining to their work at least once a week;
- teleworking should never be used as an alternative to adequate workplace or state childcare;
- all homeworkers' contracts should be collectively agreed between management and the union, ensuring that individuals do not find their terms and conditions worsened in comparison with other staff.

The public service union UNISON also has guidelines which include the following additional points:
- a particular manager should be assigned to ensure regular contact;
- homeworkers should enjoy the same rights as other workers to join trade unions and have their own representatives;
- all teleworkers should be entitled to an annual review of their working arrangements.

The Society of Telecoms Executives made the point in their agreement with BT that: "Teleworkers can expect a career in BT. Their managers must give them feedback on their performance, including an annual appraisal, and must identify development needs. Teleworkers have access to all appropriate training packages and courses. They should also be notified of current vacancies within BT, via the same channels as office-based workers."

The Communications Workers Union has also created a model agreement in relation to BT's teleworking arrangements where it requested that it should also have access to the technology linking teleworkers to management (such as email) in order to provide member services on an equal basis.

The National Union of Journalists provides members with subsidised email and online information services, and is moving into providing relevant training in software skills for members. Over 25% of NUJ members are self-employed.

US telecommuting consultant Gil Gordon believes that all communications over a company network would have to be considered insecure, as they could be monitored by the company, and that employees should consider this if contacting union representatives over company email systems.

The European umbrella body for white-collar unions, FIET, is lobbying for rights for online workers:

- The right of free access by employees and by trade unions and works councils to corporate email systems so that employee members can receive information and communicate with their representatives

- The right of free access to the Internet (and to corporate intranet networks) by employees to enable them to access trade union websites and other information relevant to their rights to work

- No electronic monitoring by employers of email sent or websites visited by employees.

The CWU in Ireland has been involved in representing freelance teleworkers and developing teleworking – a development that is in line with the move by a number of European white-collar unions to begin representing the self-employed as well as PAYE workers, although as writer Andrew Bibby points out: "There will remain a core philosophical area which will separate unions from simple commercial information and advice services. There is still the concept of solidarity – the idea that individuals who join a union do so not just to help themselves but also to help each other."

Acknowledgements

Thanks to Croner Publications for allowing us to refer to text from *Flexible Working Practices* – a comprehensive guide for employers.
Tel: 0181 547 3333 Fax: 0181 547 2637.

The TCA is also indebted to the following people for their guidance in preparing this section:

Maurice Parry-Wingfield of Touche Ross Tel: 0171 936 3000;

Mathew Brown of Independent Accountancy Services
Tel: 0171 375 1001 Email: mail@iasltd.co.uk

Contributions Agency and Inland Revenue local offices and press office;

Chris Ridgewell of VIP Consultants **www.vipconsultants.co.uk**

Stephen Jupp, New Ways of Working consultant
http://freespace.virgin.net/stephen.jupp/.

Bibliography

Telecommuting Review   Periodical
Editor: Gil Gordon
Source: Gil Gordon Associates, 11 Donner Crt, Monmouth Jn, New Jersey, USA
Tel: +001 8852 732 329 2266
Comment: US periodical publication available at www.gilgordon.com

An evaluation of homeworking in ACAS   *Date:* 2000
Author: Ursula Huws
Source: ACAS Tel: 020 7396 5100 www.acas.org.uk

Business guide to e-work   *Date:* 2000
Authors: Imogen Bertin, Brian Goggin and Brian O'Kane
Source: Enterprise Ireland www.e-work.ie

The Work-Life Manual   *Date:* 2000
Authors: Lucy Daniels and Lucy McCarraher
Source: Industrial Society ISBN 1–85835–875–2 www.indsoc.co.uk

**Teleworking and Local Government
– assessing the costs and benefits**   *Date:* 1999
Author: Ursula Huws
Source: Local Government Management Board
Tel: 020 7296 6756 Email: david.maycock@lgmb.gov.uk

An Organizational Guide to Telecommuting: *Date:* 1998
Author: George M. Piskurich
Source: American Society for Training and Development
ISBN 1–56286–086–0

Directions for Teleworking   *Date:* 1998
Stoke City Council £20
Tel: 01782 232889 Email: dennis.a.marsh@stkoe01.stoke-cc.gov.uk

Flexible Working
Source: The Eclipse Group, 18-20 Highbury Place, London, N5 1QP,
Ref: ISSN 1360-9505. Tel: 020 7354 5858
Web: www.irseclipse.co.uk/publications/flexi.html
Comment: Periodical

Managing Telework: strategies for managing the virtual workforce   *Date:* 1998
Author: Jack M. Nilles (www.jala.com)
Source: John Wiley and Sons, Inc. ISBN 0–471–29316–4

Manual of Remote Working   *Date:* 1997
Authors: Kevin Curran and Geoff Williams
Source: Gower Publishing Ltd, Gower House, Croft Road, Aldershot, Hampshire
GU11 3HR

New Information and Communications Technologies at Work   *Date:* 1997
Source: Trade Union Congress Publications, Congress House,
Great Russell St, London WC1B 3LS

Changing Places – A Manager's Guide to Working from Home   *Date:* 1996
Source: New Ways to Work, 309 Upper Street, London N1 2TY Tel: 020 7226 4026

Flexible Working   *Date:* 1996
Author: Steve Simmons
Source: Kogan Page, 120 Pentonville Road, London N1 9JN
Ref: ISBN 0–7494–1713–7
Comment: practical guide to flexible working including tick-box express implementation guide for the project manager in a hurry

Guide to Teleworking *Date:* 1996
Source: Surrey County Council, County Hall, Penrhyn Road,
Kingston-upon-Thames, Surrey KT1 2DN

**Homeworking: Guidance for employers and employees
on health and safety** *Date:* 1996
Author: Health and Safety Executive
Source: HSE Books, PO Box 199, Sudbury, Suffolk CO10 6FS
Tel: 01787 881165 Fax: 017187 313995.

Teleworking and Gender *Date:* 1996
Author: Ursula Huws
Source: European Commission DGV, Brussels

Trade Unions and Telework *Date:* 1996
Author: Andrew Bibby
Source: Fiet, Avenue de Balexert 15, CH-1219 Chatelaine-Geneva, Switzerland
Web: www.eclipse.co.uk/pens/bibby/fietrpt

Working at Home – A Study of Homeworking and Teleworking *Date:* 1996
Author: Celia Stanworth
Source: Institute of Employment Rights Tel: 020 7738 9511 Fax: 020 7738 9577.

A Manager's Guide to Teleworking *Date:* 1995
Author: Ursula Huws on behalf of Department of Employment
Source: Dept of Employment, Cambertown Ltd., Unit 8 Goldthorpe Ind. Estate,
Rotherham, S. Yorks Tel: 020 7273 6969

Employment of Homeworkers: Examples of Good Practice *Date:* 1995
Authors: Ursula Huws and Sarah Podro
Source: International Labour Organisation

Guide to Remote Working – A Practical Manual *Date:* 1995
Authors: Tynedale Network
Source: Tynedale Network, 362 Durham Road, Low Fell, Gateshead, NE9 5AP
Tel: 0191 420 0280

Teleworking and the Labour Movement *Date:* 1995
Author: Labour Telematics Centre
Source: 3Com Europe Ltd, Eaton Court, Maylands Avenue,
Hemel Hempstead, Herts HP2 7DF

Flexiplace Scheme *Date:* 1994
Author: Oxfordshire County Council
Source: Commercial Services Print Unit, Oxfordshire County Council
Tel: 01865 815672 Ref. C21-17

**Self-employment and Labour Market Restructuring –
the Case of Freelance Teleworkers in Book Publishing** *Date:* 1993
Authors: Celia Stanworth, John Stanworth, David Purdy
Source: Future of Work Research Group, University of Westminster,
35 Marylebone Road London NW1 5LS Tel: 020 7911 5000

Homeworking Strategy *Date:* 1993
Authors: Borough of Blackburn, Economic Development Department
Source: Shaheen Sameja, City Challenge Access Point, Brook House Business Centre,
Whalley Range, Blackburn, Lancashire, BB1 6BB Tel: 01254 676796

Teleworking Explained *Date:* 1993
Authors: Mike Gray, Noel Hodson, Gil Gordon
Source: John Wiley & Sons, Baffins Lane, Chichester Ref: ISBN 0 471 93975 7
Comments: Extremely comprehensive teleworking guide

Contacts and URLs

Blackburn Borough Council Tel: 01254 260736 Web: **www.blackburn.gov.uk**.

BT's Working from Home site has information from its Workstyles consultancy
Web: **www.wfh.co.uk**

Communications Workers' Union of Ireland, 575 North Circular Road, Dublin 1
Tel: +353 1 836 6388 Fax: +353 1 836 5582 Contact: Chris Hudson
Email: chris@cwu.ie Web: **www.cwu.ie**

Coventry City Council, Homeworking Officer, Economic Development and Planning, Tower Block, Much Park Street, Coventry CV1 2PY Tel: 024 7683 1285
Web: **www.invest-in-coventry.co.uk**.

Gil Gordon's excellent website: **www.gilgordon.com**

Jack Nilles website with information on selecting and managing teleworkers
www.jala.com

Irish development agency Enterprise Ireland has a comprehensive website including a business guide to telework and video clips at **www.e-work.ie**

Labour Telematics Centre, GMB National College, College Road, Whalley Range, Manchester M16 8PB Tel: 0161 860 4364 Fax: 0161 881 1853
Email: labourteladmin@mcr1.poptel.org.uk
Web: **www.labourtel.org.uk**

Trade Union Congress, Congress House, 23-28 Great Russell Street, London
WC1B 3LS Tel: 020 7636 4030 x1305 Fax: 020 7467 1317 Contact: Janet Williamson
Web: **www.tuc.org.uk**

European Foundation for the Improvement of Living and Working Conditions, Wyattville Road, Loughlinstown, Dublin, Ireland.
Tel: +353 1 204 3100 Fax: +353 1 282 6456
Contact: Eberhard Köhler, Research Co-ordinator
Email: eberhard.kohler@eurofound.ie Web: **www.eurofound.ie**

MSF Union Contact Peter Skyte at MSF, 40 Bermondsey Street, London SE1 3UD
Tel: 020 7939 7086 Fax: 020 7403 2964 Email: skytep@msf.org.uk
Web: **www.msf.org.uk**

Ursula Huws Web: **http://dialspace.dial.pipex.com/town/parade/hg54**

www.eclipse.co.uk/pens/bibby/telework.html is journalist Andrew Bibby's home pages which contain a number of articles on teleworking including the FIET report.

The Institute of Employment Studies website has a number of reports relating to teleworking including several by Ursula Huws – **www.employment-studies.co.uk**

Rochdale Borough Council Homeworking Office, PO Box 15, Town Hall, Rochdale, OL16 1AB Tel: 01706 864377.

www.collaborate.com is the address for Collaborate Strategies, a CSCW consultancy that maintains a useful site with info on Workflow and Groupware/Teleworking systems. They also produce a commercial newsletter.

www.isi.gov.uk is the address for the UK's Dept of Trade and Industry's new "Information Society Initiative", targeted at raising business awareness and use of internet, open electronic networking, *etc*

www.energy.state.or.us/telework/telehm.htm has information produced by the Oregon Office of Energy about telework and telecommuting.

www.voffice.com is a site for virtual offices in London.

Consultants

There are a number of consultancies in Britain and Ireland which specialise in teleworking and related issues. Brief information and contact details are given here.

BT Workstyles Consultancy Group (WCG) www.wfh.co.uk
WCG evolved from BT's much publicised Workstyle 2000 programme which began in 1993. WCG's client base includes diverse organisations such as Microsoft, the AA, Surrey and Kent County Councils, Barclays, Littlewoods, Eli Lilley and the BBC. WCG tries to provide a holistic perspective covering operational change, technology, human resource and property considerations. There are bespoke consultancy services as well as standard packages such as:

- Flexible working audit: how do your people work and how could they work?
- Change management: planning to overcome resistance and involve all stakeholders
- Virtual Call Centre: exploiting the operational benefits of agents based at home
- New Property Infrastructure: developing a strategy to incorporate hotdesking, touchdown and project rooms.

VIP Global Consultants www.vipconsultants.co.uk
VIP has three founding partners who have all previously run major flexible working programmes in the IT or Telecoms sectors. The organisation is run on a "virtual company" basis from the partner's home offices and other facilities.

- David Markby has held various positions for UK subsidiaries of US companies such as Computer Sciences and Leasco Software Ltd
- Chris Ridgewell has run management consultancy services for Mercury Communications and change-management programmes for France Telecom.
- Peter Thomson is an expert in personnel management and held senior posts with Rank Xerox and Digital amongst others. He founded the Future Work Forum at Henley Management College.

The Home Office Partnership www.hop.co.uk
HOP believes the key to successful introduction of new ways of working is to get traditionally distinct departments such as personnel, marketing, facilities, IT and finance to work together with a shared commitment to common objectives. HOP sees its role as providing good external advice and support to overcome barriers to change, bringing perspective and experience from other organisations that have faced similar strategies. HOP staff include Bob Crichton, who previously had long experience with consulting group PA; Andy Lake, editor of HOP's Flexibility magazine and

a number of reports on teleworking in local government. Their programmes include:

- Awareness and training programmes including seminars, workshops and practical guides
- Audits, analyses, surveys and studies with fully justified recommendations for management
- Development projects to pilot and evaluate recommendations before planning large-scale rollout.
- Implementation programmes where HOP can act as advisors, monitors, trouble-shooters or project managers.

Small World Connections (SWC) www.smallworldconnections.com
SWC has been assisting large organisations and local/central government departments in the UK with their teleworking strategies since 1992. They have organised awareness raising seminars and workshops for clients and run telework training programmes. Between 1995–1998 SWC organised and ran the UK Corporate Telework Forum – a discussion group for telework specialists representing many major UK organisations including four of the "big five" clearing banks. SWC has carried out three surveys on corporate telework in the UK and developed a complete set of telework training materials suitable for teleworkers and their managers.

Others
The TCA has conducted a number of teleworking consultancy projects – usually where these coincide with the aims of the association.
Email: info@tca.org.uk

Louis Wustemann, editor of *Flexible Working* magazine, specialises in advice on flexible working and teleworking for the public sector.
Email: lw@sivill.demon.co.uk

Ursula Huws of Analytica carries out research and report writing for private companies as well as academic institutions, governments, the EU and UN bodies focussing on social and economic aspects.
Email: analytica@dial.pipex.co.uk

Imogen Bertin of Cork Teleworking focuses on the practical detail of implementation plans – presentations, surveys, induction training and monitoring of telework programmes. **www.cork-teleworking.com**

IHM Solutions mainly focuses on training and the introduction of ecommerce to businesses but has carried out some teleworking projects with organisations in the public sector.
Email: info@ihmsolutions.co.uk

Stephen Jupp, formerly of HOP and Digital, is now operating as a "new ways of working" consultant **Email: stephen.jupp@iee.org**

Survival guide

This chapter is based mainly on the experiences of members of teleworking associations, contributors to the TCA's web board (**www.tca.org.uk/forum/**) and former users of the Telework Europa forum on Compuserve.

Should you be teleworking?

This section is freely adapted with permission from Irish telephone operator eircom's teleworking literature (**www.eircom.ie**), which was written by Paul Healy, who is also a contributor to *Teleworker* magazine.

The first step is to be sure why you want to get involved in teleworking. Here are some common reasons – more than one may apply to your own situation, or you may have a reason not listed here:

- I'm very short of time and looking for ways to be more productive and use my time better;
- The office is too distracting for the sort of work I have to do;
- I want to live in my town/village and not in a city;
- I want to combine with work caring for my children/elderly relative/family member and it will be easier if I can work from home;
- I am spending too much time commuting;
- My customers are all over the place – it's easier to work out of a home base, or to move from one customer to another, than to keep returning to the office;
- I have a disability/illness which affects my work. It would be easier to cope and work as well if I could work at home;
- I'm setting up a business and I need to keep the overhead costs down;
- I want to be more independent and manage my own time and tasks.

Next, you need to think about how you want to telework. There are four main types of teleworking:

- Full time from home
- Splitting your time between home and office
- On the move – at customer sites, in the train, in the car, hotdesking
- From a telecentre or telecottage.

You may find that more than one of these methods suits your job. Only a minority of people work full-time at home, and most research shows that if possible you should be spending at least one day a week in the office with your colleagues. Spend some time thinking about how many days or hours you want to telework, and what equipment you will need to carry out your

Lewisham goes location-independent

Sonia Steele, a childcare facilities registration officer for Lewisham borough council gives her personal view of her section's teleworking scheme. Home is now Sonia's main workplace though she visits the office two or three times a week and makes inspection visits to client premises. Her office has been reorganised from 16 desks to four bookable desks and a soft furnishings area for meetings with colleagues.

"There are always reports and casework to write up. I'm never short of work to do at home. It's very calming. I enjoy it. I'm fortunate in that I've got a suitable area in my house to accommodate home working, which has plenty of natural light and looks out on the garden. When you have a large and difficult report to do, it's easier to do it without interruptions.

"The employer supplies us with a PC, chair, table and drawer. We're given a BT chargecard for telephone calls we make from home, and we get an allowance of £100 for the heating and lighting costs. The council carries out a risk assessment of the house and we're advised to tell our insurers that we're now working from home. I think we were all apprehensive when the pilot scheme started. It felt lonely at first, especially when the desks were taken away. An office is like a second home – you create your own little space and take little things in to make yourself comfortable there. But you have to make a positive decision to make homeworking work. You have to think there's no turning back. You need to mentally adjust to it.

"The vital thing is to keep in contact with your colleagues. We had an awayday recently and it was really enjoyable getting to know each other again. Three of us also arranged to take flexitime to go for a six-mile walk but it's up to you to keep in touch and do things together.

"You're inclined to work longer hours at home. At work, you physically leave everything behind at the end of the day. At home, work is there and you think, perhaps I should finish this first. You sometimes have to discipline yourself and say no – hang on a moment, this is my own time. On the other hand it provides greater flexiblity to organise your personal and work life. If you want to take a long lunch hour, time can be made up later. There needs to be trust between the manager and staff to achieve success with homeworking."

Adapted from an article in Flexible Working magazine
www.irseclipse.co.uk/publications/flexi.html

work when you are out of the office – if possible begin a list.

The third step is to analyse your situation critically and see if you are suitable for teleworking. The key qualities are:

- Good self-discipline
- Strong communication skills

Voices of experience...

"I find that it's important to juggle workload according to mood. Some days I am good for nothing but administrative tasks such as catching up on the bills. When I'm working on something involving major writing or creative input, there is always a stage of displacement activities I have to go through before I can start. This is quite stressful at the time because you are ticking yourself off for cleaning out the fridge when you should be in front of the computer racing a looming deadline, but over the years I have realised it is a necessary part of the creative process – whilst I clean the fridge, some sort of composting process takes place in the brain and then the structure, idea or phrase will come that allows me to face the blank screen and get going."

"I used to complete and deliver jobs well ahead of the deadline. Now, I may well finish the job ahead of time but I've learned not to deliver it until close to the deadline. That way, people think I'm busy and leave me alone! It's not a matter of planning your work but of planning your life, setting yourself targets for both the personal and professional spheres and aiming for the proper balance."

- Ability to work independently
- Trustworthiness
- Mature attitude

If you are an employee, your employer will also be considering:

- commitment to the company
- personal productivity in the office
- the suitability of your line manager to supervise you at a distance.

Of course, you have to have a job which has within it some tasks that are suitable for teleworking. The main attributes of job suitability are:

1. high information content
2. comprised of autonomous (separate) tasks
3. can be supervised by setting objectives, (or time deadlines and financial budgets) rather than by face to face contact

To assess your job, try to keep a log of how you are spending your time during the day, divided up into 30-minute intervals. For each half-hour section record what you were doing – telephone calls, working alone at your desk, meetings, breaks and so on.

Now score each half-hour section based on the three suitability points above. Give a 1 for low information content, a 5 for high information content and so on. Average your scores to give an overall mark for each of the three points – information content, autonomous tasks and management supervision. If your job is suitable for teleworking, you will get high scores for all three. You may find that if you do a lot of teamwork, your supervision score suggests that your job is not suitable for teleworking – unless perhaps you can arrange for certain elements of the job to be carried out on "at home" days, while others are carried out when you are "in the office".

Be realistic about the downsides to teleworking – it doesn't suit everyone. Some people miss the company of their office colleagues. Occasionally teleworkers find that they are overlooked for promotion or training opportunities. More commonly, people find it hard to separate work and home life, so that there is never a space in their lives when they can truly "switch off". Once you have read the advice in this chapter, try to outline for yourself how you would cope with some of the negative aspects of teleworking, such as isolation or noise and interruptions.

How do I convince my employer?

Deciding that you would be a good teleworker is less than half the battle: you still have to convince your employer, or if you are planning self-employment, create a business plan (see Chapter 4, *Getting Work*). The best way to convince an employer is to spend time preparing a cost/benefit case to show that it will be helpful for the employer as well as for you. It may not be possible for you to include all the information you need (for example you may not know what "overheads" figure your company uses to cover the office space, heating, lighting, IT facilities that you use while working for them at the moment) but if you can prepare a clear document they will be able to fill in the gaps for themselves.

Research carried out over the past 20 years in Europe and America indicates that teleworkers are:

- More productive (between 10% and 40% more productive)
- More reliable
- More loyal
- More likely to produce better quality work
- Less likely to take time off
- Likely to stay with the organisation for longer.

In addition, allowing telework can help an employer to:

- Attract and retain quality staff as part of a family-friendly human resources policy;
- Relieve space in cramped offices, if it is combined with a hotdesking policy;
- Reduce office overheads – though the saving will not be large if you are also retaining a central office desk;
- Provide coverage outside normal hours.

Of course there are also costs – you will need IT equipment at home, the employer may need to pay for extra telephone lines or different equipment

Telephone communication skills

If you are **imparting information:**

- *don't assume the receiver sees the conversation the same way you do or hears exactly what you wished to say*
- *don't use irritating words and repetitive phrases*
- *don't use inappropriate language (swearwords, sexism, jargon) which the other person doesn't understand or feel comfortable with*
- *don't mumble, fidget, or use distracting mannerisms – speak clearly*
- *don't interrogate the receiver aggressively*
- *avoid jargon*
- *ask one question at a time*
- *listen carefully to the answer*
- *be concise.*

If you are **receiving information** try to avoid:

- *jumping to conclusions and interrupting*
- *changing the subject*
- *talking too much*
- *thinking about what the other person is going to say next rather than listening to what they are saying now*
- *switching off or ignoring what is being said*
- *seeking to score over the other person*
- *competing rather than cooperating*
- *pretending to understand when you don't to avoid embarrassment*
- *being judgmental*
- *being defensive rather than open to the information you are receiving.*

Active listeners try to:

- *signal their interest*
- *listen between lines*
- *ask questions for clarification*
- *avoid criticism*
- *summarise the message before the end of the call.*

such as laptop computers or routers to allow remote access to central computers. There will be management time involved in setting up the teleworking arrangement, and it is important that both you and your manager receive appropriate training for teleworking.

Most of the information you will need to prepare a cost/benefit case for your employer is in this book. Keep your document as short as you can but spell out:

- A brief introduction explaining teleworking and its spread as a working practice, perhaps giving examples of companies using teleworking in your industry sector
- Your job and why it is suitable for teleworking
- Your personal reasons for wishing to telework
- What sort of teleworking arrangement you are proposing (hours, location, etc.)
- The suitability of your home or other premises for teleworking (covering issues like security, availability of a room for use as a home office, discussions you have held with your family, etc.)
- The benefits to your employer of teleworking
- Any disadvantages that you foresee both for you and for your employer
- The cost savings (*eg* if your employer had to replace you, a recruitment company would probably charge 10% of your salary as a finder's fee for your replacement)
- The extra costs (home office equipment, telephone charges, training etc.)

If you think that the teleworking idea is going to be fairly new to your manager it may also be useful to give a brief reference list of books and websites on the subject.

When the report is completed, the normal procedure would be first to approach your line manager, and then for the two of you to approach the human resources department. In exceptional circumstances you may wish to bypass your line manager and approach human resources directly but bear in mind if they feel that your line manager is unsuitable for supervising a teleworker, or is not fully "behind" your application it is quite likely that they will not approve the request unless you can be reassigned to another manager. Management opposition or lack of support is the biggest factor in the failure of teleworking arrangements.

Getting the job done

In articles about teleworking, journalists often ask teleworkers: "How do you make yourself sit down at the computer and start work in the morning? Why don't you just stay in bed?" Any self-employed teleworker can give them the reason: no work – no pay. You need to pay the rent or mortgage, buy food, buy paper and so on. Behind the simplistic journalist's query is a real dilemma: organising your work when there is no-one physically hammering on your office door to ask where that report or memo or piece of software has got to. To avoid upsetting clients or employers, teleworkers need to be very good at managing their time and the projects assigned to them.

One invaluable aid is to buy a personal organiser package which runs on your computer. The groupware packages Microsoft Outlook and Lotus Notes contain a lot of the necessary functions. Not everyone gets on with these (and it has to be said that a well-maintained handwritten list can do the job equally well), but the best of these packages will keep track of your tasks as well as holding information like contact addresses.

Typical teleworker tasks that need to be covered include:

- urgent deadline-based tasks
- major projects that may contain a number of sub-tasks
- routine work such as monthly reports
- regular administrative tasks such as backing-up computer data or preparing VAT returns
- calls to be made
- appointments and meetings.

To carry out this range of tasks you will need:

The transatlantic bank manager

Liz Codling spent 25 years working for the Bank of Montreal's Institute for Learning in Canada before deciding to return to her roots in Britain in 1994. Liz had been involved in the creation of the bank's Learning for Success scheme since 1991, and led a team of eight people: her employers were loathe to lose her.

Now she is a transatlantic telecommuter, working from her home near Dorchester, and has to cope with a five hour time difference from her colleagues. "I attend to my correspondence between 6 am and 8 am. I then have the mornings with my husband and start my working day at 12 noon, or rather, 7 am Toronto time. My colleagues know to book meetings in the morning if they need to include me."

"I miss out on the 'water cooler' conversations but colleagues are good at remembering to let me know about changes. I also found it particularly hard after tough meetings or conversations, because after I hang up I am on my own – I am unable to grab a coffee with a colleague to discuss the outcomes. I've accepted that my decision to become a permanent international telecommuter may well limit career opportunities but I am not complacent. I am always looking at how I can make sure that my job continutes to be of value to the organisation."

- a diary function (with meeting alarms and planners)
- a contacts database (addresses, phone, fax and email numbers)
- a "to do" list which is prioritised and which allows automatic prompting of regularly scheduled tasks.

It's also a big help if the time manager has a function that allows you to record what time you spent working on which project for billing or cost centre purposes. Perhaps the most important piece of advice in this chapter is to ensure that you log every hour that you spend working, whether or not you can claim for it. Do it on the same day, or in the morning of the next day, before you forget. This will also help you to monitor whether you are overworking. You can use Microsoft Outlook's journal function and then export the results to an Excel spreadsheet for calculations at intervals, or use specialist software (see **www.timesheet.com** or projclock at **www.cyber-matrix.com** for a couple of examples).

Motivation is, surprisingly, not reported as much of a problem by most teleworkers, although overworking often is (see "Maintaining the worker" section, pages 108–10). One contributor said: "I add up how much I owe my creditors or how much I still owe on the mortgage. This does wonders for my motivation". Another commented: "My main incentive to work is the arrival of the childminder so I know I've got to get stuck in while I've got peace and quiet!" The voice of experience shines through this contribution: "Try and plan your work so that the first thing you have to do in the morning is not difficult or unpleasant. Break off in the evening at a point which leaves you an easy start first thing the next day. This means that if you do run into a problem the following day you will already be in full swing."

Good tricks for adapting to a new teleworking arrangement without a loss of motivation include:

- Mark the start and end of the working day – walk the dog, water the plants, read the paper;
- Dress for the office if it helps – even if your audience is a toddler and the cat;
- Understand that teleworking is more productive and intense than standard office work – give yourself proper breaks for lunch, coffee, *etc*;
- Prioritise your tasks: don't try to tackle everything and get depressed by the volume of work undone;
- Set yourself a "treat" target – if you reach it you can have the treat;
- Beware of snack attacks and fridges that "talk" to you while you are trying to concentrate on work. Eat sensibly and try to discipline yourself.

Start your day by collecting your email, post, and any messages, and working through your "to do" list in the light of the new messages, prioritising tasks. It is well worth taking the time to eradicate junk mail from the post you have to open by subscribing to the Mailing Preference Service, and its companion the Telephone Preference Service, so that your name is removed from the marketing databases. For information on preventing or filtering junk email see Chapter 10, *Email and online services*.

Next, log your incoming post in a book, or better on a spreadsheet, so that you have a record of what came in. Stamp it with the date it was received and file it immediately before it clutters up your work surfaces. Your filing system does not have to be complex – it could be just the classic in, out and pending, or action now, action later and information – but if you have one you'll be able to find what you need without having to excavate the piles of paper taking over your home office.

Beating the deadlines

Successful time management is about achieving important goals in your life and in your work. You can't do this unless you know what your goals are. Know your goals – even spend time discussing them with a professional counsellor if needs be – write them down and read them regularly to keep yourself on track.

Once you have a list of goals – which can be diffuse, unmanageable items like "pay off the mortgage" or "get promoted" – the next step is to divide your goals into smaller, manageable tasks such as "request performance review meeting" or "request quotation for early repayment of mortgage". The tasks then have to be prioritised:

- Important and urgent
- Important and non-urgent
- Not important and urgent
- Not important and not urgent.

Focus only on the first two. Some time management trainers would even suggest that you don't bother with unimportant and non-urgent tasks at all because you'll probably never get round to them – so why stress yourself out by listing them?

In addition to task lists, you need to start logging your time – both so that you can get paid, and so that you can spot patterns and plan properly. Do you know what you did yesterday? In detail? Probably not unless you are already logging your time. But it's important because most people underestimate by 10–20% the time that tasks will take. So start working out how long regular tasks are taking – and don't forget to record the time you took for coffee breaks, fixing computer software crashes, and so on. This will also allow you to begin spotting your peak productivity time. Some people work best early in the day, others only after the coffee break, or late in the evening. By focusing work into these productive periods you can get more done in the same amount of time.

At the end of the day, go through your task lists and plan for tomorrow. Try to keep your list to no more than ten tasks – otherwise you are probably spending too much time on your lists. Long lists may also mean some of the

Turn it off – controlling the anytime, anywhere office

Gil Gordon, probably the best known consultant on teleworking worldwide, has recently turned his attention to the problem of how to switch off from all the new forms of work. A new book by Gil on this subject is due out in spring 2001 accompanied by a website, www.turnitoff.com.

"This technology (voicemail, fax machines, email, laptops, pagers, cellular phones and so on) has changed the way we work – that's the good news. The not-so-good news is that this same technology has made it more difficult to get away from work. We seem to have stretched our workdays and workplaces to the extreme; sometimes we find it hard to leave work behind as much as we'd like, and pay attention to the rest of our lives.

That's why I've developed the "turn it off" slogan – to remind us that we do have lives beyond the reach of all that technology. However, this isn't an anti-technology, anti-work, anti-commitment or anti-anything campaign. It's meant to remind us that we'll probably do better work if we get in the habit of letting go of work even for a little while now and then. I encourage you to try to do what I'm trying to do – give ourselves a break from all this great technology."

Gil's concerns are born out by other recent research. The 1999 survey by US association Telework America suggests that American teleworkers typically work 9 days each month at home but of that time only 3 hours per week is during normal business hours – the remainder is work outside conventional hours. The survey also found 42% of teleworkers work long hours – 50–75 hours per week. A December 1999 survey by Stanford Institute for the Quantitative Study of Society in California looked at 4,113 adults and found that over a quarter of workers who use the Internet for more than five hours a week said it increased the amount of time spent working at home without cutting back at the office. (**www.telecommute.org** and **www.stanford.edu/group/siqss**).

items on the list are really non-urgent or unimportant. Try to clear your desk at the end of each day – a lot of leftover, undone tasks at the end of the day can be a turn-off.

Most people's filing tasks can be reduced to three:

- Bin
- Action – so write it on your task list!
- Filing – do it now, don't just shuffle paper between piles.

Perhaps the hardest time management topic is learning to say no to interruptions unless they are very high priority. "If you're working to a serious deadline, put the answerphone on. You can always interrupt it if an important call comes in, otherwise you can call back after the deadline work's completed."

Be realistic about your time estimates. If it's obvious something isn't going to get done by the deadline, inform the customer or client. Often a deadline can be stretched, or the customer or client can rearrange their workload – it is much better to let people know what is happening than to let them down at the last moment.

"Make sure you know all the last posting times and courier pickup times. There's nothing worse than panting into the post office after a day racing a deadline and then finding that you've missed the van because they changed the pickup routes."

When agreeing deadlines with clients or managers, don't forget to take account of regular tasks that have to be fitted in to the working day, such as filing, backing up data, accounts and so on, otherwise you will find that these tasks always get pushed into evenings and weekends to make room for deadline work, and you end up overworking.

Thinking through the home office

Detailed information on teleworker equipment and home office issues is given in chapters 7 and 11.

General considerations

In principle all equipment should be supplied by, and remain the property of, the employer, if you have one. As a ballpark guide to costs, a survey by Bill Murray reported in *Flexible Working* magazine gave an estimated average setup cost per teleworker of £2,250–£3,500, with annual costs (heat, lighting, use of home as office) ranging from around £1,000 to £1,500 per employee.

Equipment should be assessed to be ergonomically sound especially where repetitive movements are likely to occur. Furniture needs to be adjustable to provide correct working heights – a good quality, comfortable, adjustable chair is especially important. Lighting should be reviewed as home lighting is unlikely on its own to be adequate for office work. As part of health and safety requirements, employers should consider inspecting all home office equipment for ergonomics and safety and organise regular inspections to test for electrical safety as with all other company equipment.

Ian Fletcher-Price of ergonomic office furniture supplier Posturite UK Ltd comments: "Invest some time in getting the ergonomics right. You will not only increase your productivity without creating fatigue but also eliminate unnecessary stress, which after all is the reason many of us choose to work from home in the first place. If you only make one ergonomic investment, buy a good quality office chair. The position of the computer on the desk is also vital – make sure you are sitting directly face on to the computer screen. Position your screen at the right height so the top of the visible screen is at eye level."

Veteran teleworkers favour a separate building for the home office to provide a work environment away from the potential distraction of the home, assist with "switching off" at the end of the day and prevent work material becoming distributed around the house. Failing a separate office, the space for the home office should be carefully chosen to take it out of the main family thoroughfare – ideally it should be lockable.

Home offices are often characterised by lack of space, so good use needs to be made of available room. Both office and home furniture manufacturers are beginning to recognise the home office as a new market and produce special ranges such as lock-away desks and cabinets where computers can be kept, space-saving furniture (*eg* wall beds, high-level shelving) and home-friendly office furniture (for example made of pine to match home decor).

Security

Physical security and insurance issues are covered in detail in Chapter 7, *Staying safe and legal.* Many commercial insurers have developed specific home office policies to reflect the move to teleworking, and the lower risk involved in insuring home offices. Domestic insurance policies will not normally cover home office equipment including PCs, so employees should notify their home contents insurers of their intention to work from home.

Security surveys show that the most likely causes of home office problems are not viruses or hacking, but more basic issues such as power cuts, hard disk crashes or fire damage, all of which can be minimised as risks by appropriate procedures. Make sure you know the procedures for backing up data, and any specific instructions concerning the storage of important or sensitive papers such as locked storage space.

Hints for homeworkers

Homeworking has its good points –
Forget about that bus
And the rush-hour crowds and tube strikes
Have no effect on us.

The downside is the effort
It takes to fill each day
When all you've got ahead of you
Is work to earn your pay.

The routine I've developed
Is big on washing up.
Take each item separately,
Wash, rinse and dry each cup.

Another thing I'd mention
That really helps time pass is
Tightening up those little screws
On specs, if you wear glasses.

Some people check their cheque stubs
Other clean their shoes
Displacement chores are plentiful:
It's up to you to choose.

You'll find your own distractions,
(And don't forget the phone).
There's nothing like a day to fill
When you are on your own.

Simon Rae
(first published in Guardian Weekend section)

Communications: it's good to talk...

Teleworkers have to make maximum use of all the communications tools available to keep in touch with the people who pay them. Because you are not physically in the same office, it is vital to respond quickly and effectively so that your client or employer feels secure that you are on top of your work for them and they can rely on you to complete the task. It's good to talk, as the advert goes, but for teleworkers the secret of success is to pick the right communication tool for the job. Telecommuters may well have a corporate policy laid down about when email should be used, when face-to-face meetings are needed and so on, but the self-employed usually have to learn by their mistakes.

Teleworkers don't have the luxury (or nuisance, depending on your view) of constant face-to-face meetings, with all the nuances of body language and time for discussion, or of informal chats in the corridor. It is very easy to pick up the wrong end of the stick and make an expensive mistake, or develop a grudge or irritation with a colleague which would never happen in the conventional office environment. Learning to be a teleworker requires good attention to communications tools and skills. On the other hand, face-to-face meetings for teleworkers often take on new and more interesting roles – they may become about team-building, training, developing relationships and discussing possibilities rather than about imparting routine information.

This section focuses on the communications and productivity aspects of teleworking equipment – technical details and information about purchase options are dealt with in Chapter 11, *Teleworking Equipment*.

Telephone

A separate line is vital in order to ensure that personal and work calls are distinguishable. This is desirable for both professional and psychological reasons. Phone costs should be paid for directly by the employer so that there is no perceived tax benefit. Additional services now available for standard telephone lines include call diversion, caller ID, divert on busy, and conference calling, all of which are available at minimal cost and assist the teleworker in handling calls. Where insufficient lines are available, a recent innovation from BT may be helpful. Call Sign allows two numbers to be handled from one phone, with each line distinguished by a separate ring (*eg* home and office calls or voice and fax calls). Where a lot of time is spent on the phone, hands-free operation should be available and in some work situations such as technical support, a headset allowing more comfortable operation and less risk of strain injuries can be a boon. A cordless phone may also be useful to give you the freedom of the house without missing calls.

Corporate voice mail systems are often used to take messages for teleworkers, but call minding (digital answerphone on your home line) is flexible and easily controlled and sometimes a simpler solution. Make sure your voicemail message is dated, states when you will be next available, and if an alternative number can be called. Some service companies offer message-taking services, which use call diversion from the teleworker's home, and caller line identification tools to create a customised, human response which can be important in certain occupations.

You need to know to call forward using the company's PABX (switchboard) to ensure your calls will follow you home on a day when you are teleworking. Forgetting to set call forward the night before is a common, practical teleworking problem and teleworkers should assign an "office buddy" who knows how to redirect their extension to overcome this difficulty. Many PABXs now allow you to call in from a remote location and redirect calls after you have given an identifying PIN number. Increasingly, transferable personal numbers are also being used. A permanent or personal number is rented by the company which can be linked to various different locations – mobile, home, office – as appropriate by the teleworker.

The telephone is a vital way of reinforcing other communications – for example details passed through by fax and email can be followed up with a phone call to talk through and develop a greater comprehension, or to negotiate a problem where fax or electronic mail are too constraining, formal, or unambiguous. The main disadvantage of the telephone is that it requires the simultaneous presence of both callers, leading to the familiar syndrome of "telephone tag" between busy people as messages replying to messages are left to pile up. Some teleworkers may also find continuous calling from the employer causes interruption to their work and is irritating.

At the end of a phone call, without some kind of written backup it is possible for two different interpretations of the topic to persist. To make sure there has been no breakdown in telephone communications, take written notes of telephone calls. Where possible restate any information received before finishing the call to check that you have understood correctly. When imparting information, it often helps to write down before starting the call the points you plan to make, ticking them off as each one is discussed. Check the following:

- are you talking to the right person?
- do they understand who you are? Did you introduce yourself and your work context?
- have they received the document you are supposed to be discussing?
- is your communication timely? (have you already missed the deadline for applications? If so there's no point in going further with the call).

When communicating with your manager or client:

- check if people have time to talk and if not, make an appointment for a long call at another time;
- have the relevant documents to hand before you start;
- ensure that your message is clear and unambiguous;
- keep it short – their time is precious;
- don't use excessively costly communication methods such as videoconferencing unless they are necessary;
- always try to imagine yourself in the other person's place – empathy.

Often calls made by telephone are discussions or negotiations, or the development of an idea. Be concrete to reduce the possibilities for confusion – use examples of what you mean wherever you can.

"When working alone, it is important to establish trust in your answering machine. Clients must feel confident that leaving a message on the answering machine is as good as a direct contact. This confidence may be established by acknowledging messages quickly, even when it is not necessary to do so and explaining to clients that the presence of the answering machine may only indicate an absence of a few minutes. I, for example, may simply be sitting in the garden with the laptop and will check the machine frequently." (Another option for this teleworker would be to get a cordless phone...)

When leaving messages, always state your name, the time and date of your message, your telephone number and leave a clear, brief message – try not to burble when faced with someone else's voicemail. Keep a duplicate message book by the phone, for writing brief notes of telephone calls, whom from, time and date. This gives you a record of information from the telephone call, and also provides a method for other people in the house to take messages and leave them for you in an agreed format and place. Using message books in conjunction with listening to your voicemail messages can also be useful – otherwise if you get interrupted by another call you may forget the content of the first message.

Mobile phones are hugely convenient but you need a way of recording the salient details of the message while pulled over at the side of the road, or walking along a railway platform. Most phones now have a message taking utility. You can record the details of the mobile call straight away, and play back the recording for action when you return to the office. Mobile messaging is also useful for that brilliant idea, or task you've forgotten, which strikes you while sitting in a traffic jam. You can also use your mobile phone to dial your home or office answerphone and leave there details of the message or idea for collection and action later.

Mobile workers will benefit from spending a bit of time with their phone manual and their mobile service provider's website to work out how to do some of the following (available on most current models):

- Use playback/voicemail functions – your mailbox number is usually one digit different to your normal mobile number;
- Switch on EFR (Enhanced Full Rate) technology which improves call quality on many phones;
- Divert calls to a message minder or alternative number when your phone is out of signal coverage or battery life to avoid your clients finding that your mobile number rings out;
- Use call waiting and call hold to answer a second call coming in when you are already talking;
- Restrict the phone's dial-out usage to a small range of numbers (useful if your mobile is ever likely to be used by other members of the family). You can also bar international calls being made or received;
- Use your phone to programme in caller line IDs so that the identity of frequent callers appears on the phone before you answer (*eg* you tell the phone that number 123 456789 is your important client Sam, and Sam's name will then pop up on the phone's screen whenever he calls so you can answer "Hi Sam – how can I help you?" or whatever;

- Send SMS text messages to other mobile users from your phone or through your service provider's website (such as a short message telling the recipient to find a computer and pick up an urgent email message waiting for them);

- Send and receive fax calls (if you have a mobile which can do this) or divert faxes to a suitable number as appropriate (many providers offer a fax mailbox service which can store messages until you have a fax number available for redirection);

- Use your phone with a laptop computer to send and receive email or access the Internet;

- Use voice recognition functions to "tell" your phone who to dial (it's quicker than picking out the numbers).

For details of the new services becoming available that use WAP technology try **www.nokia.com/wap.html**. Many are location-related, as your service provider can tell which "cell" your phone is in, such as services that tell you where the nearest cash machine or restaurant is.

Considerable development work has recently been put into making CTI technology (computer telephony integration) widely available through packages such as Goldmine (www.goldminesw.com) which can use features such as caller line identification to allow your PC to produce relevant information from your database about a caller, and to record and make calls without physically having to dial. This is useful for people involved in the areas of sales and support.

A telephone communication method which is often overlooked as "low technology" is the audio or telephone conference. Audioconferences for up to three people can be arranged through basic call services available to anyone on request from most telephone companies. Audioconferences for more than three people can be arranged through telecoms companies or, if you are working in the voluntary sector, through Community Network (020 7359 4594). Theoretically up to 20 people can join in an audioconference, but from the point of view of running an effective meeting, audioconferences work best with up to 10 people. An effective "chair" who works round the participants collecting views, resolving conflicts and summing up the meeting decisions is vital. Audioconferences are extremely cost effective for a group of people who need to discuss a topic but don't want the time and expense of a face-to-face meeting – costs have come down to around £9/hour/person.

Fax

Where a fax machine is required more than occasionally, an additional line rather than a line shared between telephone and fax is recommended. This has the advantage of allowing the teleworker to receive and send faxes whilst using the telephone and avoids annoying busy lines due to fax traffic. If significant online work is being performed a separate line for the Internet should also be installed. If the use is not significant, sharing Internet access with the fax line should be adequate. It may be worthwhile to consider installing one ISDN line which can be used for different purposes (fax and voice calls) simultaneously (see page 99). Telephone companies may also offer "faxminding" services where faxes are stored by the company and can be retrieved by dialling a special number with a fax or PC-based fax from any location.

Fax provides a good method of getting short, sometimes urgent, instructions across and delivering copies of documents that may be held in one location but not the other. However, fax limits the subsequent processing of the information as it is not delivered in a computer-readable form (even if you use a fax modem, the fax transmitted to the computer is a graphical image, not editable text, though some fax packages now come with OCR software which can be used, sometimes not too successfully, to convert the image).

There can be a temptation to fax everything to save taking it to the post office. But faxing large documents is wasteful and if the recipient does not have a plain paper fax, then the document needs recopying from easily-damaged thermal paper in order to preserve it. If your fax is not plain-paper or computer-based, be sure to copy important documents received onto

---

The *Teleworker* gadget wish-list

Teleworker magazine asked its readers what would make their working lives easier. Here are some selected suggestions:

- *Trousers with banana holsters (saves trips to the kitchen)*

- *Brainstorming software – when you need an idea and are on your own. You put a general theme in and it creates bizarre ideas and random buzzwords*

- *A foot control for the radio – you've got the radio full on and you're shaking it around to All Spice when the phone rings – kills the radio dead without taking your hands off the radio or reaching for it over the other side of the room. (AIMS labs have a radio card for your computer with a mute button for silencing with a mouse click. 065 339 7761)*

- *Timelock on the fridge to avoid snack attacks during working hours*

- *A space you step into at coffee time for ten minutes where you talk to holograms of other teleworkers about nothing in particular – notworking as opposed to networking*

- *A good view is essential. Preferably one with Robert Carlyle in it*

- *A cordless headset to avoid neck cricks and allow you to move around the room to consult files and computers while talking. Needs to have the cradle switch on the headset*

- *Cat-proof keyboard guards*

The 10 commandments of successful email communication

(Received from various sources including Denise Cox and David Fitzpatrick)

1. Thou shalt include a clear and specific subject line.
2. Thou shalt edit any quoted text down to the minimum thou needest.
3. Thou shalt read thine own message thrice before thou sendest it.
4. Thou shalt ponder how thy recipient might react to thy message.
5. Thou shalt check they spelling and thy grammar.
6. Thou shalt not curse, flame, spam or USE ALL CAPS.
7. Thou shalt not forward any chain letter.
8. That which thou findest hateful to receive, sendest thou not unto others.
9. Thou shalt not rely on the privacy of email, especially from work.
10. When in doubt, save thy message overnight and reread it in the light of day.

ordinary paper, otherwise when the client tries to sue you a year later and you go to look in the file, all you may find is a blank piece of paper. When you receive a fax, do check that all the pages have arrived before filing it, especially if it is not something you are going to take action on straight away.

Many people now use computer-based faxes, saving the cost of a separate fax machine though they may have the disadvantage of slowing your computer considerably when a fax is being received. Also, unless you have a scanner, you will not be able to send graphical pages such as sketches or diagrams, except where they have been created on the computer. As the computer fax modem is usually also used for email, if you handle a lot of messages on the same modem and telephone line you may find the fax is occupying the line when you want to send email and vice versa. You will need to leave your computer on all the time so that faxes can be received on a 24-hour basis. If your computer crashes it will prevent further faxes being received until it is reset.

ACD (Automated Call Distribution systems)

ACD systems are widely employed in call centres to distribute calls to agents, giving an even loading amongst operators and equalising the caller response time. They are often closely integrated with company databases. They can also be used to distribute calls to homebased teleworkers, at the same time providing connection to the company database if an ISDN line is used.

ISDN (Integrated Services Digital Network) lines

Where teleworkers need access to company databases, or require larger amounts of data transfer, a high-speed digital ISDN line may be best. This allows faster transfer of data, high-quality voice communication and videoconferencing. A number of devices (up to six) can share the same ISDN line, so only one is likely to be required per teleworker. However, only two devices can be used at any one time on standard "basic rate" ISDN. ISDN is not available on some older exchanges, and enquiries will need to be made with your telephone supplier for specific locations, especially in rural areas – ISDN will not normally work if you are more than 4 km from the local exchange.

ISDN can also be used for personal videoconferencing equipment though take-up of this technology has been lower than predicted. The equipment is fast reducing in cost and consists of a camera which is attached to the PC monitor or stands on a separate stalk, an ISDN connector, cards which fit into the PC, and software. The videophone, in addition to providing visual images, can transmit files and allow application sharing between remote users.

Email

Email is a great way of transmitting information that needs to be reworked by the recipient, and of keeping tabs on documents involved in multiple projects, since most email readers provide an electronic filing system for messages. Other applications for email include documents which need collaborative work, detailing progress against a plan, circulating general memos to a large group and maintaining regular background contact. It is also a good way of providing quick technical fixes for software. Most systems will provide on request receipts which return a message to confirm the original document has been picked up – this can prove a useful project management tool. If at all possible, resist changing Internet service providers or domain names where this requires you to change your email address. You will lose a lot of messages and upset your colleagues and clients.

Email is excellent for developing documents and technical specs through the use of different fonts or colours or annotations in a mutually used word processing package. The annotations show the additions and developments in a document passing through a team evaluation. Email is also a highly cost effective communications medium to international locations.

However, some people are notoriously bad at reading and dealing with their email, whereas they will handle a fax or telephone call with no problem – you need to be sure that the person at the other end of the communication is happy with using email. Many people are quite able to send short plain text messages, but aren't clear on the ins and outs of attaching files such as reports or spreadsheets (see Chapter 9, *Email and the Internet*), a crucial skill for effective teleworking.

It's frighteningly easy to take the wrong "tone" in an email and end up with an unintended dispute on your hands (hence all the "flame wars"). Email requires a high level of facility with written communications, yet it is an informal method – abbreviations and cyberslang abound – and therefore is often used for communications which might better be handled face-to-face or by telephone.

There are three keys to successful use of email:

- use a mail reader which allows filing of messages by project, and which will allow you to sort or search messages by sender, subject and date. This allows easy retrieval of information or instructions relating to a project;

- use a mail reader with an easy-to-use address book function, which allows you to quickly "lift" an email address from an incoming message;

- keep a pad by the computer when you are reading your email to write down information such as instructions received which you need to act on. Of course you can print out the whole message, but usually it's only a couple of words that you actually need. Either way, do something to put the information on your action list, or you may forget the contents immediately after reading the email.

Many companies now have their own web servers that can be used to supply teleworkers with a "library" of corporate information and documents which can be browsed from the teleworker's remote site when needed and downloaded onto the teleworker's computer. Web servers are also useful for providing software tools, a general noticeboard, news and other functions to staff. Internally-focused company web servers are usually called intranets, and can also be used to link workers at a number of sites. Where an intranet is not available, widespread distribution of corporate notices can take place by email, and these communications have largely replaced the traditional office memo in many organisations.

PCs and technical support

Technical support mechanisms should prioritise the teleworker who may well be isolated and unable to work without a functioning PC – in contrast to central office-based colleagues. For companies without their own means of nationwide equipment support, it may be worth looking at subscribing to a technical support service which can ensure speedy repair, assistance or replacement of equipment at teleworkers' homes.

Windows software provides a simple way to make sure that you always have the most up-to-date version of your data while you are on the move. The Windows Briefcase appears as an icon on most PC screens. Copy into the briefcase the files you want to take home and then move the briefcase onto the floppy or zip disk or laptop computer that you plan to take home. When you get home, pop the disk in or switch the laptop on and work away. Back in the office, the disk or laptop containing the briefcase and edited files can be reconnected back to your main computer and by choosing "update all" on the Briefcase menu all files are updated as appropriate.

The Psychologist's take on homeworking

Linda A Doe is an Occupational Psychologist who is also a homeworker. She spent two years researching how people work at home for her MSc thesis – which can't be boiled down into a short text panel – but agreed to let the TCA extract a few pointers from her work.

"There is no one "personality" suited to homeworking. Personal motivation and emotional intelligence are the most important factors for making homeworking a success. Emotional intelligence is being aware of your own feelings, and the ability to control them. If you know what makes you tick then you can learn to develop strategies and structures that build on this knowledge.

Isolation, while a potentially negative aspect to homeworking, is something which can be overcome. If you know your job really well, you will be less vulnerable without the support of others. You can phone colleagues for a chat or to let off steam – replace the coffee machine conversations in a way that suits you. Some people compensate for isolated work by being more sociable in other aspects of their lives – such as through voluntary work or spending more time with their family or friends when not working.

A lot of people find creating a structure that divides work and home important – the method of "containing work" can be as complex as an exercise routine or as simple as spending half an hour watching a soap to wind down. Spatially, a division between homespace and workspace helps too, even if a separate room is not available. Have an active plan to contain work – 'I don't want work leaking into my evenings and weekends'.

Every homeworker emphasises the need to be self-disciplined – and this applies to anyone else living in the house, not just the teleworker. "If you've got children, say: 'during this time keep the door shut, do not disturb me'. If you don't feel self-disciplined, but have the emotional intelligence to realise this, you can put in place structures, such as dressing for work or sticking to a tight schedule, that will help.

The homeworkers saw work achievements as being output rather than time-based – not how long you spend but what you produce. This approach suits some people more than others but you can adapt and use strategies to train yourself.

Appreciate the benefits of flexibility – enjoy the positive changes that homeworking can bring to your life. Control of workstyle and output can be a major contributor to psychological health."

Email: lindadoe@cix.co.uk

Software for helping teams of people to work together is known as groupware. An example of groupware in action is the use of Lotus Notes by the Henley Management College in its global classroom project to overcome the geographical barriers to distance learning. Henley has adopted groupware technology to support its 7,000 distance learning students worldwide, providing interaction with peers, tutors, staff and other information sources and has used Lotus Notes since 1994.

Students can send electronic mail, search databases and retrieve and send files, as well as being able to participate in electronic discussions led by Henley faculty. They can read profiles of other Notes users, and network with those with similar interests. Notes is used for the electronic booking of workshops and ordering of papers. The electronic submission and marking of assignments and course works was introduced as long ago as 1996. A tutor from New Zealand explains: "When I receive a query from a student on Notes, I have time to give a full answer with accurate references, indeed I can give the student a mini-tutorial, and it will also be available to other students. The student raising the query gets the benefit of one-to-one tuition but other students can get involved if they wish."

Videoconferencing

Videoconferencing can allow effective meetings while avoiding travel costs, but has not taken off into widespread usage yet except to allow contributions at conferences from people who cannot be physically present, or for recruitment companies to carry out interviews at a distance. If you are fortunate enough to have access to videoconferencing, you will find that although the technical standard of affordable systems today is no replacement for face-to-face meetings, it offers a big improvement over the audioconference, especially for delicate meetings or negotiations where a face-to-face meeting is not possible. Most ISDN PC-based systems are still a bit jerky and this means you need to learn to moderate your body language. Also, on many systems only one person can "speak" at one time (rather like a VHF radio system). This means it helps the flow of the conversation if you can indicate clearly by your voice tone or other gesture when you have finished making a point. Otherwise conversations can either degenerate into a staccato cutting from one participant to another as you accidentally interrupt each other, or to a Quaker-like silence at the end of each point while the person at the other end tries to work out if you've finished talking. Videoconferencing facilities are covered in Chapter 11, *Teleworking equipment*. Although they are still beyond the pocket of many teleworkers, a number of telecottages and other bureau services provide videoconferencing on a local basis (see Chapter 6, *Centres for teleworking*).

Post and couriers

In many situations work still needs to be sent by post – even if it's on disk! Unless you have access to ISDN file transfer, the practical limit in cost and time terms for moving files around by email is about 2–3 megabytes. The postal service (or courier where extra speed is required) provides a largely reliable and fast door-to-door service.

If you are working for a company, they should instigate a method of ensuring that company mail is regularly delivered to you – for example pigeon holes can be allocated and regularly swept by the internal system. It may also be necessary to make arrangements for urgent deliveries via courier on occasion. The Royal Mail quotes that 92% of first class deliveries arrive next day, but it is reasonable to assume that the 8% that don't are to locations off the beaten track – such as to rurally-based teleworkers.

It is important to be clear on issues such as the last posting time at your local postbox or office, the time at which your post arrives (in some rural areas this can be as late as 3 pm, causing problems for teleworkers who need to turn work round fast) and the different services available, such as Swiftair, registered post and Mailsort. Equally, courier companies will have last pickup times for your area, and different delivery times for areas of the world. You don't know when you'll need them, so make sure you have up to date pricelists and contact numbers for all your delivery services.

Log all incoming and outgoing post so that if anything goes missing, you can show when and how it left you. Where disks arrive by post, check immediately that they are readable, even if you don't plan to work on that project for a few days. That way, if there is a problem, you can request a replacement disk without disturbing your schedule, and the client won't know that you "sat on it" for a few days – it can be difficult to explain phoning up to request a new disk the day before the deadline...

Cybersupport for work-at-homes

http://telecommuting.miningco.com/smallbusiness/telecommuting
– a list of useful resources

www.svi.org – the Smart Valley project. Telecommuting guide with focus on personal issues (see Family and Home chapter)

www.wahm.com – short for Work At Home Moms.

www.en-parent.com – community and career resource for parents looking to use self-employment to balance work and family

www.homeworking.com – community site with info and news

www.momsrefuge.com/telecommute – working mothers focus

The housekeeping

There are four chores self-employed teleworkers must find time for regularly in order to survive:

- **keeping timesheets** should be done daily and the hours added up at least monthly. If you don't know what hours you worked on each project, how can you tell whether you are achieving sufficient reward for your work? And why should your employer or client pay you?;

- **preparing bills** regularly and chasing payments (at least monthly). Usually regular phone calls will ensure prompt payment (bother the accounts department, not your client within the company, who probably has no control whatsoever on when your invoice will be paid). The next step for non-payers is usually a stiff solicitor's letter, which may have to be followed by use of the small claims court;

- **backing up your computer data** (at least weekly). Most backup programmes can run unattended and automatically, perhaps in the evening after you have finished work for the day. Do not ignore this chore or you will regret it. The average time between failures for computer hard disks is just over two years. Sooner or later it will happen to you – you will lose all your data – so make sure you have backups, that some are kept offsite to avoid fire risk, and that you test and update backups regularly. Be sure to create an emergency startup disk which can boot your computer in case of disaster. Windows users – you should also backup your registry data;

- **marketing or researching new opportunities** – if you are self-employed you should be devoting somewhere between a quarter and a third of your time to marketing. For the PAYE teleworker, substantial time should be devoted to keeping in touch with the office, knowing what is going on, and ensuring that people remember you and what you do.

If you are unwell or on holiday, let your most active clients and contacts know in advance or leave a message to this effect, but try not to invite burglars through a detailed answerphone message. However, if you normally use a business name, an answerphone message may be OK – how is the burglar to know you work from home, as opposed to in a busy office block? While you are away, Royal Mail Keepsafe service can hold your mail at a cost of £5 for a fortnight or £15 for two months. One week's notice is required – ask at your local post office or telephone 01345 740740.

Balancing "home" and "work"

Although a formal, written family agreement may be excessive, prospective teleworkers should discuss and suggest ground rules as to how the family can best help and least hinder the process of working from home. For example, children's voices or pets barking in the background of telephone calls create a bad impression to customers and put strain on the teleworker intent on creating a professional image. On the positive side, the teleworker is much more available (by virtue of being there in emergencies and no longer spending time commuting). Over time, a greater appreciation by the teleworker's family of what they do usually develops. Here are some starting points for discussion:

- where is the office?;
- is it out of bounds to partners, children or pets? All the time or just at certain times? (Final reports have been decorated by older children with pictures of elephants… children discovered playing frisbee with backup disks while another feeds disks into the CD player "because they fit, Mummy"; pet fur tends to disagree with computer disk drives but cats in particular love to sleep on a nice warm photocopier or printer);
- who tidies the office? (Desk is tidied and important paper filed in bin; computer dies during crucial email of final report as it has been unplugged to make room for the vacuum cleaner);
- is company equipment available to the family? (If not, how can you explain the disappointment to games-mad children?);
- is the teleworker available for domestic chores? Which ones and when? Who does the school/childminder runs? ("What are you doing here? You're supposed to be picking the kids up from swimming!")
- who pays for the extra food needed for the teleworker's lunches and snacks? Who makes sure the food is available? ("But darling, what do you mean we've run out? I *always* have Boaster biscuits with my tea…" "Yes, darling, and if I'd known you were eating a packet a day in the office I wouldn't have bothered giving you that Weight Watchers subscription".);
- can the teleworker expect help from the family *eg.* with mailings? What's the "quid pro quo" for help? A family treat or money?;

Alan Denbigh's seven survival tips for stress-free teleworking

TCA executive director Alan Denbigh has been teleworking for ten years. This is what it's taught him.

1. Never on a Monday. Never install software in the morning, particularly Monday.
2. Teach the family to "shaddit" when you're on the dog and bone.
3. Build in some exercise or you'll become a tubby-teleworker.
4. Avoid meetings. Use phone, email, fax and post but don't waste time on meetings except at the start of a business relationship.
5. Don't meet customers at home or you'll suffer extra stress trying to give the entire house and office an instant makeover (unless you need something to force you to get tidy).
6. Le Weekend is Sacred. Yes, you can enter the 24 hour society and spend your entire life working now that you're a teleworker but your partner will leave and the kids will run away when the strange creature from the attic comes to call.
7. Start the day by writing a list. Always include something you don't want to do. Feel smug when ticking items off.

■ how are business calls and visitors to be handled by members of the family? If the teleworker is out, do they let the answerphone go off, or do they answer the phone?

When planning the home office it may be a good idea to draw up a sketch plan, with paper templates representing the various items to be fitted into the room, and get the family to help in designing what should go where. Bear in mind the realities – a loft office may have steep steps where children just love to leave toys to trip up the teleworker, whereas a room which is a pathway to others will always cause the teleworker to suffer interruption. And remember: "There is never enough room. The paperless office – the biggest joke of all time!"

It's also worth discussing how you see the teleworking routine working. Some teleworkers report that they need to keep to a strict schedule in order to maintain their work discipline. Changes in routines can cause strains if they are not talked through, leading to interruption problems such as neighbours dropping in too frequently, or conversely the "ogre in the spare room" syndrome, with children creeping round the house unnaturally quietly because "Dad's working".

Most parents find if they are to telework successfully that they need either to arrange for the children to be out of the house at school or a childminder's, or to arrange for a childminder to be present in the home . Stresses can arise if the burden of childcare shifts from one parent to the other and everyone is living and working in the same space. "I found I couldn't concentrate because I didn't believe my husband was looking after our daughter properly while I was working. She was at a demanding, toddler stage and he would just watch the telly in the same room instead of attending to her. If I heard her crying it was almost impossible for me to stay in the office. Things did improve when we changed the glass door of the office to a solid one so that she couldn't see me when I was working, but it was still stressful for me." To add to the stress, childcare costs are not currently tax deductible and must be paid in full.

The support organisation Parents at Work publishes a guide on *Balancing Home and Work* – contact 020 7628 3565. Housework duties may change as a result of one or both adults teleworking. Ursula Huws, in her study *Teleworking and Gender*, 1996, found that in households with more than one adult, only 11% of men had taken on primary responsibility for housework, whereas only one-third of the men in the sample contributed more than three-quarters of the household income. Around 45% of the men contributed less than half the household income, so overall it appears that men are doing less income earning but are not replacing this with housework responsibilities to any great extent. The women in Huws's sample were more likely than men to work standard office hours, and women were also three times as likely as men to be interrupted by children when working. Men, on the other hand, were three times as likely to be interrupted by friends when working.

On the bright side, once teething troubles have been resolved, teleworking allows far more opportunity to integrate home and work: "It can be hell when they're small, and friends tell me boys are worse than girls. Always say goodbye and greet them back from school – never be too busy – put the answering machine on instead. Do the taxi runs such as guides, music lessons, *etc*. Make them feel that there are times when they can use the equipment (under supervision when tiny) and that there are things they must not do (such as "format c:"); but they must also understand that there are times when you are not to be disturbed." It's also a good idea to decide on a review of the situation after an agreed initial period so everyone in the family can have their say about whether teleworking works for them.

"Plan your day around the family. There is no point in getting frustrated with the children coming home from school and interrupting you. Plan breaks at times such as these and enjoy them rather than try to battle on irritably. One of the joys of teleworking is surely that you can have more time for the family when it needs your time."

"I enjoy teleworking because it means I have more time with the family through not having to commute. Also a lovely rural setting and a roomy office make working from home very attractive. The downside is that work is always there, lurking in the corner of your mind and you feel yourself inexorably drawn to it. However, in any conflict with the housework, work wins hands down. I'm often glad of the excuse it gives me to ignore the dust for a bit longer!"

"Not everyone may agree, but interruptions from family members need not necessarily be unwelcome if you organise your work properly and establish ground rules."

"It is very important when working at home to keep your business and family phones separate. Nothing is as frustrating as continually answering calls for your teenage daughter or discovering that an important caller could not get through because the phone was engaged by family members all afternoon."

Maintaining the worker

A number of physiological complaints can result from long-term use of computers and include eye strain, blurred vision, burning eyes, back pain, sore shoulders and repetitive strain injury (RSI). Teleworker home offices need to be designed with appropriate desks and chairs to minimise these problems, and teleworkers need to be aware of their existence (see Chapter 7, *Staying safe and legal*, pages 195–9). It usually helps to arrange the work place to face outwards towards stimulating views, and to take sensible breaks at regular intervals.

"The BT directory enquiries experiment in Inverness found that although teleworkers suffer less stress than their office-based counterparts, they suffer more snack attacks. I can relate to this totally. The only way I cope is by banning biscuits from the house, and allowing myself one chocolate bar when I take the post to the shop at 4 pm."

Many teleworkers report stress due to overworking.

"An important problem I find – and it may seem a curious one – is a tendency to overwork. Your work is always there and it is easy to be tempted to do it rather than something else. I think it important, therefore, to have a clear idea of why you are teleworking in the first place (living in the country, more time for the family, *etc*) and carry out periodic audits to see if you are effectively achieving your aims. Resist the temptation to overwork. Make your breaks real breaks away from the computer. Stop and eat; don't nibble and keep going. Plan your social and family life and make your leisure commitments as binding as your professional ones. Comfort yourself with the quantity of work completed rather than worry about the work remaining to be done. Take that walk in the morning if the sun is shining. You can always catch up in the evening when it may well be raining. Set yourself reasonable targets (daily, weekly, monthly) and learn to relax when you have reached them."

"Don't feel guilty about breaking off to make a drink and relax a little. Working from home is more intense and it is good practice to take a break and unwind."

"These comments are backed up by a Joseph Rowntree Trust report which found that over a quarter of working fathers in Britain already work

> **Useful URLs for DIY technical support**
>
> Microsoft: **www.support.microsoft.com** for support,
> **www.computingcentral.com** for tips and tricks
>
> Corel: **www.corel.com/support**
>
> Lotus: **www.support.lotus.com**
>
> Symantec: **www.symantec.com/techsupp**
>
> Comprehensive help and how-to: **wwww.zdnet.com/zdhelp**
>
> Bulletin boards on Windows, DOS and Linux issues: **www.virtualdr.com**
>
> Forums and some free preventive maintenance services:
> **www.pcsupport.com**
>
> Email support from an expert: **www.ask-a-tech.org**
>
> Free help, step-by-step walkthroughs, dictionary:
> **www.computerhope.com**
>
> Helping Mac users since 1994: **www.macintouch.com**
>
> Mobile mac users: **www.go2mac.com/powerpage**
>
> With thanks to Irish computer magazine PC Live (www.techcentral.com)

more than the 48 hours maximum prescribed by the recent European Working Time directive. The report looked at a series of domestic tasks, who did what and how often families socialised together. For men who worked over 50 hours a week these activities dropped right down. The report also identified a minority of mothers whose partners provided little help in the home. These women were discontented and vulnerable to depression – a possible indication of the future for workaholic teleworkers.

"The one thing a teleworker should strive not to be is what I have become. I am addicted to personal computers much as someone could be said to be addicted to crack cocaine. I have two PCs in my home office and they are on from 0700 to 2000 six days a week. The day off on Sunday is my wife's idea but you should see me get the jitters at 1700 on a Saturday. Holidays away from home and the office can get hairy. Whatever you do, make sure you can walk away from your work without thinking about it."

At least this teleworker has insight into his condition – others become tedious workaholics, unable to see that what should be a method of introducing freedom and balance into life has become an excuse for self-imposed slavery. An old hand recommends: "Set yourself a limit on the number of hours a week you will normally work except in exceptional circumstances."

"Make sure that you don't push yourself too hard and that you "leave" work at a regular time. Don't forget how lucky you are to have escaped the commuter lifestyle. But don't forget the bumper sticker that says: 'Even if you win the rat race, you are still a rat!'"

"Take advantage of the flexibility of teleworking by arranging at least one exercise session a week during "normal" working hours – it breaks up the routine and makes you feel privileged to be a teleworker – you get empty pools, cheap horseriding and so on."

"If you're working alone, put the answerphone on or take the phone off the hook when you go for a toilet break."

Another area where "maintenance" is required is the updating of skills through appropriate training. Teleworkers have to adapt to three new areas of skill:

- communication
- handling customers and clients
- networking to find work and opportunities.

These areas represent significant challenges to the new teleworker and formal training can ease the transition considerably. However, after a period of years teleworking, it is likely to be core skills such as software packages and professional qualifications which will need updating. For the self-employed, this means planning budget and time to take courses. For those in PAYE employment, training is an issue which needs regular discussion with your manager to ensure that you don't end up in a skills backwater.

Loneliness of the long-distance teleworker

Teleworkers, particularly those who are disabled or based in rural areas, can suffer from isolation if they work from home for long periods. There are a number of online services which provide "coffee shops" for teleworkers, including Internet listservs and the TCA web board **www.tca.org.uk/forum/**. Professional associations such as the TCA that provide helplines and conferences can also assist in reducing isolation. Telecottages and telecentres provide an alternative workspace where contact with peers can be maintained. Some teleworkers choose to share an office with a neighbour or colleague who is teleworking for companionship and because they find that being "observed" makes them work, even though their companion is not their boss and may well work in a completely different field.

"Based on my experience as a freelance translator, I found that one of the key aspects was the relative lack of praise and positive feedback when working alone. Customers call when there is a panic to sort out, or when they want an urgent piece of work, or when they get a bill and want to whinge. Creative work requires constant positive feedback if it is to maintain its spark. I think most lone workers suffer from a definite lack of professional backslapping. I don't know how to solve this other than by establishing a kind of mutual admiration society for lone workers which sounds dreadful."

"I make a point of getting out to see someone in a business capacity at least once a week face-to-face. It doesn't really matter who they are – client, suspect, prospect, supplier – but it meets the need for face-to-face networking and avoids teleworking cabin fever, especially during the early spring. It may even lead to some business!"

"There was one occasion when I was tempted to use the Samaritan's online service. I was owed a lot of money, the work was piling up and my concentration was just shot to pieces. I found I was just reading and rereading my email messages instead of getting anything done and things were getting out of control. In the end I went to my GP and that solved the problem, but the Samaritan's email address is jo@samaritans.org for anyone else who gets that way."

"Translation is a lonely business at the best of times – you do not really need much contact with your clients and don't want it from anyone else while you are working – so that it is necessary to get the balance right. I find

Local groups and telework clubs

The TCA encourages the formation of local groups and a list of co-ordinators can be found in Teleworker magazine. Here freelance journalist Pete Hawkins, who is based in the Peak National Park, describes the setup of "SAD GITS" – Sad and Dysfunctional Group in The Star.

"Two Christmases ago I started to get worried about loneliness when I realised around the country thousands of employees were having Christmas parties and I was at home with a cup of tea and a biscuit. Sometimes the daily walk to school with the kids is my only link with the outside world. So I put a note into the village newsletter calling anyone interested to a meeting in the local pub. Half a dozen folk turned up and we spent an enjoyable evening sinking pints and chatting about what we all did.

At the second meeting we discovered one person had managed to access special Peak Park grants towards the cost of their home office. A visit from the local business advisor to the third meeting has led to a number of small grants and training projects accessed through the local TEC. Some of us have also cooperated to set up a website despite our eclectic mix of professions. However, we decided we didn't want the group to be organised formally – we were there to have fun. If we wanted to have formal meetings with chairs and secretaries, then we could have stayed as employees. The most important thing is that the sense of isolation has gone. I have the benefit of working from home but now I have links with others who are willing to bash ideas around. I have access to information and training through Business Link and another excuse to go to the pub once a month! Last Christmas we all met one lunchtime and after a pub meal toured our individual offices, eating mince pies and drinking sherry around the filing cabinets. Almost like every other office party."

it useful to visit my clients, circumstances permitting, even when it is not really necessary. This puts phone contact onto a human basis afterwards and you get the feeling of belonging to a group of real people."

"I've been a teleworker for more than a decade and have prided myself on being able to keep customers and have a good working relationship with them from a distance. But this spring a grant from an enterprise group allowed me to bring over two people from one of my export customers and I was amazed what a difference it made to work with them face-to-face for a day and then go out and relax with them over a good meal. It's surprising how much you can get the wrong impression of people over email and the phone – now our calls are much more relaxed and chatty."

Other activities that can help to reduce isolation include attending workshops, exhibitions and seminars (these also help to keep your skills and contacts up), joining professional associations, and seeking out discussion groups on the Internet.

On the other side of the isolation equation, city-based teleworkers report plagues of neighbours dropping in to borrow envelopes, stamps, use photocopiers, browse the web and so on. A quiet word, or the imposition of a nominal fee for the facility, usually solves this problem.

Technical support is an area of isolation which directly affects all teleworkers at some time or other. There must be a law about why software problems always develop after office hours. PAYE teleworkers will often have access to company IT specialists to solve their problems (and may have priority over their onsite colleagues in use of these services). But self-employed teleworkers are usually dependent on their computer or software supplier: "The main reason for using a reliable small local computer dealer rather than buying mail order." A number of computer manufacturers operate premium phonelines for support which do cover evenings and weekends, but often these give limited help after a purchase (famously, Microsoft only offers "two instances" of free support before you have to start paying).

There is definitely a gap in the market for competent IT support personnel to provide effective premium rate support services to teleworkers. The problem is that teleworkers often have high-specification systems with many add-ons which can make it difficult to diagnose the fault even where a modem is available for the engineer to use for dialling in.

Support organisations

Teleworkers can get support from a number of trade unions who are starting to look at how to support self-employed people and freelancers as well as conventional employees. The concept of employee mutuals, which are groupings of employees who use their mutual power to access discounts on items like insurance and travel, is gaining ground in the US and can provide practical support for teleworkers in some areas.

Recruitment companies specialising in the IT area are also looking at providing discount services and access to training for their candidates in these times of skill shortage to promote loyalty. However, the first port of call for teleworkers is likely to be telework associations. A number were reviewed by Bill Murray of Small World Connections in the May 1997 edition of *Flexible Working* Magazine. Bill recommends that in deciding which group to join for support you should:

- Talk to the group's administrator and find out how many existing members come from organisations with similar profiles to your own;
- Find out how often you will have a chance to share experiences with other group members;
- Request samples of the group's published material;
- Ask for the names of one or two members you could approach for an opinion on how useful or not they find the group.

National Association of Teleworking (NAT)

NAT was formed in 1992 to foster and promote best practice in the development and application of teleworking and associated flexible working practices. NAT is currently re-organising. All corporate and voluntary sector enquiries should be sent to:
Tel: 01275 333862 Fax: 01275 333515 Email: enquiries@teleworking.org.uk

Telework Ireland (TWI)

TWI works on a transborder basis promoting telework and representing the interests of teleworkers and telework-based businesses. Activities include:
– Panel of trained mentors assisting developers of telework-based business;
– Representation on the Irish government's e-work Action Forum;
– Consultancy services to organisations implementing telework policies.
– Development of distance learning course in IT, teleworking and software testing.

Membership benefits include:
– Starter pack of "The Teleworking Manual" in choice of format;
– Email list and website "members only" area;
– Newsletter and TCA *Teleworker* magazine;
– Networking opportunities;
– Online skills register;
– Discount offers on SOHO products (*eg* insurance, publications, furniture);
– Access to mentoring, training and consultancy services at concessionary rates.
– Affiliate membership of Small Firms Association with access to helpline
Individual membership is £95 a year with a concessionary rate of £50
Tel: +353 61 921121 Freefone in ROI: 1800 421426 Web: **www.telework.ie**

CWU Ireland

The Communications Workers Union in Ireland has a special "virtual membership" for teleworkers launched in 1997 which costs £99. Members get the TCA *Teleworking Handbook*, an advice line including legal assistance, access to union sickness benefits and insurance schemes, and a free web advertisement for their services. There are plans for a virtual work agency for teleworkers and training programmes. CWU also acts as a lobbying group for teleworkers and is represented on the Irish government's e-work Action Forum. Tel: +353 21 887300 Web: **www.cwu.ie**

The Telework, Telecottage and Telecentre Association (TCA)

Established in 1993, the TCA has around 2,000 members, including individuals, corporate members, telecentres and telecottages. The aim of the association is to help make teleworking an accepted way of working. Much of the information available through the TCA is aimed at the individual but the association also encourages telework take-up in the corporate world by emphasising the business benefits of teleworking. The TCA has been something of a pioneer – the *Teleworking Handbook* has been adapted and translated into French and Italian, the *Teleworker* magazine received a European Teleworking Award, and the first independently accredited teleworking qualification was also supported by the TCA.

Individuals pay around £30 to join the association and receive the *Teleworking Handbook*, the bimonthly colour magazine *Teleworker,* and the weekly e-zine *TCA Online* which provides regular news updates and information on work opporunities. Members have access to a web forum and get discounts on events and relevant products as well as being able to consult the TCA member helpline. The TCA is a not-for-profit organisation and supports itself through membership, product and consultancy income. Tel: 0800 616008 Web: **www.tca.org.uk**

The Future Work Forum

Established in 1992, the Future Work Forum is run by Henley Management College and costs around £2,000 a year. It provides quarterly seminars, workshops, visits, an annual dinner, published proceedings, research reports and an information service. Aimed at corporates, it specialises in providing expert speakers and thinkers in the area of flexible working.

Bibliography

Teleworker Magazine
Editor: Alan Denbigh Tel: 01453 834874 Fax: 01453 836174
Email:info@tca.org.uk Web: www.tca.org.uk
Source: TCA Tel: 0800 616008 or 01203 696986 Fax: 01203 696538
Comment: Bi-monthly magazine for TCA members

1999 Telework America National Telework Survey   *Date:* 2000
Author: Joanne H. Pratt
Source: International Telework Association and Council
Web: www.telecommute.org and www.joannepratt.com

Don't stop the career clock – rejecting the myths of aging for a new way to work in the 21st century   *Date:* 1999
Author: Simon Collin
Source: Virgin Publishing Ltd ISBN: 0–7535–04103

The procrastinator's guide to success – a 7-step program for taking action now *Date:* 1999
Author: Lynn Lively
Source: McGraw Hill ISBN: 0–07–0383073

Do it now! Break the procrastination habit *Date:* 1998
Author: Dr William J Knaus
Source: John Wiley & Sons ISBN: 0–471–17399–1

Follow your heart: finding purpose in your life and work *Date:* 1998
Author: Andrew Matthews
Source: Seashell ISBN: 0–646–31066–6

How to change your life with technology *Date:* 1998
Author: Anthony Capstick
Source: Management Books 2000 Ltd Tel: 01285 760722 Email: m.b.2000@virgin.net
Practical and realistic guide to using technology to streamline working life.

30 Minutes... to boost your communication skills *Date:* 1997
Author: Elizabeth Tierney
Source: Kogan Page, 120 Pentonville Rd, London N1 9JN ISBN 0–7494–23676

Corporate Telework Survey *Date:* 1997
Authors: Small World Connections
Source: PO Box 162, South District Office, Manchester M20 3BB Tel: 0161 445 0630
Fax: 0161 445 1403 Email: small_world@compuserve.com
Web: www.smallworldconnections.com

Hebridean Teleworker *Date:* 1997
Source: Western Isles Project Office Tel: 01851 880225 Fax: 01851 880386
Email: itproject@sol.co.uk Web: www.work-global.com
Comment: Networking newsletter for teleworkers in the Western Isles with database of 500 skilled people which has been built up by the Western Isles Project Office.

Get Yourself Organised! (60 minutes Success Skills Series) *Date:* 1997
Author: Mike Levy
Source: David Grant Publishing, 80 Ridgeway, Kent TN2 4EZ ISBN 1–901306–00–3

Maximise Your Time (60 minutes Success Skills Series) *Date:* 1997
Author: Ronald Bracey
Source: David Grant Publishing, 80 Ridgeway, Kent TN2 4EZ ISBN 1–901306–02–X

Teleworking and Gender *Date:* 1996
Author: Ursula Huws Web: http://www.dspace.dial.pipex.com/analytica
Source: Institute for Employment Studies, Mantell Building, University of Sussex, Brighton BN1 9RF Tel: 01273 686751 Fax: 01273 690430.

Lone Parents & Their Information & Communication Technologies *Date:* 1995
Authors: Leslie Haddon & Roger Silverstone
Source: Science Policy Research Unit, University of Sussex, SPRU, Mantell Building, Falmer, Brighton BN1 9RF

Contacts and URLs

Freeagentnation ezine – Dan Pink's throughts on the change to increased self employment over the net. Subscribe at
www.freeagentnation.com/newsstand/newsletter.html.

www.kendlebell.co.uk – Personal call-handling service for people who don't like to use voicemail when they are out.

Parents at Work – formerly the Working Mothers Association, 77 Holloway Rd, London N7 8JZ Tel: 020 7628 3578

Royal Mail – details of postal services and conditions, a two-way postcode lookup table, tariff calculators, track-and-trace facilities **www.royalmail.co.uk/atwork**

Telephone Preference Service – to register your wish not to be contacted by direct selling organisations Tel: 0845 070 0707

Fax Preference Service – to register your wish not to be faxed by direct selling organisations Tel: 0845 070 0702

Posturite – ergonomic office furniture including chairs, desks, wrist supports, ergonomic mice, document holders, back supports. PO Box 468, Hailsham, East Sussex BN27 4LZ Tel: 01323 833353 Fax: 01323 833999 Email: support@posturite.co.uk Web: **www.posturite.co.uk**

Uninterruptible power supplies – try the Radio Spares (RS) catalogue **www.rsc-components.com** stock numbers 331-6465 (£95), 331 6471, 326-8108 (£65) and 234-2615 (£195) or **www.upspower.co.uk**.

www.bt.com/timesmart – BT site aimed at helping you to save time by collecting together useful tools such as currently calculators, world-time clocks, UK phone directories etc.

www.gator.com – downloadable software that allows you to fill in your personal details (usernames, passwords for websites) so next time you sign on to a website you don't have to retype information. A similar UK product is available from Royal Mail at www.mailme.co.uk.

www.yac.com – "free" but ingenious system which assigns you a personal number that you can switch from mobile to email to voicemail to office – YAC can forward your voicemail to your email and vice versa. The catch is that those who call you get charged mobile phone rates even if you're on an ordinary landline.

Getting work

This chapter is aimed at teleworkers who are, or wish to be, self-employed or to run a small business. For ideas on services which can be offered by self-employed teleworkers, see Chapter 5, *Ideas for telebusinesses*. This chapter is not relevant to companies implementing telework for employees (see Chapter 2, *Company Teleworking*). If you are already employed and wish to remain in your job but begin teleworking, you will need to read Chapters 2 and 3, and then draft a cost/benefit case for teleworking to put to your employer. Chapter 3, *Survival Guide*, gives a draft cost/benefit case which you can adapt to your situation (see page 85).

Marketing yourself as a teleworker

Many teleworkers have excellent skills in their areas of expertise, but know little about sales and marketing. Think about getting professional help with marketing if the whole idea makes you nervous. In the UK, your local Business Link would be a good place to look for help. In Ireland, talk to the Enterprise Line (1850 353333), FÁS and your local County Enterprise Board or LEADER group. But perhaps the first thing to do is adjust your mindset.

From your customers' point of view, they probably aren't interested in whether you are a teleworker, even though you may see teleworking as a central issue. So begin your marketing review with a simple resolution coined by Horace Mitchell of telework consultancy MTA Associates:

"Don't mention the T-word (teleworker...)"

There is a second T-word which is very important: trust. The big issue for most prospective customers is not technology – it's whether they trust you, because they probably aren't that used to working with people at a distance. They need to know that you have the skills, are reliable, will turn the work up on time, will be easy to deal with and will complete the job within the estimate or budget. They don't want to end up looking stupid in front of their colleagues for having suggested you. So you will need to provide them with plenty of reassurance about your competence.

What your customers are probably searching for is higher quality and lower cost than they can get elsewhere, or for a job completed within a timescale they cannot manage themselves in-house. How are you going to convince them that you can achieve this? Here are some quotes from a TCA conference on marketing teleworking:

"If people are sending work out of their office they expect it to be done better than if it was done in their own office. Everything has to be slicker and more efficient. You have to have a control system that makes absolutely sure work doesn't get mixed up, that it's done in the right order, on time and accurately. You have to be more careful than if you were working for one particular business." *Judith Verity, Office Ghosts*

"I looked at what the competition were charging for their reports and tried to get in at that sort of level. People tend not to take you seriously if you are not expensive enough. And when people ring to place an order, we answer the telephone in exactly the same way. To the customer it is a unified response although it may be a different voice. It is like a corporate image over the telephone line." *Anthony Capstick, Instant Search*

The third change in mindset you need to make concerns marketing. Marketing is not selling or public relations. Marketing is the process of adjusting what you are selling (your product or service) to best fit the demands of your customers. It can cover all kinds of strategies, including the timing and method of delivery of work, the pricing and the technical details of the work (such as the software packages used). Successful marketing is the key to a successful small business.

Establish your objectives

Objectives can be difficult to define for teleworkers. Some want a way of working which allows them more time with their families. Others are concerned with improving profits through lowering overheads. Others may be motivated by the desire to avoid commuting to work or office politics. This chapter limits itself to looking at business objectives, but anyone considering starting up a teleworking small business should consult the bibliography, and spend some time with their family working out a set of objectives – which might cover profits needed to cover living expenses, number of hours to be worked each week, circumstances under which the teleworker can be disturbed in the home office – and which everyone in the family understands and agrees to. You need a clear business idea and set of objectives before you start thinking about marketing. Equipping yourself with the computer and internet connection is not enough.

You need to know:

- what services will be offered? See Chapter 5, *Ideas for telebusinesses* if you're not already sure;
- who is going to use the service?;
- how do people buy it? By phone and fax or over the web? Then pay attention to voicemail messages, website performance and fax presentation – the "shop window" of a teleworked business;
- when do people buy it? Are there peak periods (such as pre-Christmas) that need to be covered in terms of staff levels?;
- where do people buy it from? Through the Yellow Pages, or through a personal recommendation, or from their PC over the web?;
- do others already offer a similar product or service? Is your service an improvement on these competitors? Is there any evidence that customers want an improvement?;
- how much is it going to cost? Are you going to be cheaper, on a par with, or more expensive than your competitors?;

- what is the business going to be called? The name will depend upon your target market. People offering a teleworked professional service may prefer to use a version of their own name as the business name since the clients are essentially "hiring" that person;
- what happens if a contract goes badly wrong? Do you need professional indemnity insurance in case a customer sues you? (N.B. It is often a condition of professional indemnity policies that you do not tell your customers that you are insured because that could make them more likely to sue.) Do you need to take legal advice to draw up a general contract for signature with clients?;

Brian O'Kane's guide *Starting a Business in Ireland* suggests two exercises which help to further clarify your business idea.

1. **Write your own CV** for the position of managing director/administrator of your business. What are your skills and experience? Build on these. Look at your technical, personal and business skills.
2. **Write a short description** of the processes which must be completed before you have something for which you can invoice a customer (eg receive enquiry, discuss with client, give quotation, use software package on computer and so on). Throughout, keep a list of every item which will be required, from paper to printer right down to the chair you sit on.

Market research

Once you have your business idea clearly set out, you need to do some market research. If you are applying for any kind of outside assistance in starting up a small business, the questions which grant-giving bodies or banks will want answered include:

Location, location, location

There are plenty of case studies giving examples of people working far from their clients or employers such as programmers working from Australia, or Irish call centres servicing the North American market. Teleworking can allow work to be independent of distance. But all the evidence is that most companies prefer to use teleworkers who are located close enough to be able to pop in and discuss work face-to-face when needed. The *TeleFutures* study in Ireland (1996) found that over 80% of companies would prefer their teleworkers to be situated within 25 miles. The exception to this is people with rare skills or combinations of skills, who can usually lay down their own conditions on how they will work. Some people promote teleworking by having two different prices for their work – a lower price if the job can be teleworked without on-site client meetings. Overall, however, the lower your skill set (eg secretarial), the more likely it is that your clientele will be local, so build this factor into your business plan.

- what is the total market for this service and what are the overall trends in this market area (static, expanding, contracting)? Look for national surveys on market share and size – many are available from good reference libraries or on the web;
- how much of that total market is practically accessible to your service (*eg* if it is a geographically limited service, check out what percentage of the national market is in your "catchment area")? Research basic figures in your local library or on the web such as the population in your area, the percentage of people unemployed, the breakdown of types of employment into service, manufacturing, agriculture, and so on);
- how much of the accessible market could you reasonably hope to capture? This answer should take into account practical constraints (*eg* maximum number of productive hours in a year which you expect to work) and will look more convincing if you give a minimum and a maximum and then show that you are selecting a fairly conservative figure between the two;
- what competitors do you have? Their strengths and weaknesses? How much do they charge? To provide information on costs, there is little alternative to ringing around competitor companies to check out prices – few give this kind of detail on their websites. This is a horrible job but vital. Make sure you have a "project" for them to quote on or they will quickly realise that you are not a *bona fide* customer. Look through Yellow Pages to see how many companies are working in your area. Don't forget that your competitors may be listed in different sections of the telephone directory such as secretarial services, computer graphics, desktop publishing, computer training, computer consultancy and so on;
- ask existing customers, family, friends. Why would (or do) people use your services?

The information from your market research will be used to prepare your business plan.

Business planning

There are many books and guides available which will help you to put together a formal business plan (see bibliography). Many Business Links have advisers who can help with business plans, as do high street banks. The purpose of a business plan is to produce a document, probably only around 10 pages in length for a simple small business, which has four basic functions:

- to help you clarify your thinking – focusing your thoughts and making sure you have done the calculations needed to ensure your plan is realistic;
- to establish that your business idea is financially viable;

Couldn't an agency just get the work for me?

A common query from would-be teleworkers who don't relish the self-employment option is whether there are any employment agencies which use teleworkers. Although there have been a couple of forays into this area none of the major employment agencies have tackled this market area yet. In their absence, some smaller specialist companies have targeted teleworking such as Homebased, a new service located in Dublin.

Homebased is a recruitment service which introduces companies to individuals working from home or from a remote location, and supports the company and the teleworker through telephone helplines and training to develop the employment relationship. The company is run by Karl Llewellyn, who also runs Phonenet, a telemarketing company which uses some remote workers. Karl explains:

"We hold a database of hundreds of teleworkers throughout the country, filed and formatted to provide candidates with specific skills for employers' requirements. Employers can interview a suitable candidate within days. Any candidate who is offered a position is given full training on all aspects of working from home, including motivation, structure, reports, development and negotiation skills. Both the individual and the company get a manual dealing with home-based working including issues like breaks, dealing with the family, overworking, legal and insurance issues. We also offer the candidate and the employer three months' telephone support. We can provide full IT support to set up reporting structure, email communication and data synchronisation with "head office"." Of course the service is not free to the employer – they have to pay a recruitment fee, currently £IR1250. but Karl guarantees that, if the candidate resigns their position or proves unsuitable, then Homebased will replace them at no extra charge to the employer.

Another recruitment agency based in south-east England, stresses the higher end of the market: "We tell everyone what our margin is – up to 20%. We don't handle assignments paying less than £20/hour. We can only represent people if they work wholly from home otherwise we would become their employer. The only exception is freelancers who set up limited companies".

www.phonenet.ie or karl@phonenet.ie

Samantha Jones of the Home Employment Agency is profiled in Chapter 5, *Ideas for Telebusinesses* – **www.hea-online.co.uk**

- to provide an accessible, clear document which contains all the relevant information about your business idea for outsiders including advisers such as accountants, and people you want to invest in your business such as bank managers;
- to provide a baseline against which the progress of your business can be measured.

There are many different structures for business plans. Here is a simple one which covers the basics.

1. **Principals:** who are you? Why should anyone believe you can do this? Brief history and objective of your business. Past performance (if available).

2. **Product:** what will you sell and what processes are involved before you have something to sell to the customer? How is it different from other competing services? Is it ready to sell now or do you need to develop it in some way?

3. **Location:** where will you carry out the business? Why have you chosen that location and how does it fit in with how you need to carry out your business? Do you have specific premises in mind? Indicate the purchase cost or rental. If you are working from home, estimate the reduction in overheads compared to a conventional office.

4. **Equipment:** what is needed for your product or service? Give cost estimates and indicate if you already possess any of the relevant equipment.

5. Are any **raw materials** or consumables needed?

6. **Employment:** who will be employed by the business? On what basis? Full-time, part-time, subcontracted? Don't forget all those boring administrative tasks vital to continued successful operation, such as chasing debts and completing VAT returns

7. **Management:** what will the management structure be? Outline the qualifications and experience of the key personnel

8. **Finance:** where will you get the money from? How much will be invested by the principals? How much will be borrowed and on what terms? How much are you looking for in terms of grants (if any)?

9. **Profitability:** the figures bit. Provide audited accounts for the last two years if you have them. Give projected profit and loss acounts and balance sheets for the first two years of the project

10. **Marketing:** how will your products or services be sold? Do you have any firm contracts or orders? Market surveys? Competitors?

Setting prices and quoting

Preparing a business plan can seem to be a bit of a circular process – how can you know how much to charge until you know what the running costs are that you will have to cover? Or how successful your service will be? But in fact, a combination of estimating running costs and researching the prices charged by others for similar services will probably give you a fairly good guide to what you should be charging. This may, in turn, get you to refine your ideas about your start-up costs – what you will really need to get going.

So start by doing the cashflows and other business calculations to find out what you need to earn to cover your running costs. If you aren't sure of how to do this, refer to some of the small business guides in the bibliography or get professional help from an accountant or business adviser. Your selling price must be higher than this breakeven cost. Selling price in turn affects your choice of target market, means of communication, choice of name and so on.

Many teleworkers find quoting for jobs nervewracking initially. Applying common sense is the best advice. If you aren't sure, ask to prepare a small section of the work as a "free sample". Work out how long it takes you, and multiply up to the size of the whole job. Use the trial section of work to get the exact details of the job agreed with the customer. Novices tend to underquote – so think about adding on 20% to the final amount you arrive at. Some customers find it reassuring to know the underlying cost per hour that you are calculating from. Others want you to quote a fixed price for the whole job. Ask other established teleworkers for advice on quotes.

Raising finance

The next step once you have a business plan is to raise the necessary finance for starting up. Double check your business plan figures with the checklist of items at the end of Chapter 11, *Teleworking equipment*, which you may need just to get started. Decide which are priority items, and which non-priority or unnecessary. Can you reduce costs by buying secondhand or borrowing? Remember to include VAT in the prices unless you are VAT registered, in which case you will be able to reclaim many VAT amounts.

One important item you will need to decide on with your accountant or financial adviser is whether to register for VAT. You are required to register for VAT if your business turns over more than £52,000 in the UK, or more than £20,000 in Ireland for service-based businesses (the Irish manufacturing threshold is £40,000 but teleworkers by definition will be service providers). However, it may be worth your while registering even if you turnover is lower in some circumstances. For most teleworkers, the issues are:

- if you register then you can reclaim VAT on equipment you purchase;
- if your customers are VAT registered, it will not inconvenience them that you charge VAT; but if they are mainly *not* registered (private clients), then it is actually going to cost them more to use you if you do register;
- if you register, you will need to set up, learn and keep VAT accounts and make regular returns. In some ways this is a pain, in others it is a blessing in disguise because it forces you to keep your accounts up-to-date.

You are more likely to be successful if you take a conservative approach to start-up costs and "make do" rather than going for expensive items and incurring large financing charges, but beware: a common error is to underestimate start-up costs. Your financing will also need to include working capital – the money you need to start up and keep going until the first cheques come in. Bear in mind that, unless you are doing basic secretarial work where people call in to collect their work, and you can extract money as you deliver work, you are unlikely to be paid until at least 30 days from the date you invoice a customer. In many cases the delay between completion of the job and invoicing, and payment of the invoice, will be 45 or 60 days. Don't strangle your business at birth by failing to accommodate these delays with adequate finance. The most common cause of business failure is cashflow – so make sure that you invoice at the earliest possible instance, follow up with a statement to remind them, and then chase payment.

The options for raising finance are:

1. Your own equity (ability to buy shares in the business)
2. Other people's equity (other shareholders apart from yourself)
3. Borrowing money
4. Grants (almost without exception, grant-making bodies will require that you raise at least half of the cost yourself).

Start by thinking about what finance you yourself can raise, and by taking a careful look at which of your assets you would need to retain if your business went under. You may not want to mortgage your house as collateral for a business bank loan, but if you are lucky may have other assets you are prepared to risk such as shares, jewellery, paintings, cars or land.

Now consider the possibility of investment (other people's equity). In general small businesses have difficulty raising equity capital or venture capital except from friends and relatives because the amount of money is too small (normally around £500,000 is the minimum that investors want to look at because of the expense of checking and setting up the operation).

Whatever the source of your equity finance, be very clear on the following points outlined in Brian O'Kane's book:

■ are you prepared to allow other people to own (and therefore control) part of your business?
■ what reward can they reasonably expect for their investment?
■ can your business offer the kind of return that would attract outside investors?

The amount of debt finance which you can raise will almost certainly be defined by what your bank manager is prepared to lend you and will be based on your business plan and available security. Bank managers will be looking for the three Cs – **character** (your track record), **collateral** (security against any inability to repay) and **cashflow** (evidence that your business is financially viable). Arnold S. Goldstein's American book *Starting on a Shoestring* suggests that unless you know the answer to the following points before you go to see your bank manager you may not get very far:

■ why do you need the amount requested?

Business advice and funding for Teleworkers

The sources of advice, information and possible funding are currently undergoing changes which are planned to provide a simplified structure in the long term, but in the short term it's all change.

Business Link advice centres: A collaboration between Training and Enterprise Councils (TECs, or in Scotland, LECs), Chambers of Commerce, local authorities, enterprise agencies and government departments. However, TECs and LECs are currently being abolished and replaced by Learning and Skills Councils. The government is introducing a new Small Business Service in 2001, and how these changes will affect the Business Link structure remains to be seen. If your Business Link still exists it's a good first point of contact. Services are aimed at two stages: businesses which are thinking about starting up or have just started up, and those which are past their first 12 months of existence. In both cases a range of supports are provided including start-up courses, strategic consultancy and some forms of subsidy. In some areas of the country this is supplemented by extra grants such as economic development funds aimed at businesses which are going to employ people through expansion. Contact details for the new Small Business Services will be available from the Information Society Helpline on 0345 152 000.

Countryside Agency The Rural Development Commission has been replaced by the Countryside Agency. Some of the RDC's activities have been taken on by the new Regional Development Agencies.

Regional Development Agencies These co-ordinate inward investment and other funding for specific regions. Businesses in rural areas should contact them to find out about schemes such as small business grants, redundant building grants and job creation scheme. A big effort is being made to provide web-based information on these new agencies – see **www.local-regions.detr.gov.uk/rda/info/index.htm** or telephone the Department of Environment, Transport and the Regions on 020 7944 3000.

Princes Youth Business Trust Assistance for businesses being set up by people under 30. Tel: 0800 842842 or see www.princes-trust.org.uk

Chambers of Trade/Commerce – details of your local organisation are available from British Chambers of Commerce Tel: 020 7565 2000.

- what will you do with it?
- how do you know that it's enough?
- how much less can you live with?
- who else will you borrow from?
- how do you propose to repay it?
- how can you prove that you can repay it?
- what collateral can you offer?

Don't overlook banks as a potential source of finance – most of the high street banks have overhauled their services to small businesses within the last few years and many produce packs of useful information. The Co-operative Bank offers a direct loan scheme to readers of *Teleworker* magazine on an "instant decision", unsecured, phoneloan basis for amounts between £1,000 and £15,000. Phone 0800 591 682 and quote reference 791/775. If you are unable to obtain conventional finance due to a lack of security or track record, you may qualify for the Small Firms Loan Guarantee scheme in Britain. This scheme provides loans of £5,000–£100,000 (and up to £250,000 for established businesses) over a period of two to ten years (Tel: 08700 010 172).

Advertising and PR

Few start-ups include sufficient marketing and PR budgets in their business plans. Begin by formulating some idea of who you need to address, breaking down the audience into distinct groups. You need to create a short, clear explanation of how your service will work, be charged for, have its quality guaranteed, be delivered and so on. Then work out the most cost-effective method of contacting the different audiences – postal mailing, phone, website, email, listings in directories, trade shows or a combination.

Antony Capstick of Instant Search gives the following advice: "With PR and journalism one has to think of a peg to hang the idea on when you are selling it to journalists. When Companies House opened up its service to people from the outside, I marketed the idea for my Instant Search business through that 'peg'. I sent faxes off to the newsdesk saying 'Companies House has opened their computer to the outside; however, you can get the service if you don't have a PC because Instant Search are offering it as a mail order instant-access service'. The best publicity I got from that was the Manchester Evening News. They quoted me and I was flooded with calls from Manchester, lots of orders – it was very good."

"It also helps in background credibility if your name is mentioned for example in the FT or a quality paper; somehow people think you are better. There may be direct sales as a result of editorial coverage, but it also helps when you approach people directly if they have already heard of you."

You may want to advertise at first so that customers will be aware of your existence. Think carefully about which media (newspapers, local radio) will work best for you, and compare prices. Contact details for most publications are available at **www.mediauk.com/directory/**. The basic options are:

- newspapers
- trade magazines
- web – include costs for professional design, search engine registration and maintenance, and help with publicising your website unless you are already an expert in this area. If you are determined to do this yourself see Chapter 10, *Email and the Internet* for further advice.

- local radio
- TV (if your budget is huge…)

Try to think about how you will measure response to your adverts so that you will know where to spend your money next time. Keep asking new customers where they heard about you and record their replies.

Directories and networks

Many businesses use directories to market their services. The best known and most widely accessible publication is the telephone directory (Yellow Pages, or Golden Pages in Ireland). Before advertising in Yellow Pages take a good look at the entries for your area. A problem that many teleworking businesses come across is that there is no obvious place for their services in Yellow Pages at present – or rather too many. Teleworkers would often need to make entries in a number of categories to cover all their services, including office services, desktop publishing, graphic design, bookkeeping, secretarial services and so on. Yellow Pages may be a good option if your business fits into a niche – such as market research – but very expensive if you cover a range of categories. Remember that you are entitled to a free basic text entry in Yellow Pages if you pay the business, rather than residential, tariff on your telephone. Make sure that you get that and that it is correctly worded – Yellow Pages entries for the whole country are becoming widely available on the web and via CD-ROM so this constitutes a useful form of advertising with nationwide coverage.

If you decide to pay for a more complex Yellow Pages ad, think through the different options and prices. Often a plain text advert in bold type will be more cost-effective and practical than a graphic. In general, companies are more concerned about reference clients than they are about the size of your Yellow Pages advert. Think of it in plumbing terms. If you are looking for a plumber, you might use Yellow Pages to find the number of a particular plumber, but you are more likely to select that plumber based on personal recommendation or reference from friends and neighbours than "cold" through any directory. So while it's important to have your contact details accessible, it may not be so important to take a large ad.

Local business directories may also be worth buying entries for – your local chamber of commerce or library should be able to give you information on the directories operating in your area. Chambers of commerce and other business networking organisations also often publish local directories and encourage their members to use the services of other members.

Individual teleworkers may find it worthwhile to register with employment agencies or recruitment websites as some are now taking on board the task of getting in contract work for teleworkers – though they will usually require you to have set up your own limited company. A number of agencies advertise on the World Wide Web, but most of the requests are for permanent staff, not for temps or teleworkers.

Responding to customer concerns

Whatever the package of information you decide to distribute, you will need to collect responses – perhaps by phone or through a website contact form. Some of the responses will be fears, some criticisms, some good ideas, *etc*. They need to be analysed and responded to appropriately and promptly. Your prospective customers may list a number of common anxieties about using teleworkers. You could turn the following organisational suggestions into selling points with your customers.

- computer viruses – can you guarantee that the disks you send to your customers are virus-free?
- equipment backup – what would happen if your computer went down? Is alternative equipment available quickly? Do you have ample data backups of work in progress in case of disaster?
- people backup – if you are a small operation, how will you deal with the inevitable peaks and troughs in demand? What happens if you are flattened by 'flu? You can deal with fluctuations in workload through a network of associated teleworkers, perhaps through online systems such as the TCA email broadcast list. Set the system up before you are in a crisis!
- confidentiality – what happens if another teleworker accesses commercially-sensitive information? Could somebody unscrupulous get hold of the client company's stationery?
- data security – make sure that your computer system is secure. Use security features such as passwords and file-locking to prevent unauthorised access of client's files. Make sure that your office is secure. Lock away customers' stationery and files if they are sensitive
- delivery methods – can you help your customers to get used to teleworking, for example by offering to help them to set up modems and learn to use email? If they aren't on email, do you know everything you need to about collection and delivery services for finished work? (*eg* what is the cut-off time in your area to get a parcel to DHL for delivery next day in Brussels? How much does it cost to get a motorbike delivery to London?)
- presentation – look at your fax cover sheets, letterheads, business cards. Do they reflect a professional image? How does your office look if a customer drops in unexpectedly? Can customers hear radios in the background when they ring up? Are all staff trained in telephone answering?

These issues are related to quality control which is covered in Chapter 8. If your organisation is large enough to bear the time involved, look into achieving formal quality control to ISO 9000. Use project management software to track progress on all jobs undertaken. Measure your response time to enquiries.

IWS: a telework job agency for Wales

Innovative Work Solutions is providing what it describes as a "high quality temp service" using teleworkers from west Wales. According to the website: "Companies don't have to limit their activities to skills available locally. Teleworkers can take the strain of a direct mail campaign, or fill in for staff during peak holiday periods. Using our services also allows companies to expand output without increased premises costs." IWS also ensures that:

- the teleworkers are qualified and trained
- they have access to suitable hardware and software that matches the company's requirements
- full in-house technical support is provided to the teleworkers
- job specifications are checked and the job is completed to ISO 9000 quality standards.

Each job carried out by IWS has a worksheet which specifies the requirements for the job such as spacing, tabs, paragraph styles, preferred spellings, page layout, fonts and formats. Typical administrative services (eg word processing by someone with RSA II or III qualifications and a minimum of three years' office experience) costs about £5.50/hour.

Over 90% of the work carried out at IWS is translations (especially Welsh) from companies like TV station S4C, who deliver and collect their work entirely by email. Rates for translation work are about £10.00/hour. However, despite a 100% increase in turnover for the last year, manager Malcolm O'Brien says that business is static. This is because funds for their marketing consultant dried up, so that the only active marketing currently carried out is a Yellow Pages ad.

Initially IWS had over 100 teleworkers on its books, but quickly found that only around 20 of these were "really useful" with about another 20 "fringe". The rest were deleted after a period of inactivity. Malcolm describes translation as an admin-intensive business where work has to be checked rigorously, and sometimes disputes arise over subjective issues like dialect and expression. He's also worried about the new IR35 regulations and feels that these may prove a major impediment to IWS's teleworking and consultancy services.

www.telecottages.org/iws

Handling press and publicity

Properly handled, your relations with the local and business press can be one of the most cost-effective forms of marketing, but they need to be seen as part of your marketing strategy – just as with direct mail or advertising

Skills registers – success or space waste?

Many projects have been carried out over the last decade which aimed to provide work for teleworkers via skills registers. Most have languished except where they have:

- Aimed at high level skills
- Actively sold the teleworkers through a dedicated marketing operation
- Taken steps to control the work quality of the teleworkers on the register.

Examples include:

Shetland Enterprise 01595 693177 – register of 54 teleworkers, 21 with degrees, 33 with HNDs. Successes include two teleworkers preparing Autocad electronic circuit diagrams and process schematic diagrams, both tasks requiring specialist knowledge

IWS – see previous page. Register restricted to active teleworkers producing high quality work. **www.telecottages.org/iws**

Work Global Western Isles – register of 550 people, not all teleworkers which has "created, enabled or retained 150 jobs since the start of the project in 1994, not all simultaneously". The register is actively marketed by manager Donnie Morrison who travels extensively to meet potential clients in Europe and the USA. Currently around 20 people work with local company Lasair on a self-employed basis and a further 68 will be employed by an ISP which is locating in the area. Future plans include virtual call centres and a Java-based workflow system. Winners of the 1999 European Teleworking Award **www.work-global.com**

---

campaigns, identify the target and then look at the most effective means to reach it. Apart from reaching new customers, press coverage can assist with the following:

- reminding existing customers of your existence
- a morale booster for employees or subcontractors
- improved service from suppliers if they think of you as an important customer
- bank managers, planning officers (always useful to have them on your side).

To get to these audiences you have to convince an intermediary target – the journalist. The key to success is to treat press relations as a partnership in which both you and the journalist want to reach the same people – the journalist wants to give them an interesting, useful read. You want to make the audience aware of your product or service. Helping journalists to achieve their objective is the secret of success.

Step 1: identify the publication. It could be a business to business title, or a specialist trade paper. Be careful not to confuse business and consumer counterparts – mountain bikers don't necessarily read Cycle Trader, and turkey farmers may not have much interest in BBC Good Food magazine. If you're unsure, the reference bible is the voluminous and expensive monthly *BRAD* (British Rates and Data) which gives information on almost every periodical in Great Britain and some in Northern Ireland and the Republic of Ireland (also try **www.mediauk.com/directory/** and Willings Press Guide, available in many libraries).

Step 2: draft your press release, always keeping in mind the famous acronym KISS – Keep It Simple, Stupid:

- try not to exceed one page of generously-spaced A4 on your business letterhead;
- use a short, clear headline that sums up the story in a few words;
- get all the main details into the first paragraph. Further down, include an interesting quote;
- avoid journalese – you are writing to attract the journalist's attention, not to do their job for them. Expunge words like "revealed" or "shocked" and keep in mind the news angle – why might your story generate interest?;
- avoid jargon and stick to clear, quantifiable facts such as "This is the third government contract won by Anytown Design in two months" not "this places Anytown Design as an industry market leader";
- if you enclose a photo, try to ensure that it is a print, not a transparency, label it clearly on the back with the name and job title of each person,

---

The importance of being answered

Anthony Capstick of Instant Search comments: "One of the most important things we decided was that we would answer the telephone in a uniform way. Our standard greeting became: 'Good morning, Instant Search, Anthony speaking, how can I help?'. When you are working remotely from your customers it is vital to give the right impression. It is a bit like the impression you get going into a shop or restaurant. You are completely put off the place if there is a full ashtray sitting on the counter or a black plastic bag full of smelly rubbish in the doorway.

"In the same way it is completely unacceptable to answer the telephone by simply saying 'hello' or without introducing yourself. It gives off an amateurish air. Same goes for children screaming, dogs barking, doorbells ringing in the background. Completely unacceptable, along with voicemail messages that say 'Please leave a message and we'll get back to you' – oh yeah? In which century?".

Anthony Capstick's book *How to Change your Life with Technology* can be ordered at **www.instant-search.com**

and briefly describe what they are doing. Do not use felt pen or biro for this label – in a pile of photographs the ink may come off the back of your photograph and on to the front of the one below, and biros can also cause indentations that damage the photograph. Use pencil or a typed label. Don't expect to see the photo again, whether or not it is published;

- date it and include your contact details and telephone number at the bottom;
- many journalists now prefer press information by email – don't send the information as an attachment such as a Word file. Use plain text in the body of the email because you don't know what software attachments they can read and they may not bother to find out if they can read yours.

Step 3: make sure you're sending it to the **right person.** A call to the paper to find out, for example, who covers local business may get you a name. If you don't have a name, send it to a relevant-sounding job title such as Industrial Correspondent.

Step 4: if a journalist calls you for further details, remember they don't bite:

- be courteous and don't patronise in explaining your story. Today's trainee journalist could be a valuable contact on a national paper in a few years' time;
- don't lie or exaggerate – journalists aren't particularly interested in the skeletons in your cupboard until you lie to conceal them;
- avoid going "off the record" – giving information which you do not wish to be published. Although journalists rarely abuse this privilege, mistakes sometimes happen;
- understand that you have no veto over what is printed – there is little point in demanding to see an article before it's published;
- don't antagonise journalists by complaining. Errors are sometimes made – if they are trivial let it lie rather than be branded as a time-waster. For a major mistake, write a polite letter to the editor.

Step 5: If at first you don't succeed, try again. Keep your name in the eye of the public, and in the eye of other journalists. If there's a subject where you have expertise, you may gradually become established as what's unkindly known as a "rentaquote", so that whenever a feature in your area comes along, you're the first person who comes to mind as an interviewee.

Mailing lists

The mailing list is both a junk-mail curse and a vitally useful tool in the right hands. Today's software tools allow records of contacts to be easily held, and the production of vast quantities of marketing materials which can be personalised to the addressee. However, they can have a negative effect if they are not correctly written and targeted, or waste your resources if they are not well planned.

First, you need to know whom you are going to contact and why. Use your business plan and market research to build up a profile of the likely customer. If you are selling to businesses, your next step will probably be to purchase a mailing list from companies such as Kompass, which hold regularly updated and indexed lists of companies. As you pay "per name" you will need to build up a brief for the mailing list company which may include parameters such as:

- number of employees;
- market sector (most mailing list companies have a series of ID codes for different market sectors);
- person to contact within the company (*eg* finance director, human resources/personnel);
- service, manufacturing, or export sector;
- number of years established;
- ownership (*eg* foreign owned or domestic);
- geographical location;
- telephone number (vital for qualifying the list – see overleaf).

Mailing list companies have an incentive to get you to buy as many names as possible, whereas you want the smallest number that will give you a good response rate. To avoid this poacher/gamekeeper conflict you may wish to use a mailing list broker. Bill Moss, an experienced broker, explains: "Mailing list brokers get a discount from suppliers such as Kompass because they buy in bulk. They also know the various mailing lists extremely well. So you can get professional advice from a mailing list broker to produce a well-defined list, get the broker to obtain the list for you, and pay the same amount as you would have done buying direct – the broker pockets the difference between the discount and the standard retail price as the fee for his or her advice."

The broker will also be able to help you ensure that you get the names in a format that you can use. The safest format to ask for is CSV (comma separated variable), which will work with most spreadsheet and word processing programmes. You will probably need to put the list into spreadsheet format whilst you qualify and sort it before using it with your word processing mail merge feature. Some suppliers will provide lists in mail merge format for specified word processing packages. Bill also gives a checklist for those buying mailing lists, whether direct or through a broker:

- Does it matter where the client is located?
- What contact name (job function) is needed if any?
- Do you need telephone or fax numbers?
- How is the list you are buying compiled, and how old is it?
- Is the list owner registered for data protection?
- Is the list owner a member of the country's Direct Marketing Association. If not, think twice about employing them.

Before you even consider the logistics of sending out your mailing, you must qualify the list. This is a tedious process which consists of telephoning the company and checking that the person on your list is indeed still the managing director/human resources manager or whatever, that you have their correct title, and that they are responsible for the area of activity you are interested in. Be polite, patient and persistent with receptionists – they get many such calls each day and sometimes can be a bit short with the latest enquirer, whom they may well think is either a salesman or yet another jobseeker. If they offer to put you through to the person in question, grasp the opportunity. Briefly explain why you are contacting them and tell them you will be sending a mailing shortly. Don't get depressed if they express no interest – you've just saved yourself a wasted stamp and follow-up call.

The next step is to set up a sensible schedule for mailing and follow-up. Be realistic – most mail-outs have a very low response rate of around 3% so build this into your workload projections. For business-to-business services it is highly unproductive to send out several thousand mailings at once, a large proportion of which will go straight in the bin. Instead, send out small batches in stages, and follow up by telephoning again a few days after the mailing to ask whether the mailing was received, and whether they are interested in your product or service. If they are not interested, ask whether they would mind explaining why, so that you can better target your marketing in future. This approach may elicit useful information about what's wrong with your service; however some respondents will treat this tactic as a hard-sell technique and refuse to elucidate – don't push.

For consumer or retail services, it may be more effective to use geographical mailings to all houses in a district, usually organised through the Post Office on a cost-per-copy basis. Such campaigns are almost always more effective if press coverage or advertising is used at the same time.

In either case, before embarking on a mailshot be sure you have costed

Measuring advertising response

Anthony Capstick of Instant Search comments: "The next area I went into was direct advertising in newspapers. I tried all the national newspapers, the *Sunday Times*, *Times*, *Telegraph* and the *Observer*, particularly the small ad section in the back.

We run, for example, a six line ad in the *Sunday Times* advertising our services which costs something like £70 resulting in something like 10 or 15 orders per week, and it's generally busy Monday or Tuesday. You need to run the ad for a specific period of time. I went in and out a couple of times at the beginning because I didn't want to spend too much. But I did notice that when I left it in, I was getting a much better response. People often browse papers, and may see the same ad again and again. The fourth or fifth time they may ring you up. If they have just see the advert once they may think the company is not very reliable. Persistence pays.

But the whole thing is wasted if you do not ask every single person who rings in where they saw your service advertised, where you got that enquiry. Otherwise you are just throwing money away. I constructed a spreadsheet with the cost of the advert, when it appeared, the number of enquiries and the number of conversions from that enquiry. When people call in and their orders are taken, a code is entered about where they saw Instant Search advertised. At the end of the month, when I'm booking the next level of advertising, I can see, for example, that a £200 ad in the *Sunday Times* brought in £500 of business, whereas the Daily Telegraph only cost me £80 but brought in only £60 of business. Stick to the Sunday papers if your business can go overseas – we have agents in Moscow picked up from a three-line ad in the *Sunday Times*."

it properly and that you have put aside resources for the follow-up, and for capturing details of any prospective customers who contact you as a result. Amongst the costs are:

- mailing list purchase;
- time and telephone costs for qualifying the mailing list;
- design, editing and printing of the mailshot material;
- envelopes, laser labels and postage;
- responding to enquiries – as a rule of thumb, you should expect around a 10–15% response rate if you also follow up the mailshot by phone – have you planned for the expected increase in demand for your services? If you send out 100 mailings, and you get 10 jobs as a result, will half the new contacts be wasted because you aren't able to give a timely service due to overwork?

As well as keeping track of your responses, you will need to have some method of estimating the overall conversion rate between the money you have spent on the mailing and the increased business which directly results from it.

Bear in mind that as long as you have affixed a clear mailing address label and postage, it is quite legal not to use an envelope, but to fold the document neatly and secure with a small adhesive label easily broken open by the recipient. Mailing labels can be printed in sheets on most laser printers. To save licking all those stamps, most post offices can arrange to frank large mailings for you but normally you will have to prepare the mailings with all envelopes the right way round. For mailings of over 2,000 you can use the "Mailsort" service which considerably reduces postal costs, but is only available if the postcode is clearly included in the address labels. Some companies can act as bureau services for Mailsort.

In Ireland franked mailing is available at main sorting offices only and must be paid for in cash or by banker's draft – no cheques.

Some companies are now using fax shots, although professional marketing people are divided about whether the level of negative reactions from people receiving unsolicited faxes outweighs the value of fax shots. Keep the message short and simple – one A4 page or less. Fax numbers can be found in directories available from telephone companies, and from local business directories. Many specialist business associations will sell their directories to non-members for a price, or have reasonable membership prices that give you access to the listing.

E-work

The Internet provides limitless opportunities both to find work and to waste time. First a warning: do not send unsolicited cvs to people by email. It is most unlikely to result in any work but will probably annoy the person you send it to. If you think, perhaps from looking at their website, that they are likely to have suitable telework to outsource, send a short, polite enquiry first (not more than two paragraphs) explaining your skills and asking if you can send your details. The obvious exception to this warning is a jobsite that asks you to upload your cv. Many of the more sophisticated jobsites also have features where you can specify what kind of work you are looking for and receive email notifications or alerts when any suitable job comes up. Unfortunately few of the jobsites specify whether jobs are suitable for teleworking, so dealing with the resulting email can be time-consuming.

The TCA runs its own mailing list detailing teleworking job opportunities which is published weekly – this is part of the TCA subscription. For more details see **www.tca.org.uk** or ring 0800 616008. TCA Online also provides news items on teleworking, and lists press coverage relating to teleworking. The jobsites listed in this chapter all have some relevant opportunities at the time of writing. However do take care – there are also many "get rich quick" sites as American telecommuting expert Gil Gordon summarises:

"I think there are three things going on.

1. Because demand for these jobs – sometimes from legitimately desperate people – vastly exceeds the supply, alarm bells go off for every

sleazy operator under the sun. I think it is nothing less than unethical preying on the desperation of others.

2. Slowly but surely there are some semi-legitimate sites developing, mostly in the area of freelance networks of sorts. They try to act as brokers or intermediaries rather than information providers. But these are few and far between.

3. Nobody is monitoring all of this. The sleazeballs operate well below the radar of the enforcement agencies. By the time someone makes a complaint to a local authority, it's too little too late.

What really surprises me more than anything is that here in the US where the unemployment rate is under 4% you would think that even the dumbest employer would wake up to the fact that there are scads of willing and able people out there who won't make themselves available for full-time in-office work. But it's not hard to overestimate the intelligence of most employers.

Oddly, one of the missing links is that neither the employers nor the would-be telecommuters know how to make the marriage. The workers envision that they can magically submit their resume to a company clear across the country and then start working for a huge salary from the comfort of their bedroom. The employers envision that this same unknown entity will want to live crosscountry and never show up"

*Gil Gordon (***www.gilgordon.com***)*

Gil's site contains a compendium of links – as he says "I have a bunch of these listed and have tried to screen them but don't vouch for them." Sites aimed at freelance teleworkers seem to fall into three categories:

■ auction sites where a project is listed and teleworkers "bid" for the contract

TCA Online – weekly news and work opportunities

The TCA produces a weekly email bulletin of news and telework offered, compiled by executive director Alan Denbigh. TCA Online goes to around 1000 TCA subscribers – if you are a member of the TCA, joining instructions can be found on the Opportunities page of *Teleworker* magazine. In addition to summarising any news coverage of teleworking issues, TCA Online also provides two-way communication between the association and its members. If an issue arises TCA Online provides a quick way for the TCA to find out whether it is something affecting a lot of teleworkers or only a few.

The work opportunities are also listed in the TCA's bimonthly magazine *Teleworker*. One employer commented: "it's very encouraging. We were really struggling to find people to work in a remote position and when you put something in the magazine we had a stream of good people. The quality of what was coming through was very good indeed."

Sites for job hunters (mainly non-teleworking, IT industry)

www.contracts365.com
www.contractwarehouse.com
www.exp.ie – Ireland
www.homeworkers.org
www.headhunter.net
www.jobbase.net
www.jobfinder.ie – Ireland
www.jobserve.com/index.html
www.jobsite.co.uk
www.jobsonline.com
www.job-hunt.org/ – US and Canada
www.infolive.ie/jobfinder/jobs – Ireland
hwww.indigo.ie/softskill – Ireland
http://members.aol.com/telwebsite
www.monster.com
www.peoplebank.com
www.reed.co.uk
www.skillsgroup.ie – Ireland
www.taps.com
www.tks.co.uk – UK only.
www.topjobs.ie
www.ukdirectory.co.uk/employ/it.htm
www.yahoo.com/Business_and_Economy/Employment/Telecommuting–catalogue where you may find more recent sites

- job-sifting sites that go through everyone else's jobsites, pick out the teleworking ones and often charge you for providing the details
- "support" sites offering access to work opportunities alongside forums for teleworkers, access to distance learning, *etc.*

Many of the sites do charge and it can be hard to work out what you are being charged for. Almost all require you to "register" your contact details before you can access most of the site features. Some have clear privacy policies, but others may make some of their income by selling email addresses. Overall, as with all homeworking schemes, the advice must be that any site which looks for the worker to pay a fee rather than the job advertiser (particularly during a time of skill shortage) should be treated with caution. Also beware of getting involved in contracts outside your area of expertise as it will hard to be sure that you are getting the appropriate remuneration.

Email marketing

Email marketing isn't about junk mail or just about creating a website (see *Email and the Internet* chapter). Using targeted e-zines (email newsletters) to keep in contact with your customers, or to provide useful snippets of advice that show your expertise, can be a very good way of reminding potential clients that you are there. Email marketing expert Denise Cox (**www.allrealgood.com**) gives the following marketing uses of email:

- To sell products and services
- To up-sell and cross-sell to your own customers
- To confirm orders
- To welcome or good-bye
- To announce
- To apologise
- To drive people to your website
- To have one-to-one customer relations.

Where possible you should ensure that your email software sends plain text ASCII messages without HTML or RTF formatting because some of your customers won't be able to read the formatting. The emails should be about 65 characters per line with a hard break following each line. Avoid using

---

Sussing out the scams

People looking for telework business ideas can be vulnerable to a number of well-tried and tested homeworking scams. The National Group on Homeworking identifies a number of common types, and warns there is no legislation to protect you from misleading schemes:

● *Kit scams usually appear as ads in local press and shops. They invite you to send money for a kit costing £20 to £200. Whatever you send back, they will reject on the grounds of inadequate quality and you will not be paid;*

● *Recruitment scams usually involve your placing ads in local shops. Let's say you pay £15 to join the scheme. For each extra person you persuade to part with £15, you get about 30p. So the only way you can recoup your £15 is to help the company rip off a further 50 or so people;*

● *Directory scams are often targeted at teleworkers. The ads ask you to send in the typical £15 fee and in exchange they will send you a directory of companies offering work to homeworkers. This turns out to be photocopied addresses each of which in turn ask a registration fee of a further £10 to £200;*

For advice on how to deal with any scams you discover or to check out a company contact the National Group on Homeworking Freefone 0800 174095. Never pay to get work. Be wary of box numbers and ads which don't give a phone number.

the tab key – use spaces if you have to – and if possible don't use columns. To ensure that email software creates "live" links where you have entered a URL or an email address, put mailto: before the email address and http:// in front of the URL. Avoid sending uninvited attachments (especially if these are large). Do include automatic signature text which gives all your contact details (most email software has a signature function).

Denise suggests you might consider using the following email communications with your customers:

- Updates – new services or contacts
- Special interest mailings – subdivide your customers and provide them with useful, relevant information
- Order confirmations – many people find that they get no response to enquiries sent to websites, and are unsure whether or not their order has been accepted. Follow up by email
- Autoresponders – if you receive too much email to provide a suitably speedy personal response use autoresponders to give information or to let the customer know that there will be a delay before they receive a reply.
- E-zines – (email magazines) but make sure the information is useful and give people an easy way to unsubscribe if they don't want it
- Participating in, or originating, discussion groups

There is a very fine line between the responsible use of email as a business tool and blatant spam. Collecting email addresses is something which has to be done tactfully and constantly – always request permission to add an address to your database. Ask customers to fill in registration forms on your website – but bear in mind that this may put some people off using the site at all. Include a query on email addresses with your bills. If you are exchanging business cards, ask if you can add them to your list. Try to ensure you are giving something useful in return. And keep your list current – at the moment about 50% of people change email addresses every two years. The figures are even more drastic for web-based email services like Hotmail.

Finding email contact details

Welsh email addresses – www.email.wales.com

Yahoo people search – http://ukie/people.yahoo.com

People and other searches – www.surfsearcher.net

Business and people finder – www.192.com

Business address CD available from www.thomson-directories.co.uk

Sites aimed at teleworkers, particularly freelancers

www.freelancecentre.com – Roy Sheppard's excellent and eclectic site aimed at teaching freelancers the vital tools for survival, getting work and getting paid.

www.jobserve.com – not purely telework but has a search facility for jobs which can be teleworked or are based from home.

www.elance.com – auction site.

www.smarteric.com – freelance support and a chance to input your cv.

www.brainbid.com – auction site based on sealed bids.

www.smarterwork.com – auction site focussing on telework but restricted to Internet research, document production, website design and support, graphic design or writing and editing.

www.workcenterplus.com – site focussing on homeworking with database of opportunities. Mainly US, mainly IT sector. Has an e-zine.

www.wordmarket.co.uk – aimed at media professionals – artists, web designers, illustrators, writers, photographers, picture researchers, *etc*.

www.jobswarm.com – aimed at freelancers. No useful information unless you register.

www.workaholics4hire.com – US site focussing on telecommuting. You have to register to see the opportunities database but it is free. Also offers a project management service to employers.

www.tryads.com – when we looked many of the jobs were out of date.

www.tjobs.com – mainly North American but site operators say some Italian teleworkers have got jobs on this site. Job descriptions are very short "listings similar to classifieds in the newspaper".

www.cyberworkers.com – multilingual, fast, nice graphics but we couldn't find the jobs...

www.homeworkers.org – also looking to act as a support organisation providing training and buying and reselling business reports, among other services.

http://members.tripod.co.uk/homeworking – advice site and some opportunities, mainly telesales for financial companies.

www.homeworking.com – sample jobs only when we looked, some advice also provided.

www.ivc.ca – Canadian telework association site with links to many North American work opportunities.

www.yahoo.com/Business_and_Economy/Employment/
Telecommuting–catalogue where you may find more recent sites.

In the "get your credit card out now" section you may also have a look at:
www.work-at-home-dot.com
www.outsource2000.com
www.jobs-telecommuting.com

Denise gives the following tips for ensuring effective content in e-zines:

- Make sure it's free;
- Strive to be friendly and entertaining, but pitch the content correctly for the audience's level of expertise – not too techie, not too newbie;
- Get the frequency right – too often and people will unsubscribe;
- Avoid blatant self-promotion and encourage feedback from readers, recognising any contributions they make;
- Limit the size to 15K (maximum 2,500 words);
- Include URLs where additional information is available;
- Ensure that it's easy for people to subscribe and unsubscribe – also give phone and fax contacts in case of problems with email;
- Give the recipient numerous reasons to revisit your website.

Get out there and sell!

Many teleworkers have found conventional advertising or mailing too expensive in the long term, and insufficiently rewarding. This is probably due to that second t-word – trust. People need to feel they know you before they are going to trust you enough to send work out. The people who already trust you are those who have worked with you before – whether on a face-to-face or a teleworking basis. So your time and money may be better spent on chasing up former colleagues and employers (*eg* through web searches for their names, or just asking around about where they may have moved on to).

Other suggestions include:

- prepare a brochure or prospectus of your services for selected mailings. If you want to give names of your existing clients to add weight to your

material, don't forget to ask permission. Even better, see if you can get endorsed statements from your clients to use in your marketing material;
- work out how much it will cost you to actively promote through the web (passive "brochure" type sites won't do the job). (See Chapter 10, *Email and the Internet* for further information.);
- teleworkers can form umbrella organisations to market their services co-operatively;
- "piggyback" your mailings with those of local computer equipment suppliers by agreement, sharing costs;
- speak to local business and community groups;
- if you have suitable premises, think about organising occasional social get-togethers for your customers and workers so that people can put faces to names, and be aware of all the services you are offering. How about a working lunch involving a presentation?;
- personal visits. No-one likes cold calling, but if you can talk to businesses on a one-to-one basis you could get a trial piece of work that will get your foot in the door. Try writing to your prospective customer, then telephone to say you will be in the area, and could you call in?;
- if you specialise in a particular area, is there a relevant software user group with a newsletter? These newsletters are often cheap to advertise in and hit direct to your target market;
- editorial copy is free but you need to do as much of the journalist's work for them as possible in order to get your story into a paper. Talk to all local journalists – press, freelancers, local radio, TV. Keep up the contact. Phone them, write to them, send them press releases and good photographs. Just keep your name in front of them too often for them to ignore. Invite them to visit your premises. Try holding an Open Day. Take photographs of all events – remember you need black and white photos for some newspapers, not colour;
- follow up professional contacts such as former workmates or employers where appropriate;
- the best of all advertising is word-of-mouth. Keep up the quality of your service and you will be repaid by personal recommendations. On the downside, it has been estimated that if a customer has a bad experience of your service, he or she will probably report this to 26 other people.

Tying up the loose ends

So you've made the sale, agreed the brief for the job and the price – what next? In some situations, for example if you are working for a large company or government agency, they will probably send you a contract outlining the work, the payment schedule and other factors. You read it and sign on the dotted line if you agree. But for most business-to-business transactions, unless you act to ensure that there is a written agreement, the job may go ahead on an *ad hoc* basis which leaves you in an extremely vulnerable position.

The Irish government's Code of Practice on Teleworking suggests that you draw up your own description of the job including the following information as appropriate:

- Clear contacts identifying the purchaser and supplier and their addresses
- General description of the work to be carried out including purpose and scope, timetable, delivery format and delivery date
- Details of the payment and payment timetable during or following the completion of the work including VAT liability
- Details of any systems or procedures to ensure the confidentiality and security of the work *eg* responsibilities under the Data Protection Act
- Statement on the ownership of any resulting copyright or intellectual property rights
- Arrangements for loan or supply of equipment, including insurance
- Arrangements for cover in the event of illness, incapacity, holidays or other absences, and for subcontracting if permitted
- Quality assurance procedures. If group working is involved, identify the individual responsible for quality within the group.

You can get more detail on these issues in Chapter 7, *Staying Safe and Legal* and Chapter 8, *Quality for teleworkers*. It may be worthwhile to ask your solicitor to help you to draw up a "template" contract document. Send the document to your client by fax, post or email, ask them to read it, sign a copy and return it to you to indicate their agreement *before* you start work. This kind of clear written agreement will help you to avoid disputes, unnecessary work stress and nonpayment of bills.

Keeping your customers

Working long-term for a company but not being an employee requires diplomatic, constant attention. The rule of thumb is that 80% of your new business leads will come from existing customers, so look after them! If your contact moves job or leaves, you've probably lost the contract, so if you can, try to pick up work from other people in the same company to make your position more resilient. This should be easier than approaching new companies because you already have a reference client (the first contact) to establish that you are competent and trustworthy.

Keep a good eye on corporate politics if you can – who's in, who's out, who's moving departments. Spend extra time building up relationships with new staff – go in for face-to-face meetings, explain in detail what you are doing by email because they probably know less about the procedures in place than you do. They may also be new to managing teleworkers so you have to politely train them in what information you need so you can get your part of the job done. Overcommunicate and reassure them of your reliability. Assess their level of competence in IT and email – if the new person only likes to deal by fax, then that is what you are going to have to do because they are the customer, even if you think it's timewasting.

Also keep your receipts – archive all email and other communications so that if there is a dispute about an instruction or any aspect of a job, you can show exactly what communication your received from the client. It's an unfortunate fact that non-employed teleworkers can end up in the middle of in-office disputes because they are in a weak position and are "expendable". Once people know that you always keep your receipts they are much less likely to try to scapegoat you for problems encountered.

Cultivate receptionists, secretaries and accountancy staff – make their lives as easy as possible and ensure they have a favourable opinion of you. Be sure you understand the client company's purchase order and billing systems and stick to them. If they only do one cheque-run on the last day of each month, then don't hassle for an early cheque unless there's some overriding reason why you need that money. If they require your invoices or quotations in a certain format in order to assign them to a particular cost centre in the company, make sure that that information is clearly on every document.

If your business is one where customers are likely to have a number of transactions, build a customer database. Give everyone a customer ID and let them know their number so that when they phone or email you can have their record in front of you immediately.

Acknowledgments

The TCA thanks Brian O'Kane for permission to use material from his guide *Starting Your Own Business in Ireland*, third edition, published by Oaktree Press, ISBN 1-86076-091-0. www.oaktreepress.com.

The TCA also thanks Denise Cox for her assistance with the email marketing section (www.allrealgood.com).

Barnaby Page, former editor of *Teleworker* magazine, originally contributed the sections on handling the press.

Bibliography

Code of Practice: Telework *Date:* 2000
Source: Department of Enterprise, Trade and Employment, Ireland
Web: www.irlgov.ie/entemp/telework/tele-cop.pdf

loyalty.com: customer relationship management in the new era of Internet marketing *Date:* 2000
Author: Frederick Newell
Source: McGraw Hill ISBN: 0–07–135775–0

Doing business on the Internet *Date:* 1999
Author: Simon Collin
Source: Kogan Page ISBN: 0–7494–3109–1

**Zen and the art of making a living – a practical guide to
creative career design**　　　　　　　　　　　　　　　　*Date:* 1999
Author: Laurence G Boldt
Source: Penguin ISBN: 0–14–01.9599–8

A Guide to Help for Small Businesses　　　　　　　　　*Date:* 1998
Comment: Department of Trade and Industry free booklet of practical information, support and advice for new and existing small businesses.
Source: Tel: 0870 1502 500 Email: dtipubs@echristian.co.uk Ref: 98/942

How to Change Your Life with Technology　　　　　　*Date:* 1998
Author Anthony B. Capstick
Source Management Books 2000 www.mb2000.com ISBN 1–85252–239–9

Tales to Knock Your Socks Off Service　　　　　　　　*Date:* 1998
Authors: Kristin Anderson and Ron Zemke
Source: Amacom, 1601 Broadway, New York, NY 10019
ISBN 0–8144–7971–5

30 Minutes… to write a Business Plan　　　　　　　　*Date:* 1997
Author: Brian Finch
Source: Kogan Page, 120 Pentonville Rd, London N1 9JN ISBN 0–7494–2364–1

30 Minutes… to write a Marketing Plan　　　　　　　*Date:* 1997
Author: John Westwood
Source: Kogan Page, 120 Pentonville Rd, London N1 9JN ISBN 0–7494–2363–3

The Complete Guide to Quick and Easy Marketing that Works　*Date:* 1997
Source: Tel: 01252 317700

Marketing your Consulting and Professional Services　　*Date:* 1997
Authors: Dick Connor and Jeff Davidson
Source: John Wiley & Sons ISBN 0–471–13392–2

The 24-Hour Business Plan　　　　　　　　　　　　　　　*Date:* 1997
Author: Ron Johnson
Source: Random House, 20 Vauxhall Bridge Road London SW1V 25A
ISBN 0–7126–7779–8

The 4 Routes to Entrepreneurial Success　　　　　　　*Date:* 1997
Author: John B Miner
Source: Berrett Koehler, 155 Montgomery Street, San Francisco, CA 94104–4109
ISBN 1–881052–82–6

The Complete Idiot's Guide to Starting a Home Based Business　*Date:* 1997
Author: Barbara Weltman
Source: Alpha Books, 1633 Broadway, 7th Floor, New York, NY 10019–6785
ISBN 0–02–861539–5

**Stop Telling, Start Selling – How to use Customer focused
dialogue to close sales**　　　　　　　　　　　　　　　　　*Date:* 1997
Author: Linda Robertson
Source: McGraw Hill ISBN 0–07–052558–7

Webonomics　　　　　　　　　　　　　　　　　　　　　*Date:* 1997
Author: Evan I Schwartz
Source: Penguin, Harmondsworth, Middlesex. ISBN 0–14–026406–X

**Starting a Successful Small Business/ How to Set up your Own Business/
Successful Marketing for the Small Business** (three publications)
Source: Kogan Page, 120 Pentonville Road, London N1 9JN

Running your own Word-Processing Service
Author: Doreen Huntley
Source: Kogan Page, 120 Pentonville Road, London N1 9JN Ref: ISBN 0-7494-0344-6.

Work for Yourself – A Guide to Self-Employment and Setting up a Small all Business/ Earning Money at Home (two publications)
Source: Consumers' Association, Castlemead, Gascoyne Way, Hertford

Daily Telegraph How to Set Up and Run Your Own Business *Date:* 1996
Source: Kogan Page, 120 Pentonville Road, London N1 9JN 12th edn
Ref: ISBN 0–7494–1969–5

TeleFutures – a study on teleworking in Ireland *Date:* 1996
Authors: Imogen Bertin and Gerard O'Neill
Source: International Services, Forbairt, Wilton Park House, Wilton Place, Dublin 2
Tel: +353 1 660 2244 Contact: International Services – Declan Murphy
Web: www.forbairt.ie/about/publications/telefutu

Contacts and URLs

www.know-how.org.uk TCA members Roger Pett and Pat Quinn have designed a website to help freelancers and small businesses sell their products and services by offering help and advice in the form of electronic books for sale.

IWS: Tel: 01437 766441 Email: co-ord@iws.cymru.net
Web: **www.telecottages.org/iws**

Teleworking Associations

See page 113, Chapter 3, *Survival Guide* for contacts of associations which may be able to provide you with further practical tips and contacts for getting work.

E-marketing links

(With thanks to Denise Cox, dcox@allrealgood.com)

Ezine search engines:
www.e-zinez.com/cgi-bin/hyperseek/directory.cgi
www.ezineseek.com
www.meer.net/~johnl/e-zine-list/index.html
www.zinebook.com

Article on advertising in email newsletters:
www.promotionworld.com/newslet/ezine.shtml

Comparative analysis of the four major listserver products:
www.lyristechnologies.com/compare/comparingls.html

Software for archiving your emails:
www.seemdirect.com/eoxupgrad.htm (Outlook Expresss)
www.seemdirect.com/backdora.htm (Eudora)

E-zine on maximising use of email in your business:
subscribe@allrealgood.com

Ideas for telebusinesses

This chapter lists ideas for services, some of which are only suited to telecentres. For teleworkers, many occupations not listed here, ranging from quality management to market research can be teleworked, but you must already have the relevant skills and industry contacts to make them work. General issues of how to sell teleworking services are covered in Chapter 4, *Getting Work*. When considering what services to offer, be careful to evaluate the cost of software that will be required, and avoid substantial investments in this area without thorough market research on the demand for the proposed service.

Abstracting, editing, proofreading and indexing

Many teleworkers have skills in the publishing area such as copy editing, proofreading and indexing. There is strong demand for these skills if they are combined with the ability to handle scientific subjects. A much-publicised example of a teleworking business based on these is skills is Crossaig in Scotland. Crossaig arranges abstracting and indexing of biomedical articles for Elsevier's EMBASE database. The printed journals are OCR-scanned into computer text files at the company's offices and then sent by ISDN file transfer to the teleworkers around Scotland. The teleworkers work on a piece rate, but many have specialist skills and PhDs in areas such as marine biology or pharmacology and can earn up to £17.50 per hour for their work. This arrangement gives Crossaig access to the skills it needs, and the teleworkers access to work from remote rural areas.

Preparing press cuttings to clients' briefs is another related niche business area – you may have to work slightly unsocial hours and be in a region where you can get the relevant papers or magazines early if there is a time limit set (*eg* that cuttings must be faxed through before a specific deadline each morning).

Audio typing, remote typing, document formatting

This market is under threat from advances in systems which allow direct dictation to computer. However, there is still scope for audio dictation in specialist areas such as medical and legal transcription, where a detailed knowledge of terminology may be required. Also, in any situation where accuracy or human intelligence is important, or where the quality of the audio recording is poor, humans are needed for the transcription process. If you plan to go into this area you will need to specialise or add value to your transcription services, and consider related tasks such as proofreading, indexing, editing, and translation.

Work arrives by fax, or on audio cassettes, is transcribed onto computer and returned as disk, printout, email or all three. For audio typing you will need a transcribing machine. This is a tape recorder with a foot pedal for playing the tape, stopping it and rewinding where necessary while leaving

The Dyer Partnership

Mark and Bill Dyer have been profiled in publications about Britain's Information Society Initiative for the way in which they have used the World Wide Web to expand their accountancy partnership. Mark Dyer explains: "Our website has generated interest from all over the UK and the world. For example, we've had contacts from the British Consul in Messina, Italy, and quite a number from the US, Canada and even Australia. We're doing business with people through email, acting as their accountants."

The Internet also helps with client credibility closer to home: "Where clients use the technology themselves, the minute you say you have email it establishes a lot of credibility and provides a good way of conducting business – we can send data files attached to email." Setting up the website took around 150 hours of work, and a further 100 hours has been spent marketing and maintaining the site. "Of course we are not the only accountants on the Internet, but we have interpreted the information, giving people a taster of what we can do on items such as why companies should pay dividends rather than bonuses – rather than putting up a page of detailed corporate tax law on the web."
www.netaccountants.com

the hands free. There are three main sizes of tape: standard audio (C-size), Philips mini cassette and Dictaphone mini cassette, so talk to your prospective customers about the sizes they use before buying. The work can range from correspondence to whole books or conference proceedings. Perhaps you could link up with conference organisers in your area?

Bookkeeping and accountancy services

Accountants may be prepared to send out the more tedious areas of their work such as putting purchase receipts and invoices onto computer. You will need specialist accountancy skills to succeed in this area. There is a multitude of software packages in this area, and every company has its personal favourite. Be careful to check this out before investing in expensive software. Accountants who plan to telework from home themselves need to take account of the likelihood of client visits, and provide suitable parking and insurance cover.

Computer programming/software support

Several telecentres have been started up by small computer dealers who offer tailor-made programming services to customers as well as software training and support. If you have specialist skills in this area it could be for you. Offering technical support over the telephone to new computer users could also be a winner. But beware – you should think about getting professional indemnity insurance to cover yourself in case your advice leads to a financial loss for one of your customers – what would happen if you recommended a backup procedure that led to the loss of vital data?

This kind of insurance can be very expensive. Specialist areas for computer programming and software include CAD/CAM (Computer-aided design and manufacturing), computer design of PCBs (printed circuit boards), mathematical and financial modelling, stress calculations for engineers, quantity surveying and project management.

Conferencing

Conferencing services help with "telemeetings". Telecentres can offer videoconferencing and audioconferencing facilities. For videoconferencing, you must have an ISDN telephone line and suitable conferencing hardware and software. Audio conferencing for up to three people is available using standard digital telephone services. For larger numbers, you will need to use either BT's audioconferencing service, or if you are a charity or resource centre, Community Network. Organisations using conferencing regularly may want to invest in a high quality telephone loudspeaker unit.

Data conversion

Converting data from one disk format to another, or from one software package to another, is a commonly requested service in telecottages. Software format conversion does need some knowledge of the package involved, and it's important to quiz the customer on exactly what they want to do with the resulting file in order to provide an appropriate format.

Data input

Many of the first generation of telecottages financed themselves with contracts from companies and government institutions to put large volumes of data onto computers. The more basic end of this kind of work is less available now because most historical data needed by companies has already been entered, and because of strong competition from low labour cost regions of the world. However, many companies need to continue to process data on a regular basis and, if you can offer low cost and high quality, they might be interested in a teleworking arrangement. The KITE telecottage in Northern Ireland won a contract to put customer records held by the SpecSavers chain of opticians onto computer. Data input work is not generally well paid, and is usually quoted as piece-work. However, specialist areas such as the construction of mailing lists can be more remunerative and could be tied in with preparing mailshots or faxshots (mailings by fax). An experienced person can design the database while the less skilled enter data.

Call centres

Call centres, where staff handle large volumes of telephone traffic, have been highly successful in the commercial sector and are used to deliver a wide range of services which fall into two major categories – telemarketing and data processing.

A virtual approach to computer consultancy

Talington UK has 10 full-time staff, up to 25 occasional temporary workers and no offices. The company operates mainly as an administrative consultancy, "picking up the pieces after the consultants have been in", work which leads to extra tasks for their external office services, and to training contracts.

Talington contracts have included one where their suggestions reduced the cost of automating a client's accounts from £10,000 to £6,000 and another where the consultancy work led to a contract to reformat 2,500 documents for the National Grid.

Talington make clear they are not just a network of contractors subcontracting: "We have all the procedures you would have in a normal company, such as health and safety. It is a normal business except we do it from home because the people who work for us are tied to the home." Core staff are employed on a full-time basis while the remainder are on employment agency-type short-term contracts.

The minimum pay rate is £5.50 an hour, and employees who work for Talington consistently for more than a year get a shareholding which entitles them to make suggestions at AGMs. "By employing people as part of a team and involving them we get a good response – if we are good to our staff they are good to us".

Talington use a Centrex telephone system to redirect calls between teleworkers seamlessly, giving the impression of everyone being in one building, and providing a business line for each employee. Mail goes to a central PO box before being redistributed as appropriate.

The Willow "cyber-agent" network

In the US, Willow CSN has tried to provide contract call centre work to "cyber agents" working from home for inbound call centres. Traditional call centres use the cyberagents both on a scheduled and on-call basis to cover peaks in demand. Willow works with Dade County (Florida) School Board to train the agents, who must have their own PC with a 1.6 Gb hard drive, 15" monitor, CD-ROM and 33.6 ksb modem. Special software and circuit boards are installed on the PCs.

Agents get 20 half-days of training followed by up to two weeks of applied training (theoretical and simulated call handling) for particular tasks. Willow works with client call centres to estimate their "full time equivalent" need for extra call handling, and to arrange connection of the call centre to its call distribution system. It then multiplies the number by four to get the number of Cyberagents. The client call centre can only schedule each agent for 2.5 hours per day to prevent overload.

To attract clients, Willow offers the following guarantees that:

- Cyberagents will rank in the top 20% of the call centre's agents or Willow will replace them and pay $500;
- Clients' network costs for switching calls to the cyberagents will be 10% less than in-house costs or Willow pays the difference;
- Clients' lost or abandoned calls and on-hold call time will be reduced by at least 50% or Willow will reduce the client's network access cost by 10%;
- The attrition (rate of loss) rate for cyberagents will be 50% less than the in-house rate.

Call centres are charged 15¢ for each call connection followed by an extra 10¢ for each minute of agent time thereafter. These are the only costs which the client call centres pay. Things are going well with Willow's first anchor client, Signature, but the real test for the system will be when several client call centres have to be managed at once.

(Adapted from Call Centre Management Review – **www.incoming.com**. More information on Willow CSN at **www.willowcsn.com**)

Telemarketing

- central reservations services for hotels, airlines and car hire
- technical support centres for computer hardware and software
- outbound and inbound telesales
- order processing
- consumer information centres
- market research.

Data processing
- abstracting and indexing
- health claims processing
- banking administration
- financial analysis
- magazine subscription administration
- medical transcription
- VAT reclamation
- central order processing (*eg* stationery, computer hardware).

Distributing the call centre work to "agents at home"

Online Travel is a "virtual" travel agency that employs 40 travel consultants, who handle between 400 and 1000 calls per day. Only ABTA-qualified travel consultant are employed, and all work from home full-time.

Managing director David Speakman explains that applicants are given a psychometric test as part of the recruitment process to provide an insight into their personality and skills. "We look for people who want to work independently from home for a better quality of life, who enjoy speaking to customers and selling travel, who are disciplined enough to work to schedule and adhere to our procedures whilst working within a virtual team".

Online Travel provides all the equipment that the travel consultants need but each consultant has to provide a deposit of £1,000 for the equipment. Consultants are paid monthly, on a commission-only basis. The calls that they answer come in from teletext advertisements placed by Online Travel. Calls are to an 0800 number, and are distributed from Online Travel's "Remote Service Manager" server, supplied by GemaTech, to the consultant's homes. If a call is not answered within 15 seconds, it is switched to another consultant.

Consultants get one day's training during the first month, and a second day about a month later. After that, training is only on a needs basis but a personal trainer will go out to their home and work with them if they are having difficulty converting calls to sales.

The Gematech system provides David with comprehensive monitoring information including conversion rates for each agent, call lengths, *etc*. He acknowledges that management is more complex than in a conventional call centre – "you have to create extra bonds because you have to impose yourself more and bring discipline and friendship on a one-to-one basis, building a rapport with each agent". He operates a stick as well as a carrot, barring consultants from receiving further calls for an hour if they leave the phone to ring for more than 15 seconds. Adapted from an article in *Call Centre Focus* June 1999

The development of computer-telephony integration (CTI) is now making it possible for call centres to become smaller and more specialised – previously the equipment required meant that large operations, usually with mainframe computers, were important for paybacks. CTI distributes calls to operatives, brings up appropriate customer records on screen, helps staff to fill in information correctly according to a pre-prepared script, and to enter appropriate data. CTI systems also provide statistical monitoring of call handling.

Call centres are a highly specialist area, both in terms of technology and marketing, and in the appropriate training of staff. Call centre projects are best approached through the services of a consultant, and it's also worth bearing in mind that the industry as a whole in Europe is starting to move towards higher-skill services and offering integrated offerings such as "shared services centres" which handle administration and accounts as well as calls. This is because basic call centre services can be provided more cheaply from low labour cost regions of the world.

Equipment rental

This is a minor source of income for many telecentres. It can take several forms:

- hire of computers and software on site (*eg* for people who want to use word processing, either for private use or to offer a service)

- hire of computers for private study for those who want to start using computers on an informal basis, perhaps before attending a formal training course, or who want to use software-based tutorials

- hire of equipment to teleworkers such as high quality laser printers and colour printers

- hire of equipment to "take away" such as portable PCs, small inkjet printers, for occasional teleworkers or overload work.

Sometimes this kind of service can be tied in to an existing shop or business such as a printshop. In the case of U-compute in Keswick, computers and photocopiers are on hire in a back room attached to the post office and craft shop.

Farm skills

Farmers need secretaries, bookkeepers and people who know how to fill in complex EU forms and maps. A teleworker with specialist knowledge in these areas could prove invaluable to a rural community, though many farmers are uncomfortable about using someone who also works for their neighbours and knows details of their plans. The WREN telecottage initiated a scheme whereby four farmers clubbed together to buy some crop management software and used it on a collaborative basis rather than each having to buy their own computer and software. It may be worth contacting suppliers of specialist products such as Farmplan and Optimix to discuss possibilities.

Faxing/photocopying services

Copying charges average about 10p/sheet for low volume. Fax varies at £1–£2.50 per sheet. Colour photocopying or high quality laser photocopying comes in at about £1/sheet. Think about your location before buying equipment for bureau services. If you are based half way up a remote valley, are people really going to drop in for a few photocopies? On the other hand, if you have the only decent photocopier on an island, you could be in business.

Information broking

Almost every business sector needs facts of some description. Information brokers are experts at accessing paper and online information sources and distilling the results into a product they can sell to clients. Stepping Stones, based in London, provides information on European tenders through its TED and BC-Net agencies. Alert Publications, also based in London, used to summarise online sources for telecoms news and provide the summaries to clients via daily fax bulletins. This business idea was overtaken by the customers beginning to use the Internet directly to get their information, a timely warning on the need to keep up technologically with your customers. Most brokers are specialists who know intimately the resources in a particular subject area. Good personal contacts are also important. Charges are usually via an hourly or daily rate, or by subscription to a briefing document. (See information about Instant Search in Chapter 4, *Getting Work*).

Information services/booking agency/tourist information

Telecentres can provide box office services for professional and amateur theatres. They can arrange bookings for coach services, village halls and sports facilities. Other related ideas include registers of business services and local organisations. Tourist information such as B&B lists, sites of interest and events diaries are provided by several telecottages in holiday areas. This seems to be a service that fits in well with other telecottage

---

The Virtual Office

Richard Nissen has been running the Virtual Office for nearly fifteen years in Piccadilly, London. His business provides serviced offices, meeting rooms, telephone answering, fax forwarding, a mailing address and secretarial backup such as diary management. Charges are £150/month for call answering, and £50/month for use of the prestigious London mailing address. The Virtual Office looks after 260 companies and over 1,000 people.

Office manager Rebecca Benbow explains: "We have a lot of customers who have left large corporations and are used to having a hundred people running after them. They are there to make money, and we do the menial things."

activities, and can attract funding or sponsorship from government agencies. A number of telecottages manage tourism web sites on behalf of local tourism development groups.

Internet-based services

Internet services offer a wide range of opportunities for the dedicated (and technically knowledgeable) pioneer. See page 258 for the example of Mark Francis-Jones and his jewellery-over-the-net service. Or page 129 for Malcolm O'Brien and the IWS Internet-based organisation for teleworkers. Many consultants and workers in the publishing industry use the Internet to market their services. Others advertise and sell rare goods. See if you can find John Eagle, who sells his dramatic photographs, posters and postcards of Irish lighthouses over the Internet – he's based in a remote village where employment opportunities are few. The main problem with Internet-based services are charging mechanisms. More people are now prepared to send their credit card numbers to "secure" commercial Internet sites, but there is still concern about this area, so providing a scheme for alternative payment methods is vital.

Office services

A number of virtual office services have grown up over the past five years providing an official "front" for businesses including telephone answering, accommodation addresses and meeting space. These services aim to fulfil all the functions of a traditional receptionist/secretary, without of course the expense.

Kendlebell offers work opportunities on a franchise basis to provie personal call handling services for businesses which don't want to use voicemail. Franchises cost from £25,000 for one or two people working from home up to £75,000 for a centre. The cost to the clients is from £29 to £250 per month (**www.kendlebell.co.uk**).

Telecentres can also be used as accommodation addresses by very small businesses. As well as correspondence services, think about message taking – the advantage to the businessperson is that their customers do not have to leave a message on a machine, they can speak to a real person. The telecottage can help the small businessperson to present a more professional image. Local enterprise agencies can often help telecottages by handing out cards to those enquiring about starting their own businesses.

Publishing, design and multimedia

There are a number of areas where teleworkers can be involved in publishing, including preparing diagrams on computer, editing text, layout work, proofreading and graphic design. However, they all require specialist skills. It is not just a case of buying the desktop publishing software! Related areas include computerised presentations incorporating sound, graphics and animation (multimedia). Telecentres often act as the focus point for community publishing operations such as local newsletters or business directories.

Samantha's only interested in finding work for homeworkers

Samantha Jones enthusiastically points out that the figure for people working from home rises daily. And that many of the work schemes advertised for homeworkers are scams of one description or another. She spotted a growing market opportunity and set up HEA – Home Employment Agency – determined to stick with some basic principles:

- *Everyone has the right to work from home if they so wish;*
- *No-one should have to pay to find work;*
- *Rates of pay should be fair and in line with the National Minimum Wage;*
- *HEA will only do business with genuine employers;*
- *Homeworkers provide substantial benefits to employers.*

Like most agencies attempting to service the home market, Samantha has had no difficulty in finding candidates and provides a candidate profile form on her website that you can use to add to her growing database. But she's also putting in serious work to finding employers. "Each week I go through all the local job papers from Thursday to Saturday, and spend my weekends doing all the national papers. On Monday our sales manager phones round prospective job opportunities and discusses whether homeworking might be a possibility. This is exactly what the recruitment agencies do. Then we carry out a candidate match. If it all works out, we receive a fee from the employer of 5% of the salary. For permanent positions the fee is 5% of 12 months' wages, but for shorter term contracts it is 5% of the salary for the time of the contract. We also offer a 50% refund if the candidate leaves within the first four weeks, and if the employer is within one and half hours' travel of our Merseyside base then I also visit to check out the employer and get a feel for their business free of charge."

To date almost all the appointments Samantha has handled have been sales-support oriented, such as telephone sales for particular sectors, appointment-setting for other sales personnel, following up on quotations or offering free product trials. To see the jobs currently on offer try **www.hea-online.co.uk**.

Remote office services

A few corporations have created telecentres remote from their main offices where much routine correspondence and administration is done. Examples are GlaxoWellcome in Teesdale, and Rank Xerox. The advantages for the companies are that, rather than relying on disparate teleworkers with varied equipment, they can specify the equipment to be used and the procedures to be carried out, as well as controlling the teleworkers more closely. By locating these centres in rural areas, they can reduce labour and premises

Lasair lights Lewis telework flame

Donnie Morrison is one of a number of returners to the Western Isles of Scotland. Formerly the sales and marketing director of a computer company, Morrison set up the Highlands and Islands Enterprise (HIE) board's skills register, followed by the start-up of Lasair (which means "red hot" or "flame" in Gaelic), a limited liability company providing editing services. The first client was an American company indexing and abstracting business journals. Currently Lasair has about 20 people, mainly women, carrying out the work.

Other Lasair clients include the Metropolitan Police Forensic Laboratory and the legal journal Scots Law Times, as well as various scientific publishers. "At first we made the mistake of restricting the register to IT skills – it is now just a skills database – we look for example for people with language skills and then give them the IT skills", says Morrison. The Lasair teleworkers got grants of up to 70% for their equipment, are self-employed and have to "bid" for any available contracts. However, commercial margins are tightening for this type of work with competition from low labour cost locations, and there is also the threat of "smart software" that could make some of the work obsolete.

Training has also proved to be too costly when carried out on a one-to-one basis, so Lasair requires teleworkers to come to a central office for induction sessions and training. Teleworkers keep in contact and support each other through the First Class conferencing software package which runs over the Internet. Donnie is now moving on and leaving marketing for Lasair to those who have become expert in the work such as director Kathleen Turner.

(Tel: 01870 602757 Email: kathleen.turner@compuserve.com)

costs. The French company Telergos, which specialises in providing back office services opened a subsidiary on Tyneside to exploit these opportunities.

Scanning

Scanners are used for three purposes: to scan text, to scan line graphics and to scan photographs. For text scanning, you will need a flatbed scanner with an automatic feeder, and OCR (optical character reading) software. Text scanning works well on clean, typed manuscripts. It does not cope well with heavily edited typescripts, or with handwriting (yet). For scanning line graphics such as simple company logos, a cheap hand-held scanner will be sufficient. To scan photographs at high resolution you need a high quality scanner, and specialist knowledge of printing processes such as halftoning to get best results. For colour reproduction, expensive colour separation drum scanners are used. These are normally provided on a bureau basis by reprographics or typesetting companies. Standard desktop colour scanners do not provide sufficiently good quality for high volume colour printing, although they are excellent for adding interest to short print run documents such as report covers, local newsletters and brochures.

Skills register

Telecentres often maintain a local skills register of individual teleworkers and can refer work to them. Sometimes the telecentre takes a percentage of the value of the work if a contract is arranged through the telecottage. In others, because the teleworkers are using telecentre equipment, no commission is taken. Some telecentres simply maintain a skills noticeboard that teleworkers can advertise on, whilst others hold social events such as lunches where teleworkers can exchange ideas and form business relationships.

Training

Most telecentres offer a variety of training courses introducing people to information technology. Other areas which you can consider include training in specific software packages (particularly word processing, spreadsheets and databases), training in business skills and special vocational qualifications for teleworkers. Much software training is now done by means of interactive tutorials, often based on CD-ROMs.

Funding may be available for these courses from Training and Enterprise Councils (TECs). Larger telecentres could think about becoming examination centres for qualifications such as the RSA word processing examinations, the City and Guilds diplomas and the Cambridge syllabus information technology modules, including teleworker training qualifications such as the VQ in teleworking.

Telecentres should also consider linking up with their local Further Education college as TCA member Su Pointer did, following up an article in *Teleworker* magazine: "I immediately contacted a senior member of one of the colleges in the area, some 30 miles away. He was more than willing to meet and discuss possible developments. Three months further on, and we have already run, and been paid for, three successful subsidised computer courses."

A number of colleges are starting to look at providing courses supported by remote means such as modem and videophone (*eg* Open University, Stroud College of Further Education). A telecentre can provide a learning base for students without these facilities.

A related area of opportunity is the production of training courses and materials. Such documents can run to hundreds of pages, and command high prices, especially where they are prepared for professional bodies or large corporate clients. The preparation of distance learning materials is a major growth area, but requires skills in editing, teaching, high level word processing and/or desktop publishing.

Translation services

Translation services are increasingly in demand, and translation work is often received and delivered via email these days. Translations can be tied

Evergreen – the benefit of 25 years experience

Gill Price of Evergreen Services has employed several of her staff two or three times over. Firstly in the financial services industry, where Gill worked for Equitable Life and secondly when she set up the Scottish Widows "virtual life office", a network of teleworkers carrying out back office administration. When changes in technology led to the closure of the virtual life office, Gill put her long experience to work setting up Evergreen and re-employed some of her former colleagues again.

"We now have six full-time and two part-time employees. We've specialised in three areas I know well – transcription, press review and translation services. The transcription services involve a remote windows-based dictation service that customers phone. Evergreen staff produce the documents as required and return the work via email, post, courier and fax. On the press reviewing, we screen many quality and popular titles in the early morning, seven days a week and 365 days a year. The press clippings are taken to fit detailed client briefings and because we have been focusing on financial services, we find Wednesdays and the weekends are the busiest days. With translation, we're providing a one-stop shop with text proofing, accuracy and speed."

"We recently got a large new contract after a feature on Evergreen in *Teleworker* magazine. The work involves the transcription of confidential legal work, and we've had to strengthen our existing confidentiality agreements with the clients and with our employees to take account of the sensitivity of the work, as well as looking at our data protection and data security measures."

Gill believes that a "virtual" organisation is a big advantage – her customers buy a service and the location of the staff is irrelevant. "My literature does not refer to home-based staff because to some people it would be perceived as a distinct disadvantage". She also believes her long track record in the financial services industry has been a big advantage in winning work: "I have experience built up over the years and my staff also all have financial services experience. Outsourcing is the future. I am convinced that more companies will become virtual and simply buy in the services they require. One major client which relies heavily on outsourced functions and services says that Evergreen is the most efficient service they utilise and perhaps more importantly they tell me that it is the most effective service that they buy in."

However, she hasn't quite managed to relax into a flexible workstyle in her Wakefield office. "I am looking forward to expanding enough to take on an operational manager but at the moment I do the marketing and run the operational side and in addition I like to actually do some of the work myself on new jobs so that I understand what the staff are being asked to do, where the problems lie and how to be more efficient".

www.evergreenuk.freeserve.co.uk
or email gillprice@compuserve.com

in with word processing and desktop publishing services. By connecting together a number of language teleworkers, telecentres can provide a complete European service.

Word processing and desktop publishing

Word processing (typing) services can be offered to home workers, businesses, political parties and pressure groups, community newsletters and societies. If you are in a university area, see if you can get involved in typing theses and academic papers. Another area which is more within the skills range of most telecentres than full-blown publishing services is the use of desktop publishing to prepare brochures, newsletters, pricelists and instruction leaflets for local companies.

One telecentre combines producing the local community newsletter with training exercises for word processing trainees. Another, Daily Information, arguably the first telecottage in the UK, began by combining word processing training and services with the production of the *Daily Information* free broadsheet covering activities in central Oxford. Think about making commission arrangements with a local printer to provide printing of documents as well as typing and layout. You may also want to invest in cheap forms of binding such as a comb binding machine, or a lamination machine which provides a protective plastic surface for documents such as menus and price lists.

Web page design

The production of web pages is something that many teleworkers have tried their hands at. It is still "flavour of the month", with many businesses requiring help to advertise their services on the web. To produce web pages, you need appropriate authoring software and a working knowledge of HTML, the programming language used. It is a big help if you have graphic design or information editing skills, as many client companies are not good at putting together clear information, or understanding how to structure it for use with hypertext. Some websites include forms and other areas for users to enter information. Programming skills in cgi scripting, database related languages such as ASP, and in Java, the programming language used to send small, self-running programmes over the Internet, are in high demand but the market for basic web page design is highly competitive.

Bibliography

How to series: Freelance Teaching and Tutoring   *Date:* 1997
Author: John T Wilson
Source: How To Books Ltd, 3 Newtec Place, Magdalen Rd, Oxford
ISBN 1–85703–407–4

30 Ways to Make Money at Home   *Date:* 1996
Author: Jennie Hawthorne
Source: Rushmere Wynne Group Plc, 4–5 Harmill, Grovebury Rd, Leighton Buzzard, Beds LU7 8FF ISBN 0–948035–25–0

Ideas suitable for telecentres

Sales force support centres: National sales forces often have a far flung group of people who may need to meet up with regional managers, hold small conferences or drop in and use the facilities. Telecentres have been approached to offer these facilities and can network with other telecottages to offer coverage of an entire region.

Homework club: Some telecentres have offered access to computers for children for homework or games usage. By adopting a fixed timetable, disruption to other telecentre users can be avoided.

Internet access: Usually charged on a time basis of £1 minimum to around £5/hour. Telecentres could offer an Internet education package – a getting started course followed by a number of sessions at the telecentre.

LETS: The Local Enterprise Trading System (LETS) allows local services to be exchanged in cashless trading, with different services attracting different rates of LETS. Each subscriber gets a cheque book for their LETS tokens, and abuse is discouraged by monthly statements showing the indebtedness (or otherwise) of each subscriber. The system encourages local trading, and re-enfranchisng people on low incomes by allowing them to exchange services and goods without money. Telecentres can operate as administrative centres for local LETS systems.

Local council information centres: A number of county councils are keen to develop on-line information access points or satellite offices in rural towns and might welcome a site for an additional terminal which could be rented to them. The Post Office scheme Open for Business has been adopted by some local authorities. Four East Anglian telecottages host kiosks under this scheme in addition to sites in post offices and libraries.

CD-ROM or distance learning library: Some telecentres offer access to CD-ROM information resources. Recently the explosion in Internet or CD-ROM based IT learning has opened up new opportunities, such as provision of the "self service" version of the ECDL computer literacy qualification, or the Microsoft certification programme. It seems likely that a role as local "campus" or learning support centre will become increasingly important for many telecentres, especially as some course providers now also provide their examinations and results online.

Job club: Telecentres can provide a site for job information, a noticeboard, latest job information faxed over or jobs information available on-line. Contact your local Job Centre for information.

Business adviser outpost: Business Link, your local TEC, council or regional development agency are all potential clients for use of facilities to meet customers.

Online Business Information and Business Information Basics (2 publications)
Source: Bowker-Saur Tel: 01342 330100
Comment: Useful publications for those interested in information broking.

Online Notes
Source: ASLIB Tel: 020 7903 0000
Comment: Useful publication for those interested in information broking.

Contacts and URLs

ASLIB, 44-45 Museum Street, London WC1A 1LY, Tel: 020 7831 8003, is a useful organisation for those interested in information broking. Web: **www.aslib.co.uk**

The Dyer Partnership, contact Mark Dyer Tel: 01420 473 473 Fax: 01420 487 695 Email: info@netaccountants.com Web: **www.netaccountants.com**

Internet magazine keeps a listing of British cybercafes at **www.internet-magazine.com/resource/cybercafes/index.html**

Centres for teleworking

Prospective teleworkers are often concerned about isolation problems if they work exclusively alone. There are many forms of telework which involve working alongside other people including telecentres, telecottages, cybercafés, neighbourhood offices, bureau services such as the US chain Kinkos and serviced or "virtual" offices like those provided by the Regus chain.

A **telecottage** provides its local community with low cost access to computer and telecommunications equipment, which in turn give access to information services and work. Most rely on provision of IT training for their main income and tend to be community- rather than business-oriented. Telecottages also support teleworkers and small businesses and are sometimes called electronic village halls.

Telecentre is a term that often overlaps with telecottage but is sometimes used to refer to small call centres or "back office" operations where work is carried out away from the employer's main location. They are usually commercially-run operations servicing one company. A related idea is the "neighbourhood office", a telecentre run for company staff to use as a base away from the main office. A number of councils in Britain now have neighbourhood office/telecentres to reduce time spent travelling by their staff.

Teleworkers often need facilities which they cannot obtain in their home office, such as meeting space, complex photocopiers or expensive software used only occasionally. Some printshops provide access to such services, but US chain Kinkos, which now has three outlets in south-east Britain as well, is considered the expert in supporting what is known in the US as the "free agent" movement – self-employed people including teleworkers.

Kinkos opens around the clock and provides opportunities for "self service" access to technology as well as expert staff who can carry out tasks as required. A more "corporate" version of this idea is the European chain Regus, which provides services ranging from receptionists offering a personalised answering service to meeting spaces and fully serviced offices for businesses of all sizes.

Teleworkers on the move also need support – from suitable meeting space in hotels and airports to easy ways of picking up email. A cybercafé recently opened in Gatwick airport where anyone can get online and use web-based email services such as **www.hotmail.com** or **www.twigger.co.uk** to collect their email. Most cities now have a variety of places where you can pay to get Internet access. Internet magazine keeps a list of British cybercafes at
www.internet-magazine.com/resource/cybercafes/index.htm.

Telecottages

The first centre claiming the title telecottage in the UK, the Moorlands Telecottage, was set up in 1989, but like many good ideas, it appears that telecottages were being independently "invented" in a number of places. A TCA survey turned up examples which predate the first Swedish telecottages in 1985, such as Daily Information in Oxford. Numbers of telecottages grew to a peak of 165 in 1998. The TCA now requires all telecottages shown on its map (published in *Teleworker* magazine and on its website **www.tca.org.uk**) to be members and currently lists around 140.

Many different forms of telecottage have been set up. Some are community-orientated and offer training and use of resources for community groups. Others are highly-equipped commercial enterprises. Experience suggests that centres need to adopt a commercial attitude if they are to survive beyond an initial grant-funded start-up. A key to success appears to be creation of a core business, usually software training, around which other complementary services are offered. Because rural areas are often short of resources, telecottages can become a focus of community and commercial activity where teleworkers can network, using each other's services to provide backup on larger contracts.

Telecottage statistics

At the end of 1994, the TCA supported a survey of telecottage activities by Bill Murray of Small World Connections which was repeated in early 1998 –

Services offered at Daily Info (www.dailyinfo.co.uk)

- Computer use – PCs and Macs charged per hour, with up-to-date software for Internet access, word processing, spreadsheets, desktop publishing, webpage authoring

- Laser printing – A4 and A3, charged per page plus computer time

- Colour printing – A4 and A2, charged per page plus computer time

- Photocopying, A2, A3 and A4, colour and black and white, volume discounts and prepaid photocopier cards available

- Scanning and OCR text recognition – included in computer time charge

- Staff consultancy charged per hour – software installation, disinfecting viruses, recovering trashed disks, advice on machine purchase

- Lamination for frequently-used documents like menus

- Faxing – per page, rate depends on destination

- Email – included in the per hour computer hire charge

- Digital camera for hire

> **Wrong number for Wiltshire**
>
> A report from the Community Development Foundation on the demise of a network of four telecottages in Wiltshire concluded that some of the problems encountered were:
>
> - Tension between community and commercial sectors of the network
> - Poor communication between the telecottages and the Community Council for Wiltshire, which set up the network
> - Unrealistic expectations of what could be achieved commercially by a rural telecottage
> - Unsuccessful marketing of the telecottage services
> - Cost of renewing skills and equipment became a problem
> - Insufficient financial, resource management and strategic support
>
> Three of the telecottages were sold out to a commercial concern in 1995 which later closed them down. The fourth continued on a voluntary basis, but in 1998 the two key staff members had to leave and set up a separate business because they could not obtain funding without becoming an independent entity unrestricted by the charitable status of the village hall committee. More information at **www.uk.ibm.com/community/uk171.htm**

about one third of the 165 telecentres and telecottages surveyed replied. The results give a snapshot of the "typical" telecottage which can be useful to those thinking about setting up. All the figures are averages or approximations.

- Over 20% of centres have over 50 regular users and 50 occasional users though seven centres reported no drop-in users at all. The average was 30 regular and 30 occasional users. Only three centres reported that over ten people other than staff used the centre as a regular place of work, and over two-thirds had no-one using their centre for regular work.
- 40% subcontract work to local teleworkers.
- Around 20% see themselves as "telecottages" and 15% as "telecentres" with a further 15% describing themselves as "business centres"; other titles given include Community Resource Centre, Computer Resource Centre, IT Centre, Telematics Centre, Office Bureau.
- The vast majority (88%) are located in rural areas or small towns (rural villages 38.8%, small towns 36.7%, remote rural areas 12.2%, city centres 4.1%, city suburbs 2.0%, large towns 6.1%).
- Most centres have two full-time staff, one part-timer and one volunteer. Over 60% have no volunteers.
- Half are "breaking even" financially, with one-third making a loss (usually the most recently set-up telecottages) and about 28% making a

profit. Only six centres which were loss-making were operating outside their own financial plans. Incomes ranged from £6,000 to £180,000 with an average of £50,000 in the 1994 survey.

- Facilities vary widely. All have Internet access and 82% have a website. Over half have ISDN lines. However, only 20 centres responded to the initial email version of the survey questionnaire.

- In 1994, over half saw one of their main functions as training, with provision of office facilities a close second. In 1998 the responses indicated more emphasis on training and internet activities, and provision of local services being more important than originally thought. Predictions for the future were increased emphasis on training, the Internet and commercial work. Two centres reported they were likely to close.

- About 30% of the responding centres are privately-owned, with a similar figure funded mainly by central or local government. The remaining third mix public, voluntary and co-operative structures. Of the privately-owned centres, almost all started life privately-owned, suggesting that public centres die rather than go private. Startup funding included grants, equipment or other assistance for almost three-quarters of the centres.

- Income comes from commercial operations for over one-third of centres, but 40% rely almost entirely on continuing public funding. About a third pay no rent. The median level of grant was £29,750, with median turnover of around £60,000 and income of about £25,000.

Niche business services providing income included: language translation, bookkeeping, recruitment, abstracting, website development and maintenance, computer hire and consultancy, commercial and tourist information provision, and to a lesser extent, call centre and message taking services.

Telecottage services

Telecottages usually offer both formal and informal training, computer hire (some offer "take-away" computers too) and access to the Internet, photocopiers, printers and faxes. Other facilities include use of workspace, and meeting rooms. A more complete listing of services which could be provided through telecottages is given in Chapter 5, *Ideas for Telebusinesses*. Trained staff are often available to provide secretarial assistance, word processing and desktop publishing, which can be invaluable to teleworkers who need additional help.

Telecotttage case studies

During the 1990s it became increasingly apparent that successful telecottages fall into one of two models. Under the first model, they develop a core niche business which often provides the infrastructure (equipment and premises) which subsidises the economically-priced services of the telecottage. Under the second model, they receive their support from various agencies in exchange for providing training services. Within these two models, there are some interesting variations, such as telecottages which also manage a number of start-up business unit premises, telecottages attached to sub-post offices or tourist offices, and integrated telecottages, such as KITE, and WREN, which work to provide training, commercial work and childcare facilities on one site. WREN has pioneered the "jigsaw" approach where telecottages broaden their services towards general community development.

Barnham Telecottage

Barnham Telecottage near Bognor Regis was set up as a private venture in June 1995 by husband and wife team Jane and Eric Pascal. Jane is a retired teacher, and Eric had sold off his computer bureau business though he still sells, upgrades and repairs PCs. The centre is run from a shop at the front of the Pascal's house and follows the pattern of telecottages which run the telecottage on the back of an existing core business. Eric's work, which

---

Rural Areas Videotelephone Access Network (RAVAN)

The RAVAN project was backed by the DTI's Multimedia Demonstrator Programme and organised by the TCA. Over a period of eighteen months it installed PC-based videotelephone equipment in a group of UK telecottages and performed demonstrations to over 1000 people of how the equipment can be used to enhance business performance. The target was one user demonstrated to in each centre per week.

In Lanarkshire, a local textile designer showed scarves to Italian clients over the screen, a tour company courted US clients, and steel workers relocating to Wales held face-to-face interviews. Another local firm has secured a £100k deal to supply recycled laser cartridges to Italy, partly assisted by demonstrating products onscreen and sharing a costs spreadsheet showing pounds and lire. At the KITE telecottage in Co. Fermanagh, videoconferencing has been used to enhance a contract where New York emergency room notes are processed, and as part of the peace process. In Norfolk MPs held constituency 'surgeries' by videoconference from Westminster. In Durham a local photographic agency got to know US clients without the expense of conventional business travel. In East Kent, the chamber of commerce held video meetings with their opposite numbers in Lille, France. The RATIO project in Plymouth used videoconferencing equipment to link telecentres for remote learning. WREN Telecottage in Warwickshire has developed a protocol for demonstrating videoconferencing, while in Cumbria the equipment is being used by one local business to save travel time on face-to-face meetings in Newcastle.

However, follow-up to the demonstrations did not lead to a big increase in take-up of videoconferencing. According to ICUA, the videoconference users association, "People still don't understand what the technology is about or what use they could make of it. It hasn't yet reached critical mass."

also includes website design and maintenance, provides an income of around £25,000. The telecottage income amounts to a further £6,000, which is expected to grow to £10,000. The telecottage makes use of the equipment amassed through Eric's business.

One of the largest income earners for the centre is training, and the majority of the trainees are women returners, though Jane says that there is now considerable competition in this area from local colleges. She sees their client base as private and business customers who don't enjoy the college environment. Other services include photocopying, printing, Internet access, desktop publishing and business support. The telecottage is a boon to local home-based businesses as Jane Pascal explains: "There are lots of small business converts to the telecottage – people who work from home but probably wouldn't call themselves teleworkers though most of our customers are homeworkers or run a business from home. Also we get students in to type their work, or if they've left it too late, to get it typed by us!"

The value of the centre is also backed by an enthusiastic local user: "I think telecottages are an excellent concept – I have been setting up a business venture from the dining room table with no resources. The telecottage has been ideal – I don't think I would have been able to get this far without help from them. I use their email number on my letterhead which has added credibility. I intend to get computer trained in the future – they have put everything they do for me on a space on the computer – and I look forward to the point when I can get going on this myself."

Because they have a core business interleaving with the telecottage, the Pascals have been able to provide economically-priced training to the community without any subsidy. Eric is keen to stress that the telecottage would not exist on its own, but it appears to work well with the existing business supplying the basic infrastructure of premises and equipment. Both Eric and Jane believe that the number of teleworkers in the area is definitely increasing.
Tel: 01243 553725 Email: barnham.telecottage@saqnet.co.uk

Cape Clear Telecottage

A tiny telecottage on Cape Clear Island off County Cork in Ireland with three PCs provides office services, Internet access, photocopying, faxing and word processing from its North Harbour office. The same premises acts as a bookshop and tourist information centre, as well as helping the co-op that runs the island's ferry service. In past years the telecottage also provided administrative services for the Electricity Supply Board, and the local turbot fish farm had its accounts and records provided by telecottage staff. The island has a population of 150, swelled to 1,000 by tourists and students attending courses in the Irish language during the summer which provides plenty of usage for the Internet connection. Computer literacy levels on Cape Clear were helped by ECDL training courses funded through the EU's New Opportunities for Women programme. The telecottage received a small amount of startup funding from the economic development agency for Irish-speaking areas, Udarás na Gaeltachta. Email: ccteo@iol.ie

Daily Information, Oxford City

Daily Information in central Oxford began as an adjunct to a privately-run broadsheet listing of events, which was published daily in the university area of the city. Owner John Rose invested in three giant Philips word processors and a number of IBM electronic typewriters in 1979. "For the first six weeks, the Philips machines didn't work. For the next six months, we had no idea what they were really for. They cost £10,000 each, with annual maintenance costs of £1,000", recalls John. He offered free learning time to customers and soon found that demand was so great that the computers had to be available 24 hours a day for thesis and book preparation. The Philips machines were retired in 1985, and Daily Information quickly built up a stock of 30 PCs for hire on-site or to take away. Daily Information probably did more than the University's computer department to introduce PCs to the students. John now turns over £200,000 a year, selling PCs and laser printers, as well as disks, cartridges and paper, and offers access to sophisticated photocopiers and colour printers. "Now that the machines are small enough to take away, we don't have to open overnight. The biggest problem is that technology changes so fast that the business eats up capital just to keep it going", says John.

In the past few years, business for printing out theses has fallen as more people have their own printers, but the sophisticated photocopiers and scanners at Daily Information are still a draw for customers though John is worried that the bureau services are no longer breaking even. Access to the Internet is popular, especially with foreign language students, but many language schools have started their own cybercafes. The broadsheet is also available on the web, along with a computer exchange for secondhand equipment. A recent innovation is "serve yourself" ads which can be entered on the web and are then included in the printed broadsheet. Daily Information long ago achieved the status of an Oxford institution and is now in its 21st year.

Web: **www.dailyinfo.co.uk** Tel: 01865 310011

East Clare Telecottage and Training Associates

East Clare Telecottage was established in 1991 in Scariff, Co. Clare, to provide computer-based office services to businesses and community groups. Drop-in access by people wanting to use IT equipment amounts to about 10-15% of the income of the telecottage unit. Services supplied include design and printing, translation, computer training, software development, Internet access and web design

The training is provided by a related company, East Clare Training Associates, which provides courses and consultancy in a wide range of topics including management, team building, group work and facilitation, materials development, European project management, an Introduction to Enterprise, working with volunteers, personal development and fundraising. Fifty people are currently on ECDL computer literacy courses at various stages, and an introduction to computer literacy is also offered. East

> **HM prisoners do it in Styal**
>
> Ten women in Styal prison are teleworking from the "comfort" of their own prison cells. The ten have studied for vocational certificates in teleworking, and have worked on a number of projects including a mailing list for a national charity, a database for a government department and Christmas card designs for prison service charity shops.
>
> Prison governor Mike Goodwin said the women had gained experience of the world of work and gained self-confidence as well as supporting each other as a team. The project has been funded by Prison Enterprise and the European Commission, and was the brainchild of Manchester consultant Bill Murray of Small World Connections.
>
> Call centre and fulfilment operations are planned for the future. Murray comments: "The programme provides women prisoners with much better prospects when they return to society – and we believe it means they could be less likely to re-offend."

Clare also offers the Teleworking NVQ (see Chapter 12, *Training for teleworkers*).

The training centre has six workstations, and East Clare was recently designated the National Farm IT Training Centre. Training manager Martina Minogue finds that ECDL is not really sufficient to get people work and is currently working to get certification as a MOUS (Microsoft Office User Specialist) and MCP (Microsoft Computer Professional) training centre. There is also a small call centre with three workstations set up initially with European funding as a training project. The call centre can offer order processing, reservations, data distribution and market research

East Clare operates a network of translators who take on contract work. They keep a register of 75 local translators and work amounts to perhaps 15 man-days each week (3 full-time equivalents). The network receives a commission on work obtained. They see translation of websites as a new area of opportunity.

Telecottage manager Nana Luke agrees that the service offering is a wide one, but says that the main theme of success is being able to provide a one-stop shop – either for the printing services of the telecottage, or for translation. The telecottage plans to do more website development and hosting in future. They are also working on a European-funded plan to develop the Teleworking NVQ further, in particular by providing training for managers of teleworkers. There are 9 people directly employed by the various operations at East Clare though not all are full-time. They include one training manager, one trainer, one accounts person, two part-time subcontracted assistant trainers, a receptionist, a full-time staffer for the telecottage, a transport consultant and the telecottage manager.

Phone: 061 921121 Email: bealtaine@bealtaine.ie

Eccles House Telebusiness Centre

Eccles House is the brainchild of the Peak Park Trust and arose because Trust member Godfrey Claff had visited telecottages in Scandinavia. Blue Circle Cement donated a Grade II listed farmhouse with outbuildings to the Trust, which spent £400,000 and several years converting the buildings using monies from both the public (Rural Development Commission and European Social Fund) and private sectors. The site was opened in February 1992 and is managed by Contract Data Research (CDR), a data processing company specialising in GIS systems and software development.

The old barns and outbuildings now provide twelve individual offices and small workshop units, which vary in size from 179 sq ft to 880 sq ft. These units are used as accommodation for start-up businesses or for professionals. Previous managers of the centre offered meeting room hire, some training projects and secretarial services but these proved unprofitable in a remote location. When CDR took over, tenants were drifting away. They cut the telecottage-type services, dropped prices on the units and carried out a strong advertising campaign to reverse the trend. Manager John Ievers believes that for telecottage enterprises in remote locations to succeed, they need subsidy through government-funded training services. Tel: 01433 621427

Isles Telecroft, Shetland

At Unst in Shetland, Laura Baisley runs the Isles Telecroft, one of six telecottages set up in 1991 by the Highlands and Islands Enterprise (HIE) with funding from British Telecom under a three-year project. Two of the telecottages were schools-based, the others were attached to existing community organisations. "One member of our community co-op was keen on IT, which was how we got involved initially", explains Laura.

Isles Telecroft began by running two telework training projects. On the first, four women who live on remote islands were trained in telework both through conventional courses and by carrying out a telework project to put museum records onto a database. The four women had computing equipment provided by the project at home, along with modems for communicating with Unst and elsewhere. Funding for this project came from the local authority, Shetland Islands Council and from Shetland Enterpise. On the second project, seven people with disabilities who live in rural areas of Shetland were trained to achieve an IT qualification.

These projects were succeeded by four courses funded through the European Social Fund (ESF) and the local enterprise company. One catered for disabled people, the second provided training to unemployed and women returners in a socially-deprived area, and the third provided IT skills to members of the Shetland Tenants' Association. The fourth project supplied IT training for 10 local women as part of an integrated training scheme for women returners.

As ESF funding cannot be used for capital purchases, re-equipping as equipment becomes obsolete has been a problem. However, depreciation

Urban alternatives – Kinko's and Regus

Two retail chains seem to have cracked the market for urban services to teleworkers. Kinko's is an American success story founded in 1970 by Paul Orfalea which now has nearly 900 branches in 8 countries, including three in London run jointly with the Virgin Group. Kinko's stores are open 24 hours a day, seven days a week and offer a wide range of services including:

- *Computer hire and internet access*
- *Digital copying – black and white and colour, collation*
- *Digital on-demand printing*
- *Presentation and finishing services, binding*
- *Oversize posters, dtp services*
- *Videoconferencing*

Unlike high street printshops, you can use the computers yourself. There are Macs (set up as "design stations" with software like Quark and Photoshop ready installed) as well as PCs, and helpful staff, who are known as "co-workers". US commentator Dan Pink describes Kinko's as "the Cheers bar for the Free Agent Nation – a place full of quirky and compelling characters" and Kinko's staff as "the yeomen of the Information Age. People trust them with their ideas. They do more than make copies. They manufacture dreams". UK press officer Michael Taylor says the next move will probably be expansion to a chain of stores in Manchester or Leeds.

Regus aims squarely at the corporate market, offering meeting rooms with presentation facilities, answering, secretarial and reception services, offices, videoconferencing and "touchdown" space in major cities around the world. The company advertises that you can "walk in, sit down, start work" and avoid meetings in crowded lobbies and bars. Space can be booked by the hour or day by phone or online, and all the centres have a variety of room sizes. It promotes videoconferencing as a way of saving up to 75% of the costs of business travel to meetings and says business people are increasingly concerned with confidentiality issues of meeting in public places.

Regus also operates serviced business centres and business space for companies with longer-term space requirements such as temporary office expansion or special projects. The advantage is billed as an all-inclusive price covering security, maintenance, IT facilities, the avoidance of capital investment in property, with additional features such as catering or reception services also available as required. Reception services include dedicated lines, mail and fax forwarding services, and the use of prestigious business addresses for mail.

Kinko's 326/333 High Holborn, London Tel: 0171 539 2900
Regus **www.regus.com**

> **Cybercafes go easy in the high street**
>
> The fortunes of cybercafes have been mixed in recent years, with their market for Internet access being crowded by increased home access, Internet kiosks, and more public access points in libraries and council offices. Stelios Haji Ioannou, the founder of affordable airline easyJet has now turned his attention to making the Internet cheap and accessible for all.
>
> There are five easyEverything centres in central London locations such as Oxford Street and Trafalgar Square providing a total of 2,300 terminals, and the facilities have been widely advertised on Underground posters to attract tourists and business people as well as new Internet users. A centre has opened in Edinburgh and others are planned for Amsterdam and Rotterdam.
>
> A company spokesman said that previous cybercafes had been on a small scale: "Cybercafes have tended to be one-off owner managed establishments without the capital or business skills to set up a bigger operation. Most of them survive whilst charging more than £5 per hour. On the other hand people don't really want to spend £1000 updating their hardware at home every year and even in the world's most wired countries less than a third of households are connected. We've broken the mold by appealing to all age groups and avoiding the bohemian, techie style of cybercafes. The easyEverything name reflects the fact that products as diverse as books, clothes, music, videos and air travel are available at bargain prices on the net, and email has made this kind of centre the post office of the twenty-first century. We've been getting more visitors than the Millennium Dome."
>
> The easyEverything centres have PCs with 15 inch flat screen monitors and 2 megabit connections to the Internet providing high speed access. They are open 24 hours a day, 7 days a week. The price of access fluctuates depending on how busy the centre is – a screen at the front counter details how much access you can get for £1. (**www.easyeverything.com**)

    charges and maintenance costs are allowed, so Laura does a bit of creative accounting and tries to upgrade the existing machines instead. Separate grants have also provided the telecottage with a colour printer and flatbed scanner, and ISDN has finally arrived in the past year. She would like to improve her own IT skills, which have been restricted to the level of the training she delivers, and sees the lack of training and development opportunities for staff as one of the pitfalls of operating on a shoestring.

    The telecottage derives some income from telework services, but sources of income are limited, especially since the closure of the civilian airport which formerly serviced the oil industry on the island. "We do get pressure from the local enterprise company to increase the income from telework, but we have no budget or resources to do the marketing required at the moment, so it's not easy. About 80% of our income comes from training, especially providing assessment services for vocational qualifications", explains Laura. The other 20% is from business services such as desktop publishing, web authoring and word processing. She sees the ISDN videoconferencing equipment as particularly useful for the island environment as it allows the replacement of meetings for businesses which would otherwise involve complex ferry trips.

Her advice to other community telecottages is not to worry about the technological aspects: "People are much more important. You can buy technical expertise when you need it. Try to tack the telecottage on to an existing service such as a post office, and make sure there really is local support, and it's not just the brainchild of a couple of boffins. And do a good business plan. That's vital." She is concerned about the future, and feels that the local college is now competing with the telecottage in the provision of training services.

Email: isles.telecroft@zetnet.co.uk Tel: 01957 711224

KITE, Co. Fermanagh, Northern Ireland

Kinawley Integrated Teleworking Enterprise is located in West Fermanagh, close to the border between Northern Ireland and the Republic. It is a highly successful enterprise which sources 60% of its work from North America, and offers childcare facilities as well as training. The purpose-built telecottage is the brainchild of Sheila and Michael McCaffrey, both of whom have substantial managerial and and business experience. Sheila identified the basic requirements to set up the enterprise – premises, childcare facilities, training, equipment and a market for their services.

The telecottage occupies a purpose built centre which was established in 1993 and has a predominantly female workforce which has received training in both managerial techniques and ICTs. KITE focusses its business on remote management of data and has customers in the US, UK and Ireland. KITE believes industry standards, specifications and requirements are very important so it has involved partners to assist in ICT training and development for both the corporate and community sectors. The training emphasis is on high levels and end results.

Equipping a centre like KITE is a continuing issue and Sheila comments: "We invest in the tools of the trade which are relevant and necessary – this is a key to success and growth in any profession. However our decisions are based on customer needs, not on flash new technologies which may not be relevant to our customer base".

One of the key features of the KITE development is the provision of on-site childcare to supply "family friendly work". The childcare provision was originally covered pre-school care but has been developed to include after-school and holiday care as well as a variety of play and learning opportunities based on ICTs.

Tel: 01365 348943 Email: s.mccaffrey@btinternet.com

Moorlands Telecottage

Moorlands Telecottage is attached to the local school and is a classic example of the telecottage as rural IT training centre. Simon Brooks, Community Education project officer, explains that Moorlands courses focus on various aspects of information and business technology – and that around 50% of the training offered is now paid for by businesses on a commercial basis. "A lot of businesses prefer to send their staff into the telecottage, away from distractions in the office. Many courses are held in the evenings at the request of clients." Simon favours the RSA IT qualifications because he feels that these are the ones best accepted by businesses, and thus produce the most employable graduates. Moorlands also offers some unaccredited courses and some CLAIT courses.

"One problem that a rural telecottage must plan for is that if the local population is small then eventually you will run out of trainees. We get a lot of repeat business – people coming back for retraining – especially from small businesses. They might start off learning word processing to do invoicing, move on to Powerpoint to get work from clients, and then learn Excel so they can do their own accounts."

The telecottage also gets contracts from organisations like ADAS, the farming advisory service, to train farmers with alternative holiday businesses in specific skills such as how to prepare confirmation letters for holiday bookings. The telecottage also offers community development courses, and these are run at locations around the area using a suite of eleven laptop computers. "We have got over problems with setup times for the laptops by teaching the students how to set up their own computers in the first week of the course. After that, they do their own!" The laptops are also used in the telecottage to provide extra course places. "We were having trouble reducing our waiting lists – now we can offer 140 places a week instead of 77. This has also helped with the development of new courses. Currently we're working on a course in family learning with our LEA aimed at giving parents skills so they can help their children with after school computer-based learning".

The telecottage is also used as a referral agency by local businesses looking for teleworkers. "We don't do this officially or gain any income for it because we don't want the hassle of being an employment agency, but local businesses know that people we have trained are going to be competent and high quality, so they come to us when they need work done. We contact suitable teleworkers and tell them to get in touch with the businesses – it's up to the businesses which teleworker they pick and to sort out the details of the job."

SPIC: Standon Parish Information Centre

SPIC, set up in early 1995, is truly owned by its own community – the main financial support comes from an additional £4.50 on the council tax of local residents. The centre was set up with grants from Herts County and East Herts District Councils but running expenses were initially covered by the Parish Council grant. The first telecottage manager worked on a Community Action programme which paid for 18 hours a week of his time – additional time was provided by volunteers.

Once it had established a local presence, the centre moved to more convenient premises, again funded through the council tax, that include rooms which can be let to the Parish Council and to other local service providers for field operations. The Citizens' Advice Bureau uses the centre once a week, and it is also used for Parish Council meetings, and for meetings with other local councilllors. There is a book order point for purchase and delivery, and the local library catalogue and county council information services can also be accessed through the centre.

For a while SPIC was managed by a local web design business which unfortunately went bust. Now the centre gets rental income from the Citizen's Advice Bureau and from providing an "oasis point" for county council workers. There is plenty of drop-in trade to use the photocopiers, fax and Internet services, but SPIC relies on volunteer help to staff the centre although manager Barbara Norris is paid for one of the days that she works each week. A service to allow local residents to inspect planning applications is very popular.

The telecottage provides courses in Word, Excel and the Internet and has participated in the BBC's Computers Don't Bite campaign and the DTI's IT for All project. Barbara says the telecottage needs to rent out more space to be viable, and has recently found a new tenant through a local charity. Getting enough volunteers is a continuing problem, but she has hopes of new plans to offer tourist information services through SPIC.

Tel: 01920 824900

Ottery St Mary – Project Cosmic

"What we are basically is an Internet café", explains Ian Clifford from Project Cosmic, located in an old railway station in the Devon village. Ian applied to the National Lottery for funds to start up the project, and received

£85,000 over three years on condition that he found matching funding. The matching funding has come from the county, district and town councils, the local Lions club and the Rural Development Commission. The cybercafe, which has a fast Internet connection serving 8 PCs, is open five and a half days a week and focuses on helping young people.

The project runs various computer training programmes for people in the local area and hopes shortly to have a mobile training facility available. Income also comes from authoring websites, often using the skills of local young people. Ian offers informal, impartial advice to members of the public about computer-related issues and has been working to get a telework agency off the ground.

Tel: 01404 813226 Web: **www.cosmic.org.uk**

Community resource centres – Herefordshire and Worcestershire

The Herefordshire and Worcestershire community council originally created a network of 22 resource centres located in village halls, community centres and schools with help from the county council. The centres were provided for non-profit making organisations, the unemployed, small startup businesses and youth businesses. Most centres are run on a self-help basis by a volunteer coordinator, often a retired person, who could show users how to operate the equipment. Opening hours vary and the resource centre equipment usually consists of a computer, printer, photocopiers, combined scanner/printer, and in some centres binding and stapling machines.

A recent funding bid by the Community Council and the Southern Marches Partnership was successful in supporting nine of the original centres further. The Southern Marches Area Rural Telematics project (SMART) was started in 1999 with funding aimed at making computers and the Internet accessible to country communities. Project officer Steve Palframan explains that the project has three years' funding, but hopes to extend it beyond that period. "The idea was to introduce computers into rural areas using the existing community resource centres", he comments. The nine centres were already offering services such as photocopying, typing and printing, and have been upgraded with computers, access to the Internet and email. "We have also set up a website with Hotmail so people can have an email address. The centres are in a variety of locations from village halls to a prefabricated cabin on a caravan park. They are provided by the local community and people use them for typing up work, producing parish magazines, *etc*. It varies from place to place." SMART has also provided two part-time centre co-ordinators, and the New Deal with Community pays for two other centre co-ordinators. The total of centres has now reached 25.

The SMART project has also provided a lead centre in Ross-on-Wye which will be used for training as well as public access to IT. This centre has two part-time members of staff and a network of seven PCs. A further three training centres are planned under the SMART 2 project, based in secondary schools as "opportunities to learn in a friendly environment at your own pace", and there is hotmail email access via the website. (**www.srcnet.org.uk**).

WREN Telecottage

Once established, a telecottage can act as a platform for various additional services. The WREN Telecottage was founded as Warwickshire's first telecottage in 1991. WREN belongs indirectly to the Royal Agricultural Society of England (RASE), and received start-up grants from ARC, BT and Coventry and Warwickshire TEC. Through RASE, WREN has educational charity trading status. Any profits from trading are used to subsidise local services.

WREN pioneered one-stop access to a range of business and community services: IT and the Internet, training, open learning, business services, and local community projects as well as social and networking functions. This jigsaw approach – taking into account both local needs and global opportunities – ensured that WREN has survived in a fast changing field. It continues to advise on a range of flexible models for similar centres, as ideas have moved on, for example into Healthy Living Centres and a University for Industry.

WREN has moved with the times on limited resources, and is now involved, often with its national arm, the NREC, in a wide range of projects in both the private and grant-funded sectors. Projects may be short- or long-term, are usually based on partnerships, and often – but not always – use ICTs. One current example helps villages in Warwickshire and Worcestershire save their shop, or establish a new hub for online services. The telecottage is a DTI Local Support Centre, works with an EU-funded business support partnership, and is also part of the DTI's IT for All initiative. WREN is closely involved in RuralNet, a Lottery-funded intranet supporting the rural voluntary sector, and with supporting a range of networks and organisations, from small businesses and social entrepreneurs to government departments.

WREN's equipment includes the usual computers and office facilities but in addition it has a leased line to the Internet (through partnership with Internet UK), its own email and information service (RuralNet) and videoconferencing equipment. It also offers a nursery where telecottage users can 'park' their children while they train or work. WREN has developed a national and international role as a demonstration telecottage, facilitated by its location at the National Agricultural Centre, Stoneleigh, and by its work in combining community and commercial functions.

Success factors

Key features for success from these case studies include:

- Leadership
    - team management
    - business acumen

- networking
- strategic planning
- marketing
- cooperative partnerships
- Having a clearly-defined focus
- Local knowledge (research, profiles, community needs, other resources)
- Structures in place on which developments and programmes can be built
- Community linkages (locally responsive and accepted)
- Networking (again!)
- Being able to adapt to change
- Adequate funding
- Professional development and training for the organisation and its staff.

The global perspective

Bill Murray of Small World Connections is currently preparing a global study of telecentres to be published under the title *Telecentre Models around the World*, funded by the International Telecommunications Union, a UN body. He outlines the best-known telecentre model, the Swedish telecottage or "multipurpose community telecentre", and looks at different stages of development with the help of international authors. What follows is an interpretation of some of the draft material and does not necessarily represent Bill's view or those of the ITU.

The first stage is using telecentres to provide any access at all to ICT facilities – currently telekiosks, providing just telephony and possibly fax services, are growing in number in Africa, while Hungary is seeing explosive growth of telecentres, with over 500 planned to open. In the second stage, once access becomes reasonably cheap and widespread, telecentres must reinvent themselves through offering training or commercial services, otherwise they die because there is no longer widespread need for access (and where there is a need, it is supplied by small businesses such as printshops). This pattern can be seen in Sweden, Newfoundland, Brazil, Finland, Germany, Holland, the UK, Ireland and parts of Australia and usually sees a considerable reduction in telecentre numbers.

In the third stage, rurally-based telecentres must work out what to do once they have trained the people in their area, and often face competition from existing training providers such as local colleges which want to provide IT and open learning offerings. Solutions involving state funding have included becoming open learning support centres with sophisticated facilities such as videoconferencing, or broadening activities to become general centres for community development. Where income is partly or entirely commercial, the solution has often been based around call centre services, as these services do not require workers with as high a level of basic IT skill as professional or niche teleworking businesses.

In the US Murray notes that there have been two separate movements – the Community Technology Centres, which aim to help develop technology based skills among economically marginal minorities, and the neighbourhood work centres, which try to provide facilities for telecommuters. He stresses that "one model does not fit all – fit your model to your objectives and use existing infrastructures".

He also points out that political, geographical and financial factors impinge – this is very clear in Australia where political and financial support continued in the western part of the country but not elsewhere, so that now Western Australia makes up 71 of the 87 Australian telecentres – the others collapsed due to lack of financial and political support, despite the extremely isolated population and the huge importance of distance learning common to all rural Australian areas. California has continued to support neighbourhood offices in the belief that they contribute to traffic reduction,while in Hungary, support is offered in exchange for telecentres providing services for the citizen such as access to government documents and grants. Murray concludes that telecentres are stepping stones which allow less-developed regions to catch up and that successful models must be adapted to local conditions.

If you are considering setting up a centre, it is important to realise that some commentators think telecentres are not currently a good use of public funding. Werner Korte of German consultancy Empirica in his 1998 paper "Telecentres in Germany and abroad – top or flop?" argues that common problems have been seen in all countries including:

- lack of commercial focus (*eg* projects with several aims, some non-commercial)
- lack of access to state funding from a single source necessitating excessive time spent negotiating with a range of grant-giving bodies
- offering services which did not add any significant value to what was already available on the market (*eg* secretarial services)
- location in a remote area with access only to low skill levels and basic IT training, resulting in service offerings suitable only to local sale (not high-level enough to attract distant customers) yet there is no local market due to the remoteness of the area.

Korte also noted common success factors including

- an income anchor such as a regular large customer
- entrepreneurial spirit, usually through a single person, the "local champion"
- good business ideas aiming at market niches or alternatively
- broadly based attractive service ranges.

Korte concluded "for the not too distant future I do not expect [telecentres] to become a 'hot growth industry'. Rather we should identify how they could further be developed to serve specific functions for society and industry that we want them to fulfil and leave new business creations to the market."

Donnie Morrison, the force behind the Lasair and Western Isles teleworking project in Scotland, is also pessimistic about centres. "The bottom line is that telecottages as originally envisaged have now moved on. They were absolutely the right thing to do at the time but could never be economically viable as they were. Now we have commercial companies setting up in rural areas and the better availability of good telecommunications. That means the centres are not an essential part of the equation. For a telecottage to survive it needs to have a commercially-focussed manager with appropriate skills. These are the very people who are now setting up commercial operations and the old telecottage is left to struggle."

But don't be put off if you are determined! According to Bill Murray there are over 700 telecentres in the western world plus rest-of-world figures collected over the Internet by Paddy Moindrot that tot up to 847 cybercafés, 112 multipurpose community telecentres and 557 organisations that "don't quite fit" the usual telecentre description.

Setting up a telecentre

Start by defining your aims. Telecentres can take many different forms and serve a variety of purposes, ranging from community education through economic development to purely commercial ventures. Those who use telecottages include self-employed and employed teleworkers, unemployed people improving their skills and community groups. You need to decide the function of your telecottage and then keep checking that your activities are directed towards that purpose.

Sources of reconditioned PCs

- *Many large computer manufacturers and asset managers now refurbish PCs or take trade-ins including Dell, ICL, Technical Asset Management (www.tam.co.uk) and Frazier International.*

- *The Charities Aid Foundation publishes a directory, Waste Not, listing organisations in need of computers, printers and faxes. Tel: 01732 520000 www.caf.org.uk*

- *Bytes Twice will put you in touch with local community computer re-use projects. Charities, community organisations and schools can apply to receive free PCs but delivery incurs a charge. Tel: 0171 248 0842 www.wastewatch.org.uk*

Source: *Personal Computer World* magazine **www.pcw.co.uk**

Networks and training – the way forward?

The £5m RATIO programme used EU "Objective 5b" funding matched by local and central government funding to set up 40 IT "drop-in" centres in the south-west of England for people seeking information, work and training. Each centre had PCs, videoconferencing, digital satellite reception and email. They were run by volunteer facilitators from a variety of locations including council premises, libraries, village halls and commercial sites. RATIO, co-ordinated by Plymouth University, finished in June 1999 and the centres were left with the problem of how to continue.

Anne Woodhams of Praa Sands explains that the centres were valued for their different approach: "They suited people who aren't happy in a traditional training environment, who preferred individual coaching." Those centres which chose to take over their equipment from Plymouth University were immediately faced with the cost of relicensing the training materials and upgrading them. "Our approach has been to spread our offerings to attract more funding. We are providing family learning, and a dedicated room for people from the travelling community. We've had help from the Pathfinder organisation, a North Devon Trust which supported several of the centres, to apply for further EU funding but that's coming to an end. We still provide access to training in computer literacy (CLAIT) and desktop publishing and general access to PCs is popular but we're still depending on people being prepared to work long hours for little or no reward".

Lindsey Svensson of Okehampton centre says staff found adjustment to the end of RATIO hard. "Previously RATIO picked up running costs such as telecoms bills for Internet access. Our usage was substantial with 14 PCs, and certified courses like CLAIT. We got an extra 12 PCs with funding from the Lottery and the Rural Development Programme, and we relocated to provide better disabled access. But the manager had a high sense of ownership of the project and could not readjust to the reality that we had taken on the running costs. Ninety percent of our clients are on benefit and cannot afford to pay high fees so we have had to restrict Internet access. The software on the PCs is out-of-date and our Pathfinder grant is about to run out. We tried running a cybercafé but found staffing was a problem on our limited resources – if they were good they got commercial jobs and left, and if they weren't, then they weren't the kind of people we wanted either. I have to ask, where is the government funding for Lifelong Learning?"

Geoff Curry from Ilfracombe, who co-ordinated the Pathfinder funds, is more positive. "We are hoping for funding from the government's new University for Industry and its related project the Learning Connection which will be developing tutorial support centres. Our main source of funding at present is the Further Education Funding Council which will be replaced by the new Learning and Skills Councils – they will be focusing on small pieces of training, and not just on certification, which is more appropriate for the IT area. We operate a mix of paid and volunteer staff, and our centre is always full, mainly with people on computer literacy courses. Networks of centres are easier to fund than standalones."

Lloyds TSB funds top £30m

Telecottage start-ups could do worse than to apply to the Lloyds TSB Foundations. There are four foundations, covering England, Wales, Scotland and Northern Ireland. The Foundations receive 1% of Lloyds TSB group's pre-tax profits in lieu of their shareholder dividend. In the year 2000 the Foundations received £31.3 million, making them one of the largest general award-giving organisations in the UK. The Foundations have a programme of small- and medium-sized grants for charitable activities at local, regional and national level. The Foundations for England and Wales also have a new collaborative programme which has a focus on three areas: family support, challenging disadvantage and discrimination, and promoting effectiveness in the voluntary sector.
Tel: 020 7204 5276 or **www.lloydstsbfoundations.org.uk**

Interested parties

The first step is to gather together interested people into a management or steering group. This could be an informal group of like-minded people, or a more formal working group. Try your parish council, chamber of commerce, local politicians and community school. Discuss the services that could be offered, and the premises and equipment that will be needed for the services. Don't forget all the bureaucratic issues – planning, insurance, tax, financial structure. Check that you will have access to a digital telephone exchange, and preferably to ISDN services. Get expert help on the equipment issues.

Visiting a telecottage

Visit an established telecottage. Many hold occasional open days including:

- WREN Telecottage: based at the National Agricultural Centre, Stoneleigh, Warwickshire. This centre is something of a showcase, and is housed in an adapted exhibition building. Open Days are held quarterly for 5 to 15 people, though special visits can be arranged where there is demand. The cost for the half-day is £10 per person including VAT, refreshments, online demonstrations and an information pack, or £35 an hour for a special visit. Casual drop-in visitors are welcome to look around the displays and equipment. Contact Sue Lewis or Jane Berry on 024 7669 6986.

- Moorlands Telecottage: based in school premises in the small village of Warslow, Staffordshire. Users come from a series of villages in the surrounding area, and the telecottage has specialised in developing training materials for teleworkers. Visits are by prior arrangement and cost £30 for up to 10 people. The visit lasts about 90 minutes, and covers what the telecottage does, how it was set up, its training courses and support for the local community and local enterprises. Visits by educational organisations and small community groups are free.

Moorlands Telecottage has branded itself the UK's first telecottage and was responsible for the development of the TCA Teleworking VQ. Contact Simon Brooks on 01298 84336
Email 100135.2516@compuserve.com

- KITE Telecottage near Enniskillen in Northern Ireland provides training, childcare and commercial work for around nineteen staff. KITE likes to have a detailed advance discussion with prospective visitors on what they want to see, which can cover childcare facilities, obtaining European funding, the teleworking operation (which works for US companies using ISDN links), and initiatives to promote US/Northern Ireland trade sponsored by the US State Department. Prior discussion allows the visit to be tailored to visitors' needs. The cost is £50 for up to 10 people, and the tour normally takes just over an hour. The price includes an information pack. Contact Michael McCaffrey 02866 348943 Email s.mccaffrey@btinternet.com

Try contacting a centre in your area using the list and map at the end of this chapter to see whether they would take visitors or offer consultancy on setting up a telecottage. As you are taking up valuable time, remember that you may be charged for a visit.

Market survey

Next, assess the need for the centre by performing a market survey of the locality up to a radius of fifteen miles. Try a questionnaire targeted on individuals working from home, small business and community groups. Assess any similar services in the area. You could combine the market survey phase with an open evening to discuss the idea locally. Contact potential sponsors and relevant local authorities as early as you can. Then prepare a business plan (see Chapter 4, *Getting work*, and the end of this chapter) and examine the available funding sources.

Private funding sources and fundraising

Raising money will involve a search for innovative funding methods. In addition to funding from local and central government and educational institutions, many different sponsors, including equipment manufacturers, telecommunications companies and high street banks, have seen the potential of the telecottage idea. Think about linking up with a local bank to provide meeting rooms for their customers who run businesses from home, or charging local agencies for using the telecottage as their base in the local community. You might also offer to act as a local representative for an office supplies wholesaler.

Try to make sure that your sponsorship idea would create commercial value for the sponsoring company. An equipment dealer may consider a telecottage an excellent place to display equipment so that it can be seen and used by potential customers. A large company which is laying off staff may wish to balance this by helping to create a local service that can train former employees in new skills, and support new businesses. They may

European funding programmes

Richard Warren of training telecentre Steppingstones has kindly provided the following guidance:

"The days when merely mentioning telework was enough to guarantee funding from the European Commission are over. Individual teleworkers have little realistic chance of accessing research funds in their own right unless they are experts in a particular field. For these specialists, information and leads are given on the Commission's Cordis website which lists tenders and requests for experts, and provides a partner-finding database.

For telecentres the picture is more rosy. The Lisbon Accord refers to the need to encourage Europe-wide networking between these centres and looks forward to having such effective systems in place by the end of 2002 although there are no hard proposals yet. Keep an eye on Cordis. It is never to early to think about partnerships and projects – EU expansion also means there should be exciting possibilities for work helping Eastern European countries to catch up.

Telecentres should check out some areas of the current 5th Framework R&D programme such as "Quality of Life and Management of Living Resources", "User Friendly Information Society" and "Improving human research potential". Have a clear idea of what you want to do and why you want to do it before you start searching. If your project has some benefit to Europe, and can be described in terms reflecting at least one of the "key action areas" and you have the skills and support to make it work then you should be able to obtain European support. Look at the list of officials on the website, select the one whose area most closely covers your ideas and send him or her a short email – nothing ventured, nothing gained...

Education and training activities are mainly supported through the European Social Fund and funding is usually channelled through local and national government agencies or chambers of commerce – do some research on the situation in your area. There will be more than one agency and each will have its own set of priorities so if your first contact is unsuccessful don't give up. Be aware that these agencies will probably "take a cut" from your funding. Depending on your location you may be able to get from 45–90% of the costs of the training programme you want to run. The remaining amount (10–55%) is called match funding, and can be real cash (from a donor or local government) or "in kind" such as depreciation of equipment, or contributions from a local employer in terms of employee time lost whil studying. It is vital that you have good record-keeping systems in place – the paperwork involved can be horrendous."

Cordis: **www.cordis.lu**
European Commission Information site: **http://europa.eu.int**
European Training (Eastern Europe) site: **www.etf.eu.int**

also have redundant equipment. One Irish telecottage persuaded a bank that was closing a rural branch to loan the premises to them.

Because telecottages often use software for training, they may be entitled to educational discounts on software prices. Companies may be prepared to offload equipment that is obsolete for their uses, and which has low secondhand value. Such equipment is often perfectly functional for telecottage use.

A subscription scheme can be designed to raise money for capital equipment. Once the money has been raised and the equipment bought, the subscription is redeemable against a number of hours of free use of the equipment.

Draws, raffles and lotteries are old stalwarts for the fundraiser. Try to add a twist to the prizes to gain interest – for example, games that children can play on the telecottage computers, business or personal stationery to be designed by the telecottage for the winner and so on.

If you have written a credible business plan and cashflow forecast, don't be frightened to approach your local high street bank. It may be prepared to offer cheaper banking services, or loans, or suggest other sources of funding. Keep in contact with government business support agencies.

Some telecottages think about using professional consultants to find funding for their startups. Before taking any such step, it is worth consulting a checklist produced by the Forum for Private Business which warns against consultancies which claim 100% accuracy or claim special relationships with government. Much of the information offered by consultants may be available free from various sources including economic development agencies. Contact FPB on 01565 634 467.

The National Lottery Charities Board (NLCB)

Any organisation set up for charitable, philanthropic or benevolent purposes is eligible to apply for national lottery funding. Grants cannot be given to individuals. Applications can be made for capital or revenue funding. The programmes for lottery applications are under constant review and in Summer 2000 they are focussed on "community involvement" and "poverty and disadvantage". A straightforward application for the establishment of a telecentre is unlikely to score highly without direct attention to the aim of the NLCB programme and should included a distinct project addressing at least one of the following issues: provision of training, providing a service for those otherwise disadvantaged, or training opportunities. Guidance on completing forms can often be obtained from charity support organisations such as CVS or local councils. To get an application pack, phone 0845 7919191.

John Lakeman, a former director of the TCA and former assessor for lottery funding, points out that because bids exceed available funds, you must put in a high quality bid that satisfies strict criteria. Consider your application in the light of:

- how well-planned and financially sound a proposed project is;
- the value for money it offers;
- whether there is adequate management and staffing;
- whether it includes an appropriate commitment to equal opportunities;
- the level of user involvement and encouragement of community participation;
- plans for the project's future survival, or an exit strategy once lottery funding expires if the funding is requested for more than one year.

Other state support

The key is to talk to movers and shakers in the area and get an idea of which schemes are available to help fund some of the centre's activities. There seems to be a trend of better success in achieving support for networks of centres (*eg* Hereford and Worcester, Powys, Shropshire), rather than centres trying to "go it alone". Some local councils in geographically isolated areas have been very supportive of telecentres, which can also act as support centres for the council's economic development strategies. Council-supported activities may have access to funding from the Single Regeneration Budget (SRB). Chambers of commerce may also be helpful where the centre plans to deliver business support.

In Britain, the Training and Enterprise Councils (TECs or LECs in Scotland) which are responsible for training workers, have used telecentres as a platform to deliver TEC services to rural areas. This may change as they convert to become "Learning and Skills Councils" during 2000. FÁS and the VECs provide similar services in Ireland.

There are a number of EU schemes which can provide funds to telecentres that deliver specific training services. Obtaining EC funds requires specialist help – for example from County Council economic development departments. The EU is interested in many areas of teleworking and related technologies (usually grouped together under the terms such as "telematics" or "the information society").

A scheme developed by the Department for Education and Employment is very much in the ethos of telecottages – "The Information and Communications Technologies (ICT) Learning Centres Initiative" is a new programme designed to help bridge the gap between those in society who have access to ICT and those who do not. The aim is to establish around 700 centres across England to provide access to ICTs and learning for disadvantaged communities. For more information Tel: 0845 6022 260 or **see www.dfee.gov.uk/ict-learning-centres**. The University for Industry (UfI) initiative, due to launch in Autumn 2000 and also known as Learndirect, may provide some funding opportunities (see **www.ufiltd.co.uk**). Further Education colleges and universities may also be involved in outreach or distance learning plans which can include telecentre activities.

The Regional Development Agencies have taken over some of the grant schemes from the old Rural Development Commission (now replaced by The Countryside Agency). These include small business grants, redundant building grants and job creation schemes. The Countryside Agency can provide assistance for services that might form part of your plan, such as setting up a shop, post office or village hall. A list of RDAs is on the web at **www.local-regions.detr.gov.uk/rda/info/index.htm**. One such is Yorkshire Forward (**www.yorkshire-forward.com**). For more contact details call the Department of Environment, Transport and the Regions Tel: 020 7944 3000.

Rural Community Councils exist in England, with sister organisations in Wales, Scotland and Northern Ireland. RCCs work at parish council level to assist community development. Some RCCs have become involved in telecentre projects. For details of your local RCC, contact ACRE (the Association of RCCs) Tel: 01285 653477.

Highlands and Islands Enterprise, in conjunction with BT, has sponsored six telecottages. The Welsh Development Agency and the Development Board for Rural Wales have also supported telecottages. The Department of National Heritage has two schemes that could be used by community groups wishing to find out about funding a telecentre – the Local Grants scheme, which helps groups to learn from each other through study visits, and the Support Grants Scheme, which helps large voluntary and community organisations to support smaller groups.

Yortel – a teleworking pilot action for Yorkshire and Humberside

Yortel is a project led by Calderdale and Kirklees TEC, working with the TCA and funded by Compris Adapt, a European Social Fund initiative which is part of the RISI (Regional Information Society Initiative). The project is supported by TECs around the Yorkshire/Humberside areas and the regional TUC, and there is a working group which includes representation from business, education and trade unions.

Yortel was launched in 1999 and is raising awareness about teleworking through events held in partnership with local business groups. Yortel is also running a training programme that has put 25 people through the ECDL (see Chapter 12, *Training for teleworkers*) as well as some NVQ modules at Dewsbury College. In addition there is a research project investigating suitable structures for support of freelance teleworkers. As a result of response to the awareness-raising events, a forum of interest has been created, including a web-based forum and an e-zine. The project will end in June 2000 – further information at **www.tca.org.uk**.

Telecottages and telecentres
March 2000

To be included on this list, updated bimonthly in *Teleworker* magazine, a telecentre must offer public access to IT equipment, provide training facilities, and supply services to assist other businesses. The telecentre must also be a paid-up member of the TCA. The location information indicates the nearest post town to the telecottage. However, telecentres come in many different flavours, so, to get exact details of services, please telephone the telecottage in question. To add to this listing or make a correction contact Alan Denbigh (Tel: 01453 834 874, Fax: 01453 836 174, Email: info@tca.org.uk). To see an updated version, check out **www.tca.org.uk**.

1 Hyfforddiant Ceredigion Training
2 Sprint Telecottage
3 Antur Tanat Cain Llangedwyn
4 Welshpool Telecottage
5 Antur Teifi
6 BOON Ltd.
7 Dereham Digital Centre
8 Telework Northampton
9 Connemara West
10 Fakenham Telecottage Services
11 Daily Information
12 Telelink
13 Vocational Training Project (West Lothian)
14 NewComm UK Ltd
15 East Clare Telecottage
16 St Columb RATIO Centre
17 Eccles House Telebusiness Centre
18 Praa Sands RATIO Centre
19 Highland Business Networks
20 Alford IT
21 Instant Search
22 Ecom Business Learning Centre
23 Mizen Telecottage
24 CITU Belfast
25 Llanbadarn Fynydd Telecentre
26 Pathfinder Open Access Centre
27 Wingrave Telecottage
28 Strathcarron Centre
29 Adur Resource Centre
30 Bournemouth IT Services
31 Colne Valley Trust
32 Comharchumann Chléire Teo.
33 Mass Mitec
34 GTI
35 Blueprint Business Centre
36 Tarbert Community Teleservice Centre
37 Isles Telecroft
38 Business Space Ltd
39 Stornoway Telecentre
40 Hereford & Worcester Resource Centres
41 The Lovelace Centre
42 Moorlands Telecottage
43 PATCH, Dublin
44 North Tyne Telecottage
45 The Westmorland Business Centre
46 Sennybridge Resource Centre
47 Inishowen Technology Centre
48 SIMTRA Aberaeron
49 SIMTRA Crymych
50 SIMTRA Fishguard
51 SIMTRA Llandeilo
52 SIMTRA Narberth
53 SIMTRA Saundersfoot
54 SIMTRA St Davids
55 SIMTRA Tregaron
56 Firth and Mossbank Community House
57 Tele Teach
58 The Irthing Telecentre
59 Southwater Business Resource Centre
60 WREN Telecottage
61 Wolds Enterprise Bureau
62 Services to Business
63 Upper Nithsdale Community Initiative
64 Sitca Scoraig
65 Rhyader Telecottage
66 New College Durham
67 Enterprise Tamar
68 Midhurst Resource Centre Ltd
69 CROW Ltd
70 Manchester Womens EVH
71 Northern Rural Training
72 Ilkley Telecottage
73 Innovative Work Solutions
74 Gaundle Teleworking Cottage
75 Dee Valley Telebureau Ltd
76 Machars Action
77 Kington Connected Community Co.
78 Daventry Tertiary College
79 TheColour Shop
80 Caia Park Partnership
81 Network Personnel Ltd
82 Longton Telecottage
83 Naver Teleservice Centre
84 Clarendon College
85 Skills Station
86 Newport Advanced Teleservices
87 Flexit
88 Lingfield Telecottage
89 U-Compute
90 Clydesdale Telecentre
91 Kinawley Integrated Teleworking Enterprise (K.I.T.E.)
92 Moira Telecottage
93 Chumleigh Resource Centre
94 Mevagissey Telecottage
95 Strathyre IT Centre
96 Rothbury Community IT Centre
97 York Telecottage
98 W.C.E.I.R.D.
99 Paqua Accountants
100 Leek Telecottage
101 Voluntary Action Barra
102 The AWITT Group
103 Sedley IT Centre
104 Honeybun Secretarial Services
105 RNIB Teleworkers
106 Skyedat Services
107 Kingsfield Centre
108 Resource Solutions Telecentre
109 Varitech Telecentre
110 Castell-y-Dail Telecottage
111 Romney Resource 2000 Ltd
112 Computer Advisory Services
113 Basford Hall CFE
114 Ewart Library Cybercentre
115 Llanwrtyd Wells Telecottage
116 Slamannan IT Centre
117 Barnham Telecottage
118 Support Shop
119 Project Cosmic
120 Castle Douglas Community IT Centre
121 Selsey Regeneration
122 Beara Community School
123 Business Focus
124 Webtel Telecentre
125 SPIC
126 Cennin Ltd
127 Bude Business Centre
128 Tecniche
129 Phoenix Telecentre
130 Action for Blind People

CENTRES FOR TELEWORKING

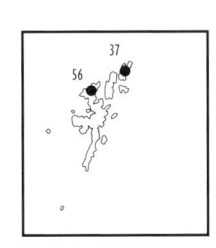

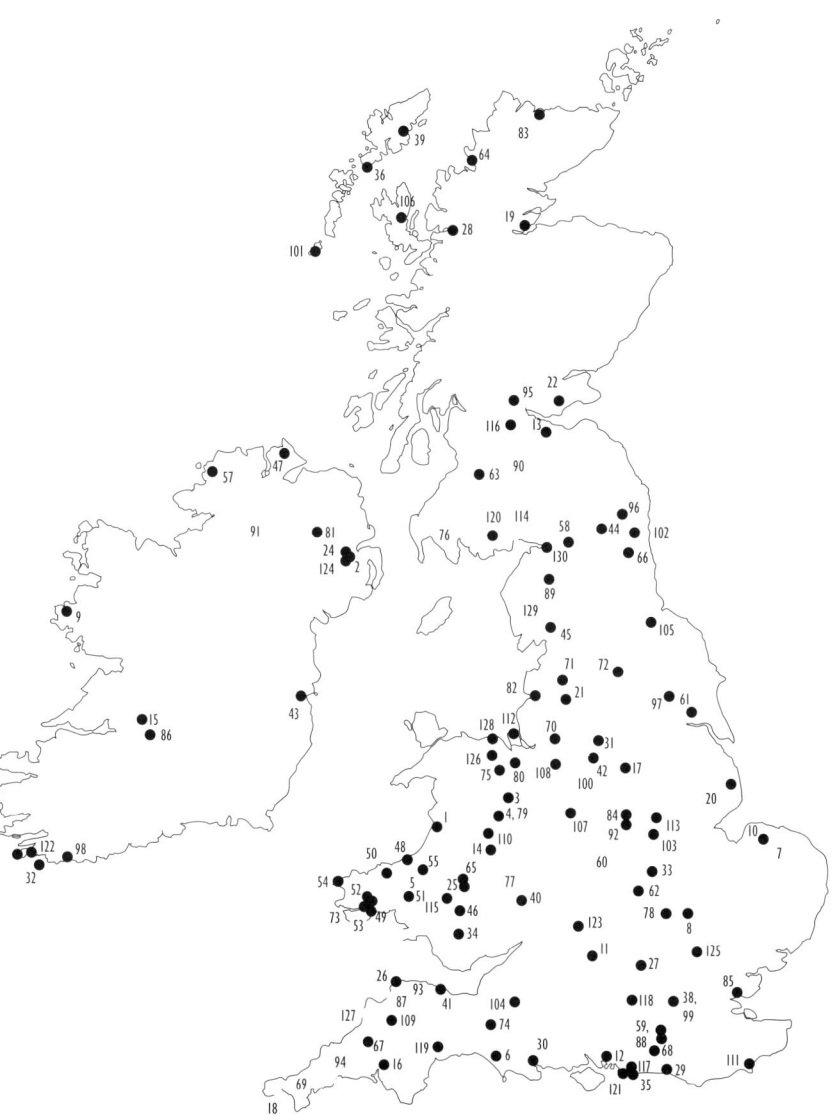

191

Telecottage cashflow: year 1

	Start	Jun	Jul	Aug	Sept	Oct	Nov	Dec	Jan	Feb	Mar	Apr	May	Total
INCOME														
Grant or Capital	10000													10000
Sales														
Copying/binding		72	96	108	120	144	144	72	168	192	240	240	240	1836
Fax/messaging		80	125	125	200	200	250	250	250	300	300	300	300	2680
Equipt/Hot Desk Hire		20	30	30	100	100	100	100	100	150	150	200	200	1280
Commercial training			350		525	700	875	175	875	1050	1225	1225	1225	8225
Community training		250	250	250	500	500	500		250	500	500	500	500	4500
Internet access		50	80	80	120	120	200	200	120	120	120	200	200	1610
Telework		0	0	750	750	750	750	750	750	750	750	750	750	7500
Publications		50	50	80	80	60	50	50	30	30	30	50	50	610
Room hire			150	150	300	375	375	300	375	375	375	375	375	3525
Business Services		100	100	200	400	400	600	400	400	600	700	800	800	5500
Retail sales		50	100	150	300	400	600	700	500	700	850	1000	1250	6600
Total	10000	672	1331	1923	3395	3749	4444	2997	3818	4767	5240	5640	5890	53866
EXPENDITURE														
Retail sales cost	1000	33	65	500	195	260	725	455	325	455	552.5	650	813	6027.5
Wages														
Manager/Trainer		1000	1000	1250	1250	1250	1250	1250	1250	1250	1250	1250	1250	14500
Assistant										400	400	400	400	1600
Teleworkers				600	600	600	600	600	600	600	600	600	600	6000
Freelance Trainer			100		200	400	500		500	600	650	650	650	4250
Support worker										100	100	100	100	400
Staff costs		200	200	250	250	250	250	250	250	350	350	350	350	3300
Overheads														
Rent/Rates		500	500	500	500	500	500	500	500	500	500	500	500	6000
Light/heat/power		100	100	100	100	100	100	100	100	100	100	100	100	1200
Insurance		75	75	75	75	75	75	75	75	75	75	75	75	900
Promotion	850	120			250		120		100	80	80	80	80	1760
Telephone	137			300			425			475			475	1812
Stationery	300				400			400				400		1500
Subscriptions		170												170
Postage	50	25	25	25	25	25	25	25	25	25	25	25	25	350
Copier/fax Lease		75	75	75	75	75	75	75	75	75	75	75	75	900
Consumables/software	700	30	30	30	45	45	45	45	50	50	50	80	80	1280
Repairs/servicing														0
Premises fitting	6000													6000
Equipment lease		260	260	260	260	260	260	260	260	260	260	260	260	3120
Bank charges/fees		20	50	50	50	50	50	50	50	50	50	50	50	570
														61640
TOTAL	9037	2608	2480	4015	4275	3890	5000	4085	4160	5445	5117.5	5645	5883	61640
Opening balance	0	963	-973	-2122	-4214	-5094	-5235	-5791	-6879	-7221	-7899	-7776.5		-7781.5
Plus/minus		-1936	-1149	-2092	-880	-141	-556	-1088	-342	-678	122.5	-5	7	
Closing balance	963	-973	-2122	-4214	-5094	-5235	-5791	-6879	-7221	-7899	-7776.5	-7781.5		-7774.5

Notes: This cashflow is for illustrative purposes only. Adapt based on local conditions, service offered and market research. The centre begins to break even by end of year one if sales targets are reached; overdraft should be cleared by end of year two — realistically this level of activity would need considerable pre-start promotion and contract development. It's assumed another body supplies overseeing/senior management function. Alternatively, in a self-employed situation the manager's wages would be drawings against profit and would be half that shown to avoid overdraft. For a community initiative the deficit shown might be carried by a sponsoring organisation. Lease payments are for fax/copier on 3 year lease. Service contract and repairs begin in year 2. Equipment leasing based on £8000 worth over 3 years (say 8 PCs with software £6,400 plus printers/scanner). Rent/rates reflect a property big enough for multiple activities including room hire.

Bibliography

Setting up an IT Centre in a Village Hall *Date:* 2000
Source: Acre Tel: 01285 653477

The Wired Habitat *Date:* 1999
Authors: Jan Simmons and Dot Gavin
Source: Morrison House Inc. Old Hereford Road, Mt Evelyn 3796, Australia
Email: mhouse@eisa.net.au Web: www.vicnet.net.au/~morrison

Community Economics *Date:* 1995
Source: The New Economics Foundation, Tel: 0171 377 5696

Survey of Telecottage Activity and Finance *Date:* 1995
Authors: Small World Connections with support from the Telecottage Association
Source: Bill Murray, Small World Connections, Tel: 0161 4456 0630.

Sussex Telecentre Network *Date:* 1995
Authors: Sussex Rural Community Council
Source: Sussex Rural Community Council, 212 High Street, Lewes, East Sussex BN7 2NH, Tel: 01273 473422 Ref: ISBN 1 873850 13 1

**Telecottages: How the Usage of Information Technology
can counter Rural Disadvantages** *Date:* 1995
Author: Tatjana Gosau, MA in European Business Administration
Source: University of Northumbria

Marketing Telecottages and Teleworking *Date:* 1992
Author: Various
Source: TCA/ACRE, Somerford Court, Somerford Road, Cirencester, Glos GL7 1TW

Telecottages: the UK Experience *Date:* 1992
Author: Various
Source: TCA/ACRE, Somerford Court, Somerford Road, Cirencester Glos GL7 1TW

**Telecommuting Centers and Related Concepts:
A Review of Practice** *Date:* 1994
Authors: Michael Bagley, Jill Mannering, Patricia Mokhtarian
Source: Institute of Transportation Studies, University of California, Davis, California 95616 Ref: ISBN UCD-ITS-RR-94-4

Telecottages, Teleworking and Telelearning *Date:* 1994
Author: Lilian Holloway
Source: Teldok, Sweden, Tel: +46-8-23 00 00 Fax +46-8-10 13 27

Final Report on the Evaluation of Community Teleservice *Date:* 1993
Centres in the Highlands and Islands
Authors: John Bryden, Stuart Black, Frank Rennie
Source: The Arkleton Trust, Coulnakyle, Nethy Bridge, Inverness Tel: 01479 821 393, Fax: 01479 821 441 Ref: 0 90 6724 41 4

Marketing Telecottages and Teleworking Date: 1993
Author: ACRE/Telecottage Association
Source: ACRE, Somerford Court, Somerford Rd, Cirencester, GL7 1TW
Ref: ISBN 1 871157 33 1

Contacts

Partners in the Countryside is a non-profit-making organisation established to promote a business approach to rural regeneration. The organisation provides information about rural initiatives and uses its sponsor's funds to support a range of rural projects. Contact Anne Harris Tel: 01273 205200 Fax: 01273 205220 Email: info@pitc.org.uk

Australian Rural Telecentres Association. In 1993, the Australian government awarded AUS$2.7 million for the establishment of telecentres nationwide. The resulting network has produced a best-practice guide released in 1997. Those located in Western Australia are still government-supported and the support body has some literature packs available as well as good information on its website **www.telecentres.wa.gov.au/maiin/telest.htm**

The Community Investment Fund created by English Partnerships is for projects from priority areas such as rural development blackspots, former coalfield areas, city challenge areas and so on. Grants of between £10,000 and £100,000 in value are possible and can be for capital works to buildings or for revenue projects that are expected to produce social and economic benefits. Contact 020 7976 7070.

Small World Connections Tel: 0161 445 0603.
Web: **www.smallworldconnections.com**

ACRE – Action With Communities in Rural England. ACRE can put you in touch with your local rural community council who may know of other schemes or funding awards in the area. Tel: 01285 653477 Email: acre@acre.org.uk
Web: **www.acreciro.demon.co.uk**
WCVA – Wales Council for Voluntary Action Tel: 029 2085 5100
Email: enquiries"wcva.org.uk Web: **www.wcva.org.uk**
SCVO – Scottish Council for Voluntary Organisations Tel: 0131 556 3882
Email: enquiries@scvo.org.uk Web: **www.scvo.org.uk**
NCVO – National Council for Voluntary Organisations (UK-wide) Tel: 020 7713 6161
Web: **www.ncvo-vol.org.uk**
NIAA – Northern Informatics Application Agency – aims to improve communications and information access in the Northern area including Northumberland, Tyne & Wear, Cumbria, County Durham and Cleveland. Tel: 0191 528 0039
Web: **www.niaa.org.uk**

National Lottery website with information on obtaining funding – **www.nlcb.org.uk**

Telweb is a European project funded by the ADAPT programme and set up to link Telecentres for work and information. Its website has maps of European telecentre locations. Web: www.telweb.org

Nevada Telecommunities project: **http://ctr.cstp.umkc.edu/nevada**

For details of other regional funding bodies, also see the Bibliography to Chapter 4, *Getting work*.

Staying safe and legal

This section is intended for all those involved in teleworking – employers, employed and self-employed. Some of the legislation that affects teleworkers, such as that covering business rates, is a bit of a grey area. Elsewhere, a bit of interpretation is required – for example, does a home office risk assessment require an independent home visit, or can a suitably trained teleworker self-certify? In general, the advice has to be to inform yourself and use your common sense – few authorities want the headache of regulating home offices. Get yourself a good accountant and solicitor, and ask for advice about anything you're not sure of, either from your advisers or from the relevant authorities. If you encounter a problem that is not easily solved, let the TCA know about it so that we can try to resolve the issue and warn others who may be affected.

Health and safety

Health and safety authorities have wide powers of inspection and enforcement, and all HSE legislation includes workplaces in the home. However, in reality the HSE does not have any register of teleworkers, or the resources for a large number of inspections. There is nothing in health and safety law that prevents working alone at home provided that it does not affect the worker's health and safety. Strictly speaking, all workplaces, including those in the home, should have an approved safety statement.

Some may feel the 1974 Health and Safety at Work Act means that teleworker's employers have less onerous duties as they cannot be deemed responsible for the safety of an employee's home. However, any equipment used by the employee in the course of their employment should be deemed safe by the employer. In general it is advisable that the employer should provide the teleworker with all equipment and ensure that the equipment is inspected and checked on a regular basis, and in accordance with the company's on-site practice. Unfortunately this is not happening in practice. A 1999 web-based survey by infrastructure specialists Sulzer of 362 homeworkers and 123 managers found that only 63% received health and safety advice when they started to work at home. Just under half received no advice, assistance or money to assist with remote working. Their working conditions at home were less than ideal – 30% were working in part of a living room and 5% in the kitchen (**www.si-cbx.com**).

In order to reduce risk of RSI or other injuries due to poor work furniture, the employer is also advised to supply all working furniture. The main relevant law to teleworkers is the Display Screen Directive 90/270/EEC which requires:

- clear and stable screen, bright and free from glare, which should swivel and tilt easily

- adequate arrangement of keyboard characters, adjustable keyboard with sufficient space to support the hands and arms of the user
- sufficient user space to change positions and vary movements. Work desk sufficiently large, document holder adjustable and stable
- satisfactory lighting conditions
- minimised glare and reflection at the workstation, and minimisation of radiation levels
- work chair adjustable in height including the back rest
- a foot rest available if required
- environmental factors should be minimised including effects of reflection/glare, noise, heat and humidity.

Employers should put in place a system for their teleworkers to report accidents or hazards, as there would be in a conventional workplace. Practical experience within the TCA suggests that the following are also often problems:

- insufficient power sockets leading to over-use of extension leads, trailing cables and adaptors. Home offices may need rewiring for more sockets – get your installation checked by an electrician
- shelves situated inconveniently so that when heavy files are frequently placed and replaced there is risk of stress on the spine and overbalancing
- inadequate office chairs and tables which are not the appropriate height or adjustability for long periods of work
- reading glasses not correct prescription for close work. Anyone working with computers should have their eyes tested, and the optician should be informed of the computer work
- lighting – spotlights and anglepoises are generally less tiring than fluorescents in small spaces. Light levels should be about 350 lm m^{-2}. Screens should be positioned at right angles to windows. Blinds to prevent sunlight making screens hard to read should be installed where needed
- temperatures should be as near as possible to 18.5 degrees centigrade. Small home offices can easily overheat because IT equipment generates heat – temperatures may become uncomfortably hot in summer unless adequate ventilation can be provided
- adequate ventilation is also important where equipment such as laser printers may give off ozone or other fumes
- the use of IT equipment usually requires an additional two power outlets, and one or two telecoms sockets. Safely stowing cabling is important
- electrical equipment needs to be checked for safety (*eg* all cable grips in place, no burn marks on plugs or cracked sockets)

Mobile phone use in cars to be banned?

The British government is becoming ever more forceful in warning drivers against using mobile phones except where they have pulled over. Although so far the government has resisted creating a specific offence, companies may wish to ensure their employees are given instructions on safe use of mobiles.

Research from the Transport Research Laboratory in 1998 showed that drivers using mobile phones show the same lack of control as motorists who have drunk the legal maximum – and the risk is the same for hands free phones. John Howard of ROSPA commented: "A passenger will shut up if you get into a difficult situation or understand why the driver has broken off the conversation. But if you are talking to head office or to a client there is a natural inclination to continue the conversation. There is research to show that people try to drive through much narrower gaps when they are on the telephone than they would normally."

Present legislation can fine drivers up to £2,500 plus endorsements for careless driving, and in extreme cases could impose two years' imprisonment, unlimited fines and disqualification.

- psychologically, most teleworkers prefer to be situated so that they can see out of a window if possible, although it is important to avoid problems with glare and reflection on computer screens.

Prolonged computer work can also cause discomfort and fatigue to the back, shoulders, neck, head, eyes, buttocks, legs and wrists. Maintaining posture in a static position also causes blood flow to the muscles to be restricted. Ergonomics expert Éilis Duggan of Workright Consultants advises the following guidelines to maintaining a comfortable and efficient work posture:

- feet should be flat on the floor with knees bent at 90° or 100° angle;
- the front edge of the chair seat should not be touching the back of the knee or press into the underside of the thigh as increased pressure on the back of the leg may lead to numbness, fatigue or knee swelling;
- The chair seat should be able to tilt forward slightly by 5–15° to lift your hips so they are slightly higher than your knees;
- the chair seat to chair back angle should be slightly backwards (10–20°). Try to maintain contact between your own back and that of the chair;
- the document being typed should be placed by the screen at the same distance and height, and as close as possible;
- Elbows should be at a 90° angle and shoulders relaxed and dropped;
- change body position frequently, moving feet up and down, adjusting chair and/or keyboard height;

- organise work so that you can take "mini-breaks" to stretch muscles;
- exercise regularly and eat well.

Ian Fletcher-Price of ergonomic office suppliers Posturite UK advises: "The minimum requirement for a chair is one with a five-star base, swivel action, gas height adjustment and a tilt mechanism for the seat. The chair back must also be height-adjustable to support your lower back. If you are constantly looking between your source material and the computer screen, a document holder avoids repetitive neck motions and constant refocusing of the eyes which can lead to headaches.

Employers with more than five workers have a legal requirement to carry out a conventional health and safety workspace risk assessment on teleworker's home offices. This involves:

1. Identifying hazards that may cause harm, however small (such as keeping potentially harmful substances out of children's reach)
2. Deciding who might be harmed and how (*eg* the homeworker, members of the household, visitors)
3. Assessing the risks and taking appropriate action (*eg* deciding what steps must be taken to eliminate or reduce the identified risks)
4. Recording the findings – what steps have been taken to reduce or eliminate risks? Inform the homeworker, or anyone else affected by the work, of the findings
5. Check the risks from time to time and take steps if needed, especially if there is a change in working procedures.

Union believes laptops may damage your health

Britain's biggest union UNISON carried out a survey of nearly 500 careers advisors and found some worrying statistics concerning laptop users

- *Eyestrain reported by 68%*
- *Headaches and/or back pain and/or neck pain contracted by around 60%*
- *Around 55% found laptops heavy and complained of arm pains*
- *Just under half were concerned about risks of assault while carrying the laptop.*

Keith Sonnet of UNISON commented that many of the reports are the same as for any computer equipment, but that the risks may be greater for laptops because users find it more difficult to get into a comfortable working position. He even called for laptops to be eliminated from the workplace and sent a copy of the survey to the Health and Safety Executive.

Headset research indicates health benefits

Research commissioned by headset manufacturer Plantronics indicates risks of health problems from non-headset telephone use if you use a telephone for more than two hours a day.

The research was detailed but small sample. A team from Surrey University surveyed 26 workers from a variety of occupational groups (legal, secretarial, computer support, PA, financial and administration) analysing posture and health problems followed by a cross-over study where the participants used headsets.

Nearly two-thirds rarely or never had a headache when using the headset compared to 65% sometimes or frequently using a standard handset – a reduction of 27% overall. Headset use also reduced neck pains by 31%, lower-back pain by 16% and upper-back pain by 9%.

The Chartered Society of Physiotherapy reports an increasingly common form of repetitive strain injury (RSI) – telephonitis, caused by wedging the telephone between head and shoulder. Research by the Californian Institute for Treatment and Prevention of Repetitive Motion Injuries warns that anyone combining telephone calls with other tasks can increase neck and shoulder muscle tension by up to 41%.

The Health and Safety Executive produces a booklet on safety for homeworkers at **www.hse.gov.uk/hsehome.htm/pubns/homeindx.htm**. The Institute of Occupational Health and Safety has an excellent datasheet including a telework premises assessment form on its website, stressing the importance of adequate training and of regular reassessment of the risks at **www.iosh.co.uk/inform/datasheet/telework.html**. Some consultancy firms, such as Mouchel, which has a nationwide team of experienced advisors, will carry out health and safety checks on homeworker premises on behalf of employers.

Planning and building regulations

Without doubt, setting up a home office constitutes a "change of use" in strict planning terms. However, as far as planning departments are concerned, the average teleworker is unlikely to require planning permission, particularly if they are not creating a nuisance to neighbours. Surrey County Council provides the following advice to its own teleworking staff: "Teleworking at or from home does not represent a significant change of use of a building likely to cause a nuisance or hazard to your neighbours. Unless you intend to make structural alterations to accommodate your working area, or extra noise, pollution *etc* is generated because you are working at/from home, there is no requirement for planning permission." Some other councils differ on whether home offices constitute a "material" or "ancillary" change of use (*ie* turning an outhouse into a garage and car repair workshop is rather more material than putting a computer into a spare bedroom). Material changes of use require permission; ancillary changes or temporary changes probably don't.

Decisions on whether the change of use is "material" are based on whether it will cause increased traffic, changes to the visible appearance of the property, nuisance such as noise or smells, or unsocial working hours. Unfortunately some local authorities have not yet taken into account that teleworking is a form of homeworking which reduces traffic and generally involves no alterations other than provision of electrical sockets and telephone lines. Oldham Borough Council, in contrast, recognises teleworking formally in its planning guidelines, and regards home offices as ancillary changes of use. The Oldham document is available to other planning authorities, who can use it as a blueprint for their own guidelines if they wish. Babergh District Council in Suffolk prepared its own leaflet *Working from Home – balancing the issues* because "we often get asked questions about homeworking and we are aware that there are people who don't really want to ask the question".

The Department of Transport issued guidelines in 1994 which request local authorities to encourage teleworking. The document, *Planning Policy Guidance 13* (PPG13), is currently under revision (a draft can be viewed at **www.planning.detr.gov.uk/consult/ppg13/02.htm**) and contains recommendations for local authorities to "take a flexible approach to the use of residential properties for homeworking, consistent with the need to protect the residential environment for neighbouring development". In Ireland the Department of the Environment recently issued the following guidance:

"1. Teleworking/telecommuting from home (either part-time or full-time where all that is involved is a computer terminal). In relation to teleworking, it would be difficult to argue that there is any material change of use here and accordingly it would not be an issue from a planning point of view.

2. Home as an office with staff and dedicated space for use. This is quite a different concept and would involve a material change of use and would consequently come within the scope of the planning code."

Building a workspace

If the establishment of the home office involves any building work, such as conversion of a loft space, there are strict building regulations which must be adhered to, mainly relating to means of escape in case of fire. Loft ladders and space-saver stairs are not favoured, according to Paul Kalbskopf, building control officer at Stroud District Council, because they require familiarity of use for safe passage. Roof lights should also act as a means of escape, so that you could get out or a fire officer could get in if necessary. You may also need to upgrade the floor between the loft and the rest of the house to give half an hour of fire resistance. Kalbskopf advises contacting an architect, and then approaching building control and

When teleworking upsets the neighbours... victims of success

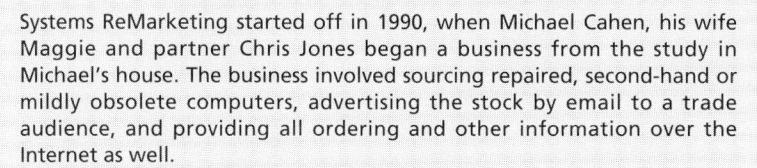

Systems ReMarketing started off in 1990, when Michael Cahen, his wife Maggie and partner Chris Jones began a business from the study in Michael's house. The business involved sourcing repaired, second-hand or mildly obsolete computers, advertising the stock by email to a trade audience, and providing all ordering and other information over the Internet as well.

"Our biggest competitor at the time employed almost 200 people and couldn't provide the same level of service. By keeping the distribution costs to an absolute minimum, the business grew very rapidly. Before long, the team of three had grown to six. The atmosphere was great. The house overlooks a golf course, the alfresco lunches, the odd bottle of wine and a very civilised working environment suited almost everyone", Michael explains.

Except the neighbours. Although the bulk of the warehousing and despatch was done from a different site, a few spares were kept at Michael's house for emergencies, and were collected by courier companies for delivery to customers. One of the neighbours in Michael's quiet, residential cul-de-sac complained to the council that a business was being run from a residential address. Following an unannounced visit from the council, SRM was threatened with an enforcement order unless the business moved or ceased trading. A planning application was made and rejected. Michael's wife Maggie was concerned about bad relations with the neighbours. If the planning application had succeeded, the cost of partial business rating would have been considerable. In the end, a small office was rented in Marlow, and the centre of the business moved there, with the Surrey office becoming a remote site.

planning departments for advice before starting work.

Another alternative to loft conversion which has been successfully used by a number of teleworkers is imported timber cabins from Scandinavia – if you have sufficient garden space to spare. These buildings are warm, well insulated and long-lasting – as a rough guide, a 12ft square cabin including electrical fittings and decoration, with a minimum of four inches of insulation will cost around £5,000.

Financial implications for your home

If you classify part of your house for business purposes, the "work" part of the house is potentially liable for Capital Gains Tax, although as the first £7,100 of any capital gain each year is exempt, it is unlikely to be a major concern for most teleworkers. Perhaps more worrying is the possibility that your local authority may try to levy business rates on the "work" part of the house on top of normal Council Tax charges (see pages 203–4). Other problems could include business rates being charged for gas and electricity, and the possibility of higher insurance charges. However, the Inland

Revenue says that it treats tax information as confidential and does not pass on information to other public bodies, so these risks may appear more worrying than they actually are.

Anyone moving to teleworking will need to notify their mortgage provider if they have a mortgage, particularly if they are also moving into self-employment. A few building societies do offer packages with a built-in payment holiday or the option to reduce payments for a period of time. Those which don't would rather discuss the situation with you now than end up with a repossession on their hands...

One company, Legal and General, have recently launched a new mortgage package aimed at the self-employed which includes a variable rate guaranteed not to exceed 1.5% over base rate, the option for payment 'holidays' and additional payment and reborrowing facilities. The company stresses that it is more interested in ability to make regular payments than in standard tax accounts required by most mortgage companies, but this mortgage is only available to existing mortgage-holders.

Another, the Ecological Building Society, specialises in providing loans for environmentally-friendly premises. According to Chairman Gus Smith, "the question we ask is: Does it fulfill one or more of the following criteria for lending? Does it contribute to 1) the saving of energy and non-renewable resources 2) preservation of buildings and communities or 3) the promotion of self-sufficiency and the most ecological use of land." EBS looks favourably on environmentally friendly ways of working – however, if the business use of the building exceeds 40%, then semi-commercial rates rather than domestic ones are charged.

Restrictive covenants

"Some properties, particularly estate houses and flats, may be subject to covenants which could in theory restrict working from home. The origin of these covenants is usually a condition put in place by a vendor selling development land to prevent business rather than residential developments. A TCA member discovered that his flat was affected by a covenant imposed by a local authority when selling land to a builder, and intended to prevent business use other than by a dentist or doctor. Another TCA member, Peter Fowler, a solicitor working on business-related legal matters and commercial property, fills in some background information on the two types of covenant, freehold and leasehold:

Freehold covenants

A typical restriction on a housing estate would be that no trade or business could be carried out on the property, and no use is permitted other than as a private dwelling house. The power of enforcement lies with the original estate owner or his successors, and in some cases owners of other properties on the estate who could be affected by physical damage or a fall in value of property. Most teleworkers are unlikely to cause damage as they are working entirely inside their home, although some problems could be envisaged (excessive parking obstruction from multiple visitors to a business). In general, it will be a case of common sense and keeping disturbance to neighbours to a minimum.

Sometimes old estates may flex their muscles and request payment for a licence to vary the original covenant, but often they have no direct right of enforcement and may no longer own any nearby property which could be affected. The threat of action is likely to be a bluff as the cost of enforcement could be prohibitive. They could also face a substantial claim from the teleworker if their claim failed, but in the interim the teleworker had been prevented from working by their injunction.

Leasehold covenants

Houses on very long leases such as 999-year leases will fall into the same category as freehold and the comments above apply. However, some small developments of houses or blocks of flats on long leases with ground rents pose a different problem. There will probably be an existing landlord or management company (possibly owned by the residents) who could enforce the covenants although, as before, they will have to prove that damage is being caused. Such proof is easier where covenants have been established for the common good. All that is needed to cause a problem is one resident who has been inconvenienced and an active residents' committee.

In general, if you are prudent and do not cause any nuisance from your business, even if you are in technical breach of an estate covenant, you will probably be safe enough to carry on teleworking. In many ways, the planning authorities are a bigger source of worry to potential and existing teleworkers."

Business rates

If you do go through the process of receiving official planning permission for your home office, then you are liable for commercial rates or council tax on the portion of your house that you are using for work.

In the UK, as far as liability for business rates is concerned, a large grey area exists. The accepted advice is typified by internal Treasury guidelines issued for the management of its own homeworkers: "Generally when part of a home is used as a workplace where the non-domestic activity precludes the use at any time of that part of the property for living accommodation, the part will be non-domestic and therefore subject to the business rate. In practice where domestic use can take place after work has finished, it is unlikely that liability for the business rate will arise." A Babergh Council rating department spokesman commented: "This is a grey area for everyone which will become more of an issue. We don't actively go looking for people working at home. We produce a local business guide and I know there are businesses in that guide that work from home – but others only use home as a base. It is difficult to enforce unless it is a separate building and cannot be used for other purposes."

This view was confirmed by another local rating officer: "We apply what we call a six o'clock rule. If, after six, the room reverts back to domestic use, then it would not be subject to business rates. Generally as most home businesses wouldn't need planning permission we would only get to hear about this if a neighbour complained. It is highly unlikely that a home office business would require business rating."

However, the same officer described an example of a publisher operating from home and using two rooms – one entirely for stock and the other as a computer room which resulted in an (amicably agreed) annual rate of around £300. TCA member Geoffrey Carter, who uses one room with a computer and a few files which the family have access to in the evenings, found himself with a bill for £450 for part use of the room after a visit by the valuation officer. After intervention by the TCA, the rating against Geoffrey was dropped. Another case, Fotheringham *v.* Wood ([1995] RA315, LT) found against an accountant working from home on the basis that the room was wholly or mainly used as an office – use of the room as living accommodation could not be envisaged.

More recent experiences suggest that "home businesses" are more of a target than employed teleworkers and if you move a business from a rated office-based premises to home, you may well be visited by a rating valuation officer as a matter of course.

In Ireland the situation is unclear though as in Britain, if there is exclusive occupation of part of the home which is of value or benefit to the occupier and is permanent (not for too transient a period), then it will incur rates. The Department of the Environment states that "The Valuation Office does not have a policing role and probably would not be aware if a domestic premises were being used for teleworking. Therefore, if rates were liable on such premises, detection would be extremely difficult and it is not clear who would take on such a role."

"Business" charges by public utilities

Unfortunately for teleworkers, many power utility companies have a policy that to qualify for the minimum tariff, premises must be used wholly for domestic purposes. The practical situation is that they would have to know that you are working from home before any change could be made, and that the exact conditions vary from company to company. Check with the relevant regulatory body such as OFFER or OFGAS, and contact the TCA if you have a problem.

For telephone service, BT does not compel people to use the business rate, but points out that the business service has the advantage of a Yellow Pages entry, and a Business Pages entry. BT also puts business users on a higher priority for fault correction than residential users. In both cases compensation is paid if the fault is not repaired within 24 hours.

When is a phone line not a phone line?

Ken O'Brien moved to Porkellis in Cornwall and planned to set up a computer business from home. He was stunned to find that he could not connect to the Internet. BT informed him that Porkellis was on a line-concentrator which allows 90 subscribers in the village to be routed through 14 trunk lines. The company told Ken that although they could provide him with a direct line they weren't prepared to because of the cost. The response galled Ken because the village primary school has an Internet connection as does a cottage two doors away which through an accident of history has a direct line. Ken did enquire about an ISDN line, but was told his house was over four miles from the local telephone exchange so neither ISDN nor BT's Homehighway service were available.

Oftel advised that there is no requirement for BT to provide anything other than a voice service but did offer a crumb of comfort – they are looking into an extension of the "universal service obligation" (USO) beyond speech transmission and there may be news later in 2000. A move in this direction would be supported both by the Telecommunications Managers Association and by the European Commission which plans recommendations to national regulators on the USO, and on local and long-distance call rates shortly.

BT said that as a line-concentrator is a recognised method of providing speech transmission, the line will not be removed from this equipment. On previous occasions BT have commented to the TCA that, although their liability was limited to voice, they encourage use of the phone for teleworking, fax services and so on. If you have difficulty with line quality they recommend asking for the complaints review manager of the unit and requesting a thorough quality check on the line.

Financial implications for you

Employed or self-employed?

Many teleworkers and telecottages have reported confusions and difficulties when they wish to get help from other teleworkers to complete work. The difficulty comes over whether the other teleworkers are employed (PAYE) or self-employed. The definition used to distinguish between self-employment and PAYE-employment is that of a contract **for** service against a contract **of** service:

- contracts for services are agreements for a specified piece of work to be completed. In teleworking terms these normally consist of the completion of a specified project by the teleworker for his or her client as a self-employed activity on which no PAYE (or PRSI in Ireland) is levied;
- contracts of service are standard employments – a teleworker operating on a payment by the hour for one single client is likely to be considered

to have a contract of service, on which PAYE and National Insurance (PRSI in Ireland) are payable, regardless of the location of the teleworker in relation to the client/employer.

On occasion the tax authorities have taken a retrospective view that regular telework contracts which both teleworker and client thought were contracts for services were in fact employments (contracts of service), and have levied back-tax and penalties. This confusion damages the willingness of businesses to use teleworkers, particularly as the "employer" can then be liable for both sets of taxes.

The erratic nature of telework contracts can also cause difficulties. Take two teleworkers collaborating closely on a project for a third party for three months and then not working together for a further six months after that – are both self-employed, or is one employing the other during the three months, but not afterwards? The answer will depend on the extent to which one controlled the other's working patterns, how many other clients each had, whether one required the presence of the other at specific premises and times and other factors.

Richard Nissen of the Virtual Office took up this issue with his local tax inspector: "The fact is that you can employ people and have them working on a self-employed basis as long as they are not directed by you. The easiest way to do this is to send the terms and conditions for the worker you want to employ on a self-employed basis to your local PAYE office for

What to do when a customer won't pay

The maximum amount that you can recover through the Small Claims Court is £5,000. The Small Claims Court offers a simpler court procedure which is swifter, less formal, less expensive and less intimidating than traditional legal proceedings. The case is heard by a judge in chambers with evidence given around a table. The judge makes an immediate decision but there is no appeal procedure – the decision is binding on both sides.

You begin by completing a standard form explaining the problem, and who the claimant and defendant are. A summons is then sent by post to the defendant who can:

- Admit the claim and pay you in full (payment can be in instalments)
- Admit part of the claim and pay you in part (payment can be in instalments)
- Dispute the claim in its entirety in which case a date is set for the hearing.

There is a ClaimsLink support service which can advise you in relation to your problem and help you complete documents. More information is available at **www.small-claims.co.uk**

Employment agencies and the law

Although it is no longer necessary to obtain a licence if you are getting work for other people, a number of legal strictures apply regardless of whether you are a commercial concern or a non-profit-making body (but charities are exempt). Full information on the legal provisions is available from the Department of Trade and Industry's Employment Agency Standards Office (Tel: 0645 555105). Anyone thinking of providing employment services is also recommended to discuss the matter with their professional advisors and to contact REC, the Recruitment and Employment Confederation, which is the main professional body and can provide detailed advice Tel: 020 7323 4399 Web: **www.rec.uk.com.** The situation in Ireland is complex – contact the Department of Enterprise Trade and Employment for guidance. **www.irlgov.ie/entemp**

Who is affected?

- an employment agency: any business providing services (whether by provision of information or otherwise) for the purpose of finding workers employment;
- an employment business: a business like a secretarial agency that provides people to act for and under the control of other people;
- the law does not affect independent contractors undertaking specific tasks using their own staff who remain under their direction and control.

What are the main issues? (This list is not comprehensive – use the contacts above for full information.)

- you may not charge fees to workers for seeking to find them jobs or offer any financial benefit or benefit-in-kind to persuade workers to use your services (there are a few exemptions eg theatre and modelling);
- you must obtain adequate information from employer and worker clients for the purpose of selecting a suitable worker;
- you must not disclose information about employers and workers other than for the purpose of finding or supplying workers;
- you must ensure workers possess any necessary qualifications required by law (such as HGV licences for lorry drivers);
- you must ensure the worker and employer are aware of any legal conditions such as work permits for certain non-EU nationals;
- you must provide employer clients with clearly legible written terms of business on receipt of an application;
- you must, if you receive money on behalf of a worker client, pay it to the worker within ten days of receipt;
- you must not prohibit or restrict workers from entering the direct employment of a hirer, or replace workers on industrial dispute, or supply workers previously employed directly by the hirer within the previous six months.

> **Proto-type's points for ensuring self-employment:**
>
> - The teleworkers provide their own equipment;;
> - The client deals with the teleworker directly;
> - There is no guarantee about the amount of work which the teleworker might expect to receive;
> - It is the responsibility of the teleworker to correct poor work at their own cost;
> - The teleworker's ability to take on other work is not restricted;
> - Separate invoices are issued from the teleworker to the main "work getter" (such as Proto-type) and from the work getter to the client company.

confirmation that you can employ them in this way before you start paying them. However, even if you cross this hurdle, then there is another problem. If you ask a teleworker to do some typing for you that is then charged out and sold on to a third party, you fall slap bang into the scope of employment agency law (section 134 ICTCA 1988), so you would have to act like an agency and pay John or Jane PAYE and National Insurance. Yet if the person you employ is from another EU country then no PAYE is payable – it's actually easier to use a cross-border teleworker."

Whatever the exact situation, where it is important that self-employed status is assured, get advice on formulating a contract and working conditions from your financial adviser and verify it with your local tax assessor.

Ann Collins of Proto-type, a TCA member, has successfully established a situation where the four teleworkers she works with are classified as self-employed. Proto-type is a remote word processing service based in Essex and operating for city-based firms. The company's main client is a quantity surveying group. Handwritten documents and audio tapes are received by fax and post, typed and returned by modem. Ann explains: "We started off with just myself and we are still small, using four teleworkers, with very tight margins. The additional cost and the time in administering PAYE and National Insurance for employed status would have been sufficient deterrents to stop us from continuing the business. From the teleworkers' point of view, self-employment gives them greater flexibility. We had to argue the point with the local tax office, but a number of points eventually convinced them."

One way of avoiding the employed/self-employed dilemma, particularly popular with contract computer programmers who tend to find their work through employment agencies, has been the limited company route. Here the teleworker sets up a limited company, which is contracted to do the work by the client. The limited company pays a salary to the teleworker,

Are you employed or self-employed?

The main criteria to be taken into account are listed in a free Inland Revenue booklet *Employed or Self-Employed?* which states that if you can answer yes to the following questions, it will "usually" mean that you are self-employed.

- Do you have the final say in how the business is run?
- Do you risk your own money in the business?
- Are you responsible for meeting the losses as well as taking profits?
- Do you provide the major items of equipment you need to do your job, not just the small tools which many employees provide for themselves?
- Are you free to hire other people, on terms of your own choice, to do the work that you have taken on? Do you pay them out of your own pocket?
- Do you have to correct unsatisfactory work in your own time and at your own expense?

Alternatively, if you answer "yes" to the following questions, then you are "probably" an employee:

- Do you yourself have to do the work rather than hire someone else to do it for you?
- Can someone tell you at any time what to do or when and how to do it?
- Are you paid by the hour, week or month? Can you get overtime pay? (even if you are paid by commission or on a piecework basis you may still be an employee)
- Do you work set hours, or a given number of hours a week or month?
- Do you work at the premises of the person you are working for, or at a place or places that they decide?

Another key, though not decisive, issue is how many clients you have if you are self-employed. In general single longer contracts will indicate employment, while several simultaneous contracts with different clients suggest self-employment. If in doubt check with an accountant. More detail on this issue is available at **www.netaccountants.com**.

which of course is subject to income tax and national insurance contributions. Unfortunately a number of contractors took to paying themselves low salaries but high dividends from their limited companies, which effectively reduced their tax and national insurance contributions.

The response of the Inland Revenue has been to issue a new regulation, known as IR35, which it says: "is aimed at engagements with the essential characteristics of employment... where these characteristics are disguised through the use of an intermediary such as a service company or partnership... There is no intention to redefine the existing boundary between employment and self-employment." The changes have caused

> **EU teleworking laws**
>
> A number of European countries are currently struggling with how to treat teleworkers for tax purposes.
>
> - *In Denmark computers supplied by employers for private (not business) use are no longer subjected to tax as long as they are also available to be used for work. Many large companies have now initiated schemes to supply computers for employees, and the schemes often involved a requirement that the employees take the ECDL computer literacy qualification.*
>
> - *In Belgium, a contract on homeworking must be signed – if it is not then the teleworker is entitled to claim 10% of the gross salary as teleworking expenses. The contract must specify allowances for heating and lighting. Computer equipment remains the property of the employer. No tax or social security applies to the payment.*
>
> - *In Holland companies can give about 363 per year (or a once-off five-year payment of about 1815) to teleworkers as compensation for furniture. There must be a written teleworking contract specifying at least one day a week working from home. The company can also supply a computer worth about 2200 or its cash equivalent without incurring tax. However some tax regions have tried to levy benefit-in-kind tax on the amounts while others don't, and there are problems about the definition of one day (as opposed to 20% of work-time) especially for people who work from home rather than at home. Telephone lines for business use are exempt from benefit-in-kind – unless they are ISDN lines in which case the tax authorities are not sure how to treat them.*
>
> - *In Germany if someone works for more than 50% of their time at home they can get tax deductions of around 1300 a year. The authorities are strict on proof that at least half of the time is spent at home, requiring letters from employers.*
>
> - *In Sweden there is a proposal to allow home-based employees an annual tax-free sum of 250–500 but again this would only be payable where at least half the working time is spent at home. As Swedish unions are opposed to people spending so much time away from the office, the proposal has not progressed quickly.*
>
> - *In Ireland the Minister for Finance has stated that home use of PCs supplied by employers is "incidental" and will not incur a liability for BIK taxes but no mention is made of other teleworking equipment or software – just PCs.*
>
> - *See page 212 for details of UK benefit-in-kind regulations.*

controversy in the engineering and computer contracting sectors and the effect on teleworkers is unclear. The TCA's financial advisers comment "Payments of dividends out of the income in such cases will become ineffective – company expenditure outside permitted expenses will be taxable under PAYE for a relevant engagement, which is one where the income would have been taxed as employment income if the worker had contracted directly with the client organisation under the same terms. The rules for detemining whether the engagement is relevant are the same as the rules for establishing whether an individual is employed or self-employed."

Tax and benefit-in-kind

So what expenses can you claim for your home office? The best advice is to talk through the issues with your tax adviser, but if you are self-employed you can claim expenses for heating, lighting, and telephone, depreciation of the fixtures and fittings, installation of extra power points, cleaning costs, business insurance, refurbishment, office equipment, postage and stationery, repair of IT-related equipment, work-related publications such as books and magazines, and membership of professional associations. For start-up self-employed teleworkers or teleworking small businesses, 100% capital allowances on investments in information and communications technology are now available in the three years from April 1st 2000.

Claiming costs of acquisition of the property such as mortgage interest, building costs, solicitors fees, *etc* could make you liable to Capital Gains Tax in future according to Mark Dyer, accountant and TCA member. "Although the domestic portion of a house is exempt, CGT could be due on the proportion of the gain related to the rooms used. If you used two rooms in a twelve-room house, then one-sixth of the gain would be due. But as the exempt band is £7,100 per person, and gains are inflation adjusted, realistically the problem will probably only occur when the gain happens in a year when other CGT gain items have been realised." The Dyer website at **www.netaccountants.com** gives further information on CGT.

If you are employed, the good news is that the provision of computers for use in the home by your employer is no longer subject to "benefit-in-kind" (BIK) tax in Britain. In theory, any item which could be considered a perk is subject to BIK – you pay tax on 20% of the list price of the equipment. However, computers, scanners, software, modems and printers are now exempt up to a maximum benefit of £500 a year. Fax machines are not included but will not incur a liability if they are only used for business purposes. There are a few strings attached – IT equipment for use in the home must be available for all staff and not just directors of the company or their families. The equipment also has to remain the property of the company. Where a telephone line is provided, there is no liability if it is only used for business purposes. The situation for mobile phones is complicated. Ideally your employer should provide the phone and pay for calls – if you own the phone and the employer pays the bills things get sticky both in regard to the apportionment of private and work use, and in relation to tax on the rental charge.

Furniture provided by an employer is subject to benefit-in-kind and strictly speaking should be recorded on the annual P11D BIK form though the low value of standard office furniture is unlikely to excite great interest from most tax officials. In relation to costs for heating and lighting, these can be claimed by employees but must be justifiable. One large company which has thousands of teleworkers has come to an agreement with the Revenue that employees can be reimbursed against receipted expenditure (heat and light bills) for up to £150 a year without payment of tax – it does not get reported on P11D forms and is not paid through the payroll. This is just an agreement and does not reflect an official dispensation or set a precedent – other companies will have to make their own arrangements. The company comments: "It was difficult to justify to the IR how anyone could spend an additional £500 a year on extra heat and light for the one room they occupied as an office. We also considered that a flat-rate payment would not be appropriate due to the difference in circumstances of each individual. The IR questioned how we would justify the same payment to a person using home as a base and someone using home as a permanent office."

There is also some good news on travel expenses. Maurice Parry-Wingfield of Deloitte and Touche explains that since the beginning of 1998 "The Inland Revenue recognises that if you have two places of work and that you are based at home for more than 40% of the time, then the cost of travelling between the two can be claimed if you are required to be based at home so that your home is treated as a permanent workplace". Proving that requirement may involve showing written instructions from the employer for homeworking.

Pensions

Those who begin teleworking are often entering self-employment for the first time and consequently losing the security of a former occupational pension. This area of financial services has been in turmoil for a number of years after the Maxwell scandal and investigations into sales advice about personal pensions given in the late 1980s. It can still be hard to get clear, unbiased advice because most pension advisers receive commissions on the pensions they sell. The best option is to look for an independent financial adviser (who should be approved by the Personal Investment Authority) whom you can pay on an hourly rate (from £30–£100) to look at your situation and advise you – that way the adviser is paid by you to look after your interests, and not by the pension company to sell their policies.

The two types of pension – occupational and personal – differ widely in their tax breaks and regulatory regimes. In general, a well-funded occupational pension scheme is likely to be preferable to a personal pension, but fewer and fewer people are eligible for occupational pensions, which were designed in the old days of "jobs for life". Both types of pensions are paid on top of the state old age pension, which is a flat rate payment available to those who have paid into the state scheme for a sufficient number of years through their National Insurance or PRSI contributions. Because of the increased number of older people in the population, and long-term underfunding of the state scheme, it is likely that the value of the state pension will fall far below the present basic level as we move into the 21st century, and contributions to an occupational or personal pension scheme are strongly recommended where affordable.

An occupational pension scheme is normally run by an employer and provides a pension based on a percentage of your final salary rate at retirement, as well as on the number of years of membership of the scheme you have. Occupational pensions cannot exceed two-thirds of final salary, and to achieve this maximum you will need at least 40 years membership of a pension scheme. Normally both the employee and the employer contribute to an occupational pension. Added benefits can include death-in-service grants and payments to widows or widowers.

When someone changes jobs they have two main options available for their pension – deferred pension or transfer value. If they become a deferred pensioner, they leave their contributions in the scheme untouched and quietly growing until they reach retirement, beginning a new occupational scheme with the new employer. If they opt for a transfer value, the pension scheme calculates the value of your pension based on existing contributions and arranges for its transfer into a new scheme. TCA Executive Director Alan Denbigh found that when he became a teleworker, by taking out his new personal pension with the company that had operated his previous company pension, he was able to avoid the normal penalties of withdrawal – his pension was "converted" from an occupational to a personal pension with minimal pain.

Personal pension plans by contrast are based on how much pension you have "purchased" by your payments throughout your working life. What you receive depends on your contributions, and how successful the pension fund managers have been in selecting good investments. The big difference is that employers usually will not contribute to a personal fund, so that the whole pension burden is borne by the teleworker.

However, contributors to personal pension schemes are entitled to tax breaks. As you get older, the amount of money you can put into a pension scheme tax-free increases up to the UK earnings cap of £90,600:

Age	UK	Age	Ireland
Up to 35	17.5%	Up to 29	15%
36-45	20%	30–39	20%
46-50	25%	40–49	25%
51-55	30%	50 and over	30%
56-60	35%		
61 plus	40%		

If you are starting a personal pension plan it pays to begin early – the rule of thumb used in calculating how much you should contribute is to halve your age and convert it to a percentage (so a 30-year old should begin contributing 15% of their income).

Many self-employed people wait until towards the end of the tax year, when they know what their total income is likely to be, and then buy single-premium pension plans to allow them to use up all of the available tax relief on the grounds that it is better to spend money on a pension than to give it to the government. The alternative is monthly regular premium policies, but these can be inflexible if your income varies – if you fail to make payments there are penalties. It is very inadvisable to stop payments in the first two years of a regular payments scheme. One company, Equitable Life, offers a regular scheme where there is no penalty if you cease contributing or vary your contributions. Equitable Life is also the only company which does not pay commission to salespeople on its policies.

To avoid a cashflow crunch at the end of the tax year when pension payments have to be made to qualify for tax relief, it can be worth looking at having two policies: one for small regular payments, and the other a single premium whose value depends on the maximum tax relief you can obtain. Single premium policies allow you to spread your investment over a number of different companies, reducing the risk that you might "pick" an underperformer, but regular premium policies are a lot less painful to the bank account.

In Ireland, proposed pension payments can be taken into account when calculating your preliminary tax liability in October. The payment must then be made by 31st January of the following year.

When selecting a personal pension plan, you are likely to be faced with a plethora of graphs and figures indicating how different companies have performed and many different options, such as with profits schemes and index linked bonds. The main points to watch for are:

- underlying trends of performance – the final value will depend partly on inflation and partly on the growth of the funds invested. Look at how your proposed pension company has fared compared to others over a period of years
- administration charge percentages (these can vary from 8% to 32% for regular premium policies, and from 13% to 39% for single premium over a 25 year period)
- commission charges, which can be more than half of the first year's payments.

Within each company there are options on funds which carry risk and growth tags, such as investment in shares of companies trading in the

Catch 22 – unemployable and uninsurable

Jane (not her real name) is a 35-year old teleworker who has been diagnosed with endometriosis, a condition affecting up to 10% of women of reproductive age where tissue from the lining of the womb migrates and grows in other parts of the body causing problems with fertility, the bladder and bowels. Symptoms vary but the disease is often accompanied by heavy periods, painful sex and depression. It's a chronic condition which cannot be cured but often can be controlled with drugs and surgery.

Jane comments: "It is impossible to know how the disease will progress. It has stopped me expanding my business because I can't take out a loan and risk not being able to pay it back. In many ways the worst problems are not the physical symptoms, but the fatigue and mental confusion that can be caused by changes in hormone levels, either from the disease or from the drugs taken to alleviate it. It's like suddenly being reduced to living your life by the light of a 40W bulb. I'm pretty much stabilised at the moment, but if I have to have a hysterectomy, the 10–12 weeks off work would be just about long enough for the business to go down the drain."

"Waiting lists make it hard to schedule an operation for a quiet part of the year, but going private would cost thousands. It would also be very hard now for me to get a permanent job because I could not pass a company medical. I looked into permanent health insurance, but it is a Catch-22 situation once you have been diagnosed. If you go to a company for income protection insurance you must declare the condition – and then they whack the premiums up so high you can't afford it. There is a massive change in your lifestyle if you have a chronic condition. It is vital people take out health insurance before they get sick. One in six people say they have a health condition which seriously affects their life – this often results from chronic diseases such as arthritis or irritable bowel syndrome."

particular regions or sectors, or in property, or in index-linked bonds. A with profits policy is a calculation based on the bonuses of the company that reflects its overall level of profitability. Ethical funds are a recent development which invest only in companies conforming to certain standards, and avoiding areas such as arms production.

At retirement in Britain currently you can take up to a quarter of your pension as a lump sum. The remainder has to be used to buy an annuity, which provides a regular income for the rest of your life. You can choose which company to buy the annuity from, and it is a crucial decision for a comfortable old age. In Ireland there are a number of options available for self-employed people at retirement and these are clearly laid out in the Revenue leaflets available at **www.revenue.ie**.

Health insurance

In Britain everyone has access to the National Health Service for free medical care but you may need to think about extra health insurance if you are opting for self-employment. You will also need access to welfare benefits or insurance payouts to replace your income should you become unable to work. Typical categories of insurance policy are:

- access to fast, private healthcare to reduce time out of work (private medical insurance)
- insurance against certain illnesses preventing you from working and earning that provides a lump sum (critical illness insurance)
- income protection insurance to provide a regular income if you are unable to work due to a serious injury or illness (permanent health insurance or PHI)
- insurance against the consequences of accidents (personal accident insurance)

Private healthcare policies are available from a range of suppliers in the UK such as BUPA and PPP. These regular payment policies are not the same as the critical illness insurance policies currently being marketed which need very careful assessment, as many cover the basic unhappy events such as heart attack, stroke or cancer, but not chronic conditions such as arthritis or endometriosis which can prevent you from working just as effectively. The small print is well worth reading!

Self-employed people do pay National Insurance, but it only entitles them to the health service, disability benefits and the old age pension – not to unemployment benefit if their business goes under, although depending on circumstances other means-tested benefits may be available. The benefits system has become increasingly complex in the past few years, and it is worth consulting your local library or Citizens' Advice Bureau on your entitlements.

Any teleworker becoming self-employed should think seriously about taking out personal health insurance (PHI) to secure their income level should they become unable to work through ill-health. PHI does not pay your medical bills – instead, it replaces your lost income. Normally the policy provides around 75% of your usual salary (to give you an incentive to go back to work…). Premium levels depend on your medical history when you take out the policy, your deferral period, and any exemptions you select. The deferral period is normally around 13 weeks, and is a time delay between the onset of illness and the date when the policy begins to pay out. The longer the deferral, the lower the premium.

Exemptions are usually created where you have a pre-existing problem (such as back trouble) which makes your premiums very high. If you agree not to claim with regard to back problems, you can get insurance for other conditions at more reasonable premiums. It is extremely important that you ensure that your medical conditions are fully disclosed when taking out a permanent health insurance policy (check your doctor's report and make sure that you let the insurer know if you think anything has been omitted). Otherwise, if you need to claim and have to undergo an independent examination, your claim may be denied. Permanent health insurance isn't a particularly remunerative sector for insurance companies, and many will only offer these policies if they are taken out in tandem with personal pensions. Western Provident Association has developed policies aimed at the self-employed and says that its premium levels are lower to reflect the lower level of claims from people who can't afford to be ill. Small businesses can also consider buying "key person" insurance for owner-managers so that the business receives a payout if the key person dies or becomes incapacitated.

In Ireland membership of VHI or BUPA is to be recommended to ensure swift treatment of health problems for the self-employed. Premiums can be partially claimed against tax.

VAT (4th schedule)

Another area of confusion concerns "4th-schedule" VAT. Where a teleworker is registered for VAT and performs data processing tasks for a VAT-registered business located in another EU member state, no VAT is chargeable despite the transaction being for a service rather than goods. The existence of this rule is particularly important for Irish teleworkers because if they were forced to charge their export clients the high Irish VAT rate of 21% and oblige their clients to go through the cumbersome process of reclaiming the difference between this rate and that pertaining in their own country, they would be at a competitive disadvantage compared to teleworkers in other EU member states with lower VAT rates.

Data Protection Act

The regulations relating to the British Data Protection Act changed on 1 March 2000 to take account of an EU directive. Previously manual records not kept on computer were exempt from the Act but they are now included. According to a spokesperson on the Data Protection helpline (01625 545740), previously about 90% of those who telephoned for advice on

> **Data protection principles and definitions**
>
> Personal data that you process must be
>
> - *fairly and lawfully processed;*
> - *processed for limited purposes;*
> - *adequate, relevant and not excessive;*
> - *accurate;*
> - *not kept longer than necessary;*
> - *processed in accordance with the data subject's rights;*
> - *secure;*
> - *not transferred to countries without adequate protection.*
>
> Personal data covers both facts and opinions about living, identifiable individuals. It includes information regarding the intentions of the data controller towards the individual though some limited exemptions apply.
>
> Data processing includes obtaining, holding and disclosing data.
>
> Data subjects are those to whom personal data relates

whether they should register did in fact need to. Now although the percentage has dropped to about half, it has become more complex to decide who should and who should not register. You are advised to contact the helpline and discuss your situation with expert staff, who can also help you to have your "notification" forms prefilled as templates before they are sent out to you for approval. It is also possible to get advice and make notifications on the Internet (**www.dataprotection.gov.uk**). There are some quite complex transitional arrangements for some bodies such as schools, and the helpline can assist you to understand these as well.

The Data Protection Registrar will want details of the data you hold and control, the purposes for which it is used, where the data is obtained and to whom it is disclosed, both here and overseas. If your information handling practices are found to be negligent, you can be liable for civil action due to damage caused by inaccurate data, unauthorised data, loss of data or destruction of personal records, including liability for related distress caused. Data subjects can request access to their personal data, and where appropriate, demand correction or deletion of a record. In return, data users can charge up to £10 for a copy of the data.

In general, if you are processing information on behalf of an employer, it is the employer's duty to register, not the employee's. If you are transferring any personal data outside the European Economic Area then you will also need to ensure that there is adequate protection for the data subject in the country that you are exporting to. Everyone is required to comply with the Act, even if they don't actually need to register. The cost of registration is £35. There are a number of exemptions from notification including:

- some not-for-profit organisations
- processing of data for personal, family or household affairs including recreational purposes
- data controllers who process personal data only for the maintenance of a public register
- data controllers who process personal data only for any one or all of the following purposes for their own business:
  – staff administration
  – advertising, marketing and public relations
  – accounts and records.

The data protection laws in the Republic of Ireland are similar but substantially simpler for laypeople to understand. Legislation to bring the same European directive into force in Ireland is currently going through the parliament.

On a practical basis, this affects you in relation to email marketing. If you send out marketing material by email you must be able to show that you obtained the email address fairly – usually by asking permission directly or because they have volunteered their email address for your website enquiry form. If someone requests to be removed from your email list you must comply with their request. It is illegal to sell personal data without the permission of the person involved. You should also ensure that you advertise and comply with a privacy policy in any Internet business dealings – do not share personal data with any third parties without permission from the person involved.

Both Britain and Ireland are currently drafting, or passing through their parliaments, laws which will deal with the evidential status of electronic writing and contracts, and look at issues such as certification (trusted third parties) and validating digital signatures.

Consumer and direct selling rules

Consumer protection directives issued by the EU also apply to electronic commerce, and to any interchange via an electronic medium such as telemarketing, or kiosk-based services. A new EU directive on distance contracts has to be in place in all member states by June 2000 and affects telephone, mail order and Internet-based sales. In summary it provides that:

- the consumer is entitled to the name and address of the company selling the goods, to details of the goods and a clear price;
- On receipt of goods, whatever the quality of the goods, the consumer has seven days in which to return them;
- All goods must be delivered within 30 days (except perishable goods,

and allowing for public holidays *etc*).

The EU's consumer protection law will also apply to electronic commerce requiring that you must:

- provide goods that are of merchantable quality and fit for their purpose;
- own or have title to what you are selling;
- provide samples that are similar to any bulk sales;
- provide services with the necessary and skill and diligence that would normally be expected;
- avoid advertising which is misleading or likely to deceive.

The EU's Unfair Terms in Consumer Contracts law applies to any contract which is not individually negotiated, such as websites which provide "click here to see terms and conditions" pages.

In Britain new regulations on the Telephone Preference Service, which allows individuals to register their wish not to receive telemarketing calls or faxes, came into effect in May 1999. However, the legal definition of an "individual" also includes businesses which are not separate legal identities, such as partnerships or sole traders. This means telemarketers and others working on business-to-business contracts can accidentally fall foul of the new rules by calling a sole trader business that has registered its wish not to be contacted and might incur a potential fine of £5,000. A service to check numbers for small telemarketing businesses has been put in place by OSL costing around 6p per number. OSL give a reference number for each number checked, and the service is backed by professional indemnity insurance.

Intellectual property and copyright

Although prosecutions for infringements of copyright and intellectual property rights (IPR) are rare, it is important to have a basic grasp of your rights and responsibilities, especially with regard to online material. In practical terms, most people don't necessarily want to be paid if you re-use something of theirs in your work. However, they almost certainly do want to be asked, and to have their IPR acknowledged in your document. Barry Mahon of information management association EUSIDIC comments: "Publishers would like you to believe that quotation is a cardinal sin, but that is because they make authors sign away their rights to allow quotation without payment. Equally, if you are an author, take advice before signing away all your rights to a publisher – it is possible only to grant limited rights." Many authors and agents distinguish rights for paper publication from those for online distribution these days.

Most countries in the world operate to the Berne Convention, which means that even if a document does not have a copyright notice or use the © symbol, the work is copyright, even if it's merely a shopping list. Pictures are covered as well as text, and it is irrelevant whether or not you charge for your publication – even if you give it away free, if you include someone else's copyrighted material without permission it's an infringement of their IPR.

If you want to assert your own copyright on a document, add:

Copyright © [date] by [author].

With regard to information on the Internet, including newsgroups and listservs, nothing is "in the public domain" and therefore free to use unless it has an explicit statement granting it to the public domain attached. This particularly applies to material from online news services; you may be able to extract information, rephrase it and sell it on in some circumstances, where it could be regarded as "fair use", but in general beware of all but the most minimal quotation.

An excellent guide to copyright and IPR by Brad Templeton is available at **www.clari.net**, and includes this summary of "fair use":

"The "fair use" exemption to copyright law was created to allow things such as commentary, parody, news reporting, research and education about copyrighted works without the permission of the author. Intent, and damage to the commercial value of the work are important considerations. Are you reproducing an article from the *New York Times* because you needed to in order to criticise the quality of the *New York Times*, or because you couldn't find time to write your own story, or didn't want your readers to have to pay to log onto the online services with the story or buy a copy

---

Beware software salesmen bearing gifts...

Modern market research and telephone sales techniques are being used to target businesses for IT theft according to the Internet Content Register (ICR), a non-profit register.

Mike Hawkes of the ICR explains that using telemarketing techniques and offering free software, the villains extract information about the home office address, the equipment in use, and when the teleworker will be out. "The offer of software means questions about the computer and its specification seem reasonable. Then they tell you that they need to send round an installation engineer. The result is almost robbery to order".

Hawkes believes the problem is UK-wide, from the Grampians to Yeovil though most incidents happen close to the motorway network such as areas of Staffordshire and Cheshire close to the M6. He also warns that a similar scam involves extracting credit card details for "carriage charges" on free software.

The Internet Content Register performs background checks to ensure websites are who they say they are, and runs a code of practice for web advertisers, publishers and designers. Registered sites can display the ICR logo and are added to the ICR register, providing a simple way for consumers to verify websites as honest, decent and committed to promoting safe Internet trading. **www.internet.org.uk**

of the paper? The first is probably fair use, the others probably aren't.

Fair use is almost always a short excerpt and almost always attributed. (Do not use more of the work than is necessary to make the commentary.) It should not harm the commercial value of the work – in the sense of people no longer needing to buy it (which is another reason why reproduction of the entire work is generally forbidden)."

Training materials do not normally fall into the fair use category, a point of particular relevance to telecottages who may be copying training modules. Always bear in mind that uploading and downloading software or graphics on the Internet may cause an infringement of someone's copyright or IPR and could lead to financial liabilities.

Defamation

Another important area to consider is that of defamation, particularly when "flame wars" break out on the Internet. In general you should resist putting anything which could be considered defamatory in an email message, even one that is sent on a one-to-one basis. In ordinary written correspondence, a letter from one person to another in a closed envelope is considered to be "privileged" correspondence and it is unlikely that a defamation lawsuit could be made to stick in such circumstances. Email is not the same at all – it is not assumed to be private unless previously agreed between the parties. It's also very easy for a slip of the finger to send an email to entirely the wrong person. If in doubt, leave it out, particularly on public forums or newsgroups.

Security

Teleworkers need to address issues of data security as well as those of physical security (preventing theft and damage). Telecentres that allow public access to premises, also need to look at the problems of supervision of visitors and casual users.

Issues of fire and theft head the likely list of incidents. Many home offices do not have fire extinguishers, smoke alarms, first aid kits or clear evacuation routes. If you are worried that an official safety inspection by the fire brigade might lead to your office being "banned", ask advice from a supplier of firefighting equipment on suitable measures.

No one is immune from crime, and in many ways a burglary has a much more drastic effect on a home office than on a conventional office. In an office, the employer takes responsibility for equipment, and can afford security measures such as closed circuit TV. At home, you will be dealing with all the consequences of any burglary.

Computers have a high resale value and are likely to be the main target for a break-in. However, the advantage of most home offices is that they do not advertise "expensive kit in here". To all intents and purposes the risks of burglary are actually lower than for an ordinary house because working from home means there is someone on the premises for most of the day and

Telecentres and security

A survey of telecentres carried out by the Telecottage Association in 1994 showed particular problems with user supervision:

- *One-third felt that people could get into their offices undetected during office hours;*
- *Once inside the building, visitors were generally supervised by centre staff or clients, but less than half reported supervision "all the time";*
- *Over three-quarters had no signing-in or visitor's badge procedure;*
- *Almost half allowed access to the office outside office hours by clients;;*
- *Only a quarter had an alarm system;*
- *Almost half described their environment as "loosely controlled";*
- *Only 30% had any kind of disaster recovery plan;*
- *Only 40% had plans for provision of alternative telephone lines;*
- *Only 20% had plans to cope with power supply loss;*
- *Less than half required users to employ passwords when accessing PCs.*

53% of telecottages reported at least one security incident, at an average cost of £1,300, although half of the cases were described as very low impact (one incident costing £10,000 substantially skewed the average cost). No incidents of hacking or computer fraud were reported, and the level of deliberate computer misuse was low compared to national surveys, although misuse incidents including loading of illegal (copyrighted) software, introduction of viruses and running up large unauthorised online charges were reported.

A series of security guidelines and policy suggestions entitled *Keep IT Safe and Secure* for telecottage managers is available from the TCA. Send an SAE with 47p stamp to KISS booklets, WREN Telecottage, Stoneleigh Park, Warwickshire CV8 2LZ.

night, but you might look at installing blinds if your office is on the ground floor so that the computers are not visible to passers-by. In general it is wise not to allow visitors into your home office unless necessary – the fewer people who know about your equipment the better. Check the credentials of utility company and local authority officials who call at the house.

Physical security advice will be available from your Crime Prevention Unit, contactable via your local police station, or from your insurers. Common sense measures include:

- five-lever mortice locks on outside doors;
- key-operated window locks;

- key-operated bolts on back doors and patio doors;
- ladders or other tools that could be used to gain access locked away;
- a separate lock which allows the home office door to be secured against the rest of the house;
- if away on holiday arrange for security *eg* lights to be switched on and off by timer, and notify police;
- leave a radio or light on in the house if popping out during the day;
- lock all doors and windows before going out or retiring for the night;
- photograph and keep a description of your IT equipment including serial numbers in case you have to report a crime or make an insurance claim.

Specific deterrence devices for computers include alarms, labelling, etching ID numbers, cables to lock equipment to fixed items like tables and lockable workstation cabinets.

The Suzy Lamplugh Trust warns that women working from home should ensure they are not running security risks if clients visit them. A survey by Barclays Bank in 1998 found that two-thirds of home-based businesswomen have client visits but 40% of these women take no steps to ensure their physical safety such as ensuring another person is present. One-fifth feel the presence of their dog is a help. The Suzy Lamplugh Trust encourages use of the mnemonic acronym PLAN – Plan to meet the first time in a busy place rather than your home. Log your visitors with a buddy by phone and phone to check in after the meeting. Avoid situations which could be difficult. Never assume it won't happen to you.

Telephone and electricity supplies are often not considered when analyses of security risks are being made, but problems in these areas can effectively stop a business from trading. For most people the cost of providing an uninterruptable power supply (UPS), or generator backup for a whole office will be prohibitive, but systems are available which at least give you sufficient breathing space to close down the computer after a power cut without losing work in progress – check the Radio Spares (RS) catalogue at **rswww.com** which lists various devices that will keep one computer powered for about 15 minutes costing around £65–£195. It may be worthwhile to pre-arrange for the use of workspace elsewhere in the area should you suffer a loss of power for more than a day. The arrangement could be with a neighbouring teleworker or office services company, or with a telecentre.

Faster repair times are probably the main reason for paying business rather than residential rates for your telephone lines. However, if you have a residential line, and no need for the directory entries provided as part of business services, but still want fast repairs, you can pay BT £8.25 a quarter to get its Total Care service, which aims at a four-hour repair time every day except Sunday.

Association member Stephen Thomas found that it is also possible to arrange with BT for an alternative number while your own is out of service, so that clients hear a message and can leave voicemail or speak to you, rather than getting a frustrating engaged tone or, more commonly, the phone appearing to ring out as though you were out. Dial 154 to ask for this service – but as it operates through call diversion, you need to have another, functioning number to which the calls can be diverted.

The most effective form of data security is to ensure that you take regular backups and that one set of your backups is held "offsite" in case of fire or other extensive damage to your computers and onsite backups. As well as physically swapping backup tapes or disks with a co-worker or local business, you could look into backing up your data remotely via the Internet or an ISDN line – a number of specialist companies offer safe archiving services in this way. Remember that on average a computer hard disk will fail once every two to three years – and that the inconvenience hard disk crashes cause can be hugely reduced by even once-weekly backups.

Fire Safety

Fire officers advise that all home offices should be fitted with smoke detectors (costs in the range of £4–£14 each – those which are interlinked by cable so all go off if one goes off are better, and mains-driven systems are preferable to battery-operated). Bryan Bates of Gloucestershire Fire and Rescue Service said: "The main thing that we suggest is for people to get interlinked smoke detectors fitted. One in the hall, one in the landing, and one in the home office, particularly if it is a converted loft space. All new properties have to have them by law, but when people convert lofts they often forget to do it. It is the biggest life saver because a smoke detector goes off at the first whiffs of smoke, giving people time to walk out of the house, shut the doors and call the fire brigade. But systems must be maintained properly. Once a week – perhaps first thing on a Monday morning – it is important that they press the test button and get into a routine. Local fire brigades can supply a free brochure, *Fire Safety in the Home*, to give further advice."

Around 500 people a year die in home fires in Britain. Ted Savill of ES Safety Supplies points out that many insurance policies are invalid if you don't have fire extinguishers. The most suitable type of extinguisher for a home office is a CO_2 (carbon dioxide) extinguisher. Ted explains: "Dry powder can be used on anything, but it's very messy and will get into the works of your computer. CO_2 extinguishers are more expensive but better suited to electrical fires. A typical 2 kg model retails for around £65 plus delivery, while a dry powder model costs around £32." Whichever model you choose, check that it is British Standard approved, and ensure that it is maintained according to the manufacturer's instructions (usually it will need servicing every 6 or 12 months).

Another issue for those with upstairs home offices is to look at escape routes if a fire were to make the stairs impassable. The most important point is that windows should be easy to open and large enough to climb out

> **Teleworking tales from the Tolson files**
>
> The TCA has had a long-term relationship with insurance brokers Tolson Messenger who specialise in the home office market. Tolson opened their files to reveal some of the stranger claims they have received...
>
> "My mobile phone came loose from its mounting on the car dash while going round a corner. It slid along the dash and flew out of the open window, landing terminally on the road."
>
> "I was using the PC outside in the garden. A dog chased a cat towards me. I moved to get out of the way and in doing so knocked over the table. The PC fell into the carp pond, which is deep. No loss of data as full back-up disks maintained. But I have not yet been able to retrieve the computer though will be part-draining the pond in order to do so very soon."
>
> "The train stopped suddenly pitching another commuter forward and trapping my fingers in the laptop. Unfortunately the screen suffered irrepairable damage."
>
> "We had set up the PC in an alcove which was a disused large walk-in fireplace. A freak storm deposited gallons of water down the chimney and into the PC."

through. Steel ladders or stairs fixed to the outside of the house may be a possibility, but could be expensive, a security risk or unsightly. They may require planning permission. In some circumstances "rope ladders" which are bolted firmly inside the house and can be thrown down to provide access may be considered, but the ladder should have metal chains, and metal steps which hold the chains away from the wall in use so you do not scrape your knuckles. These ladders are not recommended by some fire safety experts because they require agility and familiarity for use. However, if you feel confident using such an escape route, and you alone are the usual occupant of the home office, it could be worth looking into.

Insurance

The insurance market has pretty much caught up with the shift to home working. It is still the case that a standard home contents policy is unlikely to cover your home office equipment, but specific policies targetted at home offices have been produced to replace the plethora of computer, office and home policies previously designed to confuse the teleworker. These new policies also cover important business issues which can affect teleworkers such as public liability, employee liability and loss of earnings.

Standard domestic policies, even if you have remembered to inform your insurer that you are working from home, usually don't cover more than £5,000 worth of goods and may exclude single items worth more than £1,000 (which means that many PCs won't be covered). Commercial office and computer policies will cover the computer equipment – but at a high price caused by the dramatic rise in computer theft. Home office policies generally cover equipment valued in the £5,000–£20,000 range and cost about 60% of the cost of an equivalent office policy. The higher the value of the equipment, the higher the premium. Whether your office is part of the house or a separate outbuilding may also affect the premium (in the house is considered more secure because it is constantly occupied). When adding up the cost of your equipment, don't forget extras and small items such as mice and tape drives which can easily turn a £1,000 basic PC into a £2,000 replacement cost. Be sure to make your calculations on a replacement, value not current value, particularly since computers depreciate in value so quickly. Also remember to inform your insurers about any changes, such as purchase of new computers, or a change in the number of visitors or employees, which affects the risk insured. Failure to inform can cause problems if you have to claim.

If you use an insurance broker who, on your behalf, moves your policy around different insurers to get the best deal, check that the material details (such as serial numbers of equipment) are properly recorded every time the policy is renewed. Other items which affect the premium vary from insurer to insurer and include:

- client visits to your premises
- employees
- window locks
- mortice locks on doors
- presence of burglar alarm
- membership of neighbourhood watch (Community Alert in Ireland)
- age of policy holder.

Mobile phones, eminently portable and stealable, are usually excluded from home office policies. Another area often omitted is stock held for resale such as paper, disks or publications. Other areas to consider (which are usually available at the cost of extra premium) are:

- loss of data (*eg* through virus or malicious attack)
- public liability or employer's liability insurance if people visit or work at your home office (this is a must for anyone operating in the Republic of Ireland). It is also important for employers to ensure that employees other than the teleworker visiting the home office are covered (*eg* managers or those involved in health and safety checks)
- business interruption insurance, which compensates you for your time spent putting your business back together and other costs incurred after an incident
- computer breakdown insurance – in some situations this can be cheaper than holding a maintenance contract and ensures that expensive part replacements are covered
- cover off the premises *eg* portable computers on business trips.

Employers need to consider some extra issues. The usual arrangement is to extend the company's insurance to cover the home workplace. The employer will need to consider including public liability for visitors to the home workplace. Some employers offset the additional home office risk by requiring a health and safety risk assessment of the home workplace (this is required anyway by health and safety regulations). However, normally there is no great increase in the employer's premiums as liability premiums are based on wages and salaries plus previous claims experience. Because of a potential clash with domestic policies, teleworking employees must inform their home insurers that they will be working from home – most home insurers then say thanks for informing us, it's not a problem.

If, alternatively, an employer asks an employee to take out a home office policy to cover the employers' equipment used at home, they should also sign an agreement that transfers the insurable interest in the equipment to the employee.

Bibliography

Planning Policy Guideline 13 *Date:* 2000
Author: Department of the Environment
Source: The Stationery Office Ltd, National Publishing, 2nd Floor, St Crispins, Duke Street, Norwich NR3 1PD

Working from home – balancing the issues *Date:* 1998
Babergh District Council Tel: 01473 822801 Fax: 01473 825708.

Data Protection Advice on Homeworking and Computer Information *Date:* 1997
Author: Data Protection Registrar
Source: Tel: 01625 545745 Web: www.dataprotection.gov.uk

Homeworking: Guidance for employers and employees on health and safety *Date:* 1996
Author: Health and Safety Executive
Source: HSE Books, PO Box 199, Sudbury, Suffolk CO10 6FS
Tel: 01787 881165 Fax: 01787 313995. Web:
www.hse.gov.uk/hsehome.htm/pubns/homeindx.htm

Keep IT Safe and Secure (Security and Telecentres) *Date:* 1995
Author: Bill Murray, Small World Connections
Source: Send SAE with 47p stamp to KISS Booklets, WREN Telecottage, Stoneleigh Park, Warwickshire CV8 2LZ
Comment: Part of 1994 security survey analysis, available free of charge to TCA members, subject to availability.

Employed or Self-Employed?
Source: Inland Revenue Ref: Booklet no. IR56, free of charge
Web: www.inlandrevenue.gov.uk/pdfs/ir56.htm

Contacts and URLs

Danacom Headset manufacturer – UK office at 25 Broadway, Maidenhead, Berkshire SL6 1LZ Tel: 01628 676768 Fax: 01628 773806.

Personal Investment Authority – registers independent financial advisors Tel: 020 7676 1000 Web: **www.pia.gov.uk**

Inland Revenue self-assessment enquiry line Tel: 0345 161514. Web: **www.inlandrevenue.gov.uk**

UK Health and Safety Executive, HSE Tel. 01422 892 345 Web: **www.hse.gov.uk**

Data Protection Registrar Tel: 01625 545745. Web: **www.dataprotection.gov.uk**

Institute of Occupational Safety and Health – datasheet on teleworking health and safety issues and form for telework premises assessment. **www.iosh.co.uk/inform/datasheet/telework.html**

Law Centres Federation Tel: 020 7387 8570 or 0161 236 3365 Email: info@lawcentres.org.uk Web: www.lawcentres.org.uk

Oldham MBC has revised its planning guidelines to take account of teleworkers. Its guidelines are available to other planning authorities. Contact Dave Hashdi, Oldham Metropolitan Borough Council Tel: 01619 114 156 Email: dhashdi@gmnresearch.u-net.com.

Peter Fowler is a solicitor with a niche practice in businesss-related legal matters and commercial property. Tel 01202 849 242 Email p_fowler@lds.co.uk Web: **www.peterjfowler.co.uk**

Plantronics Ltd, Headset manufacturer, Interface Business Park, Bincknoll Lane, Wootton Basset, Wiltshire SN4 8QQ Sales Enquiries: 0800 410014 Fax: 01793 848853

Posturite – ergonomic office furniture including chairs, desks, wrist supports, ergonomic mice, document holders, back supports. PO Box 468, Hailsham, East Sussex BN27 4LZ Tel: 01323 833353 Fax: 01323 833999 Email: support@posturite.co.uk Web: **www.posturite.co.uk**

Tolson Messenger – specialists in home office insurance Tel: 0800 374 246 **www.tolsonmessenger.co.uk**

Sulzer Infra CBX – web-based survey on teleworking infrastructure including health and safety information **www.si-cibx.com**

Wilson Insurers – specialists in non-standard home insurance such as people who work from home, problems with subsidence, adverse claims etc. Tel: 0990 239 607 Web: **www.quotelinedirect.co.uk**

Western Provident Association Health insurance plans aimed at the self-employed Tel: 0800 783 0784.

Health and Safety issues: Eilis Duggan, Ergonomics consultant Tel: +353 45 861148

Information on trade union guidelines for teleworkers is available from **www.labourtel.org.uk** – The Labour Telematics Centre website in Manchester

EcologyBuilding Society Tel: 01535 635933. Email: info@ecology.co.uk Web: **www.ecology.co.uk**

Timber cabins for use as home offices
Accommodex – 024 7630 1301
Forest Fencing – 01886 812451
Universal Log Cabins – 0800 731 5947
Homelodge – 01962 881480
Temple Co Ten – 01223 712710

Telephone Preference Service – to register your wish not to be contacted by direct selling organisations Tel: 0845 070 0707

Fax Preference Service – to register your wish not to be faxed by direct selling organisations Tel: 0845 070 0702

www.upspower.co.uk gives information and prices on devices to provide secure power supplies or to give you breathing space to safely close down computers in the event of a power cut.

www.osl2000.com – SAFE2CALL service checking telephone numbers against the Telephone Preference Service listings so that telemarketers can avoid contravening distance selling regulations that could lead to a £5,000 fine.

www.mouchel.com – health and safety assessment service for homeworkers and web-based information service on HSE issues.

Quality for Teleworkers

Why do I need quality management?

One of the key characteristics of successful companies is a "culture of quality" – the participation of all staff to ensure that the product or service delivered constantly satisfies or exceeds the customer's expectations. Most teleworkers have limited time for sales and marketing, so building strong customer relationships and encouraging repeat business makes sense. Achieving a high level of quality is something both teleworkers and their employers should aspire to.

Attaining high levels of quality depends on many factors including:

- staff competence
- level of staff training
- availability and reliability of equipment
- quality of subcontractors
- quality of suppliers.

Many small businesses carry out work at superlative levels of quality without needing to think about these issues – quality is inherent in their method of working. But as businesses get larger, or where a company is part of a more complex supply chain, then it often becomes important to address quality management issues if consistent levels of customer satisfaction are to be achieved. Large organisations may employ a designated quality manager, and have a dedicated quality department to address these issues.

All businesses whatever their size should adopt some quality management measures. This might be as simple as putting in place some basic mechanisms for carrying out the main business functions which may not necessarily be documented. At the other end of the scale, a company may use a formal, documented quality management system (QMS) that has been audited by an independent organisation and shown to comply with a recognised standard such as ISO9000. The approach will vary depending on the nature and size of the business.

Good quality depends on the competence, dedication and thoroughness of people carrying out work. A QMS can help by making the business processes more visible, by focusing the attention of staff on quality and by identifying problem areas. However, a QMS will not turn a "bad" business into a "good" one.

Where do I start?

The first step is to understand the key processes operating within the business. Then you can put in place mechanisms to manage these processes. For a self-employed teleworker, these key processes may include:

- Estimating/quotations/tendering
- Handling of sales orders
- Tracking the progress of work
- Despatch and invoicing
- Document version control
- Checking of work before despatch.

For a one-person business operating from home, there may be no need to formally document these procedures. A simple system could be established based on a hard copy order book, or on spreadsheets for recording and progressing enquiries and sales orders. In larger businesses where teleworkers are operating in a variety of locations and where work co-ordination is an issue, having the procedures documented and understood by everyone becomes essential. Larger businesses are also likely to have a broader range of key processes that need to be managed such as:

- Purchasing
- Assessment of supplier performance
- Material inspections
- Management of subcontractors
- Payroll/HR
- Project planning
- Handling of customer returns/complaints.

Anyone involved in software production must address other processes including:

- Software design and design change control
- Software version control
- Testing.

Quality requirements need to be built into the working methods and procedures of the business. Quality is not a "bolt on" option that can be added to the company's existing working methods. In some organisations the quality manual (the documented set of work procedures) is treated almost as an ornament which gathers dust on a shelf largely unused, but dusted down yearly prior to the quality audit. In such organisations, quality management is treated as an overhead – the creation of unnecessary paperwork with no perceived added value. In contrast, a properly designed QMS need not be a burden. The quality requirements can be satisfied by defining the work procedures appropriately without incurring unneccessary bureaucracy and paperwork. An inappropriate system can become a bureaucratic overload that is expensive for a small businesses to maintain. Such systems are inflexible and stifle creativity and innovation.

Improving internal procedures using a QMS should result in greater efficiency, improved customer service and improved customer satisfaction.

A documented QMS helps the different functions of your business to work together and often results in considerable savings by preventing mistakes. A good QMS will also provide a basis for monitoring and improving the company's performance. It is therefore important to monitor the effectiveness of any QMS to ensure that it is appropriate for your business and to make improvements as necessary.

What are the quality standards?

The internationally accepted quality standards, known as the ISO9000 series, were issued in 1994 and replace the previous British Standard (BS) 5750. The ISO standards comprise a number of model quality systems together with guidance notes indicating which quality management system is applicable depending on the key processes within the business. Most teleworking businesses fall under ISO9002 except for those involving design/software activities that will need to take note of the design control requirements of ISO 9001:1994.

These standards provide a useful measure of best practice and for many companies it will be sufficient to base their QMS on an ISO 9000 standard without going for certification. However, some customers require that an independent check or certification is made of the quality management system. This check is usually by means of an audit carried out by the customer or, more normally, a third party. There are a number of third-party organisations accredited by the DTI to carry out these audits and a successful audit results in your company becoming 'registered' to ISO 9000.

PR needs override quality results for cancer testers

Faulty cervical cancer test results have led to a hospital in Norfolk ending its homeworking scheme for testers although quality checks indicated the home-based workers often had better records than lab-based staff.

The James Paget Hospital had to repeat over 9,000 cervical smears after mistakes by one tester led to 357 minor and 19 serious errors. It takes two years to train a tester, most of whom are women. As some had left to start families, the hospital allowed a homeworking solution which also freed up lab space during a time of increasing demand for the smear tests. The report which investigated the errors recommended abolishing homeworking, and retesting all of the homeworkers' samples.

The implication that the quality of the home-based workers was worse is not borne out by the evidence. According to Elayne Guest, director of corporate services, the quality assurance procedures in place indicated that mistakes by home-based testers are no higher than for lab workers. "Not all of our screeners live close to the hospital. They come in once a week and their work is supervised during the visit. Their slides are checked and a second opinion is sought when required."

In addition, companies specialising in software development could also consider registering under the DTI's TickIT scheme (ISO9000–3), which provides guidance on applying ISO9001 requirements to the software design and development process. It is possible to apply for certification under ISO9001 and TickIT at the same time. A growing number of large companies who have business-critical or safety-related software requirements insist that their suppliers operate under the TickIT scheme.

The ISO9000 standard is in the process of being updated and during 2000 the new standard ISO9000:2000 will be issued. Teleworkers and businesses seeking registration will be required to operate in accordance with this new standard. ISO 9000:2000 has been developed to overcome some of the criticisms often made of the 1994 standard. Some quality specialists claim that ISO 9000:2000, with its stronger focus on business processes and management issues combined with less emphasis on the need for quality documentation and its associated bureaucracy, will be better suited to the needs of small businesses. ISO9000:2000 places less importance on a clause-by-clause compliance with the published standard and concentrates more on the overall adequacy of the business processes in use to provide a level of quality applicable to the business.

Is quality management different for teleworkers?

In a standard industrial quality system, a company controls its subcontractors or suppliers by insisting that they deliver in accordance with a documented specification defining the scope, timescale and standards applicable to the materials or service supplied. Teleworking often relies on less formal, and more personal, relationships with customers. Many teleworkers operate on a reimbursable contract basis, receiving payment at an agreed rate for the number of hours, or days, worked. Under such arrangements, the teleworker is likely to be operating under the customer's

QMS, almost as an employee, rather than working under their own quality system.

Simon Burke of ISO9001-registered company Intermec Ireland agrees that ISO9000 is probably inapplicable to individual teleworkers or very small businesses of less than five people. "The effort involved and the corresponding documentation of the business processes could be enough to kill the business." Instead, Simon recommends making sure that you can comply with your client's vendor assessment procedures. "A company like ours divides its purchases of goods and services into primary items that can affect the quality of our own products and services, such as software developments. Other purchases are secondary, such as office stationery and consumables. All primary goods and services must be purchased from other companies that are listed on an internal Qualified Vendor List. This list is compiled by the company, usually on the basis of a quality related questionnaire, sometimes called a Vendor Appraisal Form. This must be completed prior to trade between the two companies. If the vendor is ISO9000 -registered then there is no problem. If not, samples of goods or services will be tested, or they will be accepted through a reputable third party recommendation. A vendor is normally on the list only for a given product or service. If a vendor is qualified to supply one item, it does not qualify them to supply everything."

So for small teleworking businesses, the best advice may be to be aware of your client's vendor assessment forms and make sure you can comply with their quality management system.

What kind of QMS do I need?

In order to display the ISO9000 symbol, a business must achieve third-party accreditation. This involves first establishing a QMS which satisfies all the requirements of the ISO 9000 standard and then having the system independently audited. Once registration has been achieved, annual surveillance audits are conducted to ensure that the standards are being maintained. Achieving third-party registration requires a significant commitment of time and resources and teleworkers should carefully consider whether formal registration is necessary for their business. Reasons frequently cited by teleworkers and small businesses for requiring third-party accreditation are:

■ **Customer demand**

In some cases, companies will only trade with ISO9000 registered businesses. If you wish to trade with these companies, achieving ISO9000 registration is a condition of 'joining the club'.

■ **Market differentiation**

Some small businesses operating in a price-competitive market find that quality can provide market differentiation. Holding ISO9000 registration when your competitors do not can help businesses stand out from the competition and perhaps command a premium price for their goods and services.

■ **Work in specialist markets**

Businesses operating in certain specialist markets, such as goods or services which have health and safety implications, would normally be expected to hold ISO9000 registration.

During the early 1990s, many small businesses were encouraged to seek ISO9000 registration under circumstances where the ISO9000 standard was badly applied so that registration created extra work and bureaucracy and overall had a negative impact on the business. The problems encountered by small businesses slavishly seeking ISO9000 registration have been well publicised, and today, companies tend to be more circumspect when considering the need for registration.

Teleworking companies might heed the words of Jacques McMillan, former head of the European Commission department in charge of quality policy and certification for telematics networks and systems: "There are many enterprises going bust where the last flag as they go under is their (quality) certificate. I am trying to put it back in perspective so those companies that actually need it should go for it and those that don't shouldn't. It should not be thrust down the throats of small and medium-sized companies."

Other critics say quality certification is expensive, bureaucratic and difficult to set up and maintain, and that companies mistakenly see certification as an end in itself, rather than as a step towards improving quality.

Establishing a quality system

Step 1: Determine whether ISO9000 registration is required

Determine at the outset whether you wish to achieve ISO9000 registration. If registration is required, then it will probably be necessary to employ the services of a Quality Consultant. A good consultant will understand the requirements of the ISO9000 standard in detail and will ensure that your Quality Management System complies with the standard.

However, Suzanne Flynn, Head of Quality Services at Cygnet Solutions, counsels against asking consultants to implement your Quality Management System. Flynn says "No-one knows your business as well as you. Asking a stranger to define the work procedures for your business is a recipe for failure. A good consultant will guide you through the process of setting up the QMS and interpret the rules for you. However, the working methods and business procedures should be your own."

Teleworkers and teleworking businesses that wish to avoid the costs of employing a consultant could opt to obtain a copy of the ISO9000 standard (and the many available books explaining it) and interpret it for themselves.

Step 2: Identify key business processes
Identify those processes within the business which are critical to maintaining good quality. These might be processes which involve interaction with the customer, which impact on the fitness-for-purpose of the delivered product or service or which influence the ability of the business to deliver on time. If ISO9000 registration is being sought, then that standard will define the processes which must be addressed.

Step 3: Document work procedures
In all but the smallest and simplest businesses, the work procedures used to manage the key business processes should be documented. Ideally, this activity should be carried out by the teleworker himself/herself.

Step 4: Communicate and review
In businesses with more than one employee, all relevant personnel should be asked to contribute to documenting and reviewing the work procedures. When the work procedures are agreed, they should be circulated to all staff and everyone should be clear as to their responsibilities. A mechanism should be put in place to allow the effectiveness of the procedures to be reviewed and amended as necessary.

Step 5: Use the Quality Management System
Once the work procedures are established and communicated, they must be adhered to. Before considering applying for ISO9000 registration (if applicable), the procedures must have been in day-to-day use for a period of time (usually three months) to allow a documented case history to be produced.

Step 6: Trial audit
If seeking ISO9000 registration, it is advisable to conduct a trial audit prior to the visit by the independent auditor. A quality consultant will normally be able to offer this service.

Step 7: Obtaining registration
In order to obtain third-party registration, it is necessary to apply to one of the accredited certifying bodies. It is a good idea to approach two or three and compare their costs and registration processes. They will visit your business and assess your Quality Management System. If the certification body is satisfied both that the quality management system complies with the standard, and that it is being used comprehensively within your business, you will be awarded a certificate. You can then use the certificate and the registered company logo in marketing activities. After registration, the certification body returns periodically (once or twice a year) to ensure that the quality management system is up-to-date and in use. There is normally an annual fee to be paid for continued registration. A final word of caution: there are a number of non-accredited organisations who will register companies to ISO 9000. This certification, whilst legal and providing an impressive logo for your letterhead, is worthless and is likely to be unacceptable to your clients.

The use of supporting software tools

Software tools are available to support quality management. These tools can automate some of the routine tasks but they are not a panacea. An effective QMS cannot be established simply by running a software package. These tools fall into various categories and supplier contact details are given in the references to this chapter.

- **quality management tools**

These are designed to help companies achieve compliance with the ISO9000 standard and maintain the necessary documentary evidence of compliance. Tools available include Voyager, Powerway and EQS.

- **Accounts/business management tools**

Affordable software packages are available which manage small company accounts and provide a range of additional facilities such as sales order processing, stock control, manufacturing control, despatch, invoicing, etc. The adoption of such packages can help a small business to establish a set of business procedures quickly that will form the core of the QMS. Sage and Pegasus offer some of the most popular packages in this area.

- **Process management software**

These are interactive software tools that allow companies to define their own businesses procedures and workflow requirements and help track the processes through an organisation. This process-oriented approach is particularly relevant to the ISO9000:2000 standard. Products available include Process Expert and 4TQToolkit.

- **Collaborative working tools**

Collaborative working tools use information and communications technology to help workers share information securely and collaborate on projects, irrespective of the location of individual workers. Packages include OfficeVenue and HotOffice.

For teleworkers involved in the generation of software, there is a wide range of tools available to help with the software development process including:

- **Design tools**

These allow design requirements to be specified at a high (functional) level and help in decomposing the design into data structures and modules of code. Some tools are able to generate parts of the code automatically. The tools include facilities to manage the process of applying design changes ensuring that these are properly authorised and documented.

- **Configuration Management Systems**

To control the quality of a software build, it is essential that versions of all software modules which comprise the build are known and documented. This ensures that a particular version of software can be traced to its constituent components and re-built at any time if required. Configuration

Management Systems (CMS) are available to support this task. Microsoft SourceSafe is a popular, and inexpensive PC-based package which may be used for this purpose.

- **Testing**

Commercial software is frequently rushed to market without adequate testing having been conducted. Testing can be laborious, time-consuming and expensive. Software tools are available to aid the testing process, allowing some testing to be carried out automatically, documenting the test results and providing statistics on the extent of testing conducted and on the quality of the code.

A pragmatic approach

Teleworking consultancy Cornix has prepared a code of conduct for Devon & Cornwall TEC that gives a good starting point for teleworkers:

The Telnet code of conduct

(© Devon & Cornwall TEC)

1. To carry out the assignment which the teleworker has undertaken diligently, conscientiously and with proper regard for the client's interests.
2. To apply good management and quality assurance practices to all teleworking assignments.
3. To agree with the client a written statement which clearly defines the objectives and scope of the proposed work, the timescale and fee basis, and also where necessary to agree in writing any subsequent revision.
4. To respect all information concerning the client's business as strictly confidential and not to disclose or permit the disclosure of any such information without the client's specific prior permission.

Quality on the move at Spektra Systems

Spektra Systems, a specialist software consultancy, has made its quality procedures and work practices available to staff who are teleworking or working on customer sites. The system uses Lotus Notes to provide online information, and also encompasses forms for expenses, timesheets and training records as well as for quality management. It is now being marketed to other companies as the PR1ME package. Euan Robertson, Spektra's Technical Director, sees several benefits:

- Quality becomes a banner for staff to rally around and is well-received by clients;
- The quality system has helped introduce structure and a disciplined approach;
- New staff can easily assimilate the company's methods and work practices.

5. To ensure that all property, data, text and other materials belonging to the client and held by the teleworker are stored in a secure location when not in use and handled appropriately when in use.
6. To only accept assignments for which the teleworker is suitably qualified and/or experienced to carry out to a high standard.
7. To refrain from undertaking any assignment which would result in a conflict of interest and to disclose to the client any financial or personal interest which may influence the work carried out for the client in any way.
8. To ensure that all hardware and software used by the teleworker is used only in connection with the teleworker's professional activities, is properly maintained and that all reasonable care is taken to ensure that it is free from defects.
9. To ensure that the teleworker's knowledge and skills are kept up-to-date, where necessary through obtaining appropriate training and professional development.

Contractual relationships

(© Devon & Cornwall TEC)

Agreed terms and conditions for sales should be implemented. There should be a process for defining the customer's requirements, and dealing with any conflicts or changes to the requirements. Ensure that your business can satisfy its contractual obligations for each sale. Cornix makes the following recommendations for a minimum teleworking contract:

1. Include identities and contact addresses of both purchaser and supplier, and if either is a corporate body, the names of the individuals concerned.
2. Describe in general terms the work to be carried out, its purpose and scope.
3. Specify the payment for the work, and whether VAT will be applicable.
4. Specify a timetable for both the work, and payment for the work.
5. Describe clearly the proposals for confidentiality and security of the work and its Data Protection Act status.
6. Define the ownership of any resulting copyright and intellectual property rights, if appropriate.
7. Arrangements for loan or supply of equipment, where applicable, including insurance arrangements, should be listed.
8. Specify arrangements in the event of illness, incapacity, holidays, *etc.* and for any consequent subcontracting, if permitted.
9. If the workload exceeds 21 hours per week, and is an exclusive use of the teleworker full-time, then arrangements for PAYE and NI deductions should be made, as in these circumstances the teleworker may be classified as an employee for the duration of the work.

10. Refer to the quality assurance system to be used, if any.
11. Where group working is involved, the identity of the individual responsible for quality within the group should be specified.

Lesley Carr of People, Processes and Systems lists other areas covered by quality standards:

Suppliers and purchases
All your suppliers should be vetted for the quality of the product or service which they supply to you. Suppliers with bad track records should be dropped. Purchase requirements need to be clearly laid out to avoid misunderstandings.

Production and process control
You will need a method of checking, inspecting and rectifying the product or service while it is being produced to ensure that it meets customer requirements. At the end of the production, any goods or services that are not up to scratch must be identified and dealt with accordingly. The quality system should allow the status of individual products or jobs to be easily traced or identified.

Handling and storage
Any items handled by your business should be stored, packaged and delivered to the customer in a way which protects them from damage, deterioration, loss or misuse.

Keeping records
The precise records needed for every business transaction or procedure should be specified. They should be identified, comprehensive, secure and accessible to all who need them. The records should be retained for an agreed time period and then archived or destroyed.

Financial affairs
There should be adequate control over aspects of finance that relate to the customer, such as invoice production.

Training and competency
Each member of staff should get the correct level of training, and should have the appropriate qualifications for the tasks they carry out. Records of training given should be kept.

Coping with complaints
A recognised procedure for dealing with complaints should be implemented to resolve problems.

Malcolm Lake of Effective Quality Management adds three more points:

Management reviews and audits
A regular and systematic review by the management of the business to check whether the quality management system is working well, and to monitor business performance, training needs, *etc*.

Statements of responsibilities

A clearly defined statement of management/job responsibilities. Even if the business is operated very flexibly, the owner/manager will have different responsibilities from his or her assistants.

Corrective actions

A procedure for determining what to do when a problem occurs: ways of enabling the problem to be sorted out quickly and effectively, and of ensuring that it does not happen again.

Case studies

Antur Teifi – solving a quality problem

Mike Jones, Quality Officer for Antur Teifi, an organisation located on six sites with 30 staff, including a well-equipped Telematics Centre, sums up the quality process: "It should be a bottom-up process – you need to keep your existing good practices. You have to ensure everybody owns the quality process – *ie* involve those who have to use it. Then write it down. I think anyone who is thinking about going for a quality standard needs to ask themselves the following questions:

1. Do we really need quality control?
2. Can we afford its costs?
3. Are we really committed to the work needed to maintain the system?
4. Do our customers expect us to operate to an ISO9000 standard?

If you decide to go ahead, the next step is to decide whether you are going to use a consultant, or whether you will try to "DIY" your quality system. Either way, the golden rules are:

1. Document what you do;
2. Do what you have documented;
3. Check that you are doing it.

It took Antur Teifi 18 months to become certificated, but smaller organisations should be able to do it on a much shorter timescale. "During our certification, we encountered a problem with a contract we had taken on from the Employment Department. The contract involved training for long-term unemployed people that culminated in each participant having their CV typed by our Telematics Centre. Within four days of the end of the course, the Jobcentre should receive ten correct copies of each CV. For months there were problems, ranging from late delivery of CVs to incorrect CVs, and inconsistencies in the CV format. When I initially investigated the problem, everyone involved blamed everyone else for the errors. The tutors thought the typists were incapable of the work. The typists believed the tutors did not care about their work because of the poor quality of the manuscript CVs.

We sat down and discussed the problem without apportioning blame, and the problem was tracked back to the lack of a procedure that everyone understood, that could be owned by everyone, checked independently, and where if anyone did not adhere to the procedure, non-conformance would be evident. The next step was to write down the problems and examine their causes rather than their symptoms. The tables and flow chart below show how we solved the problem and documented it for our quality system."

Problem	Reason/cause	Answer
Late delivery of CVs	• Scripts not arriving at Telematics Centre on time for typing	Scripts to be posted 1st class to Telematics Centre on same evening as course is held
	• No-one available to do the typing	A minimum of 3 days notice to be given to the Telematics Centre of the arrival of scripts
	• Some scripts unreadable	CV details to be printed by trainees and checked by the tutor for accuracy
Incorrect CVs	• Scripts unreadable	All CVs to be checked by a second person after typing and only typists with good skills to be used
		Trainees to print rather than write details
		Tutor to check script prior to despatch to Telematics Centre
		All CVs to be checked by another person before leaving Telematics Centre
Inconsistencies in format	• No trainee or tutor had a format by which a standard could be set	Each trainee to fill a standard form with CV details

This analysis was used to draw up the following quality system documentation.

> Using form 116 Jobsearch participant prints CV during the course, or presents a typed version if preferred. Form 116 is attached [not shown in this factsheet]

> Completed form 116 or typed version checked by Jobsearch Course Leader by end of course and passed by end of Day 2 to Telematics Centre for typing

> Information from form 116 to be typed in CV fashion and despatched by end of Day four (two working days from receipt). Prior to despatch, typed CV to be checked for accuracy against original by person other than typist

> Person who checks the accuracy signs and dates at item 5, page 6 of form 116 and passes copy and original through to the Training Department

> In cases where complete form 116 is unreadable or obscure, the Course Leader is contacted by Telematics Centre staff. If the day 4 deadline cannot be met the relevant Job Centre is informed by Telematics Centre staff

Intermec Ireland – picking a teleworker

Margaret Burke, quality officer at Intermec Ireland, an ISO9001-registered company that specialises in barcode readers, printers and consumables, spells out what she is looking for in a teleworker:

"ISO9000 purchasing requirements list three questions that must be answered:

1. How can we control the quality of what we buy from subcontractors or suppliers such as teleworkers?
2. How should we assess our subcontractors/suppliers?
3. How do we control the quality of products given to us by subcontractors to include in our processes?

Let's look at how we might deal with this for two teleworking examples, one simple and one complex. First, Intermec have recently developed a new software package called 'Asset Tracking', which is a generic product for the barcoding market, and will be sold worldwide. We might need a teleworker to translate our user documentation into French or German. This is a specialised job, so just as though we were hiring a new employee, we would look carefully at the teleworker's qualifications and experience. We would hope to see a sample of work, but if we couldn't, perhaps because of confidentiality agreements, then we would ask for a referee, so that we can assess the teleworker's basic ability to carry out the required work. We would then transmit our documentation electronically to the teleworker, who could retransmit the translated document. We might ask for the initial few pages of the document to review for quality of translation, correct use of terminology for the target industry, *etc*. Our contract would contain confidentiality agreements if necessary.

The second example is more complex, and one where we intend to incorporate the product of the teleworking into our own products. Let's say we are overloaded in the software area and we need to contract out some development work on a once-off basis. As in the first case, we would look at qualification and experience, but we would also have to insist that the teleworker conform to our Development Standards Manual, which forms part of our quality system. The appropriate sections and samples would be provided to the teleworker, and we would also provide the teleworker with the functional specification from which the technical specification will be developed. From there on, the teleworker must conform to our standards. Development work would be reviewed by our team leaders at Intermec, beginning at the Technical Specification stage and progressing to testing of the software. Acceptance of the review could be authorised by electronic signatures, which can be used as a form of proof for an auditor. We would not accept a teleworker who did not wish to conform to these standards."

Somerset Computer Services – quality for microenterprises

Somerset Computer Services is a "1.5 man" operation run by Kieron McGrath and his wife. Kieron has three specialities – computer consultancy for small businesses, training for the local enterprise centre in the small business area, and a desktop publishing service. Kieron decided to go for a quality system with independent certification for two reasons. Firstly he felt that it would open doors in larger companies that he wanted to sell to by giving greater credibility. "Teleworkers already have a credibility problem because they tend to be microbusinesses, and because of the roses-round-the-door media image that has been promoted. Therefore it's actually more important to have a quality certificate than for other sectors", he comments. Secondly, he felt that his business, like most small businesses, was disorganised and too dependent on one person – himself. "After installing the quality system, when I went into hospital for a knee replacement, my wife was able to run the business quite happily for three weeks using the documented systems."

Kieron was fortunate in being able to join a subsidised quality course that was run at his local TEC, occupying one day a month for six months, which reduced his consultancy costs considerably. "I think that the standard is incomprehensible, and that means you can't write your own quality manual – you have to get a consultant to explain things and to look at how your existing system conforms to the standard."

Some requirements are straightforward and sensible practice for all businesses, such as the logging of all incoming and outgoing mail. But being such a small business has caused a few absurdities. Kieron has to hold monthly quality audits taking about two hours, and quarterly management review meetings, which are attended by himself and his wife.

Size had its advantages when it came to cost, however. Kieron was able to negotiate with an organisation offering certification. "I said £2,850 for three years just wasn't on for a two-person business that was going to take them half a day to assess, not one and a half days. I was about to go for a body specialising in small business certification instead, but then the original organisation came back and offered me £450 a year over three years." Another tip Kieron gives is to double-check that your consultant and certifying organisation themselves have achieved quality standards. Kieron's advice on picking consultants and certifiers is to use word of mouth, and talk to other similar small businesses that have achieved quality standards. "It has definitely been worthwhile for us. Companies that wouldn't have looked at us are now letting us quote, and the business is run much more efficiently." The flow chart on the opposite page gives an example of one of Kieron's quality procedures.

How much does it cost?

- staff time estimates are hard to make. However, if you contact a quality consultant at the beginning of your quality programme, they may be able to help you make an estimate before you embark on major expenditure. Stephen Simmons of Cornix cautions that even the smallest group's scheme will involve at least 100 hours of effort: "The point is that the real cost is in own time expended, which is likely to be more expensive than the money cost.";

- consultancy costs vary and you should obtain competing quotes. Kieron McGrath got his consultancy 50% paid for by his local TEC, reducing the cost to £1,250. Companies in the same type of business could group together to save money on courses because the process is similar for each business. In Ireland, approved courses can qualify for grant aid under the FÁS training support scheme;

- certification costs (these are sometimes included in consultant's costs). Kieron McGrath got his certification at the bargain rate of £450/year for three years, but he was originally asked for £2,850. Approximate certification costs for a number of UK certifying bodies are given overleaf.

Dealing with enquiries, quotations and orders

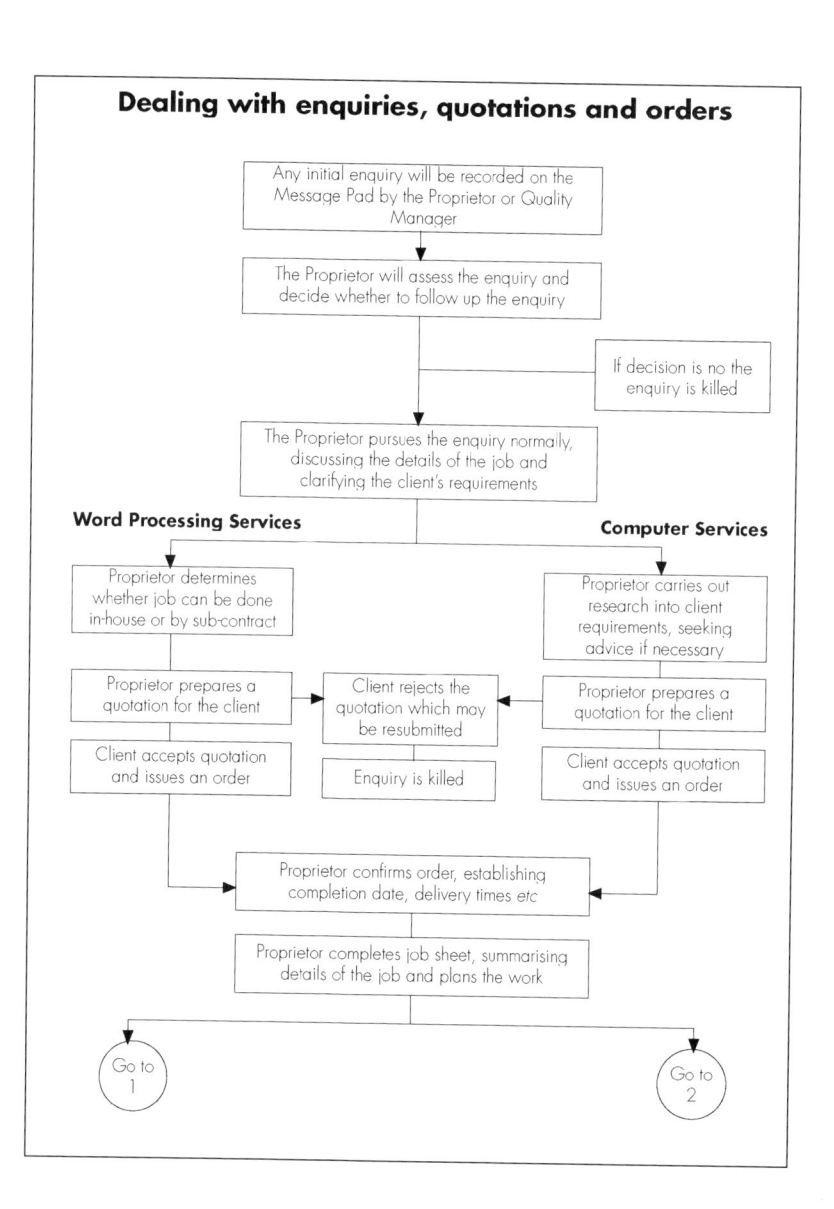

```
Any initial enquiry will be recorded on the
Message Pad by the Proprietor or Quality
Manager
            ↓
The Proprietor will assess the enquiry and
decide whether to follow up the enquiry
            ↓                          → If decision is no the
                                          enquiry is killed
The Proprietor pursues the enquiry normally,
discussing the details of the job and
clarifying the client's requirements
```

Word Processing Services   **Computer Services**

| Proprietor determines whether job can be done in-house or by sub-contract | | Proprietor carries out research into client requirements, seeking advice if necessary |

| Proprietor prepares a quotation for the client | Client rejects the quotation which may be resubmitted | Proprietor prepares a quotation for the client |

| Client accepts quotation and issues an order | Enquiry is killed | Client accepts quotation and issues an order |

Proprietor confirms order, establishing completion date, delivery times *etc*

Proprietor completes job sheet, summarising details of the job and plans the work

(Go to 1)   (Go to 2)

Certification costs

Certifying body	Contact	Telephone	Registration cost	Annual costs	Notes
BSI Quality Assurance	Neil Coole	0208 996 9000	£1,100	£795	1,2
European Quality Assurance Ltd	Linda Key	01636 611226	£630	£860	3
Lloyds Register Quality Assurance	Telemarketing Dept	0800 7832179	From £76/month over 3 yrs		4
National Quality Assurance	Steve Durston	01582 866 766	£900	£590	5
SGS Yarsley	Barry Holland	01276 691133	£1,475	£885	6,3

Notes

All prices relate to a business with up to five employees and are based on a three-year package

[1] One surveillance audit per annum
[2] Annual charge can be paid over an eight-month period
[3] Two surveillance audits per annum
[4] Fee payable monthly by direct debit
[5] Prices relate to ISO9002 only
[6] Prices shown are estimates. Actual costs are charged on an agreed day-rate basis.

Margaret Burke gives an estimate of costs for Intermec's certification: "We have over forty employees. My salary is an obvious overhead, and I would guess that over the eighteen months we have been working on ISO, each employee has probably spent 15 days on quality issues – a significant hidden cost. But there were hidden benefits. We saved money because of the stringent procedures, and looked at all aspects of our business. We have 105 procedures in place, and three manuals – Development Standards, Quality and Procedures. I feel there is a problem with certification – the amount of paperwork created. Intermec was relatively paper-free, despite operating from four different sites. All main communication and documentation was completed on our IBM AS400. All ISO9000 proof of approval, acceptance, *etc* requires sign-offs, which involve paper. I don't feel it's paperwork with a purpose – ISO does not support rainforests! "

If you decide that certification is too expensive for your business, other options are:

- use an independent scheme (this will not entitle you to use ISO9000 in your literature);

- discuss with your clients their vendor assessment and quality procedures. Make sure that you are complying with their quality system, even if you don't have certification; or

- develop a consistent quality system for your business that is compatible with ISO9000, but do not apply for certification with its extra costs.

One of Malcolm Lake's clients commented on quality: "I can now see that twelve months ago we merely "muddled along". Now we are well-organised, we know where everything is, we all know what our jobs are and we have doubled our turnover with the same number of office staff. I do not need to go for external certification but I know that if I do I will easily obtain it." Malcolm Lake of Effective Quality Management provides a free telephone advice service to any teleworking organisation that would like to know more about ISO9000 and its organisational implications. "Previously it could have been argued that quality standards represented a heavy industry, top-down approach. Now the ISO9000 models allow each organisation to be free to operate top-down or bottom-up and to choose whether or not to see certification."

Acknowledgement

This chapter has been checked and updated by Brian Higton of Cygnet Solutions.

Contacts

Many local Business Links in Britain or FÁS in Ireland keep information on quality systems, and some run subsidised workshops for companies going for ISO9000. Local offices of the DTI can also provide UK information.

Copies of the ISO9000 standard are available from BSI Standards, Chiswick High Road, London W4 4AL Tel: 020 8996 9001 Fax: 020 8996 7001 Web: **www.bsi.org.uk**

A list of quality certification bodies can be obtained from the United Kingdom Accreditation Service (UKAS) at www.ukas.com or from the QA Register, published by The Stationery Office, PO Box 276, London SW8 5DT or at **www.quality-register.co.uk**

Antur Teifi, Business Park, Aberad, Newcastle Emlyn, Dyfed SA38 9DB. Tel: 01239 710238 Fax: 01239 710358 Contact: Lynne Thomas

British Quality Foundation, 215 Vauxhall Bridge Road, London SW1V 1EN Tel: 020 7654 5000

Cornix Teleworking Consultancy, 64 Morrab Road, Penzance, Cornwall TR18 2QT Tel: 01736 369477 Fax: 01736 369477 Email: 100021.2563@compuserve.com or srs@cornix.co.uk Contact: Stephen Simmons

Cygnet Solutions, Swan House, Darvel, Ayrshire KA17 0LP Tel: 01560 323444 Fax: 01560 323432 Email: sgf@cygnets.co.uk Web: **www.cygnets.co.uk** Contact: Suzanne Flynn. Cygnet helps companies to achieve ISO9001, ISO9002 and TickIT registration.

Effective Quality Management (EQM), Lake House, Wythop Mill, Cockermouth, Cumbria CA13 9YP. Tel: 01768 776687 Fax: 01768 77629 Email: malcolm.lake@btinternet.com Contact: Malcolm Lake. This is the company that designed and developed Kieron McGrath's system.

Intermec Ireland, 19/20 York Road, Dun Laoghaire, Co. Dublin, Ireland. Tel: +353 1 280 0899 E-mail: simon@intermec.ie Web: **www.intermec.ie**

Somerset Computer Services, South View, Runnington, Wellington, Somerset TA21 0QW Tel: 01823 661544 Fax: 01823 661544 Email: 100111.3412@Compuserve.com

Spektra Systems Ltd, Spektra House, 2 MacMillan Road, Alderstone Business Park, Livingston, EH54 7DF Tel: 01506 460234 Fax: 01506 460212 Email: info@spektra.co.uk Web: www.spektra.co.uk Contact: Euan Robertson This company is now selling its own Lotus Notes quality management system adapted for use by remote workers under the title PR1ME.

Suppliers of software for quality applications

Voyager by XGL Systems Ltd Tel: 01992 638763 Web: **www.xgl.com**

Powerway by Powerway Europe Tel: 01628 672229 Web: **www.powerway.com**

EQS by Byelex Workgroup Technologies Tel: 01932 788792

Sage Line 50 by Sage Software Ltd Tel: 0191 255 3000 Web: **www.uk.sage.com**

Pegasus Capital Gold by Pegasus Software Ltd Tel: 01536 495000 Web: **www.pegasus.co.uk**

Process Expert by Ethos Business Solutions Ltd Tel: 01788 552811 Web: **www.iso9000-2000.org**

4TQToolkit byAxion Corporation Ltd. Tel: 01246 291399 Web: **www.4tq.com**

OfficeVenue by Cygnet Solutions Ltd. Tel: 01560 323444 Web: **www.officevenue.com**

HotOffice by HotOffice Technologies Inc Tel: +11 561 995 2220 Web: **www.hotoffice.com**

Disability and teleworking

Teleworking has the potential to offer some disabled people new employment opportunities. People with mobility, visual or hearing impairments can work from their own homes, or from a centre adapted for disabled teleworkers. This can be of particular benefit to people whose disability causes them fatigue or difficulty in travelling to work or moving around while at work. In addition to mobility issues, some people argue that teleworking can also reduce prejudice against disabled people due to their appearance.

In 1999, according to British Labour Force Survey figures, around 78,000 disabled people in Britain were teleworking, amounting to about 5% of teleworkers (similar to the percentage of disabled people employed overall). A further 198,000 were unemployed. For some disability types such as visual impairment, the unemployment rate is as much as 75–80%. The charity AbilityNet states that around 75% of disabled employees were able-bodied when first employed, and one in fourteen people will be eligible to be registered disabled before reaching retirement age.

The work that can be carried out by people with disabilities encompasses the whole range of teleworking, from word processing to software programming. However, the implications for those receiving state benefits need careful consideration. Recent rule changes mean that if you are earning less than £56 a week, or £3.50 an hour then any disability benefits that you receive should not be affected. If you receive Incapacity Benefit, you are entitled to undertake "therapeutic work' for up to 16 hours a week for minimal wages. But if you are disabled and seek employment through teleworking, be sure to get written advice from the Benefits Agency on how this may affect any benefits you receive, bearing in mind that some benefits are very hard won and may be hard to revive if the teleworking situation does not work out or your disability changes. In general, the benefits system is unable to cope with the variable income which is typical of self-employed teleworking.

Additionally, some insurance settlements for the disabled are paid on the understanding that the recipient will never physically be able to take up employment again, whereas others have earnings thresholds which may not be exceeded. Peter Lisney of YEP Ltd advises: "Potential disabled teleworkers should first weigh up the possible penalties against the possible gains before investing in equipment and training." Helen Suffell of Action Aid, which has a number of disabled homeworkers, believes that disabled people are reluctant to take up short-term contracts because of the bureaucracy which they have to go through to requalify for benefits at the end of a period of contract work.

The TCA/IES/Mitel 1999 survey on virtual call centres found that 10% of prospective teleworkers value the anonymity afforded by working from home, and a further 17% were attracted by the idea of not having to dress up or worry about their appearance in order to work. Some disabled teleworkers interviewed by Ursula Huws in 1986 found that teleworking could be either positive or negative for the marginalisation of disabled people depending on personal situations. Teleworking can provide a means to independence, self-respect and enhanced satisfaction, but in some situations, it can lead to isolation and fears of "out of sight, out of mind". One respondent to the 1999 Mitel survey said: "Three days per week I have the necessity to be up and out – it's very important to get out and do something."

Access to the technology

It is important to get a proper assessment of a disabled computer user's needs so that they can get the best access possible to teleworking technology. AbilityNet (formerly the Computability Centre), based in Warwick, is a nationwide charity that offers professional computer expertise to people with all kinds of disabilities. AbilityNet runs an advice and information service including a phone helpline which received 16,000 enquiries in 1999, as well as giving technical awareness sessions (3000 people attended these in 1999) and providing assessment services (1600 carried out in 1999), training courses and consultancy. There is now a network of AbilityNet centres around the country (more information from **www.abilitynet.co.uk**).

In addition to helping those who are already disabled to get better access to computers, AbilityNet helps those who already use computers but suffer from progressive problems of disability. In the case of British Gas payroll supervisor Eileen Knowles, who has Parkinson's Disease, AbilityNet "saved her job". Eileen's hand tremors were affecting her keyboarding accuracy and she was having difficulty holding a pen. AbilityNet provided Eileen with a keyguard (a template with holes for each key) and recommended moving the keyboard down to a tray below her desk. Eileen was amazed at the effectiveness of these simple adaptations.

For Jane Thurlow, a biologist at the Imperial Cancer Research Fund, severe back injury meant she could not sit down at all, and could stand for only 20 minutes in an hour. Writing and typing were causing her considerable pain. AbilityNet helped Jane to experiment with different techniques for using the computer while lying down. Jane now has a computer with voice input, and the screen is tilted through 90 degrees so that she can read it lying down.

Improvements in voice dictation software have opened up many new options for some conditions. AbilityNet saw a young woman with RSI affecting her back and preventing her from carrying on her work in data input. A voice dictation solution solved the problem and proved as productive as keyboarding. In another case an inexpensive equipment solution did the trick. An executive suffering increasing discomfort in the

A personal view on the teleworking option

Mary Duffy is a journalist and artist who lives in rural Wicklow, Ireland. These are excerpts from her talk to the 1998 European Telework Development conference held in Dublin.

"Teleworking is isolated work and it suits some of the people some of the time, often for a variety of reasons. It suits certain disabled people but it's not a panacea for the 70% or 80% of disabled people who are unemployed, underutilised, who feel disregarded and are feeling dumped in the society we live in... Teleworking doesn't eliminate discrimination but it does reduce a major element of it which is prejudice. People can't prejudge you if they don't know that you're disabled because they can't see you.

I'm convinced that if it were not for my disability, I would not have become the technobabe that I am. Nothing fazes me very much in the electronic world. I have a deep faith in the power of technology to level that playing field. Computers have made the world accessible and friendly and at my toetips. That's fine until something goes wrong. One of the problems I've had as a teleworker has been a paper jam in the printer. That leaves me nearly hysterical. Dealing with suppliers and so-called support from computer sales companies... they assume that you can just bounce around and pull out cables and stick them back in again when you get them on the phone.

To enjoy teleworking you need to be able to enjoy your morning coffee on your own. You won't have to miss the office gossip. More importantly, you have to be able to deal with the disadvantage of not being there. Not being on the spot, and not being in the right place at the right time. It's also about getting the hang of virtual reality. In my experience I feel isolated about one in every four days and feel like climbing the walls once a week."

right hand and arm swapped his standard keyboard and mouse for a small keyboard with static trackerball at a cost of £150. The change allowed him to use the mouse without the grip action which had become so painful.

AbilityNet points out that the Disability Discrimination Act now forces employers to make "reasonable adjustment" for employees with either permanent or temporary disability. In Ireland the Central Remedial Clinic carries out similar functions to AbilityNet.

Assistive technology for teleworkers

- latch keys allow users who can only press one key at once, or those who use a stick on the keyboard, to use modifier keys such as shift, alt and control on PCs;
- for users with visual disabilities, brightly coloured keytops, or those with big or bold characters can help;

- keyguards are rigid plates above keyboard keys that can take the weight of hands or arms, and have holes above each key for accurate key depression;
- personalised keyboards can be very effective for people with hand/arm difficulties *eg* smaller size keyboards, programmable keypads, switches that can be used with keyboard emulation software, and keyboards for those who have the use of only one hand;
- for anyone who has difficulty with data entry, word processors that predict word endings, and most likely next words (keystroke savers) are a boon;
- computer mice alternatives include tracker balls, which are fixed in position but you roll a ball to move the pointer, touch-sensitive pads and joy sticks. Alternative shapes and sizes are available. Highly specialised devices such as the "twiddler" operate on delicate tilting movements of the hand, while others can be operated by the head, or operated by biometrics from vestigial movements;
- help for the visually-impaired ranges from replacing old-fashioned poor-quality screens, to altering colour combinations, and installing larger

Disability and teleworking: the business case

A 1996 international survey of organisations which have telecommuting programmes involving people with disabilities found that the programmes were set up to fill employers' business needs, not for reasons of social responsibility. The survey found that teleworking schemes were introduced to:

- *Retain valuable employees and keep recruitment costs down;*
- *Respond to particular employees' family or medical situations, keep morale high and retain staff loyalty;*
- *Fill positions for which recruitment had been difficult or staff turnover high such as shift work, part-time positions or jobs in crime-ridden locations;*
- *Comply with US trip reduction and air quality legislation.*

57% of employers believed employees had become more productive since beginning telecommuting – only 6% felt that productivity had declined. Although the cost of assistive technology for employees with disabilities was sometimes higher, especially for those with visual impairment, only one in seven employers cited cost of equipment or problems with equipment as a major barrier. Nearly half (47%) said teleworking was a viable option for new employees as well as existing employees. A further 19% said they would "possibly" hire a new telecommuter with a disability. Full report available by email from the University of Texas: jarrettj@utxvms.cc.utexas.edu

Milestone case laid down in San Francisco

A US citizen was awarded $90,000 damages in compensation for not being allowed to telework – with implications for future cases in Britain. Jack Nilles, the US telework guru, was called as an expert witness for the plaintiff, Michael Faircloth, in his court case against his employer, the Bay Area Rapid Transit District (BART).

BART operates the light rail transit system for the San Francisco region. Michael Faircloth was a labour relations arbitrator for BART who is partially disabled by a neck injury which predated his employment with BART. The injury causes pain when sitting or standing for long periods. Faircloth was commuting 100 miles five days per week, causing him severe pain. He had been telecommuting informally for a number of weeks when he was refused the right to telecommute one day a week. Faircloth sued under the Americans with Disabilities Act.

Nilles reviewed the records relating to the case and administered a teleworking screening questionnaire as well as interviewing Faircloth and concluded that he could easily telecommute at least one day per week.

The TCA consulted employment law expert Jeffery Shaw of Shaw Personnel Services about the situation in Britain: "We now have the Disability Act 1995 in place which does not allow work to be refused simply because people are disabled.".

screens. Another approach is to enlarge the image, but when this is done the whole screen contents cannot be viewed at once. In some systems an enlarged image from part of the computer's main screen is displayed on a second screen (usually a closed circuit TV system that can also be used to enlarge printed material for reading);

- voice recognition software for blind and physically disabled users can act as a keyboard replacement and is available from a limited "command level" to "free text". The development of laptop computers in conjunction with speech synthesisers and voice recognition can now provide some disabled people with an easily portable communications tool. Another alternative is "screen reading" using braille output, where whole or half lines from the screen are produced on an electro-mechanical strip close to the keyboard;
- OCR (optical character reading) text scanning can be used to "read" text into a computer, producing text on the computer screen, or a synthesised voice, or both;
- text telephones can help those with hearing disabilities to communicate by displaying conversations on a small screen connected to a normal telephone line. The most commonly used system is the Minicom. Text telephones are great for communications between the hearing-impaired,

> **"Access to work" cuts Lisa's risk of RSI**
>
> Lisa Lisney is an administration assistant with Telford-based computer training company Brain Train. Lisa was born without a left hand and forearm but used a standard keyboard and mouse and worked from home providing word processing services. Lisa's employer approached the local Disability Employment Adviser who arranged an interview and assessment for Lisa and her employer.
>
> The DEA recommended that Lisa should use a special Maltron one-handed keyboard, a trackerball mouse and an ergonomic flexible arm rest to reduce the risk of RSI. All these items were available from DEA stock, and Lisa was able to obtain the equipment at no cost to herself or her employer.

but need an interpretation service to aid communication with other telephone users. The RNID offers a "TypeTalk" service where an interpreter "translates" between the spoken word and the Minicom messages;

- many items not related to computers can help disabled teleworkers, such as page turners for books and journals, lights to indicate ringing telephones, talking calculators and specially adapted work furniture.

Certain items of equipment for disabled people are exempt from VAT, but rules vary according to local VAT offices.

Access to work

The Disability Discrimination Act has the following effects:

- it is against the law for an employer to treat a disabled person less favourably, without good reason, because of their disability. It will also be against the law to refuse to serve someone who is disabled;
- it is against the law to run a service or provide goods or facilities in such a way that it is impossible or unreasonably difficult for a disabled person to use the service or goods.

The Department for Education and Employment in Britain runs the Access to Work scheme which can help disabled teleworkers and their employers. To qualify, you must "have, or have had, a physical or mental impairment which has a substantial and long-term adverse effect on your ability to carry out normal day-to-day activities". Medical evidence is usually required. The amount available varies and your employer may be asked to contribute. Examples of acceptable uses for Access to Work funding include:

- a communicator for the hearing-impaired
- a part-time reader or assistance at work for someone who is blind
- equipment or adaptations to provide help at work
- transport or assistance with adaptations to cars
- alterations to premises

Job Centres now have Disability Employment Advisers (DEAs), who can provide help with the Access to Work scheme, the Job Introduction Scheme (a chance to try out a job for an introductory period) and work preparation (such as job trials with an employer). The PACT service is therefore the first port of call for disabled teleworkers. The procedure is to call your local job centre and ask to speak to the local PACT (Placement, Assessment and Counselling Team) manager. There is an excellent explanation of the different schemes on the RADAR website
www.radar.org.uk/information/faq/employ.html.

For those already in work, but coping with a new or increasing disability, the **Employers' Forum on Disability** is the national employers' organisation dealing with disability and employment. It is non profit-making, and funded by members. It provides good publications, a regular journal, and a range of introductory literature.

The Disability Information and Advice Line (DIAL) is another good starting point for information about a range of services. There is also the Disability Information Database **DissBASE**, which is used by about 170 providers of disability information in the UK. You can telephone DissBASE and ask them to make an enquiry free of charge. The database contains information on over 5,500 national and regional organisations and services related to disability. It is also often useful to consult specialist groups who deal in particular disabilities, such as MS, as they may well have disability-specific relevant information.

Opportunities is a leading national charity working to place disabled people in employment, and staffed by secondees from commerce and industry. Jobseekers get help in identifying and developing skills, preparing CVs and interview techniques on a one-to-one basis.

The **Prince's Youth Business Trust** (PYBT) assists unemployed people including the disabled aged 18–30 to start their own business. The

> **Glittering success with Internet jewellery service**
>
> Mark Francis-Jones operates a service selling quality, British-made gold jewellery over the Internet. No stranger to self-employment, Mark had previously operated 60 vending machines around Shropshire and the surrounding counties despite the limitations of his wheelchair.
>
> Mark regards his wheelchair as the least of the disabilities imposed upon him by a road accident – other problems include pressure sores, dilation of the kidneys and migraines which can cause disturbed vision and vomiting.
>
> Some years ago, Mark was one of the original teleworkers involved in Antur Tanat Cain telecottage's contract to transcribe Weights and Measures documents for ICL. After completion of the project, he was at a loose end. He opted for an Open University course, but like a number of distance learning students, found that studying from home left him disillusioned and isolated, so he dropped out after completing one module. The vending machine venture was highly successful but the physical commitment has been huge and hard to handle. "Then I met an old school friend now employed in the jewellery trade, and identified the potential to marry his knowledge of the business with my knowledge of IT". Now, if situations dictate, Mark can operate his part of the business entirely from his bed. And he's on the expansion trail, looking for other teleworkers to earn commission by selling his jewellery.
>
> www.francis-marrack.com

support comes in the form of loans averaging £2,500, grants of up to £1,900 and test marketing grants of up to £250. Additional support is given through the services of a Business Adviser. To qualify for PYBT funding, you must have failed to achieve funding through other sources. Examples of disabled people helped through the PYBT include graphic designers and disability access consultancy.

The Association of Disabled Professionals (ADP) focuses on employment, education and training issues relating to disabled people and actively encourages the principle of teleworking. ADP calls on the experience and connections of its members to help other disabled people to meet their employment potential.

In Ireland, the National Rehabilitation Board (shortly to be replaced) administers the Workplace Equipment Adaptation Grant (WEAG) scheme through its local vocational officers. It is possible to get up to £5,000 to provide adaptations to premises or equipment in order to make a workplace more accessible or work equipment easier to use. These grants can be used in certain situations to equip home offices, and are open to registered disabled people who wish to be self-employed.

Access to training

The British government offers training through Training and Enterprise Councils (TECs). These organisations can offer information and support to people with disabilities who are thinking of starting their own business. The Training for Work scheme, which is run through TECs, is aimed at assisting long-term unemployed people to improve their skills. Disabled people are exempt from the normal qualifying period, and are given priority for training places on this scheme. You can apply for this scheme through your local Job Centre.

For people who want to learn or update job skills, the Department for Education and Employment offers Career Development Loans which can provide 80% (and in some cases 100%) of training costs for up to two years. Loans are between £200 and £8,000 and the interest is paid by the Department for Education and Employment during training.

Outset is a UK national charity which works to promote technology-based employment and training for disabled people Outset is working to create a national network of training centres, and is co-operating with telecentres where appropriate. It offers the NVQ in Using IT Levels 1 and 2 through distance learning.

The training and support gap

A conference on disability and teleworking held in Dublin in 1998 as part of the European Telework Development project looked at the problems disabled people face in obtaining telework opportunities:

- Teleworking can provide employment options for disabled people but in the main these options are suitable for those with acquired disabilities who have previous work experience, or those with third level education. It must not be used to replace the need to make conventional workplaces accessible;

- Current IT training programmes for disabled people mostly provide basic IT skills which are insufficient for teleworking where most job opportunities are at a professional level;

- There is a danger in creating skills registers exclusively for disabled teleworkers as these may encounter prejudice. Registers have to be actively marketed to companies or they languish unused. Registers should focus on cores skills like languages rather than IT skills though these should also be recorded;

- Existing disabled teleworkers report major problems obtaining technical support and repairs to equipment;

- Because many disabled people are unable to work fulltime it is particularly important to encourage the formation of support networks for collaboration, technical and social support and marketing.
www.cwu.ie/may00/library/distele.pdf

There are several schemes for training disabled people in their own homes, including the EDIT scheme (Employment for Disabled people using Information Technology) based in Derbyshire. EDIT provides courses in word processing, spreadsheets, databases and desktop publishing. Courses are provided on an individual basis to suit the learning capabilities and physical limitations of each trainee. The training can be conducted in an employer's premises or in a sheltered workplace but is usually carried out in the person's own home. Assessments are made regularly and trainees are expected to carry out a work placement from home and to reach the CLAIT Integrated Business Studies Level 2 standard and be awarded certificates. The courses are free for those on benefit.

A scheme operating in the Thames Valley is open to carers and people suffering from long-term illnesses as well as the disabled. Re-Lease provides training to people possessing or wishing to acquire skills to become self-employed. The main training package is based around the Teleworking VQ level two, focussing on computing and business administration skills. Re-Lease also refurbishes secondhand computers for trainees until they are sufficiently skilled and established to acquire their own. The training is planned for a variety of Thames valley centres, and the scheme will visit the homes of those with severe mobility restrictions.

Another option is to take a distance learning or open learning course (also see Chapter 12, *Training for Teleworkers*). To find out about suitable courses that can be completed in your own time at home, contact your local education authority in the UK, or the National Training and Development Initiative in Ireland which offers support to people so they can learn at local centres or in their own homes. An increasing number of

---

Prison service uses teleworking to assist disabled employee

Paul Dixon had the misfortune to develop multiple sclerosis some 18 years ago, but due to the sympathetic nature of his employers, the Prison Service, he has been able to continue in his work until recently. "They were very good about my condition and I received support and various pieces of equipment which made my job easier", Paul recalls. The equipment included two closed-circuit television sets – one black and white and one colour – as well as a text-reading machine, since Paul is now registered blind. The government's PACT scheme also provided a computer, printer and modem. Four years ago, his condition deteriorated and he began to work from home. Paul had previously worked as a prison governor, but was assisted to become a supervisor for distance learning training, a job which could be carried out from home. He coordinated the training, dealt with any problems arising and attended a monthly meeting. After three years, senior civil servants are expected to move posts. This was impossible for Paul so he finally took retirement on medical grounds last year.

Teleworking for carers with the NCNT

The Nigel Clare Network Trust helps people with children who have conditions that limit their lives by length, quality or both. In many cases, in addition to emotional pain and anguish suffered by parents, they must endure severe financial hardship while struggling to care for their offspring. NCNT joint founder Mairi Putt explains where teleworking fits in: "If you are the parent of a life-limited child, you simply will not be able to fit into a rigid 9-to-5 working regime. If you come to us, we will sit down and look at how you can earn money and care for your child. It's about balance". The trust is named after Mairi's two children Nigel and Clare, who both died at an early age.

The trust keeps information on hundreds of employers who already offer flexible work options, and runs self-help courses covering areas such as job sharing, flexible working, career change, redirection and retraining. It also helps employers to retain employees and ensure family friendly policies.

www.nigelclare.org Tel: 0207 256 8313 or in Ireland 024 95514

---

distance learning courses are now provided "online" – you obtain and return your exercises by email and can even do your exams over the Internet.

Teleworking networks for the disabled

Network Personnel

Ann McBride of Network Personnel in Northern Ireland is part of an organisation that provides training for 16 disabled people to learn computer skills in their own homes, and which subsequently tries to provide computer-based work for the trainees. Three of Ann's clients are now teleworking from home or at a local centre. She is very aware of the problems that people with disabilities face concerning their benefits when they wish to take up any form of employment, and suggests taking expert advice. Ann believes teleworking opportunities are out there, and it is a matter of finding a niche in the market place both locally and further afield.

Ability Enterprises (Ireland)

Cathy Cumberbeach suffered a car accident, and was left with little use of one hand and arm as well as problems with concentration. Previously Cathy had worked as a bilingual executive secretary and personal assistant, and ran her own business supplying word processing services and temporary secretaries. One of her customers, a pharmaceutical company, was extremely supportive and continued to send her secretarial work when she was well enough to start working from home, including correspondence, telephone dictation and production of bulk mailings. Cathy also got help from the Irish organisation Ability, which keeps a register of disabled people who have teleworking skills. Cathy has taken on several typing jobs for United Biscuits through Ability, but found that she could not get help with equipment or software from any organisation. She is critical of state rehabilitation services, which she feels did not assess her properly and sent her on an inappropriate high-level German course intended to train her as a translator. Another training course which she was offered would have involved spending six weeks at the other end of the country which was impractical given her disability and personal situation. Instead, Cathy borrowed money from her family to update her computer equipment and buy new software and a laser printer, which she is paying off. She has received some work for a Dublin insurance company through the EU HYPIT project, but technical difficulties with the remote access systems caused frustrating delays. However, the new equipment has also given her the opportunity to take an Open University course in technology.

RNIB

Britain's Royal National Institute for the Blind has opened a telecottage in Darlington. Tom Boyd-Smith of the RNIB points out that 79% of visually-impaired people of working age in the UK are unemployed, and says that the telecottage is part of the RNIB's interest in active job creation. He cites figures that show that on average disabled people take less sick leave than the general population. The RNIB telecottage has been founded with support from BT, the local TEC and the European Union. Paul Ham explains: "We mainly work on marketing and market research plans – projects like targeted follow-ups to mailshots. A typical one might look at why people choose certain colleges and schools. Up to four people have been involved on some campaigns but at the moment I'm working on my own."

Modifications to the standard telecottage equipment include monitors on arms which can be swung close to the face where required, speech recognition and synthesis hardware and software, access to CCTV reading equipment, headset telephones, a talking calculator, large-print dialling codes and liberal use of thick black felt pens.

Workability

This scheme is run by the Leonard Cheshire Foundation and aims to train disabled people in computer technology. According to co-ordinator Janet Epplestone, "we leave the teleworking angle up to the individual. Workability is about opportunities and choice. We would support those who choose to work from home… we would not want actively to encourage people to do this – this would rightly be seen as further marginalising disabled people". Participants in the Workability scheme get a refurbished computer and software plus access to a nationally accredited IT qualification, either through face-to-face training or online support.

Publications

Virtually There: The Evolution of Call Centres *Date:* 1999
Authors: Institute of Employment Studies and the TCA for Mitel
Source: Firefly Communications Ltd, 25/4 The Coda Centre,
189 Munster Road, London SW6 6AW

Disability and Teleworking *Date:* 1998
Author: Imogen Bertin for ETD project and the Aphrodite assistive technology project
Source: Available in .pdf format at www.cwu.ie/may00/archive.htm or by post from
Imogen Bertin, Reagrove, Minane Bridge, Co. Cork, Ireland Tel: +353 21 887300
Email: imogen@ctc.ie

Moral dilemmas and issues of providing telework for disabled people
Comment: a paper by the Ben Fairweather Research Fellow at the Centre for
Computing and Social Responsibility, De Montfort University
Source: www.ccsr.cms.dmu.ac.uk/pubs/papers/distwpa1.html.

Contacts and URLs

Ability Enterprises, Ballindine, Co. Mayo, Ireland Contact: Derek Farrell
Tel: +353 94 65054 Email: ability@iol.ie

AbilityNet (formerly Computability), PO Box 94, Warwick, Warwickshire CV34 5WS
Tel: 01926 312847 Fax: 01926 311345 Web: **www.abilitynet.co.uk**

Action for Blind People (two reports on teleworking opportunities for the visually
impaired) 14-16 Verney Road, London SE16 3DEZ Tel: 020 7732 8771 Fax: 020 7639
0948.

ADP, PO Box BCN ABP, London WC1N 3XX Tel and fax: 01924 283253 or Minicom:
01924 270335 Email: assdisprof@aol.com Contact: Sue Maynard Croft.

Association for the Advancement of Assistive Technology (US)
Web: **www.resna.org**

MS helpline uses teleworking counsellors

The Multiple Sclerosis Society is using 20 home-based counsellors to staff its helpline. All but one of the counsellors have MS themselves, and volunteer to work on the helpline. The call volume is around 17,000 a year, but prior to the homeworking option opening hours were limited and around a third of calls were lost.

Jim Glennon, the Helpline Manager explains that many people with MS wanted to be involved but could not get into the office because of mobility difficulties, or problems with intermittent relapses, or with fatigue.

Training of the counsellors including role-playing exercises also takes place by phone over a period of twelve weeks, and trainees receive tapes of their sessions. A comprehensive training programme is vital because the work is sensitive and stressful.

Tel: 0171 610 7171 Web: **www.mssociety.org.uk**

Association for the Advancement of Assistive Technology in Europe
Web: **www.fernunihagen.de/FTB/aaate.htm**

British Computer Society Disability Group focuses on the role of IT in providing disabled people with a better quality of life. Tel: 01245 242924 Email: geoffrey.busby@gecm.com Web: **www.bcs.org.uk/siggroup/siglist.htm**

CanDo – official website offering careers information for disabled university students and graduates. **http://cando.lancs.ac.uk**

Central Remedial Clinic, Penny Ansley Building, Vernon Avenue, Clontarf, Dublin 3 Tel: +353 1 805 7560 Fax: +353 1 833 5496 Contact: Ger Craddock. Web: **www.crc.ie**

Center on Disabilities, California State University (a partner in the Aphrodite Assistive Technology project) **www.csun.edu/cod**

DIAL – Disability Information and Advice Line Tel: 01302 310123 Fax: 01302 310404 Email: dialuk@aol.com Web: **www.members.aol.com/dialuk**

Disability Discrimination Act Tel: 0345 622633 for a copy or web: **www.disability.gov.uk**.

DissBASE – the Disability Information Database Tel: 01306 742282

EDIT – Employment for Disabled people using Information Technology, Derbyshire Tel: 01629 826285 Email: edit@editvg.freeserve.co.uk

Jim Lubin's disability resources – a cornucopia of disability and assistive technology information. Web: **www.eskimo.com/~jlubin/disabled/**

Madenta Internet Accessibility Center Web: **www.madenta.com/**

Training the key to employment for the visually impaired

The charity Action for Blind People has run a telework training project for visually-impaired people funded through the EU programme Disnet Step by Step. Through this project Melanie Drew-Halkyard has become the first visually-impaired person in the country to achieve the Teleworking Vocational Qualification.

Melanie lost her right eye and was diagnosed with glaucoma five years ago. "Four years ago I was computer illiterate," she says. "I was scared to switch on the computer because I thought I would do something drastic to it". Action for Blind People has re-written and redesigned all the modules of the Teleworking VQ to make them accessible for the visually-impaired. Students can attend training centres in a number of cities, and some are learning from home using online tuition and open and distance learning packages. Last October, after achieving her VQ, Melanie set up in business designing and printing wedding stationery from her home office in Cumbria.

Action for Blind People's project development manager Cath Clarke says she hopes other IT training centres will catch on to the customised training materials because it is often difficult for blind people to access mainstream education, and seven out of ten visually-impaired people are out of work. Email: afbp@enterprise.net

Matching the person and the technology homepage
Web: **http://members.aol.com/IMPT97/MPT.html**

Network Personnel, 80–82 Rainy Street, Magherafelt, Co. Derry, Northern Ireland
Contact: Ann McBride Tel: 028 7963 1032 Fax: 028 7963 1033
Email: periphera@networkpersonnel.org.uk

Nigel Clare Network Trust – 85 Moorgate, London EC2M 6SA Tel: 020 7256 8313
Fax: 020 7638 8648 Email: postmaster@nigelclare.org Web: **www.nigelclare.org**

National Training and Disability Institute (training division of the Rehab Group), Roslyn Park, Sandymount, Dublin 4. Tel: +353 1 205 7211 Email: marketing@ntdi.ie

Opportunities for People with Disabilities, 1 Bank Buildings, Prices Street, London EC2R 8EU Tel: 020 7580 7545 Email: edwa36@ibm.net
Web: **www.opportunities.org.uk**

Oscail (National Distance Learning Centre), Dublin City University, Dublin 9, Ireland
Tel: +353 1 704 5481 Fax: +353 1 704 5494. Web: **www.dcu.ie/ndec/index.htm**

Outset: contact Jean Wiltshire Tel: 020 8993 2285 Email: hq@outset.org.uk

PYBT Prince's Youth Business Trust Tel: 0800 842842
Web: **www.princes-trust.org.uk**

Princess Royal Trust for Carers, 16 Byward Street, London EC3R 5BA
Tel: 020 7480 7788.

Re-Lease Contact Scout Enterprises 0118 988 6448 or The Support Shop Ltd on 01344 485111.

RNIB, 224 Great Portland Street, London W1N 6AA Tel: 020 7388 1266. Specialist benefits advisors can be contacted on 020 7388 1266. There is a guide called Access Technology detailing available equipment for blind people and covering braille, large print and speech technology, available from 020 8968 8600. Paul Ham of the Darlington Telecottage is at 01325 267255.

RNID, 105 Gower Street, London WC1E 6AH Tel: 0208 740 9531
Web: **www.rnid.org.uk**.

Shaw Trust – champions the abilities of disabled people through providing rehabilitation, training, work tasters, employment support and occupation.
Tel: 01225 716300 Web: **www.shaw-trust.org.uk**

US National Institute of Disability and Rehabilitation Research
Web: **www.abledata.com/**

Workability c/o Leonard Cheshire Foundation Tel: 020 7802 8200
Email: a.anderson@london.leonard-cheshire.org.uk

YEP Ltd, Suite 203, Grosvenor House, Central Park, Telford, Shropshire, TF2 9TW
Tel: 01952 277077 Fax: 01952 299510 Email: rollinson@msn.com

Email and the Internet

The Internet is a global network of computer networks. The Internet began as a Cold War project to create a communications network that could protect the US against nuclear attack. It metamorphosed into a government-funded academic network and added features such as file transfer, email, Usenet news and eventually HTML, but remained a niche tool for its first twenty-five years of existence. There are now estimated to be 13 million computer "hosts" on the Internet in Europe alone.

Irish Internet consultancy Nua (**www.nua.ie**) is well known for its surveys of Internet usage and gives the following figures for Internet connections in spring 2000:

Africa	1.72 million	Middle East	0.88 million
Asia Pacific	33.61 million	Canada and USA	112.4 million
Europe	47.15 million	Latin America	5.29 million
World total:	201 million		

Through the Internet, teleworkers receive and send work to their employers or clients, get technical support or product information, and "network" socially with other teleworkers. They can also create "virtual companies" – teams of people who can be located anywhere, and who come together to work on a project, but may never meet physically. Instead, they pass around the elements of the project as messages and computer files by email. Many teleworking businesses are based around obtaining information from the Internet, reprocessing it in some way to add value before selling it on to customers.

Today anyone with the right equipment and an account with an ISP can "surf" the Web, exchange email and files or participate in conferences over the Internet. Most teleworkers connect to the Internet via dial-up links such as those provided by BT, Demon or Virgin in Britain, or Ireland Online, Indigo and Eircom in Ireland. Many ISPs are partnering with content providers to supply information, news, business, lifestyle and entertainment services.Virgin Internet (**www.virgin.net**) not only provides subscribers with free Internet access and free web space but also offers a specially customised homepage "portal" that pushes relevant content such as an online toolkit providing PC shopping advice, a computer hardware advisor and links to relevant computer websites.

There are dramatic and fast changes occuring in cyberspace as the old media (telecommunications, newspapers, publishing and broadcasting) consolidate with the "young pretenders" of the Internet. At the beginning of 2000, the world's largest proprietary online service, America Online, merged with traditional media mammoth Time Warner in a deal worth $350 billion. Time Warner can offer the appropriate print and broadcast content. AOL has the expertise in Internet technologies. Time Warner also offers high-speed broadband internet access over its cable system on a network that services 13 million customers. It is hoping that AOL will provide a new user-friendly interface and interactivity to make Time Warner content compelling when delivered to the home over a high-speed cable modems.

Improvements in Internet technology are already helping teleworkers. Assertive action from regulatory offices (OFTEL in the UK and the ODTR in Ireland) continues to erode the traditional communications monopolies, creating choice, diversifying services and bringing down costs of access. Teleworkers can choose between Internet Service Providers (ISPs) offering "free" or "premium" support, and between different speeds of access from basic dial-up analogue access over an ordinary telephone line through faster digital access using ISDN to roasting high-speed broadband access via a cable modem.

Britain and Ireland lag behind the US on Internet technology adoption, but two decisive elements in the future development of the Internet will be common to both sides of the Atlantic – increased interactivity and faster access to the Internet, providing greater capacity for uploading and downloading large files.

What you need to get online

The minimum setup is something like:

- computer
- modem
- software to control the modem
- web browsing software
- telephone line.

Computer and modem purchases are covered briefly in Chapter 11, *Teleworking equipment*. If you purchased an IBM compatible PC or an Apple Macintosh PowerPC computer within the last two years it probably includes a pre-installed internal modem as standard. The modem converts computer data into analogue sound so that it can be transported along a telephone line to your Internet service provider, and from there to any destination on the web. The standard entry-level modem is now the 56 kbs or V.90 model. Speed is measured in kilobits per second (kbs) or baud rates, which are not quite the same thing, but usually treated as identical and interchangeable units. In practice these modems usually achieve a data transfer rate of about 48 kbs. Local conditions such as the speed of the connection at the other end and bottlenecks on the Internet often restrict the practical speed at which modems can be used. If you use a 56k modem and are not able to regularly get speeds of 48 kbs get your modem and line quality checked. You can check the speed of your connection at Microsoft's home computing online resource (**www.computing central.com**).

These days software to browse the web and make connections to Internet service providers is usually provided free or at nominal charge by your Internet service provider. This software also stores your user-id (identifier) and password. Normally you can choose your own password. It is strongly recommended that whenever you have control over the choice of a password, you choose a mixture of letters and numbers, upper and lower case, that are unlikely to be known to anyone else and impossible to guess. Do not use standard classics such as Fred, God, your middle name, your partner's name or a pet's name, but do use some ingenuity to think of passwords that, while impenetrable to others, are also unforgettable to you... Never reveal your password, and never write it down, but do give people your email address so that they can contact you.

Service Providers (ISPs)

The first step in choosing a service provider is to be clear on your priorities – it can be hard to find one that meets all your needs perfectly. The main points to consider are:

Cost of access

Teleworkers rely on good quality Internet access for their livelihood, so unless you are a bit of a techie, choose a paid-for service with good technical support rather than a "free" service which is designed to provide basic access without the thrills and frills, and which makes its money either through your telephone calls to the ISP or through expensive technical support over premium-rate lines if you hit a problem.

Business services with a good reputation at the time of writing (this is a market in a state of constant flux) include Demon (**www.demon.co.uk**), Planet Online (**www.energise.co.uk**) and Level Three (**www.levelthree.co.uk**). If you do decide to go for a "free" service, well-known offerings are Dixon's freeserve (**www.freeserve.co.uk**) and BT Click (**www.btclick.co.uk**). Internet magazine gives up-to-date listings of British ISPs, their rates and contact numbers at **www.internet-magazine.com/resource/isp/isp_list.html**.

Speed of access

Assuming that you have a reasonably fast modem and a clear telephone line, your access speed to the Internet is likely to be faster if your Internet Service Provider (ISP) has a low use-modem ratio and a high bandwidth connection to the Internet. The best sources of information about this are the magazines that do regular benchmarks of all the major providers. Using the right search engine, and learning how to frame accurate searches, will also speed up access to the information you need. And remember – if you did opt for a "free" service you can't really complain about the quality of that service...

Technical support

Good technical support is the key for reliable, successful Internet use. The "free" services only provide support at a cost – it's their main revenue stream. Business Internet companies usually subsidise technical support from the subscription that you pay them – again, check the Internet magazines for reports of who currently has the best technical support.

Email facilities

The "free" services usually offer free email, but this is often web-based, which means that you browse to your ISP's homepage, enter your user-id and password and can then view your mail. What you can't do is view and store your email in a business email application like Outlook, Pegasus or Eudora. Some free services do offer "SMTP accounts" and these are the ones to look for as you will be able to set up a "POP3" email account and use a proper email package. This is also vital if you want to view your email over a mobile phone (try **www.guildsoft.co.uk**).

Web space

Most providers throw in free web space on which to create your own website, but whether this is useful depends on what kind of site you want to build. It is certainly possible to put together a simple site on your own (see Publicising your business on page 275–6), but for many applications you may need some help from your provider, which is unlikely to be free. You might be better off going to a provider who offers a specific amount of Web space at a sensible price including support, rather than one that offers you free space with no support for it.

The paid services can also host your own domain name (such as myowncompany.com or myfirm.co.uk) which always looks more impressive to customers than piggybacking off the ISP's name (*eg* mycompany@ISPname.net). You can check and buy domain names online *eg* at **www.networksolutions.com**.

A bit of backup

If you are likely to do more than just send a few email messages and do a bit of surfing, it's well worth considering using two providers, to give you backup. You can always send email in an emergency or when you are on the move using one of the web-based services such as Hotmail (www.hotmail.com) or Twigger (www.twigger.co.uk).

High-speed Internet access

Most teleworkers access the Internet using dial-up modems. But even a 56 kbs modem struggles when you are sending email with large attachments such as graphics or multimedia files. ISDN lines offer slightly faster speeds (64 kbs or 128k if you link the two lines together, though this costs more per call). Businesses that need serious bandwidth for sending data across the Internet sometimes invest in expensive T1 leased lines giving speeds of up to 1.5mbs depending on the time of day and weight of Internet traffic.

High-speed Internet technologies are becoming more affordable and widespread in Britain and Ireland except in rural areas. The Canadian telecoms company NTL (**www.ntl.co.uk**) is now offering broadband Internet access over its cable TV networks in some areas of Britain, providing download speeds of 512 kb/s. Cable modems run over 100 times faster than dial-up connections, but can slow down depending on the time of day and number of people accessing the Internet simultaneously. Cable Internet access is an "always on" connection so you don't have to make a call to your service provider every time you want to access the Internet, and you don't run the risk of dropped calls and broken connections.

Currently NTL access costs a flat-rate monthly rental fee of £40 for the cable modem and network card. Cable Management Ireland is also offering speeds of 128 kb/s in the North Dublin area, while other companies such as Irish Multichannel plan services shortly.

Don't despair if you don't live within an cable franchise area. There is also a technology which can deliver high-speed Internet access through the normal telephone wires. Digital Subscriber lines (DSL) can run at speeds 300 to 1000 times faster than dial-up connections using existing copper lines but has its downsides – it is a technology that is "fussy" about line interference or noise. You also need to live within 18,000 feet (about 3.4 miles or 5.4 kilometres) from the exchange – but as DSL tends to fade out rather than drop out with distance, even if you are close to or beyond the limit, it may still provide you with a much faster link than standard dial-up.

BT is rolling out DSL technology nationwide, NTL has tested asymmetric (A)DSL in south-east England and in Ireland another variant, 3DSL, has been tested by eircom around Dublin. DSL services are likely to be more expensive than cable, and designed for business rather than home use.

Email: cheaper, faster, better?

Why send a message by email rather than by fax or post?

- it's cheaper – the cost should be less than for conventional post;

- it's more flexible. As well as text messages, you can also send complete computer files such as spreadsheets or desktop publishing layouts. If you are working collaboratively on a project it can be much more efficient to send a computer file that people at the other end can use and edit themselves, than to send a fax which can only be read and annotated

- it's faster. Email is much faster than traditional post (usually arriving within minutes compared to a minimum of 12 hours for post), and many teleworkers deliver their finished projects by this method;

- it's convenient. Email can be sent at any time. The recipient does not have to be there to receive the message – it is stored until they are ready to receive it. It is also easy to send group communications, and many systems offer facilities for creating customer emailing lists.

Spam, spam, spam, spam, spam, spam, spam, spam, spam...

Spam, or unsolicited, junk email, borrows its name from the famous Monty Python sketch where singing Vikings repeat the name of the notorious tinned pork product over and over. It was first used in the Internet context to describe the practice of posting the same message repeatedly on different discussion lists or chat rooms. Now it has become a catch-all description for unwanted email. Spammers believe that they are just helping direct marketing to evolve. In fact spam clogs networks and slows down the operation of the Internet and it will shortly become illegal to send spam in the European Union (under the distance selling directive).

To foil spam, you can use free, web-based addresses such as Yahoo or Hotmail. You can also use a different email address (if you have two) for any public postings and website registrations, saving your main address for messaging colleagues, friends and family. The spam will pile up in the public account and can be regularly trashed. Always examine the privacy policy of a website before offering any personal information such as your email address, and be sure to opt out if you don't want to receive marketing information.

Many ISPs offer spam filtering options, but some filters may also remove legitimate email such as that from mailing lists. Most current email software packages such as Outlook, Netscape Messenger or Eudora will allow you to set up rules to sift out mail likely to be junk and send it to a separate folder (such as mail with no subject line or $$$ or sex in the subject line). You can then, if you wish, review it before sending it to the trash. Do it – it will save you a lot of time in the long run. There are also antispam software packages which can work with your email software to weed out marketing scams and other offal, as well as messages from known spammers. Try SpamScan97 (**www.webster-image.com**) or Contact Plus Spam Buster (**www.contactplus.com**) which are both inexpensive.

Also set your web browser so that it does not provide your email address as the password when you download files from anonymous ftp connections – this convention is a hangover from the academic days of the Internet and is misused regularly by spammers.

Newsgroups are a bad source of spam. If possible use a different email address for contributions to newsgroups. If you have to use your regular email address, then use your email software to insert no-spam in the From: or Reply to: parts of the email
(*eg* no-spam-jane-smith@bigisp.com). Any junk mail sent to that address can be returned to the sender.

Companies use email for internal messaging over their local area networks (LANs) as well as for external communications via the Internet. The most popular LAN-based email packages are Lotus cc:Mail (**www.lotus.com**) and Microsoft Outlook 2000 (**www.microsoft.com**). Star Nine's Quarterdeck mail is commonly used for internal messaging on Mac-based networks. Internal email systems beep or flash up a message on the screen so that the recipient can decide whether to read the message immediately or continue with their work and read their mail later.

Some packages such as Microsoft Outlook are set up by default to use more sophisticated email formats such as "RTF" or "HTML" so that messages can be made to look more attractive with different fonts, bold and italic, special backgrounds and so on. Switch them off. You don't know if the person at the other end has suitable software to be able to read these formats. Stick to plain vanilla ASCII text wherever possible.

Email for business use needs to be managed effectively. Take advantage of productivity tools such as computerised address books that avoid the need to keep retyping the recipient's email address, and computer-based filing systems so that you read and reply to your mail in a structured fashion. Like traditional mail, email has its downsides. You will, in all probability, get some unsolicited messages from rather odd people, and you will also have a depressingly high stack of messages on your first day back from holiday.

Be properly addressed

Email addresses vary in format depending on the email system used by the person you are trying to send a message to. If the recipient is on the same internal system as you, normally you just address the message with their user-id. If you don't know their user-id, there is probably a command to help you find it. On CompuServe/AOL, MSN and many other proprietary systems, all you need to know is the person's name and their location to find their user-id or email address using the membership commands. Many Internet search engines will do their best to find email addresses for you, and some Internet companies such as Esearch (**www.esearch.ie**) offer email directories and are designed to help you find business email contacts.

Most messages that you receive by email will contain the sender's address, and normally you just "reply" to the message – your software will pick up the address from the original message automatically without your having to worry about formats. In any case, 90% of your correspondents are likely to be using a standard address format, so if you're stuck take a guess such as firstname.surname@company.co.uk.

The web

The World Wide Web (commonly abbreviated the web) is a distributed information source accessible from anywhere on the Internet via "HTML browsers" such as Netscape Navigator and Microsoft Internet Explorer. It is much harder to describe than it is to use. It consists of files located on

Web browser software

Internet Explorer – www.microsoft.com/windows/IE

Netscape – www.netscape.com/uk/index.htm

Opera – www.opera.com

Internet hosts around the world. Each file looks like a page of text and graphics with certain words highlighted. These highlights are hypertext links – points which, if you click on them, jump you to another page of information. The links are often to pages located somewhere else entirely on another computer. The beauty of the web is that it hides the confusing fundamentals of the Internet, providing a standard look so that all you need to worry about is where you want to go and what you want to find. You don't need to worry about where in the world the information is or about logging in and out from different Internet host computers – you just ask your web browser to save the interesting file you've found on your computer, or to print it, and the software does all the rest. A good way to understand how the hypertext system works is to start your web browser and give the help command, which is usually held as hypertext.

For the technically-minded, web pages are written in variants of HTML, a hypertext application of the ISO standard SGML text description language. Web browser software on the user's computer interprets the HTML commands to create a graphical display of the pages. Web pages can contain graphics in GIF or JPEG formats as well as text. Audio and video clips can be stored in formats like MP3, Macromedia Flash and Shockwave. Java programmes are used to create many sophisticated interactive web pages. Increasingly web pages are being written in a specific variant of HTML called XML. To read some pages with multimedia content like animations, you need to download free plug-in software such as Flash (**www.macromedia.com**) and Shockwave (**www.shockwave.com**). Free download software for video and audio clips is available from Real Networks (**www.real.com**) or Microsoft (**www.microsoft.com/windows/windowsmedia**). Once you have this software you can enjoy streamed media such as radio broadcasts delivered anywhere in the world. Technology and business news updates on the fast moving world of new media on the web are available from techweb (**www.techweb.com**) and Bloomberg (**www.bloomberg.com**).

Browsers

The most widely used Internet browsers for the PC are Netscape Navigator and Microsoft Internet Explorer. While Netscape took the early lead in the great browser war, Internet Explorer 5 is now installed as standard on the vast majority of new PCs. There's a version of Internet Explorer for Mac, and the Norwegian specialist browser Opera has a minority of devoted adherents.

Most browsers can read email and newsgroups as well as browsing web pages. However, if you use email a lot, you may find it worth buying specialist packages such as Eudora or Pegasus, which have better facilities for handling addresses and for managing the filing of large quantities of email. Many people also use groupware packages like Microsoft Outlook or Lotus Notes to read their email because they allow close integration with diaries and contacts databases. Sales and marketing staff often favour Goldmine, because of its excellent customer-tracking abilities. Being able to keep track of your messages is a rarely-mentioned but vital element to going online. Once you become a seasoned email user, you will find yourself accumulating many trivial messages but also some that you really will need to find six months later when you need to check some small 'and could you just' add-on to your customer's specification. It's a good idea to get into the habit of printing really important messages, and filing them in the good old-fashioned way, to avoid disasters.

Mobile Internet services

Internet content can also be accessed through the current generation of mobile phones. Wireless Application Protocol (WAP) technology developed from an attempt by the world's three biggest mobile phone companies – Ericsson, Nokia and Motorola – and a small San Francisco-based web-developer to establish a standard for the delivery of Internet content to mobile phones and personal digital assistants (PDAs) over the current GSM and next-generation UTMA mobile networks (more information at **www.wapforum.org**).

Mobile phone manufacturers, telecommunications operators and Internet companies are supporting WAP because of its potential to stimulate the growth of online commerce. They also see the need to develop a universal standard for Internet access on wireless devices. "The WAP forum was stimulated out of a recognition that if we competed against each other with proprietary models, no-one would win," according to Skip Byran, director of Technology Market Development at Ericsson.

WAP doesn't involve downloading whole HTML web pages to mobile devices because mobile phones and PDAs with their small LCD screens and slow download speeds (usually 9.6–14.4 kbs) are not ideal for web browsing. Instead, Internet content design for WAP is arranged in decks of cards rather than in pages, and these cards are written using Wireless Markup Language (WML). Decks are easier to compress than HTML pages so download speeds are faster. The decks are read by a WAP microbrowser contained in special software on the phone.

You can browse through menus and services by rolling through options and pressing buttons on the phone to select particular options. The Nokia 7110 was the first WAP phone to become available, swiftly followed by the i500 from Motorola and the R320 from Ericsson. Most mobile operators are scrambling to offer WAP services. Orange in the UK has set up a typical partnership with ITN, Euronews, Reuters, the Evening Standard online entertainment guide and Lastminute.com to offer news, share prices, entertainment listings, traffic updates and bargain flight information to WAP customers.

WAP is designed to deal with the bandwidth constraints of GSM technology but the next generation of mobile telephony is just around the corner. Cellnet has already announced that it will shortly offer General Packet Radio Services (GPRS) at speeds ranging from 56 kbit/s to 114 kbit/s. GPRS also offers an "always-on" Internet connection which means that you don't have to dial up and disconnect each time you want to access the Internet from your mobile.

Finding what you want on the web

With over a million new pages being uploaded onto the web each day, it's getting harder to find the information you want. The web is not a well-organised library, but an aggregate of content both good and bad. Fortunately it has automated "librarians" in the form of search engines. Upon receipt of a simply query and mouse click they will go off and search the web, returning results both relevant and irrelevant.

The three biggest "classic" search engines are Altavista (**www.altavista.co.uk**), Hotbot (**www.hotbot.com**) and Infoseek (**www.infoseek.com**). A typical one-word search query on these engines will return about half a million "hits", or possibly relevant web references so be sure to search on combinations of words or phrases. Even so, the difficulty of finding what you want has led to a raft of new special interest directory sites or web portals.

Entries on most search engines are collected by "robots" or "spiders", software tools which roam the web indexing what they find automatically. Web designers enter text on their pages in the source code that the robots use (metatags). Some unscrupulous people unfortunately include entirely irrelevant text on their pages to boost their search engine ratings.

Yahoo (**www.yahoo.co.uk**) remains the most popular of the directory-based sites. These organise entries by category, and also use human evaluation to supplement the robots and spiders. Yahoo has categories on everything under the sun from Business and Economy to society and culture. Google (**www.google.com**) also intelligently ranks web pages based on the number of links to them from other sites. A new project, Fast Search (**www.alltheweb.com**) is attempting to catalogue the entire web, and has indexed over 200 million documents. Excite has a strong following (**www.excite.com**). Lycos (**http://richmedia.lycos.com**) can search audio and video documents such as mp3 files (**http://mp3.lycos.co.uk**). Ask Jeeves (**www.ask.com**) allows you to question a web-wise butler who answers with relevant web pages. Ask Jeeves can interpret natural language and learns from previous requests to improve the accuracy of future returns.

Publicising your business on the web

Creating Web pages

Most people create web pages either for personal "hobby" interest, or to market a service or product. The web has been the focus of a great deal of marketing activity because it is cheaper than conventional print advertising or direct mail, and the content of the "advert" can be altered at any time, although it is still extremely hard to measure the response to web advertising, or "cost per hit". Many Web sites are really PR activities rather than conventional marketing tools, despite the "buzz" about e-commerce and online trading.

Web pages are normally "hosted" by an Internet service provider (ISP) – they have to be available 24 hours a day, so renting space on existing servers is cheaper than setting up your own. ISPs will also design pages for you if you don't want to learn to use HTML authoring tools or don't have graphic design and editing skills. HTML itself can look intimidating, but is actually a clear and well-structured language. It does have strict rules, however, so most people use an authoring package which allows you to specify the structure of the document (heading levels, graphics and so on), and then inserts the correct codes to produce the desired effect, checking for adherence to the rules as it goes along. Web authoring tools include:

- Adobe GoLive – **www.adobe.com**
- Allaire Homesite – **www.allaire.com/Products/HomeSite/**
- Hot Dog Pro – **www.sausage.com**
- HoTMetaL Pro – **www.sq.com**
- Macromedia Dreamweaver – **www.macromedia.com**
- Microsoft Frontpage – **www.microsoft.com/FrontPage/**

CompuServe users can download the Home Page Wizard from CompuServe to create their own pages, an approach now being taken up by a number of local Internet service providers in order to provide customers with very basic pages. This kind of software is not appropriate for creating complex sites with sophisticated graphic design, but it can be a way to get started and make your presence known.

When designing Web pages, it is important to keep information short and well-structured, and not to go overboard with complex graphics which slow down browsing for the user. Use the facility of hypertext – instead of creating very long pages, make smaller separate pages with logical links that users can select to get more information on a particular topic.

The Web also provides facilities to create online forms for collecting feedback from users. The information in these forms has to be processed on the computer where the Web pages are hosted, so if you want to use forms you will need to create what is known as a "cgi script" to process the form information. Because such scripts can cause havoc on the local server if they go wrong, most ISPs won't let you use this approach without some help from them in ensuring that the script is bug-free.

Most people can learn quite easily to create simple web pages. But if you need to create an extensive website with much interaction between pages, especially if you do not have experience with graphics, information provision, cgi scripting and HTML, you should consider paying a consultant to prepare the pages for you.

Reaching your audience

Once you have created your pages, you need to signpost them so that people can find you. The cheap but time-consuming way to do this involves visiting each search engine site, such as Altavista and Yahoo, and filling in a request form. Or you can use a service like Submit it (**www.submit-it.com**) or Intelliquis Traffic Building (**www.intelliquis.co.uk**) – the list of similar services is growing… Whichever service you select, before posting details of your site make sure that you have used the HTML Meta tag to indicate (invisibly to the user) the content and keywords of your site on your home page – this will help search engines to index your pages properly. Use of the meta tags should be explained in your HTML editing package. The specialist website **www.searchenginewatch.com** keeps tabs on how the search engines rank sites to help you keep at the top of their listings.

Online commerce

Online shopping is growing fast in popularity, although over 50% of British Internet users are still wary of giving their credit card details over the web. Between March and June of 1999, approximately 2.1 million Internet users in Britain made an online purchase (Amárach Consulting Eir-commerce report June 1999). More than half (56%) of the Internet users in the UK bought a book online in 1999 (Continental Research). Books, music CDs and travel tickets are the most popular purchases but commerce-enabled websites can also provide teleworkers with a more cost-effective way of purchasing computer hardware and software. Online merchant auctions such as Onsale (**www.onsale.com**) and Ubid (**www.ubid.com**) provide sales of new and used computer hardware and software in a password-protected secure environment. Onsale has an automated assistant, Bid Watch, that finds, monitors and bids for items on your behalf.

However, it is estimated that business-to-business (B2B) ecommerce will outstrip business-to-consumer (B2C) ecommerce by a factor of 10:1, and there is a Klondike rush in progress to set up so-called industry portals (websites where products and information from a lot of different suppliers in the same sector are available) such as **www.chemdex.com**, which sells everything from pipettes to DNA analysers to the life sciences sector. Sites which allow businesses to compare prices on similar products are also proliferating. Once the technology is in place to link existing EDI procurement systems through the XML web protocol with buyers and sellers via the portals, a change in business purchasing habits similar to the introduction of supermarkets in the food sector is predicted. Companies which believe that they have expertise in ecommerce, such as management consultants and some IT businesses, are even offering some "dot com" start-ups free ecommerce advice or equipment in exchange for an equity share in those businesses which they think will make it big.

So how do teleworkers get involved in e-commerce? There are three main possibilities: hosting, building from scratch or working with off-the-shelf software packages. Using hosting, you pay a rental fee, usually to your chosen ISP but the level to which you can customise their offering is limited – you get a kind of template, rather like filling in an online form, and the cost depends on the number of different products you want to sell. Often training is included in the price, and a commission is taken from your income to cover the cost of secure payment processing. Usually there is also a deal with a distribution company at a cheap rate to actually deliver the goods to the customer. IBM has a home-page creator system that gives an online demo so that you can see how this kind of system works (**www.ibm.com**). Whether this kind of approach will suit depends really on your expansion plans – if you expect to expand very rapidly bear in mind that using a templated system may mean that you have to rebuild the site in future to cope with more products and higher transaction volumes.

Building from scratch is only an option if you have excellent HTML and Java skills. Off-the-shelf packages are a good compromise but there are hundreds of products on the market to choose from. John Dunne of Ireland's Sunday Business Post newspaper (**www.sbpost.ie**) gives the following guidelines to picking an e-commerce package:

- Product catalogue – can you add or modify products easily? Can you include multimedia objects such as audio clips in the product description?;

- Store – can you modify content and look yourself, remotely? Does it allow for promotions, discounts etc. Can you cross-sell products? Can you provide more than one store?;

- Personalisation – can you get users to register and then use this information to intelligently sell to them in future (eg by offering extra discounts on products they buy regularly)? Can the user personalise their own preferences?;

- Security musts – user authentication, browser to server security (eg SSL), encryption of credit card and personal details, secure online payment;

- Tax – are sales taxes such as VAT automatically calculated?;

- Shipping/delivery – does it automatically calculate shipping costs? Can it cope with third party shipping products?;

- Online payment – if possible it should support SET, cybercash, e-check, e-cash and so on. Also, if possible, you need worldwide currency support and multilingual support;

- Reports – you should be able to get statistics on most popular products, number of visitors and there should also be flexibility to prepare the reports that will be most useful for you.

Sending and receiving files

The simplest way to send or receive a file over the Internet is by attaching it to an email message. This method is usually slower than using a specialist FTP program, but not many people transfer so much information regularly for this to be a problem.

Alternatively, you can use ftp directly. "Anonymous ftp" allows Internet hosts to devote part of their disk space to public files in a way that doesn't require everyone who wants a file to have a user-id and password. You will need a piece of "ftp client software" to do this – many are available on the Internet, such as the public domain package winftp.exe or the DOS utility provided with many computers, ftp.exe, or the widely-used package WS-FTP.

You will need to know the domain name or IP address of the ftp site you want to reach. If the site is not public domain, you'll also need a userid and password. FTP has different methods of transfer for ASCII or binary files so if you have trouble transferring files, look at whether you are using the wrong one. FTP is used a great deal to upload updated web pages onto host computers.

Transferring large amounts of data

If you are planning to use email to send large text and graphics files, you will need to obtain a compacting utility such as PKZIP for the PC (**www.pkware.com/shareware/pkzip_win.html**) or Aladdin Dropzip and Stuffit Expander for the Mac (**www.aladdinsys.com**). These programmes squash your files, commonly to about half their original size. You can then email the "stuffed" or "zipped" file in half of the time, and with any luck save half of the phone call costs.

If you send your file in this form, the recipient needs to have the appropriate programme in order to unpack the file to its original size.

Some compacting programmes allow you to create "self-expanding" files – the recipient double clicks on the compacted file and it expands itself back to normal size without the need for the correct unpacking software to be installed on their machine.

It is important to use the right version of the compacting utility for your system: for example, if you are using Windows 9x or Windows NT, you will need the correct version of WinZip (**www.winzip.com**).

There are also some applications where a direct modem-to-modem link or an ISDN link is cheaper than using an email system. For example, dtp files for a four-colour magazine can easily exceed 10Mb in size. Many typesetting bureaux offer their own high-speed direct links to keep the cost of transferring such large amounts of data down. If you are involved in large-scale file transfer, it is worth comparing prices between different analogue modem speeds, ISDN lines, ADSL and high-speed cable modems to work out the cheapest methods for different file sizes. This will allow you to see whether the additional installation and rental costs are justified in your situation.

Mailing lists and listservs

The Internet has a vast number of mailing lists on subjects of special interest. As with most Internet functions, the difficulty is finding what you want in the first place but there is a website which indexes listservs – **www.lsoft.com/lists/listsref.html**. Once you have the name of the list, and the address of the computer that administrates the list, you can subscribe automatically using the ingenious listserv command. You send an email to listserv@address.of.host usually containing one line:

subscribe name-of-list yourname

The listserv programme will add you to that mailing list and send you information about a different address where you can send your contributions to the mailing list. From then on, you receive all messages that are sent to that mailing list – so check that you also know how to "unsubscribe" and how to "nomail" while you are on holiday. Do remember that the address for subscription commands is different from that for contributions to the mailing list.

Newsgroups

Usenet News is the official name of a part of the Internet known as "newsgroups", a vast and varied collection of discussions where individuals post messages and others read and respond to them. Special newsreader software can be used to access newsgroups, but all the major web browsers also offer newgroup access and can pick up your news messages whenever you log on. There are currently over 20,000 different newsgroups organised around every imaginable topic.

Mailing lists and newsgroups are easy to confuse at first, since newsgroups are really online discussion groups with very little news on

Newsgroup utilities

FreeAgent for Windows – **www.forteinc.com/agent/** – organises and filters news messages offline

NewsWatcher for Mac (**http://wuarchive.wustl.edu/systems/mac/info-mac/comm/Internet/ya-newswatcher-216.hqx**) does the same but only online

MacSlurp is at **www.macorchard.com**

Finding newsgroups – searchable index at **http://tile.net/news**

Subscribing to specialist newsgroups (fee-based but useful): **www.usenet.com**

them. Overall, listservs tend to be more specialist and have smaller subscriber lists than newsgroups. You also don't require any official "approval" to create a listserv. Newsgroups, on the other hand, are a subset of Usenet News – a set of machines that exchange articles tagged with universally-recognised newsgroup labels. Usenet receives hundreds of megabytes of postings each day. Each machine collects all the newsgroups each day and allows you to download only those groups that interest you.

Any subscriber can contribute to a newsgroup, either by replying with mail to the author, or by "following up" to continue the newsgroup messages. As well as the publicly available newsgroups, there are others, such as Clarinet, which are commercial services; your host must have a contract with Clarinet before they will be available. The main newsgroup categories are:

comp computer science, hardware, software
news news networks and software
rec   recreational activities, arts, hobbies
sci   scientific research and applications, including some social sciences
soc   social issues
talk discussion on controversial topics
misc all the rest – including the useful misc.jobs and misc.forsale
alt   alternative ways of looking at things. Includes many bizarre topics. Unregulated
biz   discussions related to business. Allows advertising, unlike many other sections of the Internet
k12   teachers, students, topics related to the "kindergarten through twelve" age group.

Remember, before you jump in with your pearl of wisdom, that you are joining a conversation which may have been going on for years. Check out the FAQ (frequently asked questions) messages which are regularly posted on most newsgroups to find the information you want, or to discover whether the topic you are dying to message about has been done to death by the existing participants in the past.

Newsgroup postings "expire" after about three days. There are some sites which archive old postings (**www.dejanews.com**) but there is no central resource which "owns" newsgroups.

Offline readers for newsgroups

Once you have done some initial exploring to orientate yourself to your on-line service, think about using an OLR or offline reader. Manually checking through Compuserve forums or Internet newsgroups for new messages can be time-consuming and therefore expensive. An OLR is a programme that creates a customised, automatic script for all the actions you would take yourself, and performs them as quickly as possible. A typical OLR script might check for waiting email, check for new forum/newsgroup messages in those areas you are interested in, and summarise any new library files. When you log on, the OLR zips through all the actions which you have requested and logs off automatically – typically taking a couple of minutes for a simple script. You can then, at your leisure and without incurring further telephone charges, peruse the messages that have been downloaded onto your computer using the OLR. Once you have composed your replies and new messages, you send them as a batch using a second OLR script, again minimising connect time and keeping costs down.

IRC – wild chatter on the Internet

Chatting on the Internet (similar to conferencing on CompuServe) is carried out using Internet Relay Chat. Once you are in IRC, commands begin with a / but everything else you type is broadcast. To join a chat, type /join channel name. Internet chats are unmoderated, and can be chaotic, but they are very useful for emergency technical support on a Sunday afternoon. The Finger command tells you who else is logged in for chatting. Millions of people now use the software package ICQ 99 ("I seek you") – a free buddy list program that lets you know where your friends and colleagues are, so that you can send them instant messages if they also have the ICQ software installed – download it from **www.icq.com**.

Specialist information services

To access a specialist online service such as Reuters 3000 Xtra financial information (**www.reuters.com/3000xtra**) or the Dow Jones Newswires (**www.djnewsplus.com**), you will need to contact the supplier either by filling out a feedback form on the web or using email or telephone to arrange contract details and payment methods. Then the service provider supplies you with an access telephone number or an Internet address, a user-id and a password. Some of these premium services offer free training on the basis that the more you know about the system, the more you will use it, and the more money you will spend.

Proprietary online services

Services such as CompuServe/America Online (**www.aol.co.uk**) and MSN (**www.msn.co.uk**) provide email and opportunities to conference with other users on topics of special interest. Using proprietary software you can communicate with colleagues and clients in real time, exchange messages in one-to-one chat features or use chat rooms in the communities area of the AOL site. You can also shop online and get technical support for the AOL/MSN software.

Netiquette

The general etiquette of online services (network etiquette or netiquette for short) is one of consideration for other users. Most breaches of netiquette are due to ignorance, rather than any desire to offend. A simple example would be that typing in capital letters is the online equivalent of SHOUTING. Instead _underscore_ words or *asterisk* phrases. Because online communications do not allow body language such as ironic grins and shoulder shrugs, some people use symbols such as <bg> for big grin and "emoticons" such as the smiley face :-) (look at it sideways) or {%—)) (cross-eyed smiling man with hat and double chin) to embellish their messages. There are also a number of acronyms such as IMHO (in my humble opinion), AFAIK (as far as I know) and BTW (by the way) in common usage.

Probably the most important piece of netiquette to understand is that blatant commercialism and marketing is disapproved of. Sales messages are likely to result in your being "flamed" – sent a hailstorm of rude replies.

A less obvious form of netiquette stems from the world-wide nature of the Web. Words that have a quite innocent meaning in one country can mean something altogether more sinister or obscene in another. A UK group with a common interest in lace-making found this out to their cost when they discovered that the term has a pornographic meaning in the USA. It's important to be aware that other people may have sensitivities of which you are unaware. It is also unfortunately true that many Web sites carry material that you might find at best distasteful, and that might be seriously injurious to children. It is possible to buy software (often from your ISP) which will screen sites for pornography or other illicit material, and which will enable you to put out of bounds altogether sites that you do not want your children to see. Filtering software has the ability to block IRC chat, email, newsgroups and selected sites. Well-known products include Microsystem Cyberpatrol (**www.cyberpatrol.co.uk**), Solid Oak CYBERsitter (**www.solidoak.com**), Net Nanny (**www.netnanny.co.uk**) and Kiddesk Internet Safe (**www.edmark.com**).

Acknowledgements

Stephen Cawley, Assistant Editor, *PC Live*, Scope Communications has updated this chapter. See **www.techcentral.ie**

Kathy Lang, Mayflower Computing, Ro Dew, West Looe Hill, Cornwall PL13 2HH
Tel: 01503 263688 Email: kathy.lang@mayflower-cc.co.uk

Peter Flynn, Academic Computing Manager, University College Cork.
Email: pflynn@curia.ucc.ie

Nua Internet Surveys Web: **www.nua.ie**

Bibliography

Internet Magazine (web site http:/www.emap.com/internet) *monthly*
Publishers: emap Business Communications
Source: Subscriptions Hotline (+44) (0) 181 956 3015 Email: custserv@readerlink.emap.co.uk

Creating Stores on the Web 2nd edition *Date: 2000*
Authors: Ben Sawyer, Dave Greely, Joe Ctaudella
Source: Peachpit Press ISBN: 0–201–70005–0

Em@il *Date: 2000*
Author: Annalisa Milner
Source: Dorling Kindersley ISBN 0751–30995–8 Web: www.dk.com

Successful Cyberm@rketing in a Week *Date: 2000*
Author: J. Jonathan Gabay
Source: Hodder & Stoughton ISBN 0–340–75815–5

The Complete Idiot's Guide to E-Commerce *Date: 2000*
Authors: Rob Smith, Mark Speaker and Mark Thompson
Source: Alpha Books Que ISBN 0–78972194–5

The Internet Rough Guide 2000 *Date: 2000*
Author: Angus J Kennedy
Source: Rough Guides ISBN 1–85828–442–2

Buying Web Services: The survival guide to outsourcing *Date: 1999*
Author: J P Frenza
Source: Wiley Computer Publishing ISBN: 0–471–31289–4

Managing and marketing your website *Date: 1999*
Author: Jim Hutchinson
Source: Oaktree Press ISBN 1–86076–091–0

Successful E-Commerce in a Week *Date: 1999*
Author: Dave Howell
Source: Hodder & Stoughton ISBN 0–340–753366

**The Clickable Corporation: successful strategies for capturing
the Internet advantage** *Date: 1999*
Authors: Jonathan Rosenoer, Douglas Armstrong and J. Russell Gates
Source: The Free Press ISBN 0–684–85553–4

The Guardian Guide to the Internet *Date: 1999*
Author: Tim Mclellan
Source: Fourth Estate Ltd ISBN 1–84115–236–6

The Virgin Internet Shopping Guide *Date: 1999*
Author: Simon Collin
Source: Virgin Publishing Ltd ISBN 0–7535–04103

**Electronic Commerce: Directions and Opportunities for
Electronic Business** *Date: 1998*
Editor: Tom Nash
Source: Director Publications Ltd for the IOD and SAP (UK)
ISBN 0–7494–2831–7

30 Minutes... to Master the Internet *Date: 1997*
Author: Neil Barrett
Source: Kogan Page, 120 Pentonville Road, London N1 9JN
ISBN 0–7494–2366–8

101 Essential Tips: Using the Internet *Date: 1997*
Editor: Irene Lyford
Source: Dorling Kindersley, 9 Henrietta St, London WC2E 8PS
ISBN 0–7513–0419–0

How to series: Doing Business on the Internet *Date: 1997*
Author: Graham Jones
Source: How to Books, Plymbridge House, Estover Road, Plymouth PL6 7PZ
ISBN 0–185703–364–7

The European Information Society at the Crossroads (FAIR project) *Date: 1997*
Source: European Commission DG13 Fax: +32 2 296 2981 Email: adb@postman.dg13.cec.be

The Rough Guide to the Internet and World Wide Webb *Date: 1997*
Author: Angus J Kennedy
Source: Rough Guides Ltd, 1 Mercer St, London WC2H 9QJ
ISBN 1–85828–288–8

Web Marketing Cookbook *Date: 1997*
Author: Janice M. King
Source: John Wiley and Sons ISBN 0–471–17911–6

Web Security Sourcebook *Date: 1997*
Author: Ariel D Rubin, Daniel Geer, Marcus J Ranum
Source: John Wiley and Sons ISBN 0–471–18148–X

Digital Business: surviving and thriving in an online world *Date: 1996*
Author: Ray Hammond
Source: Coronet/Hodder & Stoughton, 338 Euston Rd, London NW1 3BH
ISBN 0–340–66660–9

Digital Money – the New Era of Internet Commerce *Date: 1996*
Authors: Daniel C. Lynch and Leslie Lundqvist
Source: John Wiley & Sons Inc. Ref: ISBN 0–471–14178–X

The New Internet Business Book *Date: 1996*
Authors: Jill H. Ellsworth and Matthew V. Ellsworth
Source: John Wiley & Sons Ref: ISBN 0–471–14160–7

Contacts and URLs

America Online (AOL) Web: **www.aol.co.uk**

Anti-spam tools: try Spamscan 97 **www.webster-image.com** or Spam Buster **www.contactplus.com**

BT's Internet service, aimed at small businesses and home users: Tel: 0800 800 001 BT's phone directories online: **www.bt.com/phonenetuk/**

Compression utilities: PKZIP **www.pkware.com/shareware/pkzip_win.html** or Aladdin Dropzip and Stuffit Expander **www.aladdinsys.com**

Ecommerce sites – best-known examples are Amazon **www.amazon.co.uk** and CD Now **www.cdnow.com**

Free email sites: **www.hotmail.com**, **www.yahoo.co.uk**, **www.twigger.co.uk**

History of computing and the Internet: *Computerscope Online* article The Digital Century December 1999 in the Computerscope archives at **www.techcentral.ie** or Smithsonian Online **http://smithsonian.yahoo.com/index.html**

Listing of British ISPs, rates, contact numbers:
www.internet-magazine.com/resource/isp/isp_list.html

Listings of Irish ISPs: **www.dot.ie** or **www.techcentral.ie**

Greenet (Internet access specialising in community groups)74–77 White Lion St, London N1 9PF. Tel: 020 7713 1941 Fax: 020 7837 5551 Email: support@gn.apc.org Web: **www.gn.apc.org**

Dow Jones News Service, Winchmore House 12–15 Fetter Lane London EC4A 1BR Tel: 071 832 9575 Fax: 071 832 9861 **Web: www.djnewsplus.com** and **dowjones.wsg.com**

Microsoft Network Web: **www.msn.co.uk**

Submit-it is a service for sending your website URL to a number of search engines automatically. **www.submit-it.com**

www.teleadapt.com supplies adaptors and kits for linking up to collect your email or browse the web anywhere in the world.

Teleworking equipment

A note on prices

Technology changes dramatically, and prices with it. Sample prices are only given here where they are considerably higher or lower than you might expect. Often the prices stated by equipment manufacturers in advertisements are slightly higher than the 'street prices' which you will actually have to pay. To get an idea of the likely street price, check a number of retailers' advertisements for the same product, and take an average. Web-based retailers often offer a further discount for purchases made through a website by credit card, because these sales are administratively less expensive for them. Remember that quoted prices for office products often don't include VAT.

How and where to buy

Different teleworking businesses require different equipment. When you are deciding what to buy, try to get quotes and advice from more than one source, do some research on the web, and talk to other users of similar equipment. Look for tips in relevant newsgroups, or join mailing lists and ask fellow subscribers for advice. We've included a checklist at the end of this chapter to help you collate and cost your equipment needs.

Pick up a computer magazine at your local newsagent. For PCs, *Personal Computer World*, *Computer Shopper*, *PC Advisor* and *PC Direct* magazines are among the best for comparing advertised prices as well as useful information. For Macs, *MacUser*, *MacWorld* and *Mac Format* are good, reliable titles and carry thorough product surveys. Almost all these magazines have websites, including review articles from past editions, which can be useful, as well as message boards where you can post queries and comments.

Computers and office equipment are available from:

- independent local retailers, who can give you a personal service but may be relatively expensive;
- high-street chains such as Dixons and Currys;
- computer superstores such as PC World and Compustore;
- direct by phone or over the web from manufacturing companies such as Dell, Gateway, Compaq and Apple
- direct by phone or web from retailers such as Time or other direct sales organisations like Viking Direct, which mainly provides stationery but sells some computers.

If you choose to buy over the web, look for a vendor that has a reputation for fulfilling orders on time and providing good post-purchase support.

Our sixpennyworth for success when buying and using PCs

Co-authors Alan and Imogen have 25 years experience between them of buying and using PCs for teleworking – these are their tips.

- *Accept you're not going to get it right 100% of the time. We have had both good and bad experiences with direct sales operations like Dell and Gateway, and with local dealers. Unfortunately this is one area where past performance is not much of a guide to future results...*

- *Try to anticipate for the future. If in doubt whether you'll need something (eg more hard disk space) get it built into the new PC because it will cost more and cause more disruption to retro-fit it.*

- *Assume it will take you at least 40 hours spread over a period of weeks to specify, finance, order, chase up, install and completely customise a new PC for your purposes – researching magazines, comparing prices, dealing with the bank or leasing company, backing up and moving data, creating shortcuts, getting everything just so. The chances are the lost earning hours spent doing this will cost more than the PC itself.*

- *Always take at least two backups before moving data onto a new PC.*

- *Never load games on your work machine.*

- *Avoid clever little utilities that you can download free off the web or get given by friends unless they are really clever – they usually turn out to be the thing that's causing the crashes/data problems etc.*

- *Use up-to-date virus software which you can update regularly from a website. It is professionally very embarrassing to find you have passed on a virus to a customer or client.*

- *Get a utilities programme such as Dr Norton's to help you tidy up after system crashes and move programmes.*

- *Learn how to use data synchronisation programmes like Windows Briefcase – this can provide a "belt and braces" extra backup facility if you also have a second office computer, which many experienced teleworkers do.*

- *Check out any freelance PC support people in your area. Sometimes no phone helpline, however good, can replace the effectiveness of paying someone by the hour to come in and haul you out of trouble.*

- *Have a plan (like an arrangement with a teleworking neighbour) for what you're going to do if the hard disk crashes or the printer jams irrevocably when you're working to a deadline.*

- *If you can afford it have multiple methods of getting online (eg ISDN and a dial-up modem, a Hotmail or Freeserve account and a business dial-up account) to ensure you can stay in contact.*

- *Keep spare stock of printer cartridges, disks, backup tapes etc. at all times.*

In most web stores, you choose the pieces of equipment, place them in your electronic "shopping cart" and proceed to the "checkout" – the secure area of the site. You then put in your personal details, contact information, shipping address and credit card details. When you submit that form your credit card details are sent to the vendor's secure server. While in transit over the Internet, your credit card number is protected by electronic encyption. This is usually Secure Sockets Layer (SSL) technology but some merchants use Secure Electronic Transfer (SET) to protect your details.

Buying by mail order or over the web using a credit card may protect you against defective goods or suppliers going into liquidation, although interest charges can make this an expensive method of payment if you don't clear your balance quickly. Some magazines are members of the Mail Order Protection Scheme – look for the MOPS logo – which offers you limited protection against problems with advertisers. Bear in mind that, especially for complex items such as computers, a low purchase cost is no bargain if you are getting poor advice or limited after-sales service. Is on-site repair offered, or will you have to bear the expense of returning the equipment for repair? Is there a guaranteed response time? What is the service offered beyond the standard guarantee period (usually 60 or 90 days)? Some computer dealers offer access to technical support through premium rate telephone lines, but manufacturers like Dell and Gateway offer low-cost phone support once you supply your customer reference number.

An alternative to a service contract is to insure your equipment against breakdown. Then if there is a problem you reclaim the cost of having it fixed. Be wary of expensive maintenance contracts where you pay a large sum even if no problems arise. High-tech electronics do not often go wrong and some dealers advertising low prices try to crank up their profits with exorbitant service contracts. You don't have to take one at all.

Also consider whether you should rent equipment or buy; the former is more expensive in total cash terms, but your accountant may decide that it will save you more tax, and if money is tight at first it reduces your start-up costs. In essence, if you buy, then you pay upfront and you can only claim a percentage of that cost each year (around a quarter) against tax. If you buy you will probably need to negotiate a loan with your bank to cover the purchase cost upfront. If you rent or lease, the whole amount can be claimed against tax, and you do not have to stump up large amounts of money upfront. However, there are complexities – you don't actually own the equipment though there is usually a method of buying it at the end of the lease. Leases do provide a degree of security – usually they can't be withdrawn or curtailed by credit squeezes or changes in economic conditions, and are not repayable on demand like an overdraft. To work out the best option for you consult your financial adviser and bank

Many equipment purchases have hidden costs. Computer printers require expenditure on toner and paper; mobile phones and portable PCs often require extra sets of batteries to maximise their usefulness. If you're travelling abroad, you'll need power and telecoms adapters for any portable equipment. These costs are often impossible to assess precisely as your use of the equipment will change over time, but an informed estimate will save you some unpleasant shocks.

Telephony

A telephone is the only essential piece of equipment for a teleworker, and the choice of service providers is growing too fast for detailed coverage in a book. Comparisons between different operators' costs and offerings can be found at **www.tariffcentre.com**.

When buying a handset, if you can get a hands-free phone at little extra cost it's a good idea in this age of 20-minute waits to get through to call centre staff, so that you can get on with other work while "on hold". However, don't be tempted to use hands-free all the time unless the handset is very good quality – to the person at the other end your voice will probably appear distorted and tinny when you are using the hands-free facility, and some people think that using hands-free is impolite – you can't be bothered to pay attention to them fully. A headset phone can overcome these difficulties though some people find being tied down by the headset cable annoying. Cordless headsets are available but are often still expensive.

Check with your telephone company whether you are on an exchange where ISDN services are available. Don't accept a bland "everyone can get ISDN" answer. Ask them to check specifically whether your exchange does ISDN and if you are within the distance limit (about 4 km) from the exchange for it to work reliably. Whether you go for ISDN or not, you will probably want a separate telephone line so that you can easily distinguish business and personal calls and monitor business costs. Business lines are more expensive than residential, but usually guarantee a faster fault-repair service and entitle you to a free text-only Yellow Pages entry.

BT's Highway ISDN offering allows you to keep a PC, phone and fax permanently plugged in, have different numbers for each, and get Internet access speeds of up to 128kbs. The high-speed link helps with speedier network connections, faster file transfer and conferencing facilities. Assuming your PC has speakers, a microphone and the right software, you can also store numbers on your PC and use it to carry out one-touch speed dialling on your phone. BT Highway costs £119 for conversion of an existing line plus an ISDN card or £240 for a new line and quarterly rental is £138 which includes pre-paid calls (**www.homehighway.bt.com**). These prices may well change as ADSL rolls out over the next couple of years.

You can also improve the flexibility of your telephone with some low-cost enhancements. Different phone companies offer slightly different services and sometimes under slightly different names, but offerings are similar. Call Waiting alerts you when a caller is trying to get through while you're using the phone; you can switch between calls. Call Diversion redirects incoming calls to any other number, so you can receive them at someone else's premises or on your mobile. Three Way Calling lets you talk to two other numbers simultaneously for small "audio meetings" or audioconferences. Caller Line Identification allows you to see on a display who is calling your number. Call Minder sets up a voice mailbox for yourself. The mailbox works like an answering machine, recording messages when you're out or engaged, and playing them back to you through the phone. None of these services requires any extra equipment other than a standard touchtone telephone handset. Many are even free – all you have to do is ask for them.

Remote call diversion is another useful facility. This allows you to redirect your calls from any phone. You dial your number and when you get the voicemail greeting, enter a PIN code followed by the new number to divert to – this way you can ensure that your calls follow you when out of the office. Featureline is a BT system which can turn a collection of separate lines at one premises into a switchboard using facilities on the local digital exchange. Ordinary phones located within 200 metres of each other can be used as switchboard extensions, with facilities such as call diversion, call transfer between extensions, ring back when free, ring back when next used, call barring, five way call waiting and three-way calling. Call answering can be set up in cyclical hunting to ensure even distribution of calls between a set of lines. Featureline costs £99 for a new line, or £15 to upgrade an existing line, plus rental charges of £50.58 per quarter.

Computer telephony integration (CTI) is a new set of tools which use the digital facilities now available for telephones, such as caller line identification, in conjunction with computer databases and other tools such as the Goldmine customer relationship software to manage information for tasks such as telesales and telemarketing (**www.goldminesw.com**).

For directory services, it is worth knowing that you can get the entire UK business subscriber phone catalogue in database format on CD-ROM for a mere £40 from Thomson Directories (**www.infospace.com/uk.thomw**).

Conferencing

Audioconferencing (also known as teleconferencing or just plain conferencing) allows you to hold full-scale meetings over the phone. Although large numbers of participants (over 15) can be difficult to handle in practical terms, the technology will support many more. If some only need to listen in without talking, you can have an audience of hundreds on a single call. Telephone companies and specialist teleconferencing firms will set up these calls for you on a one-off basis – the technological bells and whistles are at their end, and participants can use any normal phone.

There are two flavours of audioconference – dial-in and dial-out. For dial-in conferencing, the conference participants dial a special telephone

> **Ocean rides the audioconference wave**
>
> Paul Delaney is eBusiness manager for BT's Irish subsidiary Ocean, and teleworks four days a week – two days a week at home, and two days meeting clients. Delaney uses BT's audioconferencing facilities to communicate and have "meetings" with BT's worldwide sales team.
>
> A conference is usually requested by a caller sending an email to the colleagues he wants to "meet`" with. Before the meeting takes place, a receptionist dials out to all the participants, usually six or seven people at a time, and each can intervene with comments or proposals at any time.
> **www.ocean.ie**

number and are greeted by a receptionist who checks their identity before linking them to the conference. For dial-out conferencing, an operator dials each of the participants and links them together. Dial-out conferences are more expensive for the organiser but free for the other participants.

Audioconferencing is growing rapidly and the audioconferencing market is about 20 times large than that for videoconferencing. Costs have reduced to around £9/head/person and sophisticated products also offer options to record the meeting, bringing in or blocking out specific participants as required.

Videoconferencing – using video images of participants as well as their voices – is becoming more popular and PC-based system are becoming commonplace. You need a sound card in your PC (most are built with one these days), a PC camera, preferably with USB plug and play port, costing less than £100, a microphone, an Internet connection and conferencing software. Many conferencing packages can be downloaded from the web – Microsoft Netmeeting is the most popular and is free from Microsoft (**www.computingcentral.com**). In addition to holding "face to face" conversations and collaborating with colleagues and clients regardless of location, you can send video images, and use the camera to view items. Most conferencing software also has "electronic whiteboard" features which allow you to cut, copy and paste information from other software packages such as word processors and spreadsheets to be viewed by the other conference participants. The whiteboard can be saved for future reference. Netmeeting also has a "chat" feature for swapping concise text messages, but it is usually used in practice with a simultaneous audioconference. There are also file transfer facilities so that you can send text, audio and video files to the other participants during the conference. Advanced features allow a conference to be initiated through sending an email message to the other participants.

Bandwidth is important for PC-based videoconferencing – the more you have the better. Video quality tends to be poor unless ISDN connections are available. Room or group videoconferencing systems are much more expensive, and best used where there are several people in each location. They can be used to link up international meetings or to deliver training presentations. If you are involved in a group or one-to-many videoconferences, experts advise having a separate audio (sound-only) link as a backup, in case technical gremlins cause problems with the video transmission. Where a number of ISDN lines are available (say three ISDN lines which is equivalent to six ordinary phone lines) they can be "bonded" together to provide higher bandwidth with better quality and extra facilities such as the ability for a speaker to send down presentation slides to a separate screen using part of the bandwidth.

Telephone companies, some colleges and commercial conferencing firms can provide bureau facilities for high quality videoconferencing, as can some telecentres; purchasing good quality equipment can cost several thousand pounds and it is not yet in widespread use for individual teleworkers.

Internet telephony

Assuming that your PC has a sound card, Voice over IP, aka VOIP or Internet telephony, is another possibility. VOIP calls are cheaper to make for international calls than standard PSTN calls. VOIP uses the Internet Protocol (IP) to carry the phone conversation, so voice information is broken into small packets before it is sent over the Internet. The quality is therefore never as good as PSTN but if your brother's in Australia you'll probably put up with it. Net2phone (**www.net2phone.com**) offers free download software but you have to sign up for an account, and you can then "prepay" your calls by uploading call credits using your credit card.

Bursting the bandwidth

If ISDN lines don't provide you with enough bandwidth for your communications needs then there are other alternatives. Digital Subscriber Line (DSL) provides speeds from 144 kbs upwards that run over the standard copper lines already coming into your home (as long as you aren't more than about 4 km from the exchange). Asymmetric DSL provides faster speeds for download to the PC than for upload and is currently the favourite flavour of DSL with operators. Both BT and NTL began to roll out their ADSL services in summer 2000. A new American standard, GLite, can provide DSL download speeds of up to 1.5 Mb per second.

Cable modems offer average download speeds of about 512 kbs, around 10 times fast than standard analogue dial-up, but access speeds depend on the number of users accessing the service at any one time. There are some security issues to consider – if you don't remember to uncheck File Print and Sharing in your Network Neighbourhood settings you could find strangers snooping your hard disk. Of course you have to live within a cable franchise area to get service, so cable modems are more likely to be available for city dwellers. You will need a special network card as well as the cable modem.

For the true speed freak constantly uploading and downloading large video and graphics files, you could get your own T1 leased line providing up to 1.54 Mb per second – however they cost tens of thousands a year so they are more commonly seen in companies than in homes.

Mobiles, handhelds and palm-size PCs

Many teleworkers use cordless telephones. Connected to ordinary lines, these handsets allow you to roam around within about 300 metres of the base station, able to answer the phone speedily without your client knowing you were watering the garden, not sitting at your desk. Cordless headset phones that free your hands for keyboard work or to reach up to that awkward file are also now available, such as the GN Netcom DECT headset phone, though they can be expensive, or the Siemens Gigaset range (double check the handset that you've ordered is the correct model that will work with the headset – they need two additional connection points).

Mobile phones remain pricey compared with standard fixed phones, especially if you opt for a pre-paid "ready to go" type phone. However, call charges have fallen and will continue to fall. Most services also offer a choice of connection or 'airtime' contracts, ranging from a low basic charge with high charges for each individual call, to a high standing charge offset by lower call rates. This is one area too complex and fast moving for detailed coverage in a book, but it pays to be more than usually suspicious of advertising. Try to imagine in advance how many hours per month you'll typically be using a mobile, and calculate costs of the different contracts on this basis.

Cordless and mobile phones may also be about to merge. A number of manufacturers now offer phones that can operate on both the DECT and GSM standards – so you only need one handset which switches from mobile service when you are out of your home or office to less expensive cordless connection to a landline when you are in range.

Mobile batteries need recharging. This is easily done from the mains, but if you rely on a wireless modem and may spend long periods away from a convenient mains supply, check the cost of spare batteries. Most mobiles can also be powered by an adapter in your car.

Most GSM phones can accept the SMS (short message service) two-way message protocol of up to 160 characters. Many delivery companies are starting to use the location services of GSM to track drivers and integrate logistics with location information. Other uses of SMS can be to automatically alert a remote worker when email has arrived in the office, or to cut costs as SMS messaging is considerably cheaper than voice GSM messages. Voice recognition is now becoming widespread on new mobiles – you tell the phone to dial a number instead of messing with those increasingly tiny keypads.

Matching your up mobile with a personal digital assistant (PDA) can provide a perfect toolset for remote workers. You can use the phone as normal, send and receive SMS messages, and download Internet content into the PDA, either via a GSM modem card that fits into a PCMCIA type II or III slot, or through built-in GSM capabilities.

Offerings in this area include the Palm Computing range (personal digital organisers providing a contacts database, email and diary facilities, with greyscale or colour screens, and about 2Mb of RAM). The Palm machines also have a "synchronising cradle" to connect them to a desktop PC ensuring that the data carried around is always the most current version. Palm machines can communicate with mobile phones via an infrared port.

Colour palm-size organisers have been popularised by the Compaq Aero, which has 8Mb of storage space but, although colour is nice to look at, it eats battery power. The Nokia Communicator is an all-in-one mobile phone and PDA. PDAs range in price from around £180 to £500.

Next up in size is the handheld PC, still small enough for your coat pocket but adding some multimedia functions and facilities like basic word processing. They can't compete with a laptop PC but are a lot less expensive. The most popular handheld PC is the Psion revo, though this does not run on the full Windows operating system. It has a comfortable keyboard, calendar, address book, word processor and spreadsheet applications, and comes with a PC docking station that synchronises information on the Revo with desktop information managers such as Lotus Organizer or Microsoft Outlook. Other handhelds, such as the LG Phenom Express and the HP Jornada, run the cut-down Windows operating system Windows CE, and can provide packages like Pocket Word and Pocket Internet Explorer, allowing web browsing and email delivery. Most handhelds have about 16 Mb of RAM and colour screens and cost around £400–£700.

WAP phones (as introduced in the cult movie the Matrix) allow you to access special Internet services written in wireless markup language (WML). They are now available from all the major manufacturers and have large backlit screens, a WAP mini-Internet browser, and tabs where you can store your favourite pages. Most mobile operators are now offering WAP content, though currently there seem to be more handsets available than content to browse. An explosion in WAP services is predicted because WAP "knows where you are" – the server can tell which mobile cell you are in, raising the possibility of services which take into account your location, such as information on the nearest cash machine or restaurant and traffic jam avoidance. Coming soon (within the next two years) are GPRS (faster mobile access at around 115 kbs) and UMTS (384 kbs) – UMTS will allow mobile videophones and high quality audio.

A number of services are being developed to provide seamless messaging for people on the move through the use of personal numbers. **www.yac.com** offers a facility to use one personal number for all your communications, as well as forwarding voicemails to your email (and probably vice versa) – heaven for technoheads.

Another item to think about if you travel around frequently is a telephone chargecard, offered by most major telephone companies. This can be used both in public cardphones and on any private telephones where you wish the call charge to be made to your own account rather than to that phone. International chargecards are also available though some transfer the bill to your credit-card account rather than your phone bill. Ordinary credit cards can also be used in many British and foreign payphones.

Computers

Computers change so quickly that it is never the perfect time to buy the perfect machine, and there are two schools of thought that both claim to minimise the disadvantages. One is that you should buy the most powerful computer you can afford as you will always outstrip its capacity during its lifetime. The other is that if you require your computer to perform relatively simple tasks, it is not necessary to go for the latest technology, and secondhand or low-specification computers provide a substantial cost saving. Part of the argument rests on the rapid depreciation of computer equipment – in accounting terms, a computer which is more than three years old is likely to be worthless. However, recent increases in processing power have extended computer lives a little. But even when you've only had the machine a year, and it is still useful to you, in monetary terms its value will have plummeted. This factor weighs towards the "buy expensive" option – an expensive computer may still be useful to you after three years, whereas a cheap computer not only has no financial value but becomes obsolete in practical terms more quickly because it is old and slow. Buying firsthand also often means that you get some quite powerful software bundled in which would cost a lot to purchase individually. On the other hand, if your resources are limited, you probably have no choice but to go for the "buy cheap or secondhand" option.

In reality, the easiest way to buy a computer is first to consider the software you'll need and not the computer itself – the programs with which you and your PC can actually accomplish something. Decide what task you want the computer to do, identify the software that does it, and then buy a suitable computer on which to run that software, at the same time making sure that it will be easy to add other software, extra memory and other enhancements to it. This is easy advice to follow if you are using specialist software such as CAD drafting packages, but if your needs are fairly general, you will find the major software packages for word processing, desktop publishing and so on are supported on almost all computers, so you may still find the choice confusing.

The good news, though, is that you can now buy a firsthand computer with an impressive technical specification for £1000. These machines will handle applications such as spreadsheets and databases with relative comfort. Machines costing less than £1000 will usually have "budget" processors such as the Intel Celeron or AMD K6-2 series, and less memory cache. They will not be able to load software packages as fast as the more expensive Intel Pentium III and AMD Athlon processors, and won't perform as well with number crunching or graphics applications as their more expensive big brothers.

- **the operating system or 'platform'**

This is the software supplied with the computer that manages its basic functions. Most likely, your choice will be between Windows 98, Windows 2000 and the Apple Mac OS, though on a high-powered machines with loads of memory you should consider Windows 2000 Small Business or Professional edition for its improved security and robustness. Mac OS9 is the current operating system of choice for Apple Macintosh users, though the Mac OSX is expected before the end of 2000. On the PC, Linux is the new kid on the block but has largely remained a tool of techies and programmers. Linux is an ersatz flavour of the high-end operating system Unix, and is open source software (free, open to all via the Internet, and programmers can contribute to its operating system). As a result, although extremely robust, it is not that easy to use unless you have technical savvy. You can install it on to a partitioned section of your hard disk drive if you want but be sure to get technical assistance from Corel's website (**www.linux.corel.com**) before you attempt this.

The difference between operating systems is much like that between petrol and diesel fuel – though they do much the same things, they do them in entirely different manners and you can no more use a program written for the Mac OS operating system on a Windows PC than you can run a diesel car on unleaded.

- **the processor type**

The central processing unit (CPU) chip is the brains of the computer and powers all that it does. Intel produces over 90% of the world's PC processors, and most PC users currently buy a Pentium III processor with a special instruction set for improving streaming media and better graphics. AMD has a small share of the chip market and offers the Athlon processor to compete with the Pentium III. At the lower end of the market, Intel offers its Celeron processor and AMD its K6-2. Apple Macs use PowerPC processors co-designed and manufactured by IBM and Motorola.

- **the processor speed**

Gordon Moore created Moore's Law in 1965 – it says that processor power for computers doubles every 18–24 months. So far it has held. Crucial to that power increase is the processor speed, measured in megahertz (MHz). The faster the speed, the more expensive, and usually the better the performance. Before you go mad on processor speed bear in mind that if your software has not been developed to use the greater speed it won't make much difference to you. But if you use graphic-intensive software such as Photoshop or CAD packages a lot, go for the highest speed you can afford.

- **the RAM or memory**

Measured in megabytes (Mb), this along with the processor specification is the vital determinant of a computer's speed and its capability to run the latest software. A standard offering now is 64 Mb but get as much as you can afford. It won't go to waste and it will extend the computer's life span.

- **the hard disk size**

Measured in gigabytes, hard disks have become enormous. It is not surprising to find a 25 Gb hard disk in a computer now and the standard offering is 12Gb. The disks are now so big that they usually have to be split into separate "logical" drives. That shouldn't prevent you managing to fill the hard disk long before the computer's useful life has expired.

- **CD-ROM drive**

CD-ROM drives in computers are rapidly being replaced by DVD ROM drives though they remain standard in most laptop PCs. Also, most software packages are still distributed on CD-ROM. A CD-ROM can store about 650 Mb of data. The key thing to look for is the speed. Recent drives are "forty speed" – forty times the speed of the first ones. Ordinary CD-ROM drives will only read data. If you want to write to CDs you will need a CD-recordable drive, though these come as standard with some more expensive PCs. A basic CD recordable drive (CD RW) costs around £250.

- **DVD ROM drive**

DVD stands for Digital Versatile Disk. DVDs use smaller tracks than CDs and so can store much more data. These narrower tracks need special lasers to read them so they are not directly compatible with CD-ROMs or audio CDs. DVD-ROM drives in PCs have two lasers – one reads the DVD data and the other CD data, so that the drive in a PC is backwards compatible with CDs. DVD discs hold about 4.7 Gb of data – around seven times more than a CD-ROM – and can store a full-length movie.

- **External storage**

External hard disks or magneto-optical drives can provide space to backup data from your PC or to help you transfer data to other people. Many PCs come with either a 100 Mb Zip drive or an Imation 120 Superdrive. Floppy disks are still built into most PCs, but their days are numbered. Tape drives are still popular for regular backup devices that can accept a copy of your entire hard disk.

- **Internet connectivity**

The current generation of Macs (iMacs, G3s and G4s) don't have floppy disks at all and are built to be easily connected to the Internet with a 56k modem, and 10/100 base T Ethernet port for networking. PC manufacturers are following Apple's lead and providing Internet PCs with a choice of looks and a "legacy-free" design where the older serial and parallel ports have been replaced by the faster Universal Serial Port (USB I and II) which supports plug and play peripheral devices. The advantage of USB is that you can connect and disconnect devices without having to switch off and reload the computer. The current machines also have FireWire (IEE1394) ports for digital video and fast data transfer between PCs and video cameras.

Computers are such large investments that it's wise to try before you buy, talk to colleagues, and find out about their experiences with different manufacturers. Often, such real-world experiences will tell you far more about a potential purchase than any number of reviews.

- Buy for your real needs, not to reach an abstract technological goal;
- At the same time, beware of false economies, such as a cheap computer so slow that you will spend most of your working day waiting for it;
- And if you have the cash, remember that it is usually cheaper to add extra memory or a more capacious hard disk at the time of purchase than later.

Finally, once you have taken possession of the machine, set aside time to learn about it. Commercial training courses are good for coming to grips with specific software, and it's always advisable to curry favour with computer-knowledgeable friends as many apparent problems can be sorted out that way without a repair bill.

Portable computing

Portables (laptops or notebooks) are very convenient and can be used anywhere that there is space to put them down. Traditionally notebooks were more expensive and less powerful than desktop PCs but this is changing and high-end notebooks powered by Pentium III processors offer comparable performance to desktops. As a teleworker, at a minimum you will need to use a word processor, send email and browse the web. Economy multimedia notebooks powered by budget processors (Intel Celeron and AMD K6-2 mobile versions) will meet these modest requirements. Economy notebooks usually come with High Performance Addressing (HPA) passive matrix screens. If you will need to work on large spreadsheets, databases and graphics applications go for a higher-end model using the Pentium III or Athlon chips. Higher-end laptops usually have active matrix (TFT) displays which give a sharper image that is less wearing on the eyes. Consider the weight of the whole device, including cables, spare batteries, carrying case, *etc.* if you will be doing a lot of travelling. Seven pounds may not sound like much but feels a lot heavier when you've toted it through three airports.

Recharging mobile batteries can become a chore; check how long the batteries will last between recharges. After all, isn't the reason why you are buying a notebook because you're looking for a road warrior machine? Nickel metal hydride (NiMH) batteries will last only for about 500 recharges compared to Lithium ion batteries which last for around 1000 recharges. Laptops can range in price from £1,000 to £5,000. If you will be moving between home, office and travel, consider getting docking stations to provide larger keyboards and screens when you want to carry out concerted periods of work. Many companies now provide docking stations for laptops in their "touchdown" or "hotdesking" facilities.

Printers

Choose a printer based on what and how often you want to print. Letters, bills and reports will probably be needed regularly, while greetings cards, invitations, photographs and posters may be occasional items. If your home office is small, you may prefer to get a combined scanner, copier, printer and fax machine. You may need a second mobile printer that you can take with you when you are travelling – battery operated inkjets or bubblejets are available for less than £300.

Laser printers are ideal for outputting plain text, and an inexpensive laser printer with a speed of four pages per minute can cost less than £200. Faster machines will cost slightly more – say £300 for one that can do 10 pages a minute. The lower cost of consumables is a big argument in favour of laser technology if your print volumes are high. In general you just have to replace one toner cartridge. On some models a printer drum also has to be replaced. If cost is a big issue, compare the cost per page by working out the consumable costs against the lifetime of the printers on offer.

Lasers are faster than inkjets but most are black-only printers – a colour laser printer will cost over £2,000. Inkjets are much better for inexpensive colour and work by firing tiny droplets of ink onto the paper. The smaller the ink droplet, the higher the quality of the printed output. Costs can vary from 1p to £1 a page depending on the quality and the type of ink used. Most inkjet printers have one black cartridge for text printing, and another consisting of the other three colour printing inks – Cyan, Magenta and Yellow. Some cheaper inkjets just have one cartridge slot so that you have to swap cartridges to get colour in the middle of printing a page if you are outputting a mixture of black text and colour graphics. The standard resolution for inkjets is 720 x 720 dpi. Shop around, and compare resolutions and output quality.

If you are doing professional desktop publishing or graphics, you may need a PostScript-compatible printer – these models are more expensive.

Scanners

A scanner converts images on paper, including photos and logos, to images on the computer screen which can then be edited, manipulated or inserted into other documents. You can enhance the images using an editing or scanning programme such as Adobe Photo Deluxe to brighten colours, crop, rotate, sharpen, store photos and documents for later use. You can also use optical character recognition software (OCR) to scan text documents for editing in your word processor. For a teleworker, a flatbed scanner offers ease of use. You lift the lid, lay the page on the glass, press a button and scan.

In choosing a scanner, greater colour depth (number of "bits") and higher resolution will produce richer and more accurate images. However, if the scanner's sensor captures data poorly, even the best convertor won't produce a great reproduction. A poor quality lens in a high-resolution scanner may also produce fuzzy, inferior images compared to a lower resolution scanner with a sharper lens.

Optical resolution is usually represented as two figures such as 300 x 600. The first figure is more significant – it refers to the number of scanning elements per inch on the sensor, where each element generates a dot or pixel of information. The second number represents the distance the scanner moves between each exposure – in our example this is 1/600 inch. When picking a scanner double check which of the two figures represents the optical resolution. Be sceptical of ultra-cheap models and look for a USB connection to the computer. Basic scanners are inexpensive – for £150 you can get a scanner with a 1200 x 2400 resolution, one touch scanning button, USB, bundled OCR and document management software plus image editing software.

Digital cameras

The latest digital cameras produce megapixel quality – meaning that the images produced are composed of at least one million pixels, so that you can print 5"x7" photographs. Digital cameras still can't match the quality of film-based devices, but they have plenty of advantages in speed and convenience, or if you want to quickly edit and use the end-results on your computer. Digital cameras use internal memory or memory cards to store images rather than standard film. Once pictures have been saved to a computer or printed out, the images can be erased from the memory card so that it can be reused. The cards supplied with mid-range digital cameras generally have between 4 Mb and 8 Mb of memory. This is enough for up to 100 shots, depending on the camera and the resolution.

CompactFlash cards are used by Canon, Casio, Epson and Hewlett Packard, in capacity sizes up to 128Mb. Smartmedia cards are used by Agfa, Fujifilm and Olympus, in sizes up to 64Mb. Sony has its own format in the form of a 64 Mb memory stick. Most digital cameras have a two-inch LCD digital display so you can view your image just as soon as you have taken each shot, and if you don't like it you can discard it to free up disk space.

Digital cameras are usually supplied with the cables needed to connect to a PC or Mac, as well as software, the memory card and batteries. Once the photographs are transferred to your PC, you can edit them to enhance the quality of your shots – most mid-range cameras come with software for this purpose. The software can help you to crop or enlarge images, remove blemishes and red eyes, correct colour and increast contrast and sharpness. The cost is likely to be £300–£1,000 depending on the pixel size.

Networks

A small network can increase productivity in a home or small office where more than one computer is in use by allowing file and printer sharing, internal email and the division of Internet bandwidth equally among users. You will need network cards for each PC, which are available from a wide range of manufacturers. These cards fit into a free PCI or ISA slot in a desktop PC, or into a PCMCIA slot on a laptop PC. Prices vary from £25 to £60 depending on the manufacturer. To connect two PCs together, a thin piece of Ethernet cabling, two T-connectors and two terminators are required, which can be picked up from electronics stores and catalogues. To connect more than two PCs you will need switches and hubs. A switch reads the destination of each packet of data and forwards it to the correct port on the hub. The hub is a collection of ports which act as a connection point for different devices on the network. Each PC is connected to the hub or switch, which then acts as a gateway connecting to the Internet, or to a local area network (LAN), thus forming a wide area network (WAN). For under £200 is possible to buy an eight-port 10/100mbit/s auto switching hub, which allows a network of PCs to be built up. 3Com's OfficeConnect FastEthernet Networking kit provides everything that you need to connect four or more PCs to a network. The kit includes two 10/100 network interface cards, a four-port hub, Ethernet cables and networking software.

Modems

A dial-up modem converts computer data into analogue sound (and vice versa) so it can be transferred from one PC to another over standard telephone lines. New desktop PCs, and most laptops, come with a 56k modem already installed. New modems mostly conform to the V.90 convergence standard. However, the gradual roll-out of broadband services such as cable Internet and ADSL means that in future many urban teleworkers will probably be using network cards and external high capacity modems instead. This is an area likely to experience rapid change in technology and price over the next few years.

Fax

The spread of email is gradually making fax redundant – especially standalone fax machines which are being replaced both by fax modems in PCs and by combined fax/printer/scanner/copier devices. Sagem offers a "Phonefax Internet appliance" which includes a DECT cordless telephone, a plain paper fax, a copier and a digital answering machine. The device can also be used to send voice messages over the Internet. If the recipient has a compatible sound card, they can open the email sound attachment and listen to the message. The device currently costs about £300. Phone companies and ISPs are also moving into this area, providing messaging services which allow fax, voice and email messages to be retrieved from central points.

Software

Software is as, or more, important than the computers on which it is used, and it would be impossible to do justice to such a complex subject here. There are thousands of software programs (often referred to as applications, or packages) in existence, and most are updated regularly. The British and Irish computer press covers software thoroughly, as do the specialised trade papers of particular industries.

When shopping for software, don't ignore shareware: a class of semi-commercial software which is distributed free, or at nominal cost, but for which you're expected to pay the author a small fee if you use it regularly. Shareware doesn't always have all the bells and whistles of the big commercial packages, but the best shareware certainly beats an indifferent commercial product, and often at a fraction of the cost. You'll often find it on the free disks with computer magazines; recommendations from friends, colleagues and user groups are also worth following up. Before buying any software, be absolutely sure that it will run on your computer: that it's written for a compatible model (Mac software won't run on PCs or vice-versa), that you have enough RAM to run it, and that you have a compatible monitor. All the requirements should be printed on the box in which the software is sold.

You may wish to avoid being used as an unpaid software tester by the manufacturing companies – to avoid the worst software bugs don't buy new versions of software until they have been on the market for three to six months, at which stage patches will be available on the software company's site to fix the bugs which all those other people found to their cost.

A quick tour of the generic software categories will help you prepare a shopping list. Beyond these, there are many packages developed to fill particular niches such as computer-telephony integration (CTI), which are likely to be well-known to you if they are relevant to your particular field of business.

■ **office suites**

The most popular productivity applications, usually included in the price of higher-priced desktop PCs, are bundled "office" suites that provide all the basic software functions that most businesses will need. Microsoft Office leads the way with Office 2000 while Lotus and Corel are worthy but trailing competitors with their Smartsuite and WordPerfect Office suites. Less expensive PCs tend to include a version of Microsoft Worksuite which includes word processing, a basic spreadsheet programme, home management, graphics and reference software. Most Mac owners use the Mac version of Microsoft Office 98.

■ **word processors**

Word processors are probably the most widely-used category of software, and the one that's essential to nearly every computer user. They allow you to write and edit text on the screen, providing facilities such as search-and-replace (for example, changing all references from 'color' to 'colour' automatically); style sheets (an easy way to ensure that all your subheadings, for instance, are in the same typeface and size); a running count of the number of words in a document; headers and footers (automatically placing predefined text at the top or bottom of each page); automatic page numbering and cut-and-paste (an easy way to move large blocks of text from one part of a document to another).

Many word processing packages now approach the flexibility of desktop publishing, allowing you to mix text with graphics, divide the printed page into columns, and so on. Microsoft Word 2000 is the most popular word processing application, and it also allows hyperlinks to be created in documents linking to information on Internet websites. Corel WordPerfect and Lotus Wordpro are two other popular word processors, and all three are compatible with each other. For those whose keyboard skills are lacking, voice recognition software Dragon Naturally Speaking is bundled with Corel Wordperfect when you buy the WordPerfect Office 2000 suite. Using Dragon you can dictate up to 160 words per minute to a text document on a PC. Voice recognition software has to be "trained" to a particular user's voice so there is a learning curve involved before it becomes a productive method of text entry.

■ spreadsheets

Spreadsheets are specialised tools for the large-scale manipulation of numbers, usually, but not necessarily, financial. A spreadsheet document is divided into rows and columns, forming an array or table of 'cells'. In each cell, you can enter a number, or you can define the cell in terms of other cells – for example, the cell 'profit' could be defined as equal to the cell 'sales' minus the cell 'costs'. Then, when you enter a new figure in the cell 'sales', the number in the cell 'profit' will change accordingly.

Very complex financial models, covering the operation of a large company, can be set up this way – and by changing a single figure, you can predict the effect that a change in one aspect of the company's operations would have on other areas. For example, if paper costs rose by 10% but rent fell by 5%, would your firm be more or less profitable? The most popular spreadsheet packages are Microsoft Excel, Lotus 1-2-3 and Corel Quattro Pro 9. All of these applications also provide you with the ability to create pie charts and other statistical graphs that enrich numeric and statistical presentations.

■ databases

Databases are used to store data in a structured way. Each database is composed of a large number of records, and each record is made up of fields. For example, in a database of customers, one record would represent each customer; the fields might include name, address, credit limit, and so on. Once the information has been typed in or imported from another database you can then sort and analyse the data in many ways. (For example, what are the names of customers who spent more than £500 in 1999 and live in Guildford?)

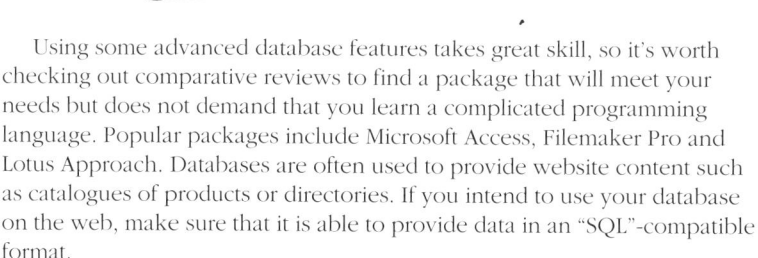

Using some advanced database features takes great skill, so it's worth checking out comparative reviews to find a package that will meet your needs but does not demand that you learn a complicated programming language. Popular packages include Microsoft Access, Filemaker Pro and Lotus Approach. Databases are often used to provide website content such as catalogues of products or directories. If you intend to use your database on the web, make sure that it is able to provide data in an "SQL"-compatible format.

■ **desktop publishing**

DTP software is used to design pages of type and images for newsletters, books, brochures, forms and any other kind of printed matter. There is great variation between the cheaper packages intended for home or casual use, and the powerful professional systems that can be used to produce a commercial magazine. Pick the right package for your level of expertise and presentation. Widely-used professional packages include Quark Xpress, Adobe InDesign and Corel Ventura. Home-use packages include Microsoft Publisher and Serif PagePlus.

■ **graphics**

Graphics software is slightly different from DTP in that it's usually employed to create or manipulate single images, such as logos, rather than entire publications. Again, there is a vast gap between hobbyist and professional-level software, and knowledge of printing processes is required to get best final results. The best-known professional packages are Corel Draw, Adobe Illustrator and Macromedia Freehand. For preparing Internet graphics, the most widely-used package is Macromedia Fireworks.

■ **image editing**

Many people get some form of image editing software bundled with an office suite (such as Microsoft Photodraw) or with a digital camera or scanner. This type of software is intended to provide the ability to edit overall qualities such as colour balance in digital photographs, or small areas (perhaps to add text or remove a blemish or crop out an unwanted area of the image). The best-known professional image editing package is Adobe Photoshop.

■ **website authoring/HTML editors**

HTML is the language used to create websites. There are several well-known authoring packages. The most widespread home-use package is Microsoft Frontpage but its use is controversial with professional web designers as it includes facilities (extensions) which work only if you use a Microsoft Internet server. The Homesite package from Allaire is very well-designed for those who want to have tight control over the HTML coding, and is often sold bundled with Macromedia Dreamweaver, a flexible editor which uses a more graphical interface. Adobe's GoLive is favoured by graphic designers because its interface is more similar to the DTP and graphics packages they use, while Netobjects Fusion is used for fast production of database-oriented sites.

■ **presentations**

Presentation software is used to create presentations that you can display on your computer or on a large screen using a data projector attached to the computer. Usually these combine text, graphics and images in a series of 'slides'. Few companies use anything other than Microsoft Powerpoint.

■ **accounting**

Accounting packages ask you to type in financial data such as your daily expenditures and sales, and then produce summarised accounts for you, saving you the trouble of sorting out which information should go where and adding it all up. It's a good idea to ask your accountant's advice before buying one of these, as not all such packages produce information in a form that's acceptable to banks and tax authorities. American accounting packages follow US norms which sometimes differ dramatically from British practice. The packages most widely-used by UK small businesses are Intuit Quicken and Quickbooks and Microsoft Money.

■ **contact managers, time and calendar managers**

Contact managers are specialised databases used for storing personal contact details, often used in conjunction with PC-based fax software, email or telephone control systems. They are usually included in Office software suites – Microsoft Outlook and Lotus Notes are two of the best-known, while Goldmine is widely used by sales and marketing staff. Time managers, likewise, are databases set up to help you schedule your diary. Advanced time management packages, called project-management tools, can be used to plan and schedule ventures involving many people, such as the organisation of an exhibition. Microsoft Project and Microsoft Schedule fall into this category, while Visio is popular for preparing diagrams that visualise a complex project process.

■ **groupware**

Groupware tools are used to help people collaborate over a network or over the Internet (see also Chapter 2, *Company teleworking*). Groupware facilities overlap with the previous section and can include editing of documents by multiple authors, electronic diaries, email conferencing, access to networked databases and electronic forms (*eg* to record customer contacts). By far the best-known package in this area is Lotus Notes and Domino, now owned by IBM, which is used by many major corporations. "Workgroup" applications like Notes integrate with POP3 email and allow you to manage information and combine email, calendaring, scheduling, contact management, task management, Internet browsing and even company knowledge management. Notes can synchronise its data with a laptop or PDA such as a Palm computing device so that teleworkers can take email, appointments, to-do lists and contacts information on the road with them.

The group calendar feature in Notes allows work colleagues to see the free and busy time slots of all team members at once. Using email, they can contact a colleague to schedule a meeting or conference call. Microsoft Exchange provides similar email, scheduling, messaging, online forms and other collaborative tools. Novell Groupwise also has a substantial following. Starter packs for each of these products suitable for small businesses cost around £1,000. Installing these systems so that they are really productive requires good service and support, so investigate this factor if you plan to use workgroup software.

Computer security

Anti-virus software

Most fears of computer crime and computer viruses are exaggerated – but then we buckle our seatbelts even though we're unlikely to crash. Do you have **virus-screening** software to ensure that text and graphics you use or receive are virus-free?

Most antivirus programmes guard against macro viruses which account for 80% of all infections. Macros are small routines that normally execute a series of instructions for you each time that you open a document. If a macro becomes infected by a virus, it could damage any Word or Excel document that you open subsequently. Multipartite viruses are less common and use a combination of techniques to spread themselves. Polymorphic viruses change themselves each time they spread, and because their signatures change, often at random, the usual technique of scanning files often fails to detect them. Antivirus programmes now also rely on "heuristic" technologies, which means that they look for virus-type behaviour.

There are well-known commercial packages such as Dr Solomon's, Command Antivirus and Norton Antivirus which will provide almost complete protection for your PC. With online facilities such as Symantec's

LiveUpdate available over the Internet, anti-virus protection can be constantly updated for a nominal fee. Remember that a single occurrence could damage vital data and, if you passed it onto a client, might cost you your good name.

Data security

Teleworking changes information security risks for companies. Allowing remote access requires a company effectively to extend their network to the teleworker's home, or provide them with a method of updating centrally held files such as databases via modems or ISDN connections. Companies are therefore anxious to control access and authenticate their users.

The risk to data security depends on the value and sensitivity of the data being handled. Start by reviewing existing procedures and identify processes which introduce an additional hazard by virtue of being remote. Procedures should cover use of PCs, remote access to central computing facilities, data transmission, backup procedures (data integrity) and viruses.

Although security threats often daunt IT staff when faced with implementing a telework programme, they should not be discouraged because there are a wide range of suitable products available ranging from inexpensive to bullet-proof. In all cases it is important to carry out a risk assessment in order to balance the budget required with the appropriate security technology to reduce the risk. One pragmatic approach to the problem may be to specify that certain tasks may not be teleworked – their associated data must remain within the company offices.

Companies often require teleworkers to secure their computers with **access passwords** so that the machine cannot be used at all except by someone who knows the correct password to enter as the machine is switched on. Passwords can also be individually applied to sensitive files to prevent unauthorised access. Blanking screen savers which switch in whenever a PC is not in active use are another common device to try to minimise the risks of people overlooking sensitive information on computer screens in public places.

A teleworker who stores email messages and other documents on their laptop's hard drive can present a risk to information security if the laptop is stolen or lost. One way to reduce this risk is to encrypt sensitive data so that only authorised users with access keys can unlock and decrypt the data. Encryption is a complex subject not covered in detail here.

Operating systems such as Unix and Windows NT offer some protection by first identifying users through passwords when they log on, and subsequently restricting their accounts to allow them to read and write data only to certain areas of a network. But in many cases simple "user authorisation" is not enough. Where the company provides remote access via modem or ISDN, anyone in possession of the company's remote access number can try to connect. The standard telephone system (PSTN) allows no real checks to determine the identity of the user. ISDN has **Caller Line ID** and also **Chap/PaP** (machine handshakes which confirm that the caller

Keeping those email viruses away

Eric Chien, Chief Researcher for Symantec, gives this advice: "The first line of defence is a bit of common sense. Be cautious about emails from people you don't know. I would delete attachments from anonymous users, and even where you know the sender be suspicious – did you expect to receive an attachment? Remember that in general it is only by opening attachments that you will run into problems. You cannot get a virus simply by reading an email. However there were some bugs in the email reader Microsoft Outlook that meant it could be exploited by some viruses. These problems have been patched by Microsoft so be sure to use the Windows update feature in Windows 98 and Windows 2000 to patch all your internet applications."

Products like Symantec's Norton Anti-virus now have online update facilities where you can update your anti-virus software regularly to ensure that you are protected against recent new specimens. In summary Eric advises:

- *Only open attachments you expect to receive;*
- *Keep your virus software updated regularly;*
- *Set up your virus software to detect viruses arriving by email;*
- *Scan your entire hard disk for viruses on a regular basis;*
- *Keep an eye on your web interface software (browser).*

is allowed to make a connection). This still does not prove the identity of the person who is using the remote computer. These days user-ids and passwords are usually stored in the dial-up networking software of the desktop or laptop, so using a password to identify an individual is meaningless – if the PC is stolen and sold on, the person receiving the stolen machine could try the dial-up networking and would find that the access number, user-id and password were all saved in the machine – thus an unauthorised person could gain access. Passwords are also fairly easy to crack – and if cracked, the computer system has no way of determining who is a legitimate user – all it sees is the authorised username and password.

To overcome these difficulties many companies now ensure that a method of **strong authentication** is used for remote access to networks. This involves two pieces of information used to identify the user. Typically in addition to a password or PIN number, the user has to carry some form of physical token (such as a card, or a device that can display numbers) which creates one-off passwords. The combination of both pieces of information (the user's PIN and the one-off password) is much harder for unauthorised users to simulate. There are two types of two-factor authentication systems: time-based and challenge-response. Time-based authentication systems generate a password every 60 seconds that is valid for only one minute.

This means that a user must send the password over the network within that time period in order to gain access to the system. Challenge-response systems generate a Data Encryption Standard (DES) encrypted password good only for a single use. DES is harder to defeat than other security methods since passwords are dynamic and they are good for travelling workers who may use different computers from different locations.

One form of security that is now "out of fashion" is **dial-back**. In this system the user would dial in and give a username and password. The network would then disconnect and dial back to a pre-defined telephone number for that person. This had the advantage of ensuring the telephone costs were picked up by the company, but the disadvantage that it only worked for people based in one place (*eg* at home), and not for roving teleworkers. However, with current telephone systems it is now simple to redirect the dial back number to another location and an unauthorised machine, so this method is no longer considered secure.

Many small businesses use the Symantec software PC Anywhere to connect to remote PCs directly via a dial-up modem. This can be a practical remote access solution for very small organisations, and allows you to "take over" the remote machine, running all the programmes and retrieving any data you have forgotten to take with you, but it is not a very secure method of access when only a simple username and password are in use.

People now telework from home, from hotel rooms, on trains and at client premises, so the requirements for flexibility and reduced telecoms costs have increased. Some large telecoms and IT companies have established themselves as providers of global "points of presence" or POPs

Some websites covering modem security issues
- www.securityfocus.com
- Common vulnerabilities and exposures list **http://cve.mitre.org**
- News portal **www.sse.ie/securitynew.html**
- Checklist **www.ebeon.com/e_business/analysis/article3.htm**
- Suppliers of security "token" systems **www.rsasecurity.com**

for connecting people to corporate networks. Using **Virtual Private Networking** (VPN) the teleworkers can establish a secure link from their laptop or desktop PC, through the POP and right into a dedicated box or server on their company network. VPN uses advanced cryptography to establish the point-to-point connection and encrypt all data during transit, preventing other users of the POPs from "eavesdropping". The encryption systems use keys which reside on the company's host servers and on the teleworker's machines and are not generally available, so many companies only use a password to authenticate VPN links. As before, this can be risky since you are identifying the computer, but not the person who is using the machine – VPNs also need "strong authentication". Many VPN products also include firewall capabilities.

Perimeter firewalls are vital barricades erected at the edge of your company's network to keep intruders from entering. These systems usually require the following elements:

- Specialised firewall software
- Firewall configuration and management software
- Dedicated hardware to run the applications
- A router to establish a connection to the Internet or other remote network.

There are two types of firewall technologies – static packet filtering and dynamic firewalls. Static packet firewalls do not perform session state monitoring, limiting your control and potentially placing your network at risk. Dynamic firewalls provide a more secure solution by creating dynamic rules and adapting them to changing network traffic. Once a session has been initiated, dynamic firewalls monitor requests to open ports. They open only designated ports and keep all others closed. When the session has ended, the ports are immediately closed, eliminating the potential for hackers to infiltrate the network and your company's sensitive data.

The move towards **application service providers** (ASPs) could provide teleworkers and small companies with an affordable security option. These systems provide software applications managed offsite at the ASP's shared central hub. Companies buy applications on a per-user basis. The ASP's job is to provide you with high availability of applications and data via leased line or dial-up networking. ASPs could have a significant effect on corporate teleworking by making applications available at lower costs to more people and companies. However, ASP use has obvious implications for security of company data prepared using the ASP facilities and only those providers with excellent security facilities are likely to be successful.

The TCA's contacts with members indicate that you should also consider the following security risks:

- Employees or colleagues who might set up in **competition** to you. Use password protection systems on your computer or network. Keep a close eye on what is being taken into and out of the office;

- **Children** who may gain access to your computer. Access-control software is needed again to protect business-related files and directories – it's easy for play to accidentally delete or alter files;

- **Stationery** that could be misused (for example, you might have a pharmaceutical company's headed paper that could be used to obtain samples of controlled substances.). Lock it up if necessary;

- Physical damage to both computer systems and backed up data. Store a set of **data backups offsite** (at the central office site or if you are self-employed, on one of the Internet free backup space websites such as **www.idrive.com**, or with a friend lest fire, theft or flood should destroy both computer and backups;

- **Shredding** of confidential paper waste or **erasure** of old disks. Don't allow sensitive material to end up on your local council dump. Take measures to ensure appropriate destruction or storage. If you are selling on or giving away old computers ensure that data has been thoroughly erased, not just deleted (in which case it can still be retrieved).

Home office equipment

There are a number of items of non-computer and telecoms equipment that you may need depending on the teleworking services you are offering. If you cannot justify purchasing the equipment outright, consider using it at a telecentre, or at a bureau or printshop. It is a good idea to try out equipment at these facilities so that you can work out what you require before you purchase.

Photocopiers

For low-volume use, photocopiers are being replaced by devices that combine fax, printing, and scanning facilities. For high-volume use and special facilities, you may be better off using a bureau service unless photocopying is an integral, everyday part of your business. Consult consumer guides on the machine best suited to your needs. Estimate how many copies you make a month and if you do decide to buy a standalone photocopier, check out maintenance contracts carefully. If you are entering into a service agreement, check what breakdown guarantees are being given and how quickly your photocopier will be returned to working order.

Tape recorders

Pocket memo machines can be used for recording thoughts or verbal 'notes' when you're away from the office. Telephone recording devices are often used by writers and journalists to record phone interviews and can be useful to others. Even where a recording is not needed as a legal precaution, preserving a complicated, technical conversation this way can be more reliable than using hastily scrawled notes. Small acoustic devices which connect a telephone handset to an ordinary tape recorder cost a few pounds from specialist electronics shops, though they are not high-fidelity.

The legal position surrounding telephone recording is complex; generally, attaching a device to the innards of the telephone (as opposed to an acoustic microphone affixed to the outside) is not allowed, but ask the phone company if you are in any doubt.

Transcribing machines are vital for audio-typing services. There are three main tape sizes, and each has different transcribers, so be sure that you know what size tapes you will be sent and that you have the correct transcriber size. The sizes are: C-size standard audio cassettes, Philips minicassettes and Dictaphone minicassettes. Transcribers usually have a pedal which controls the tape, and headphones, although if you are working alone it is great to be able to switch the transcriber on to its loudspeaker and dispense with those infuriating headphones.

Postal equipment and services

If you expect to send a large volume of mail, consider getting a franking machine which can also be used to enhance your corporate image with a pre-printed logo. Pitney Bowes produce a low-cost digital franking machine which incorporates an electronic scale. Through the Postage by Phone® service it can be securely re-credited via a 30-second phone call. Post offices will also frank bulk mailings for you by prior arrangement, without the need for investing in a franking machine, and can give you details of Freepost services (which only cost you if the reply is used) to increase reply rates to your mailings.

Other useful services include:

- **Special Delivery** (Mon–Fri) guarantees delivery by 12.00 noon next working day to "virtually anywhere in the UK". A signature is required and there is an enquiry line and website to check on whether delivery has been achieved. The main difference is the level of compensation offered in the event of loss; Special Delivery offers compensation of up to £250 for an item weighing 100g at a cost of £3.50 or up to £2,500 for an item weighing up to 10kg at a cost of £19.15.

- **Recorded Delivery** is for when you simply want proof of delivery. A signature msut be taken from the delivery address. Time of delivery is not guaranteed. Items can be tracked via an enquiry line and website. The service costs 63p in addition to normal posting, and the signed receipt can be requested by asking for Advice of Delivery when posting, for an additional £2.20p. Standard compensation does not exceed £27.

- **Swiftair** provides fast express airmail to overseas destinations. The service costs £2.85 on top of normal airmail postage, but the delivery times cannot be guaranteed. On average they are:
  Germany 2.3 days
  Ireland 2.6 days
  Belgium 2.3 days
  US 5.1 days
  NZ 5.5 days

- **Parcelforce** provides deliveries for larger packages where cost depends on the speed of delivery required. For a 10 kg package, delivery by 10 am next working day costs £24.65, but for delivery within 48 hours, you only pay £11.15 for the same package.

Whichever service you are selecting, check with your local post office about cut-off times for last collections each day.

Binding and print-finishing equipment

If you think that you will be preparing reports and prospectuses and manuals, look into binding equipment such as guillotines, large staplers, large hole-punchers, comb binders, and laminators, which provide a protective plastic covering for covers and certificates.

Acknowledgement

The security section was partly contributed by Graham Welsh of RSA Security Services (**www.rsasecurity.com**) and some material was provided for the previous edition of the Handbook by Teddy Theanne of Annixter Distribution.

Checklist

Item	Priority	Cost new	Cost secondhand
Computer/laptop			
Software			
Modem (and internet connection)			
Telephone/mobile (and headset?)			
Answerphone (or voicemail service)			
Printer			
Fax (or fax software for computer)			
Scanner			
Repair contract			
Tape drive (or other device) for backup			
Surge supressed power sockets			
Consumables (paper, ink cartridges, *etc*)			
Disks and disk storage, CD-ROMs etc.			
Insurance			
Files and shelves			
Advertising costs (directories, website)			
Desks			
Chairs			
Filing cabinets			
Suspension files			
Labels			
Postal scales			
Desk light			
Pinboard			
Reference books			
Stationery - paperclips and pens			
Envelopes			
Postage stamps			
Business cards			
Compliment slips			
Letterheads			
Brochures			
Professional fees (accountant, solicitor)			

Contacts and URLs

BT Featureline 0800 400 400. BT telephone sales and services information 152 (Tollfree UK only)

BT Homehighway ISDN **www.homehighway.bt.com**

Complete guide to PCs and the Internet: **www.computingcentral.com**

Direct sales of PCs, software and peripherals (also check computer magazines):
- Dell **www.dell.co.uk**
- Gateway **www.gateway.com/uk**
- Apple **http://store.apple.com**
- Euro IT **www.euroitproducts.com**
- Online IT **www.onlineit.com**
- Marx Computers **www.marx-computers.com**
- Microwarehouse **www.microwarehouse.com**

DSL technology information: **www.2wire.com** or **www.askntl.com**

Glossary of computer terms: **www.webopedia.com** or **www.techweb.com**

Internet phones
- Quarterdeck internet phones £49.95 plus VAT Tel: 0645 123721
Email: qsupport@qdeck.com
- Digiphone Internet phones **www.digiphone.co.uk/d2/home.html** ISDN tutorial for techies: **www.ralphb.net/isdn**

IT news services: **www.theregister.co.uk**, **www.zdnet.co.uk**, **www.electricnews.net**

Microsoft Netmeeting PC conferencing software **www.microsoft.com**

Networking sites **www.3com.co.uk**, **www.techworks.co.uk**, **www.smc.com**

Oftel UK telecommunications regulator **www.oftel.co.uk**

ODTR Irish telecommunications regulator **www.odtr.ie**

Palmtop computers **www.palm.com**

For those considering a PC security device, a good starting point is the Loss Prevention Certification Board's list of Approved Fire and Security Products and Services Tel: 020 8207 2345.

Smartcardlock – Chiplock is a smart card access system for PCs in public areas where machines are left unattended. When the card is removed the mouse and keyboard are locked and the screen is blanked out with a configurable cover page. The PC can continue background operations such as receiving fax and email. **www.orga.co.uk**.

Videoconferencing
- Picturephone direct **www.picturephone.com**
- RSI systems provides its videoconferencing via a separate box attached using a SCSI interface, rather than inserting a card into the computer. **www.rsisystems.com**
- A cheap and cheerful videoconferencing system is Connectix QuickCam for about £150. **www.logitech.com**
- Sony's Polycom system is often used for high-quality videoconferences such as conference presentations **www.polycom.com**

WAP developments: **www.wapforum.org**

Training for teleworkers

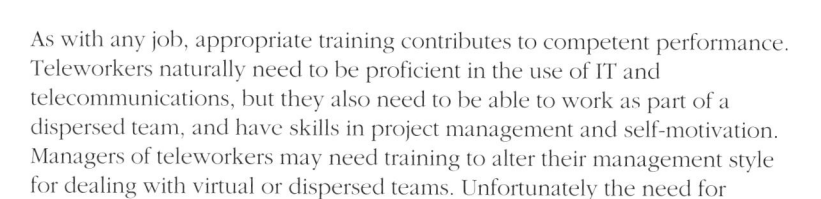

As with any job, appropriate training contributes to competent performance. Teleworkers naturally need to be proficient in the use of IT and telecommunications, but they also need to be able to work as part of a dispersed team, and have skills in project management and self-motivation. Managers of teleworkers may need training to alter their management style for dealing with virtual or dispersed teams. Unfortunately the need for training is often ignored or underestimated. This chapter aims to help you:

- identify gaps in your learning;
- plan to plug those gaps;
- look forward to manage and anticipate your learning needs.

Who are you?

Your role is going to affect what you need to learn, how you access training, whether you need certification of your learning and how you fund and organise your learning. This chapter assumes that you are in one or more of the following categories:

- trainee in a telecottage, telecentre, school or college
- employed telecommuter
- self-employed service provider
- manager or employer of others who telework.

You learn a lot outside of formal training or educational courses. So there's no point in confining your attention to formal training and education – or in getting hung up on formal definitions. For teleworkers, training means learning stuff, irrespective of how you learn it.

What do you need to know?

There are four sectors into which your training requirements are likely to fall:

- your own specialism (accountancy, design, sales consultancy or whatever it is) – this kind of training is not covered here
- entrepreneurship, business and management skills required to run a business (see *Getting Work* chapter)
- IT skills (hardware, software and Internet – see *Email and the Internet* chapter and box overleaf)
- management of virtual organisations (including self-management, managing teleworkers, working with others, project teams *etc* – see Chapter 2, *Company Teleworking* and Chapter 3, *Survival Guide*).

Take a moment to write down anything which you feel you need training in. The list will probably be quite long. You might also want to review Chapter 3, *Survival Guide* to help you think through some items, and to read the outline of the Teleworking NVQ Level 2 (page 333–8) and ECDL (page 338–9) qualifications which are given at the end of this chapter. Think about any gaps that there may be in your communication skills, and about how you will adapt to teleworking as a new way of working. Reading this book should plug many of the gaps but may point up other areas where you feel you need training.

Next, transfer to a separate list anything that you can get other people to know for you. For instance, how much do you really need to know about taxation? It's important, but (unless you're offering tax-related services to your customers) you can get by with:

- a system for ensuring you obey the law; and/or
- expert advice on call whenever you need it.

If you are self-employed and short of time, try to delegate some of the subjects to professional advisers and consultants where this is financially possible. Stick to your core work rather than spending unpaid hours researching points yourself – let the professionals quickly answer queries in their area because it will save you money in the long run, presuming that you are confident in your professional advisers. If not why not? Change them. There may also be items on your list which you could find out by being a member of a professional association, or by asking colleagues, customers or clients.

When do you need to know it?

Now that you're dealing with a shorter list, you can do some more categorisation. This time prioritise the training subjects based on when you think you will need to know about them. For example, you might need to know how to fill in a VAT return next month, how to export text from a .pdf file today, and how to code WML for WAP phones in three months' time.

Training needs analysis

You've just carried out a training needs analysis, identifying what you need to learn and when, as well as what, you can delegate. You should also plan to evaluate any training which you undertake – did the training suit you, was the money invested well-spent, was the content appropriate? This will help you to make better-informed decisions on training in future. And you'll need to keep referring back to your training needs analysis to "cross off" items you have learned and add new ones as they become important to you. Think of the training needs analysis as a continuing process, not a once-off checklist. Next, you need to know how you're going to learn, what it's going to cost and how to access the training.

Learning opportunities

The phrase 'learning opportunities' is used here because it encourages you to think of a wide range of ways of learning. Learning opportunities include:

- Full-time traditional face-to-face courses
- Part-time traditional face-to-face courses

The pre-requisites – IT skills you must have

If you are lacking in the skills listed below then it is suggested that you put on ice your plans for teleworking until you have attained them.

- Keyboarding – minimum 25 words per minute touch-typing plus ability to use a mouse
- Use of Windows (95/98/2000/NT) – particularly for file management
- Basic PC troubleshooting and maintenance – do you have a plan for diagnosing the problem if your printer stops working?
- How to store and back up files
- Word processing
- Spreadsheets
- Sending and receiving email and attaching files to emails
- Browsing the web and using search engines to find information
- Basic PC security – how do you plan to prevent children accidentally erasing files if they gain access to the PC?

The following skills are also important for many teleworkers:

- Databases
- Health and safety aspects of computers

Most computer literacy courses will cover many of the topics above but check that the detailed course syllabus includes what you want to learn. Courses described as "introduction to computers" probably won't cover all these items. Managers of teleworkers should not assume that their staff know these basics – they often know enough to get by and will ask a colleague when stuck. Check competences or look for IT literacy qualifications such as RSA, CLAIT, City and Guilds or ECDL. Self-employed teleworkers may also need to know how to load software packages and do basic hardware installation (such as adding new printers or scanners).

To be really employable, you ideally need one of the Microsoft qualifications. See the Steppingstones website for typical Microsoft training offerings explained simply – **www.steppingstones.co.uk**

MOUS – Microsoft Office User Specialist. This is suitable for secretaries/PAs, office administrators, first-level trainers and the like.
MCP – Microsoft Computer Professional. To get MCP you need to pass one of the specialist Microsoft application tests.
MCSE – Microsoft Certified Systems Engineer. To get MSCE you must first get MCP and then pass a further four similar exams plus two elective modules

www.microsoft.com/education/training/cert/default.asp
www.mous.net

Company telework training

Irish airports authority Aer Rianta provided an initial day-long orientation session for its staff who were interested in volunteering for a pilot telework programme. The session covered:

- Background to growth in telework, types of telework
- Benefits for employers and employees
- Drawbacks for employers and employees
- Suitable qualities for teleworkers and managers of teleworkers
- Home office setup
- Health and safety implications, insurance, company policy
- Technology issues
- Common reasons for success and failure of telework pilots.

Those who joined the pilot as teleworkers received a further day's training in these areas before the start of the programme, plus:

- Procedures for technical support, equipment maintenance, data backup, virus protection
- Remote access to the Aer Rianta corporate network – dialling in from home
- Interface between work and family when teleworking
- Time management and motivation
- Communications skills (effective use of email, handling misunderstandings, telephone skills)
- Administration – expenses, recording time spent, absences
- Sources of support – what to do if something goes wrong

Their managers received a half-day session including:

- Guide to selecting and recruiting teleworkers
- IT issues that may be encountered
- Managing by results – similarities and differences to eyeball management, communications agreements
- Monitoring productivity – setting objectives, schedules and deadlines
- Motivating teleworkers, keeping up the teamwork with in-office staff
- Legal, health and safety, HR, data security, expenses issues
- Assessing further training needs for teleworkers

Cork Teleworking carried out the training and comments: "We would halve the time lengths of the courses in future, and try to ensure that the training happened closer to the start date, especially the technical stuff, but sometimes it's hard to predict the roll-out dates. Emphasis on the IT training is important – if people can't connect back to base easily then their telework effectiveness is minimal." **www.cork-teleworking.com**

- Short commercial face-to-face courses
- Flexible/open learning courses
- Planned experience – such as a placement shadowing somebody from whom you need to learn
- Internet-based tutorials and flexible learning materials
- Books, magazines, videos and CD-ROMs
- Conferences, Internet discussion lists and online tutorials
- Your own experience/a knowledgebase

Consider course content and teaching quality, as well as how the course will equip you for subsequent work. One of the best ways to find out about a course is to talk to former trainees.

Full-time, traditional face-to-face courses

There's no doubt that interpersonal skills and similar topics require work with a trainer and with other participants. Thus, for courses in training skills, management, selling and the like, a good conventional course is almost essential. But for learning about such subjects as marketing, software and accounting, you may be better off with a distance learning course, perhaps supplemented by some classroom tutorials and telephone support. Keep classroom time for subjects that really need it.

Part-time, traditional face-to-face courses

Traditionally, evening classes have been devoted to adult education and to study for professional qualifications, degrees and other awards while practical courses in business-related subjects were confined to the daytime. However, many providers now run business courses in the evenings because that's what suits their customers. Courses for women returners are also often organised to fit in with school hours, and some even provide creche facilities too. It's worth checking out what's available in your area: get as many brochures and prospectuses as you can. Start by ringing your local Business Link or TEC (in Britain) or the adult education organiser of your VEC (in Ireland).

Virtual tutors switched off by students

The University of the Highlands and Islands covers a geographical region one-quarter of the size of the UK and has to use videoconferencing to provide a range of courses to its remote rural students. In early 1998, a group of geography students rebelled and refused to be taught through the video system. The students felt that time delays and interaction problems meant they would be much better off if the teacher, based 40 miles away, travelled to them and delivered classes face-to-face.

A college spokesperson put the problems down to the students and teacher not having met at the beginning of the course, and said that they had failed to sell or start the new approach properly.

Short commercial face-to-face courses

If you need to learn a new software package quickly, a straightforward commercial course is probably the best option though costs can be an issue. Make sure that the software version being used on the course is the same one that you plan to use or confusion will reign. Check that training notes are provided for you to take away, and ask about the facilities in the training room – make sure that you won't be sharing a computer. Do they provide support by phone or email after the course if you hit a problem? Can you talk to someone who's been through the course to get their opinion?

Commercial courses also cover many areas of business skills such as call centre skills, telemarketing, sales, negotiation, technical writing and so on. For getting up to speed fast, they are hard to beat.

Flexible, open and distance learning courses

There is an ever-increasing range of distance learning courses in work-related subjects. Some require you to start and finish at the same dates as other students. Others can be completed whenever you have the time to learn ("open" learning). You can do anything from a two-hour course on Excel to a full four-year professional accounting qualification or an MBA. The courses may use printed workbooks, audio, video, computer disks or multimedia materials available over the Internet or on CD-ROMs.

As well as using the Internet to search for courses you should also get the brochures of the Open University and the National Extension College. Several professional, trade, educational and training bodies have their own courses. Contact any bodies relevant to your needs and ask what they themselves offer and what they know about.

A good distance learning course is likely to structure your learning: there may be starting and finishing points, help from tutors, get-togethers (tutorials or seminars) with other learners, assignments to check your learning and other helpful arrangements. It is not easy to keep up the motivation to complete a course that you do on your own without extra support such as tutorial help and contact with other students – beware of courses which don't provide such help.

Planned experience

This term is used to cover any situation where you arrange things to allow for learning – perhaps by swapping jobs with someone else, or spending time with your customers to understand their problems, or testing new software, or looking up reviews of software packages to decide what to test. One-to-one coaching, and mentoring to solve a specific problem, often fall into this category.

Internet-based tutorials and flexible learning materials

Many commercial Internet-based courses are moving towards small "bites" of knowledge that people fit in between other aspects of their work, or else access when they need to know about a particular topic. For example the Motorola University, probably the best-known Internet-based "corporate university", is being converted to an "e-learning" system where training is broken down into five-minute learning chunks which can be customised for students by course designers, or by the students themselves. Motorola plans to deliver 30%–40% of its training through e-learning in future.

Finding training and help on the Internet

www.telecommute.org – Free set of training workshops aimed at managers who are implementing a corporate teleworking programme

www.lifelonglearning.co.uk – government website encouraging training outside conventional full-time training courses. Has information on career development loans and small business training loans.

www.tft.co.uk – Technologies for Training resource site listing centres providing training around the country, their courses and facilities

www.trainingzone.co.uk – Resource site aimed at HR staff and trainers

www.smartforce.com – one of the world's largest commercial providers of training courses

www.wbtsystems.com – company which authors many sector-specific courses

www.click2learn.com – wide range of commercial courses on a fast and easy to navigate website

www.flexible-multimedia.ie – commercial distributor of courses, some Internet based

www.edsurf.net – computer courses with free demos, ten free trial courses and a guide to online learning

www.learn2.com – wide range of courses including computer courses

The Internet can also be used to "webcast" lectures, presentations or demonstrations. Students log in and watch, using software such as RealPlayer, though the quality is not wonderful. Internet-based tutorials are particularly good for learning new features of a software upgrade.

Books, magazines, videos and CD-ROMs

Books are amongst the cheapest learning resources available, covering practically any subject which you care to mention, to any depth. They're much easier to read than anything comparably detailed on the web. Many people automatically buy a "how-to" guide when they purchase a new piece of software. Computer magazines often contain useful tips and tricks as well as information on new products and trends. Make time for this reading – train journeys may fit the bill for short "self-training" sessions through reading magazines. Training videos and CD-ROMs are to some extent being superseded by Internet-based materials but training materials on many specialist subjects are held by college libraries in these formats. They are usually quite expensive to buy but available on loan through libraries and colleges.

Conferences, discussion lists and online tutorials

All these learning opportunities are about sharing experience with other people. Although conference presentations are often interesting and provide new information, most people will agree that it is the questions that are asked afterwards, or the conversations and contacts that happen over the coffee break that are the really valuable part of attending many conferences. It's vital to swap experiences and insights with other people working in the same area, so make the effort to attend conferences – good ones will reinvigorate you, teach you new things and increase your network of useful contacts.

The Internet has many specialist mailing lists which can also provide contacts whom you can ask for help or advice. See the mailing lists and newsgroups section of Chapter 10, *Email and the Internet,* for information on how to find these resources. Remember many mailing lists have archives of frequently asked questions (FAQs) which may answer your question straight away.

A lot of learning institutions have been experimenting with online tutorials for some years now. Henley Management College uses Lotus Notes to provide documents, email discussion and chat room sessions where tutors can advise students, either on a one-to-one basis or where the communications can also be viewed by other students. US studies have shown that it takes at least one and a half times more tutorial support to successfully provide distance learning over the Internet compared to conventional, publications-based distance learning, so look for courses that offer good backup and support.

Certified courses

Certified courses are those which provide you with a certificate at their conclusion. They are not always the most appropriate for the fast-changing world of the teleworker, but it is always worth considering what is on offer.

RSA, City & Guilds, BTEC (EdExcel)

These bodies award certification for further education vocational courses. RSA has a largely secretarial bias and is well-respected by employers for its insistence on high levels of accuracy. City & Guilds has a wider remit, covering subjects from photography to IT. BTEC (EdExcel) is aimed at 16+ full-time education normally to intermediate GNVQ level (one-year courses equivalent to GCSE) or advanced GNVQ (two-year courses equivalent to A-levels).

NVQs

NVQs are not the same as GNVQs. They are vocational training courses which emphasise on-the-job training, taking into account existing skills plus some classroom and private study. NVQ students normally build up a portfolio of documentary evidence of their skills in order to achieve certification. There is a teleworking NVQ – see pages 333–8.

Degree courses and extramural studies

Degrees in themselves may or may not be useful to a teleworker – it depends on the individual's skills and profession, though few would doubt the value of an MBA for any business owner if you have the time, intellect and money to obtain one. Many universities and colleges also offer shorter, non-degree courses. On these extramural courses, students do not become full members of the institution and therefore may not have to meet normally stringent entrance requirements. Extramural courses, like NVQs, often award credits for existing skills. They are also modularised, like NVQs, with modules building towards the final certificate, and can often be "moved" from one college to another if the student needs to move.

Flexible or open learning

This is learning at your own pace, often using a workbook or taskbook. You complete an assignment and hand it in for assessment. Increasingly, such courses also make use of CD-ROM training, as well as of the Internet and email.

Commercial courses

These are normally required for software or hardware skills. They are unregulated, but many manufacturers, including Microsoft, Adobe and Hewlett-Packard, run accredited trainer programmes. Use accredited trainers wherever possible.

The KITE approach: a virtuous circle

At the KITE Telecottage in Enniskillen, six years of experience in teleworker training has given Managing Director Sheila McCaffrey a clear idea of how training and telecentre operations work hand in hand.

KITE's original mission was to use a virtuous circle of training, childcare and commercial work to provide sustainable development and employment in rural Co. Fermanagh. During the setup phase in 1993, KITE received financial support from the European Social Fund amongst other sources to provide a comprehensive initial training period for 8 teleworkers, including software skills, personal development and business administration. Training was delivered on site at KITE by the management and by the local Fermanagh College. Because most of the teleworkers were women, the availability of flexible training around school hours and the support of KITE's onsite facilities were vital. From the start, Sheila was determined to ensure that the KITE workers were trained not just in the skills, but in the practical application of the skills, doing real work for real commercial customers, so that they could understand and reinforce the training they were receiving.

Sheila believes that it takes around two years of full-time training and work experience to train a teleworker with no previous experience, but who had previously received second-level education to age 18. The methods used at KITE can halve this time to one year. KITE had difficulty with the long lead-time it experienced initially in obtaining commercial contracts; however this has recently reduced for a number of reasons including more widespread acceptance of outsourcing, cost factors and skill shortages.

From the original training plan design in 1993, KITE and its partners in Fermanagh built a successful model of rural ICT training aimed at women returners. The project has attracted over 1500 women into training in the last five years and has substantially added to the ICT skills available in the county. Funding support for the work has come from the European Social Fund.

Sheila emphasises the importance of structured personal development modules and career planning as essential components for successful training. Measuring the needs of industry is also vital to designing training content, and these needs must be constantly reviewed and updated to ensure that they are met through training. Such a process ensures that training does not happen in a vacuum but in a concerted fashion. Over 40% of KITE's trainees go directly into work. For some, teleworking is an option.

Your own experience – creating knowledgebases

Knowledge management, and the idea of creating knowledgebases – databases of experience and information – are currently trendy topics in management studies. The idea is to provide all the information normally locked up in people's heads to everyone who needs it within an organization, usually through the company Intranet. The excellent Financial Times *Knowledge Management Fieldbook* gives this definition of knowledge management: "the process by which the organisation generates wealth from its intellectual or knowledge-based assets". The result is more efficient and effective processes that lower costs, reduce cycle times and improve cashflow. However, many companies have found that it is not easy to get people to volunteer their intellectual assets – because knowledge is power, because it is time-consuming or because the person does not realise that the piece of knowledge could be valuable to the organisation.

But you can create your own very basic knowledgbase which will help you to learn from your own experience as you go along! It might just be a hardback notebook where you write down how you fixed software problems step by step so that someone else can check the book and find the solution straight away instead of repeating your research. It might be a spreadsheet or database where you record information about problem customers, or keep contact details for computer technical support services.

Certification

In considering which learning opportunities to pursue you will also need to think about whether you need certification at the end of the course. In general, the more full-time and traditional, the more likely that the course will carry a certificate, but this is not always true – for example, both the ECDL computer literacy course and the Microsoft Computer Professional qualifications can be learned using online flexible learning materials and the exams can also be taken online. Both training providers supply certificates which are widely accepted in industry. Reading a magazine may provide the answer to your problem, but definitely won't give you a certificate.

> **Learn while you shop at Gateshead's Learning World**
>
> Learning World is a computer training centre located at Gateshead's Metro shopping park which is open for 84 hours a week, over seven days, allowing students to combine shopping and learning. The project is a joint venture between the University of Sunderland and Gateshead College. Courses offered range from introductory to degree level.
>
> Chief executive Pat Robertson explains: "With so many demands on time and the increased emphasis on training and qualifications, we strive to offer a really flexible programme of learning making it easy to integrate learning into life. Our short courses and weekend programmes are perfect for fitting into a busy schedule". Take-up has been high – about 1,000 were expected to sign up in the first year, but over 3,000 have enrolled.
>
> Feedback from the students has been excellent, borne out by a 90% retention rate for courses. Most students go on to take at least three courses. There is also a video link to Newcastle University for careers advice.

It's also worth remembering that the vocational qualification (NVQ) approach, although widespread, is still controversial within the training sector. On one hand, courses such as the teleworking NVQ fit well with the British government's funding structure (see outline of the Teleworking NVQ, pages 333–8). The modular nature and practical approach of NVQs are often much easier to handle for those who do not enjoy conventional courses or who have been out of the jobs market for a period of time. On the other hand, other European countries are suspicious of the NVQ "competence-based" approach where students collect a portfolio of evidence of their skills. Surveys of British employers show that many feel that the NVQ approach is limited because it only demonstrates the ability to handle a particular task at a point in time but not that the trainee has fully understood the background to the task or committed the task to memory.

If you are currently out of work or thinking of going into self-employment, remember that teleworking is a way of work, not a job in itself. The NVQ won't necessarily get you a job because it shows you know about the way of working called teleworking. In addition you will need a core skill which employers or clients want such as translation or web design.

If you're taking learning seriously, you have to be in charge of it yourself. You decide what you need to learn and you must arrange to learn precisely what you need, when you need it. You don't have to take a package holiday just because your local TEC or college offers it; it's better to get what you want, even if it's more expensive, than to end up wasting your time on a cheap, but unsuitable, course on (say) computers or entrepreneurship. Learning is worthwhile if it helps your business or your employability. Choose your learning experiences based on their quality (fitness for your purposes) rather than on the availability of qualifications or grants. Recruitment agencies can sometimes provide very useful assessments of the value of some qualifications – is it what your future employer or client is going to be looking for?

Funding the training

Higher education courses of two years or more qualify for grants to cover fees and living expenses for anyone who has not already taken a degree or HND. Unfortunately, this only applies to full-time study. No grants are available for part-time study. However, a number of telework-related courses are funded through the European Social Fund. Usually to qualify for these you have to fall into a category of disadvantage (unemployed, women returner, rural dweller). Your local TEC will probably have free courses for anyone starting a small business, regardless of their status.

Vocational courses can qualify for Career Development Loans. These are available from certain banks and are guaranteed by the Department for Education and Employment. They are interest-free during the course itself. Training and Enterprise Councils can give you information on any funding in your local area, as well as on the range of courses available. If you are

---

Scottish Professional Development Award in Teleworking

This qualification is accredited by the Scottish Qualifications Authority and is a competency-based award which has been developed and tested by Aberdeen City Council and the Northern College. Instead of aiming at providing a basic level of competency in a number of IT skills (the NVQ approach), this award is aimed at people who already have a marketable skill (such as architects, designers, accountants) and helps them to rethink their business to take advantage of teleworking opportunities. Employees may be encouraged to work from satellite offices. Prospective teleworkers may need help to promote confidence in their clients in the use of teleworkers. The skills required will vary according to the situation of the individual course delegates. The course developers state: "Issues such as self-management and workflow assessment are just as important to the teleworker as keyboarding or knowledge of email."

There are five core modules to be assessed, plus one option taken from a range of four. The core modules are: 1) Enable use of IT solution; 2) Maintain IT solution; 3) Communicate electronically using the IT solution; 4) Contribute to the effectiveness of the work flow; 5) Develop self to improve performance. The four options are: 1) Produce documents using IT solution; 2) Produce numerical models using IT solution; 3) Produce graphical images using IT solution; and 4) Maintain data in a computer system. The modules allow considerable latitude so that the competencies assessed are relevant to individual delegates' needs. Contact Sandra Much at Northern College Tel: 01224 283500 or Donald McLean Dundee College Tel: 01382 834834

attending adult education or college of further education courses, you will normally receive a discount on fees if you are unemployed, a pensioner or a student.

For self-employed teleworkers, fees paid on training courses can be claimed as a business expense. The situation for employed workers is slightly more complex. According to Mark Dyer of Netaccountants, the cost of a "qualifying course of vocational training" can be set against taxable income (assuming that you, not your employer, paid for the course). Such courses include those which count towards National or Scottish Vocational Qualifications, and it may be possible to obtain basic rate tax relief "at source" by paying a lower amount to the training provider. Higher rate tax relief has to be reclaimed through your tax return. The expenses must be incurred "wholly, exclusively and necessarily" in conjunction with your employment. Generally it is difficult to convince the Inland Revenue that the costs were "necessarily" incurred unless there is a clause in your contract of employment or other contractual arrangement for you to undertake the specified training.

In Ireland, only courses run by certain approved, publicly-funded colleges with a duration of over two years can be claimed by employed teleworkers. The situation for the self-employed is the same as for Britain – training courses can be claimed as a business expense. The state training agency, FÁS, provides a number of free training courses for the registered unemployed. There is no equivalent to the career development loans or small business training loans available in Britain.

Keeping the focus

A course may be defined as a structured learning experience. At one level, the difference between (say) reading a textbook and studying a distance learning text is that the text may be better structured: you're shown the map of the whole course; you get an introduction and a summary of each unit (chapter) as well as of the whole module; there are various features along the way that are designed to help you to learn.

These days, the distinction between textbooks and distance learning texts is increasingly blurred. Many modern college textbooks, especially the American ones, look very like distance learning texts and use similar learning features. A properly-run distance learning course is more than just a text (or other materials). A course provides managed learning: there are events of various types to help you to get started, to tell you what's expected of you, to monitor your progress along the way and to assess your performance at the end. Much of the cost of distance learning is in this management rather than in the materials. In general, courses that provide a lot of support to learners will have greater success: a higher proportion of learners will stick with the course and complete it successfully.

If you're choosing a long course, look for one that provides significant

An experiment in distance learning training for telework

Telework Ireland received funding under the EU's Adapt project to set up a distance learning course providing teleworkers for Ireland's software localisation industry, a sector which suffers from skill shortages. The scheme drew on prior collaboration between the state training agency FÁS and the localisation industry to identify and teach the minimum skills that would take an unemployed person with little or no computer experience and prepare them for an entry-level position in localisation quality assurance test engineering. Other project partners included East Clare Telecottage, Symantec and Internet service provider Postgem/IOL.

Localisation QA is the testing performed on different language variations of a software product (*eg* French). After general training from FÁS, anyone subsequently employed in this industry would normally go through a further process of learning the particular system used by the employer, and of trust-building through working on a variety of projects so that team leaders learn what they can do and how effective they are. Localisation QA is not a particularly difficult job at novice level, but it is characterised by team interaction, deadlines, frequent changes in direction and high dependence on technology.

Telework Ireland found 120 trainees prepared to undertake a 36-week long distance learning course, which included some face-to-face workshops. Trainees were required to attend a six-week work placement at the end of the course with a localisation company to encourage "corporate acclimatisation" and build trust. The course was accredited by FÁS and by City and Guilds, included the ECDL qualification , and training allowances were paid to those eligible such as the unemployed. However, the placements were all around the Dublin area where the localisation companies are based, while the trainees were spread around the country.

Some problems were experienced with the distance learning technology with a lot of downtime on the server providing assignments and assessments for students. Project manager Joe McCormack also reports that some students exaggerated their skills to get selected for the course and then found the going tough. Of the first 64 survivors, 12 were able to take up Dublin placements; 11 did so and 10 are now employed on a conventional, non-teleworking basis in the industry. Six are working as teleworkers. A further 31% of the trainees found conventional jobs in IT-related sectors.

During the period of the project there was a change in the localisation industry to outsourcing lower level work – employing graduates and experienced localisation experts but sending out the "donkey work" to other companies (called localisation vendors), many of whom were located outside Ireland. Telework Ireland is helping some of the other trainees to set up co-operatives or small businesses so that they can become localisation vendors themselves, selling their skills to the industry. A commercial version of the training package will be available soon at **www.telework.ie**. More information from mccormackl@btinternet.com

The Teleworking NVQ

There are two teleworking NVQs with standards assembled by the ITITO (see bibiography): *Using IT for teleworking* (Level 2) and *Managing IT for teleworking* (Level 3). They are certified by City and Guilds and the Scottish Qualifications Authority. Like most vocational qualifications, they are competence-based. This means that students can supply evidence to show how their previous experience proves that they are already capable of performing skills required by a particular module, and also that the tutor is free to design modules however they like, as long as the result is that the students can perform the required elements for certification. Students create a portfolio of evidence on their skills and competence. The former Teleworking VQ, dating back to 1993 and originally supported by the TCA, is still on offer from City and Guilds but you are advised to go for the new qualifications if you can.

The NVQ approach is:

- *Relevant* – based on what people need to know and be able to do to carry out their jobs competently

- *Practical* – clearly indicates and gives credit for what people can do

- *Accessible* – open to people of any age, in or out of employment, or those working in the voluntary sector

- *Attainable* – assessment can take place at work and people can get immediate credit for the competence which they already have

- *Flexible* – candidates can achieve either unit certificates or the full qualification certificate

The NVQ Level 2 is equivalent to a GCSE/O-level and gives a good basic grounding in relevant skills. It is suitable for people with little PC knowledge as it covers the basics – word processing, spreadsheets and so on – but is probably too low level for professionals and consultants. A summary of the Small World Connections training course covering the NVQ level 2 is given opposite. Existing teleworkers may find it interesting as part of their training needs analysis to read through the modules and assess which ones they think that they could pass.

The NVQ level 3 is aimed at managers and supervisors. The ITITO states this qualification is "appropriate to anyone who controls their own business or is working in a teleworking environment or where they manage, advise and assist other teleworkers... identify and resolve problems and manage the use of IT to process information and transmit the results over a telecommunications link to a third party".

There is currently a European Commission Leonardo Programme funded project (Localnet II) being run by East Clare Telecottage to develop training materials for the Level 3 Teleworking NVQ qualification – see **www.smallworldconnections.com**.

support, in many different ways, to help the learners. That applies as much to classroom-based courses (are there tutorials? study-group sessions? individual discussions with lecturers?) as it does to distance learning courses.

If you decide to plan some learning from materials like books, videos, magazines or computer-based packages, you should try to provide yourself with structure and support. Just as you plan your work, so you should plan your learning. Set goals, monitor progress, assess performance. Build in some supports. One of the best forms of support is to work with someone else, in your own organisation or elsewhere. Discuss what you've learned. Share your insights. Question each other – and encourage each other too.

By all means find out what grants and other support you can get. But don't sign on for an unsuitable course just because it's cheap or it's grant-supported. Instead, get your customers to pay for your training. Every time you bid for a contract, include an element to cover anything new you'll have to learn for that contract — and some extra learning as well. Put that money aside; don't spend it on anything but learning.

Focus on what you need. Nobody knows your business as well as you do; the views and recommendations of course providers are their sales spiels and should be treated as such: not dismissed, but not given too much weight either. Keep managing the learning. Note new needs as you come across them; check and revise your lists of needs. Work out how best to meet each need, then arrange to do it. And remember to learn from experience; record what went wrong and how you fixed it. Don't try to learn everything yourself, by yourself. Delegate some learning to professionals and more to your colleagues and your staff. Network with others; learn from them and let them learn from you. Make arrangements so that you can call on them in time of need, but make that sure you reciprocate. Above all, keep learning.

NVQ Level 2 learning objectives

This summary of suitable course content for the Teleworking NVQ (Level 2) has been provided by Small World Connections.

Mandatory units

10.1 Health & Safety All teleworkers have health & safety duties even if they are working from home. In preparing for this mandatory unit you will need to learn

- To understand the provisions of the Health & Safety at Work Act and how they apply to your job role;
- The health & safety information you need to know as a teleworker and how to obtain this data;
- Your duties under the Display Screen Regulations;
- The health & safety features of working in a telecentre or home office;

- The importance of not ignoring hazards in the workplace;
- How to spot health & safety hazards and how to deal with them;
- How to identify which hazards pose the greatest risk.

10.2 Use and Maintain IT For Teleworking Since one of the main definitions of a teleworker is "Using IT and telecommunications to facilitate location independent working", it follows that learning how to use IT is another of the mandatory units of the NVQ. In preparing for the two units concerned with using and maintaining you will learn how to:

- Set up and switch on a PC;
- Load and format floppy disks and other media;
- Select the correct software to meet your needs and the needs of your customers;
- Take back-ups, store them and complete a back-up log;
- Ensure that an adequate supply of media and keep a media store and materials log;
- Ensure that software copyright regulations are followed;
- Ensure that you comply with relevant IT legislation e.g. the Data Protection Act;
- Deal with basic faults and know when to get assistance with more serious problems;
- Save and store files;
- Carry out diagnostic procedures to check for wear and tear and faults *eg* viruses;
- Keep up to date maintenance records;
- Power down your PC.

10.3 Electronic Communication Electronic communication is again one of the main tenants of teleworking. This fourth mandatory unit covers how to:

- Send e-mails and attachments using an electronic communication system;
- Deal with transmission problems;
- Receive and save electronic messages and files;
- Use an electronic service such as the World Wide Web to retrieve information;
- Carry out on-line information searches and download / print required data.

10.4 Project Management and Self Development The fifth mandatory unit covers self-development and planning and prioritising your work. In preparing for the self-development aspect of the unit you will need to learn how to:

- Assess your current knowledge, skills and performance and produce a plan of training and development needs;
- Undertake appropriate training and development;
- Keep records of development activities and review progress.

In the work planning aspect you learn how to:

- Identify the resources you have to carry out your work;
- Produce work plans and schedules;
- Make allowances for unforeseen circumstances when planning your work;
- Make improvements to your work environment so that you can be more effective at achieving your objectives *eg* setting up macros and creating styles.

10.5 Produce Documents The sixth mandatory unit covers the skills needed to produce documents using a PC. In preparing for this unit you will learn how to:

- Establish a customer's document requirements;
- Retrieve and save files;
- Create new files and enter data;
- Produce documents with the correct text format and page layout;
- Use application software (word processing, spreadsheet and desktop publishing) to manipulate text, numbers and graphics to produce documents;
- Output documents using either a printer, fax or email.

Optional Units

Two optional units have to be followed. These units can broadly be divided into two categories. The first three optional units are IT-based and cover the use of software applications such as spreadsheets, graphics and databases. The other four units are related to providing a service for customers. Your choice of optional units will depend on the specific training needs you have.

10.6 Spreadsheets In this unit you will learn how to:

- Ensure that the spreadsheet meets your customer's requirements;
- Create, save and input data to a spreadsheet;

London City University
"Managing change in the workplace – teleworking"

Liz Hale, a long-term experienced teleworker who has also managed other remote workers since 1987, decided to get trained after the event because she had never received any formal training for her work, and took this course, funded by the European Social Fund.

There are 18 study modules, each of which takes 4–10 hours to complete plus a course project. Each student must take 15 or 16 of the 18. The time commitment is about 10–15 hours a week, with three on-site days at the University for face to face help and group work. Liz found the time commmitment huge – essentially all weekend, every weekend for the duration of the course – and this meant students tended not to work through the course at the same rate.

The main delivery method for the course was a web-based distance learning system called Web-CT with the usual chat-rooms and message boards. Liz found it a little difficult to use as well as expensive in telephone charges. Some of the course modules are intended for both teleworkers and their managers but some are specifically for one group or the other.

Liz found the use of the Synetas profiler, a US tool which analyses an individual's profile in terms of their natural work habits, ability to work unaided, depth of reliance on interaction with others and so on, very interesting. It is used to provide indications of which elements of teleworking will probably be easy for the students to handle and which will not.

She has found the course definitely worth the effort but feels because she is a professional writer and was already familiar with some of the material the course was easier for her than for some other students. She feels the course director and materials compiler have a depth of knowledge about the subject and that the reference lists accompanying each module would take months to compile on an individual basis.

"For anyone who is planning or seriously thinking of planning a teleworking initiative I would recommend this course as an excellent 12-week investment. After all, you might find yourself teleworking for the rest of your life..."

Liz Hale is an information consultant with the KUDOS partnership
Email: l.hale@kudos-uk.com

- Manipulate spreadsheet data (*eg* move, copy and delete);
- Layout the spreadsheet and format cells;
- Carry out spreadsheet calculations;
- Print out the spreadsheet.

10.7 Graphics In this unit you will learn how to:
- Ensure the graphics document meets your customer's requirements;
- Open and retrieve graphics files;
- Enter, manipulate and edit graphics images;
- Set up page layout;
- Print out the graphics document.

10.8 Databases In this unit you will learn how to:
- Ensure the database meets your customer's requirements;
- Open and retrieve database files;
- Enter data into a database;
- Modify field characteristics;
- Carry out simple queries and database sorts;
- Set up page layouts;
- Print out a database.

10.9 Operate Service Delivery Systems For Customers This unit covers how to:
- Deliver products and services to customers;
- Maintain an effective service when systems go wrong;
- Maintain positive working relationships with customers.

10.10 Develop and Maintain Positive Working Relationships With Customers This unit covers how to:
- Present a positive personal image to customers;
- Improve customer relations;
- Deal with stressful customer relation situations;
- Meet customer needs within your own area of responsibility;
- Minimise conflict between customer needs and organisational limitations;
- Involve others in meeting customer needs;
- Respond to feelings expressed by the customer;
- Adapt methods of communication to the customer;
- Deal with communication difficulties.

10.11 Solve Problems For Customers This unit covers how to:
- Gather information on customer problems;
- Propose solutions;

- Deliver solutions;
- Check that service is being delivered effectively.

10.12 Process Documents Relating To Goods and Services This unit covers how to:
- Order goods and services;
- Obtain competitive prices;
- Check claims for payment;
- Check payment claims for numerical accuracy;
- Resolve any discrepancies.

ECDL – the European Computer Driving Licence

ECDL is gaining ground throughout Europe as a basic computer literacy qualification with wide acceptance among major employers. This section is reproduced from the ECDL Foundation's guide on the web site **www.bcs.org.uk/ecdl/index.html**

The European Computer Driving Licence (ECDL) is a certificate which states that the holder has passed one theoretical test which assesses his or her knowledge of the basic concepts of information technology, and six practical tests – which assess the holder's competence in using the computer. The Computer Driving Licence is an internationally accepted document. It can simplify employment procedures and assure the employer that applicants for a position and employees in work are competent in managing computers and using common applications. The ECDL is an Information Technology certificate for all European citizens. It is intended for those who need to, or wish to, know how to use a computer. It is suitable for people from every discipline and for people entering the job market, and for all ages from 8 to 80.

The ECDL dissemination programme differs from most national or international education programmes, since it is based on a standardised test or examination instead of a standardised teaching approach. The ECDL is awarded on the successful completion of one theoretical test and six practical tests. The domains covered are the following:

Theoretical Test

The Basic Concepts of Information Technology – the first basic requirement of competence in computing is to understand the context for computer-based applications in society and the key concepts of computers.

The Six Practical Tests

1. Using the Computer and Managing Files – it is important to understand the basic housekeeping functions required for the efficient use of the computer.
2. Word processing – using the computer for the creation, editing, formatting, storing and printing of a document.
3. Spreadsheet – similar to a manual spreadsheet, with the ability to perform calculations rapidly.
4. Databases/Filing Systems – assists in the organisation of large volumes of data to allow fast and flexible access to that data.
5. Presentation and Drawing – the use of computer-based presentation and drawing tools has grown in many application areas to support effective communication. These tools are used extensively in business and in teaching.
6. Information Network Services – the use of networks has grown from a desire to share resources and to communicate with others. Today, millions of computers are connected together around the world. It is important that ECDL holders can make effective use of the "Information Super Highway"."

Acknowledgement

This chapter has received considerable input from Cathy Murray, a Director of Small World Connections and MIPD (Member of the Institute of Personnel and Development) **www.smallworldconnections.com**, and from Brian Goggin of distance learning consultancy Wordwrights (Email bjg@wordwrights.ie). The TCA is very grateful for their expert help.

Bibliography

The Knowledge Management Fieldbook   *Date:* 1999
Authors: Wendi R. Bukovitz, Ruth L Williams
Source: Financial Times/Prentice Hall ISBN 0–273–63882–3 www.ftmanagement.com

How on earth can a computer help my business? available free from Microsoft Tel: 0345 002000 (expect a wait before connection)

Contacts and URLs

BTEC: Central House, Upper Woburn Place, London WC1H 0HH Tel: 0171 413 8400 Web: **www.edexcel.org.uk/btec**

Information Technology Industry Training Organisation is keen to help train teleworkers and has some relevant literature Tel: 0171 580 6677

Making information work for you (Part of the *Managing in the 90s* series) available at **www.bnet.co.uk**

National Council for Vocational Qualifications: 222 Euston Road, London NW1 2BZ Tel: 0171 387 9898

Prepared for the Future – The British and Technology: Motorola survey of take-up of IT: **www.mot.com**

The Stanford Learning Organization website covering information technologies and organization learning is at **www.Ieland.stanford.edu/group/SLOW**

University of the Highlands and Islands seeks to provide a "virtual university" for the remotest areas of Scotland and is receiving £35 million on Millennium funding. Its degrees are validated by the Open University. **www.uhi.ac.uk**

www.icbl.hw.ac.uk/tet/usability-guide/ is a set of guidelines for producing easy-to-use computer-based learning systems written by Carmel Smith
Email: carmel@icbl.hw.ac.uk.

Learning World Units 9–11, Allison Court, MetroCentre Retail park, Gateshead NE11 9YS Tel: 0191 488 3232 Fax: 0191 488 3111

ISI free briefing leaflets:
– How the Internet can work for you
– How networking can work for you
– How email and fax can work for you
– How videoconferencing can work for you
– How EDI (electronic data interchange) can work for you
– How CD-ROM can work for you
– How mobile communications can work for you
Available from the ISI helpline 0345 152000 http://www.isi.gov.uk

City and Guilds of London Institute, 1 Giltspur Street, London EC1A 9DD

Manchester Women's Electronic Village Hall – has an open learning course on teleworking issues on its website. The course is intended to be used in conjunction with face-to-face learning at the WEVH but you could use it as distance learning on your own. **www.wevh.org.uk**

Microsoft certification:
www.microsoft.com/education/training/cert/default.asp

Netaccountants **www.netaccountants.com**

RSA Examinations Board (IT courses and exams including word processing and dtp, held in high regard by employers because of the level of accuracy required to achieve the qualification) Westwood Way, Coventry CV4 8HS Tel: 01203 470033

Steppingstones training centre, Balham, London Tel: 020 8355 0830
Web: **www.steppingstones.co.uk**

In Britain, ASLIB, the Association for Information Management, offers a number of Internet related courses from a library/information management perspective.
Tel: 0171 903 0000 Fax: 0171 703 0011 Email: aslib@aslib.co.uk

Open University's Knowledge Media Institute **www.kmi.open.ac.uk**

Henley Management College **www.henleymc.ac.uk**

www.icbl.hw.ac.uk Heriott Watt University's Computer Based Learning centre.

Teleworking:
the flexible future with HP

The key to harmonious working in the 21st Century is all about balance – income vs. flexibility – and the realisation that the two are no longer mutually exclusive. By the year 2010, it is estimated that around eighteen percent of UK workers will be based full-time at home, well away from cities and the conventional office environment

Already, one in twenty of us now work from home at least one day a week, and the number is increasing at a steady rate. Teleworking, certainly for many larger companies, has become an accepted work style, offering both employer and employee extra choice and much desired flexibility. But what has allowed such a major shift in business culture? Quite simply, it's technology – coupled with the courage and vision of individuals and companies alike to embrace change. And technology pioneer HP is at the forefront, continuing to develop the tools to make working from home an easy and affordable option.

Surveys show that employees who work from home are up to sixty percent more efficient than their office-based counterparts, and work ten to fifteen percent more hours per week. Far from performing better surrounded by chatting colleagues and watchful bosses, it would appear that workers relish the opportunity for personal motivation and many prefer saving time and energy on commuting. But such high levels of increased harmony and productivity come at a cost, and sometimes quite a substantial one. Up until now, the speed of technological change has struggled to keep pace with demand and, especially in the case of small businesses and teleworkers, IT requirements have vastly outstripped what's on offer. Those working from home have often needed up to four or five pieces of bulky hardware to produce work of a quality comparable with their office-bound colleagues, including a scanner, printers (sometimes both colour and black and white), fax machine and quite often a photocopier. The necessity for such a large number of products, not forgetting the indispensable PC and modem, is completely at odds with the teleworker's often limited work space and – perhaps most importantly – their need for affordable, versatile and easy-to-use equipment. Earlier this year, however, HP delivered the perfect answer: a new range of All-in-One OfficeJets which can print, scan, copy or fax simultaneously.

Ideal for the home office, the networkable OfficeJet G series consists of the G55, G85 and G95, each offering complete functionality with print, fax, flatbed scan and flatbed copy – all in colour from just £399. The new All-in-Ones can now handle multiple tasks at the same time with ease through HP's exclusive user-friendly software. In addition, the products benefit from the advanced printing technology of the HP DeskJet 970Cxi with PhotoREt

III Precision. With this technology, these All-in-Ones deliver the ultimate photo quality on all types of paper (alternative mode of 2400dpi also available) with speedy printing at up to twelve pages per minute. Now, for the first time, the teleworker can now produce documents of the same quality as team members in the office – if not better.

Also, the ability of the OfficeJet G series to use two or more functions simultaneously, such as print and fax or print and scan, can save up to fifty percent of the time usually spent moving between one office machine to another. Not only does this save precious time during the working day, but also provides the user with true versatility. In addition, and answering the teleworker's demand for affordability and the need to save space, the HP OfficeJets are clearly a much better alternative than purchasing four separate products, each with their additional cost and use of valuable office space. All in all, the new OfficeJet G series (combined with a PC and a telephone line) can be regarded as a mini-revolution in the ever-changing world of flexible working.

By the time 2010 arrives (with twice as many of us working full-time from home as are now), IT is sure to have undergone many more significant changes. Whatever they may be, however, it is reassuring to know that HP will still be there, answering our Teleworking demands almost before they've emerged.

HP: Dedicated to help turn the vision of teleworking into an effective and sustainable business option.

For further information about HP products please call 0990 474747.

YORTEL

Teleworking has been identified as one of the priority pilot actions included in the Information Society Strategy for the Yorkshire and Humberside region through the COMPRIS project funded under the EU initiative RISI.

The YORTEL project, (initiated by one of the six COMPRIS Working Groups – 'Teleworking') was launched in 1999. The project includes elements to raise awareness about teleworking through events and support information, a training programme, and investigation of suitable structures to support freelance teleworkers.

YORTEL is led by Calderdale & Kirklees TEC working with the National Telework Association the TCA and supported by Compris Adapt a European Social funded initiative. The project has the support of Training and Enteprise Councils in Barnsley and Doncaster, Bradford, Humberside, Leeds, Sheffield, Rotherham, North Yorkshire, Wakefield and Calderdale & Kirklees and the Regional TUC. A working group to support the project includes representation from business, education and the trades union movements.

A series of events emphasising the benefits of teleworking have been held in partnership with local business groups. Responses to these have led to the creation of a forum of interest which has been sustained by the creation of a group forum and e-newsletter.

As part of the project 25 people have been trained in basic computer skills and have achieved the European Computer Driving Licence plus additional NVQ modules through Dewsbury College.

The project is due to complete in June 2000 but follow on information can be obtained from the TCA. Email: info@tca.org.uk.

compris
★ ADAPT

Index

Aberdeen City Council	*329*
Ability Enterprises (Ireland),	*261–2*
AbilityNet	*251–2*
abstracting	*148*
ACAS	*72*
access to	
technology	*252–3*
telework	*51*
training	*259–61*
work	*257–9*
accountancy services	*149*
accounting software	*306*
ACD (automated call distribution)	*98*
Action Aid	*251*
Action for Blind People	*264*
ADP (Association of Disabled Professionals)	*258,*
ADSL (asynchronous digital subscriber line)	*302*
advertising and PR (see also publicity)	*126–7*
response, 135	
Aer Rianta	*49–50*
agreements and contracts	*39, 49, 64–8*
AIB Bank	*20*
Alert Publications	*155*
Amárach consultants	*20, 30*
Analytica	*20, 79*
answering machines	*94–5, 313*
Antur Tanat Cain telebureau	*258*
Antur Teifi	*242–4*
AOL	*267–8*
Arizona State University	*61*
ASPs	*2, 311–2*
assistive technology	*253–6*
Association of Disabled Professionals (ADP)	*258*
asynchronous digital subscriber line (ADSL)	*302*
audio-typing	*148–9*
audioconferencing	*96, 291–3*
authentication systems, strong	*309–10*
automated call distribution (ACD)	*98*
Automobile Association (AA)	*3*
Babergh District Council	*200, 203*
backing up	*104, 128*
Baisley, Laura	*172–5*
balancing home and work	*105–8*
bandwidth	*292–4*
Bangemann, Martin,???	
Bank of Montreal	*86*
Barclays Bank	*8*
Barnham telecottage	*168–9*
Bates, Bryan	*225*
BBC	*58*
Belgium	*210*
BDG McColl	*69*
Benbow, Rebecca	*155*
benefit-in-kind (BIK)	*211–2*
Benefits Agency, the	*251*
Bertin, Imogen	*79, 288*
Bibby, Andrew	*74*
BIFU trade union	*72–3*
BIK (benefit-in-kind)	*211–2*
binding equipment	*314*
booking agency services	*155–6*
bookkeeping services	*149*
box-office services	*153*
Brain Train	*256*
British Gas	*252*
broadband	*30–1*
Brooks, Simon	*176–7*
BT	
agreement with union	*73*
business rate	*204*
flexible working survey	*20*
Homehighway service	*205, 290*
Inverness directory enquiries	*6, 12, 108*
Options 2000	*5*
train travel survey	*49*
Workstyles Consultancy Group	*78*
building regulations	*199–201*
BUPA (Ireland)	*217*
Burke, Margaret	*244, 249*
business	
adviser outpost	*162*
charges by public utilities	*204*
objectives	*118–9*
plans	*120–2*
rates	*203–4*
Business Link advice centres	*117, 120, 125, 162*
Cahen, Michael and Maggie	*201*
calendar managers	*306*
Californian Institute for Treatment and Prevention of Repetitive Motion Injuries	*199*
call centres	*29, 151–3*
caller line identification	*93, 308–9*
Cambridgeshire County Council	*25, 52*
Cape Clear telecottage	*169*

Cap Gemini	11	Contract Data Research (CDR)	172
capital gains tax	201, 211	contracts	
Capstick, Anthony	118, 126, 131, 135	and agreements	39, 49, 64–8
carers of disabled children	261	of service	206
cashflow	124	contracts,	
CD-ROMs	298	employees'	206
library	162	quality aspects of	240–1
certification of training	327–9	self-employed	67
chambers of trade/commerce	125	contractors, self-employed	67
Chartered Society of Physiotherapists	199	co-operative working,	
child care	59–60, 106–7	computer-supported	307
Cigna benefits processing	8	Co-operative Bank	126
Citizens' Advice Bureau	178	copyright	220–2
Clarke, Cath	264	Cork Teleworking	79
Clifford, Ian	178	Cornell University	29
Codling, Liz	86	Cornix	239–42
Collins Anne	208	costs/benefits of teleworking	41–3
communication procedures	62–3	counselling	263
communications		Countryside Agency	124
means, choosing	92–103	County Enterprise Boards	117
Communications Workers Union		couriers	103
(CWU)	73–4, 113–4	covenants,	
community resource centres	178–9	freehold	202–3
company teleworking	39–79	leasehold	203
computer		restrictive	202
-based faxes	98, 301	Cox, Denise	98, 139, 141
consultancy	151	Crossaig publishers	148
literacy	183, 327, 338–9	CSCW (computer-supported	
magazines	287	co-operative working)	307
prices	287	CTI (computer telephony	
processors	297	integration)	96, 154, 291
programming	149–50	Cumberbeach, Cathy	11, 261–2
security	307–12	Curran, Kevin	48
-supported co-operative working	307	Curry, Geoff	183
telephony integration		customer	
(CTI)	96, 154, 291	concerns	128
viruses	128, 307–8	retention	144–5
Computer Misuse act 1990	308	CWU (Communications	
Computerworld	1	Workers Union)	73–4, 113–4
computers,		cyber agents	152
laptop (portable)	30, 198	cybercafés	174
notebook	30	Daily Information	161, 165, 170
personal (PCs)	288, 294–6	data	
and technical support	100–2	conversion	150
purchasing	287–90, 296–9	encryption standard (DES)	310
reconditioned	182	entry	254
computing, portable	299–300	input	150–1
conferencing	96, 150, 291–3	processing	153
confidentiality	128	protection	217–9
consultants	78–9	security	63–4, 128, 225, 308–12
consumer protection and		Data Protection act	217–9
direct–selling rules	219–10	database software	304–5
contact managers (databases)	306	deadlines	88–90

defamation 223
Delaney, Paul 292
delivery methods 128
Deloitte and Touche 212
Denbigh, Alan 106, 137, 213, 288
Denmark 210
Department
  for Education and
    Employment 188, 256, 259, 329
  Employment 6
  of Enterprise, Trade and
    Employment (Ireland) 207
  of Environment (Ireland) 200
  of Environment, Transport
    and the Regions 9, 27
  of Trade and Industry 168, 207
  of Transport 25
DES (data encryption standard) 310
design services 156
desktop publishing (DTP) 161, 305
Development Board for Rural Wales 189
Devon and Cornwall TEC 239–42
dial-back security system 310
DIAL (Disability Information and
  Advice Line) 257
digital
  cameras 301
  video disk (DVD) 298
Digital 9
  cameras 301
  subscriber line (DSL) 293
  video disk (DVD) 298
direct selling rules 219–20
Direct Marketing Association 134
directories 127
disability and teleworking 251–65
  business case 254
  discrimination compensation 255
Disability Discrimination acts 253, 256–7
Disabled Drivers Association 11
Disability Information and
  Advice Line (DIAL) 257
disabled children, carers of 261
disabled persons,
  employment opportunities for 257–60
  networks for 261–3
  technical aids for 253–6
  telework jobs for 11
  training for 259–61
Disnet Step by Step programme 264
Display Screen directive 195
distance-learning 322–3, 331
  library 162

Dixon, Paul 260
document formatting 148–9
Doe, Linda A 101
Doyle, Shaun 71
Drew-Halkyard, Melanie 264
DTP (desktop-publishing) 305
Dublin Transportation Office
  (DTO) 27–8
Duffy, Mary 253
Duggan, Éilis 197
DVD (digital video disk) 298
Dyer, Mark 211, 149, 330
Dyer Partnership 149
EA Technology 28
Eagle, John 156
East Clare Telecottage and Training
  Associates 170–1
easyEverything cybercafes 174
Eccles House Telebusiness Centre 172
ECDL (European Computer
  Driving Licence) 327, 338–9
Ecological Building Society (EBS) 202
ecommerce (electronic commerce) 278–9
Economics of Teleworking, The 55
EDIT project 260
editing 148
Effective Quality Management 241, 249
electronic
  commerce (ecommerce) 278–9
  cottage 10
  publishing 305
email
  addresses 273
  contact details, finding 140
  and the Internet 266–86
  as communications means 98–100, 270
  facilities, "free" 269
  marketing 139–42
  messaging formats 272
  reader packages 100, 272
email,
  advantages of 99, 270
  computer-based 98, 301
  disadvantages 99–100
  file transfer by 279–80
  junk (spam) 271
  setting up 269, 272
  successful communication by 98
Empirica 182
Employed or Self-Employed 209
  advantages of 9–11
  disadvantages of 15–6
  financial implications of 205–11, 214

employers
   advantages of teleworking   6–9
   convincing   83–5
   disadvantages of teleworking   12–15
Employer Forum on Disability   257
Employment Agency
   Standards Office   207
employment   129, 157
   agencies   121, 207
   for disabled persons using
     information technology   257–60
   terms and conditions   64–7
endemic teleworking   39
Enfield, London Borough of   52
enterprise agencies   117
Enterprise Line   117
environment and teleworking   26–9
Epplestone, Janet   262
equipment   29–32, 93–4, 103, 154, 287–316
   prices   287
   rental service   154
   security   307–12
Equitable Life   160
environmental considerations   26–9
equity finance   124
ergonomics   197–8
equipment rental service   154
European
   Commission ECATT survey   18
   Computer Driving Licence
     (ECDL)   327, 338–9
   Foundation for the Improvement
     of Living and Working Conditions 1, 23
   funding   186
   Regional Development Fund   175
   Social Fund   172, 175, 189, 329, 336
   Telework Development
     Conference   253, 259
   Union
     Adapt programme,   331
     Disnet Step by Step programme   264
     HYPIT project   262
     New Opportunities for Women
       (NOW) programme   169
     Objective 5b funding   183
     SAVE project   28
     Social Affairs directorate   20
     Telework Development Project   74
     teleworking laws   210
     Working Time directive   23, 109
EUSIDIC   220
Evergreen Services   160

e-work   136–42
expenses,
   allowances   64–5
   tax-allowable   211
fair use and copyright   221–2
Faircloth, Michael   255
family life   15, 105–8
FAQs (frequently-asked questions)   282
farm skills   154, 177
FÁS   117, 330
Fast Search   275
fax
   cards (modems)   302
   direct mail shots   136
   machines   96–8, 302
   modems   302
faxing services   155
feasibility studies   39–41
FI group   55
FIET   74
file transfer by email   279–80
finance,
   equity   124
   raising   123–6, 186–9
financial implications,
   for home   201–4
   for you   205–17
fire safety   225–6
Fire Safety in the Home   225
firewalls   311
Fitzpatrick, David   98
Fletcher-Price, Ian   90, 198
Flexible Working   4, 12, 43, 49, 56,
   magazine   65, 70, 79, 90, 113
focus, keeping the   330–3
Francis-Jones, Mark   258
Friends Provident   217
FTP (file transfer program)   279–80
funding   113–6, 186–9
   training   329–30
furniture, telework   195–6
Further Education Funding Council   183
Future Work forum   114
Gateshead Learning World   328
Gee Publications   12, 18, 20
Germany   210
GlaxoWellcome   59, 61, 65, 157
Glennon, Jim   263
globalisation   26
Gloucestershire Fire and
   Rescue Service   225
Goggin, Brian   7
Golden Pages   127

Goldstein, Andrew S	124
Goodwin, Mike	171
Gordon, Gil	1, 28, 41, 73, 89, 136–7
Grampian Regional Council	11
graphics software	305
Gray, Mike	41
groupware	101–2, 307
Guest, Elayne	233
Haas, Christopher	14
Hale, Liz	336
Ham, Paul	262
hard disks	91, 298
Harrison, Paul	8
Hawkes, Mike	221
Hawkins, Pete	111
health	
and safety	60–1, 195–9
insurance	216–7
Health and Safety	
at Work act	194, 195
Executive (HSE)	195, 199
healthy living centres	179
Healy, Paul	80
Heidrich Centre for Workforce	
Development survey	3
Henley Management Centre	101–2, 114, 324
Hereford and Worcestershire	
community resource centres	178–9
Hewitt Associates	1
Hewlett Packard (HP)	7–8, 341–2
Highland and Islands Enterprise	
(HIE)	158, 172, 189
Hitchings, Kathryn	21
Hodson Noel	41, 55
Holland	210
home and work, balancing	105–8
Homebased	121
Home Employment Agency	157
Home Office Partnership (HOP)	25, 78–9
home-office	
equipment	30–1, 49–50, 57–9, 312–4
furniture	59
general considerations	90–1
insurance	60
planning implications	???
premises	50, 90–1
privacy	59
security	91
setting up	49–50
home PCs, estimates for	287–90
home-shopping	277–8
homework clubs	162

homeworking	101
scams	139
Hoskyns	11
hotdesk	300
housekeeping	104–5
How to Change your Life	
with Technology	131
HTML	272, 276, 306
editors	306
Huws, Ursula	9, 17, 20, 25, 52, 55, 70, 79, 107, 252
IBM	8, 11
ICL/CPS study	13
ICR (Internet Content Register)	221
IDC survey	2
Ievers, John	172
IHM Solutions	79
image-editing software	305–6
image presentation	128
Imperial Cancer Research Fund	252
indexing	148
information	
broking	155
services	155–6
society initiatives	20
Information Society Commission	20
Innovative Work Solutions (IWS)	129
Instant Search	8, 118, 126, 131, 135
Institute	
for the Future	4
of Employment Studies	17, 22, 29
insurance	227–8
integrated services digital network	
(ISDN)	205
intellectual property rights	220–2
Intermec Ireland	244–5, 249
International Labour Organisation	
(ILO)	23
Internet	
access	162
-based services	156
cafés	174
connectivity of computers	298–9
Content Register (ICR)	221
courses, certified	325
Explorer browser	273
listservs	280
mailing lists	139–42, 280
newsgroups	280–2
phones	274–5
proprietary services	283
Relay Chat (IRC)	282
service providers (ISPs)	268–9

services, mobile	274–5
specialist information services	282
statistics	266
telephony	31, 293
training	323–4
Internet,	
email and the	266–86
file transfer on the (FTP)	279–80
high-speed access to the	30–1, 269–70
setup needed to get online	267–8
Intrinsic	71
introduction of teleworking,	
endemic	39
planned	39
self-employment and the	16, 39
tacit	39
Inverness BT directory enquiries	6, 12, 108
Ioannou, Stelios Haji	174
IRC (Internet Relay Chat)	282
Irish Government	
Code of Practice	56, 143–4
ISDN (integrated services digital network)	3, 99, 205, 290
Isles telecroft	172–5
ISO 9000 standards	231–8
and purchasing	244–5
isolation and the teleworker	14–6, 101
ISPs (service providers)	268–9
IT issues and support	53–4
IWS temp service	129
James Paget Hospital	233
job	
clubs	162
satisfaction	9
job-hunting sites	138
jobs suitable for telework	4–6, 44
Jones,	
Chris	201
Ian	57
Mike	242
Samantha	157
journalism	148
junk email (spam)	271
Jupp, Stephen	79
Keep IT Safe and Secure	223
Kendlebell	156
Kinkos	164, 173
KITE (Kinawley Integrated Teleworking Enterprise)	9, 151, 175–6, 185, 326
Knight, Pauline	11
Knowledge Management Fieldbook	327

Knowles, Eileen	252
Korte, Werner	182
Labour Force Survey	16–7, 22, 251
Lake, Malcolm	241, 249
Lakeman, John	187
laptop computers	198
Lasair	158, 184
LEADER scheme	117
learning opportunities	318–27
distance-	322–3, 331
Learning World (Gateshead)	328
legal	195–230
Legal and General	202
Leonard Cheshire Foundation	262
LETS	162
Lewisham Borough Council	81
Lisney,	
Lisa	256
Peter	251
listservs	281
Llewellyn, Karl	121
Lloyds TSB Group	43, 51, 184
local	
council information centres	162
government and teleworking	52
enterprisecouncils (Scotland)	188
trading system (LETS)	162
Local Government	
Management Board	52, 55
Lombard North Central	6, 54
London City University	336
Lotus Notes	86, 101–2, 306–7, 324
Luke, Nana	171
McBride, Ann	261
McCaffrey, Sheila	
and Michael	9, 175–6, 326
McCormack, Joe	331
McGrath, Kieron	245–7
Mclocklin, Neil	5
Mahon, Barry	220
mail-order purchasing	289
mailing lists	132–6, 281
Manual of Remote Working	48
market research	119–20
survey	186
marketing	118
Microsoft	
Internet Explorer browser	73
network (MSN)	272
Office	303
Outlook 2000	86–7, 272
Minogue, Martina	171

MITEL	12, 17, 22, 29	Economics	27
Mitchell, Horace	27, 117	notebook computers	30
mobile		NOW scheme	169
data services	31	NREC	160
PCs	30	NVQs (National Vocational	
phones	197, 274–5, 294–6	Qualifications)	332–8
modems	293, 302	O'Brien,	
Moindrot, Paddy	184	Ken	205
Moore, Gordon	297	Malcolm	129
Moorlands telecottage	176–7, 185	objectives, establishing	118–9
Morrison, Donnie	158	Ocean telecom	292
motivation	13, 87	occupational pensions	213
Mouchel	199	OCR (optical character	
MS (Multiple Sclerosis) Society	263	recognition)	97, 158, 255, 300
MSF union	22, 71–2	office	
MSN (Microsoft network)	272	administration services	160
MTA Associates	117	equipment	312–4
multimedia services	156	services	156
Murphy,		remote	157–8
Elma	7–8	software suites	303
Edna	25	Office Ghosts	117
Murray,		Oftel	205
Bill	90, 113, 165, 171, 180–1	O'Kane, Brian	119, 124
Cathy	49, 56	Oldham Borough Council	200
national health insurance	24, 206, 216	OLRs (offline readers)	282
National		online	
Association of Teleworkers (NAT)	113	catalogues	278
Group on Homeworking	139	etiquette (netiquette)	283
Health Service (NHS)	70, 216	services	274–5
Lottery	183, 187–8	Online Travel	153
Rehabilitation Board (Ireland)	259	Open University	39, 258, 262
Union of Journalists (NUJ)	71, 73	Opportunities	257–8
Vocational Qualifications (NVQs)	332–8	optical character recognition	
Nationwide Building Society	45	(OCR)	97, 158, 255, 300
NCNT (Nigel Clare Network Trust)	261	Ottery St Mary (Project Cosmic)	178
Netaccountants	330	Outset	259–60
Netherlands	210	overheads	7–8, 32
netiquette	283	overwork	89
Netscape Navigator browser	273	Oxfordshire County Council	56, 61, 65–6
Network Personnel	261	Parents at Work	107
networks	127, 183, 188, 261–3, 302	Parry-Wingfield, Maurice	65, 212
New Information and Communications		Pascal, Jane and Eric	168–9
Technologies at Work	70	passwords	308
newsgroups	280–2	Pathfinder organisation	183
Ney, Lydia	69	PATRA report	9
Nigel Clare Network Trust (NCNT)	261	PCs (personal computers)	288
Nilles, Jack	1, 41, 255	handheld and palm-size	294–6
Nissen, Richard	155, 206	reconditioned	182
Nokia Communicator	295	pensions	24, 213–6
Norris, Barbara	178	insurance and health problems	215
Nortel Networks	14, 43	perimeter firewalls	311
Northern College	329	personal	
Norwegian Institute for Transport		computers (PCs)	288, 294–6

pension plans	214–5	responsibilities and	242
Phoenix 2	206	reviews and audits of	241
Phonenet	121	suppliers and purchasers and	241
photocopiers	312	supporting software tools for	238–9
photocopying services	155	training and competency and	241
physical security	222–4	quality	
pilot projects	40, 44–5	code of conduct, Telnet	239–40
Pink, Dan	173	for microenterprises	245–7
planned introduction		for teleworkers	231–250
of teleworking	39–40	management	231–3
planning		and Antur Teifi	242–4
and building regulations	199–201	system (QMS)	231–3, 235–7
planning, business	120–2	standards	233–5
Plantronics	199	system	231–3, 235–7
Pointer, Sue	159	quotes	122–3
policies and agreements, drafting	56–68	RAC	10, 27–8
postal equipment and services	103, 313–4	Rank Xerox	55, 70, 157
Posturite UK	90, 198	rates, business	203–4
Praa Sands	183	RATIO (Rural Area Training and	
Pratt, Joanne	7	Information Opportunities)	183
presentations software	306	RAVAN (Rural Areas Videotelephone	
press		Access Network)	168
and publicity, handling	129–32	recruiting costs	45
Price, Gill, 160		Recruitment and Employment	
pricing work	122–3	Confederation	207
Prince's Youth Business		Regional Development	
Trust (PYBT)	125, 258	Agencies	125, 183, 189
printers	300	Regus	164, 173
print-finishing equipment	314	remote	
productivity	83	office services	157–8
Project Cosmic (Ottery St Mary)	178	typing	148–9
proofreading	148	renting	
Proto-type	208	out equipment	154
Prudential Insurance	3, 45, 55	repetitive strain injury	
public relations (PR)		(RSI)	108, 195, 199, 252, 256
and advertising	126–7, 129–32	RNIB (Royal National Institute	
public utilities, charges for	204	for the Blind) telecottage	262
publicity (see also advertising		Robertson,	
and public relations)	129–31	Euan	239
publishing services	148, 156	Pat	328
publishing, desktop (DTP)	305	Rose, John	170
Putt, Mairi	261	Royal	
QMS(quality management		Agricultural Socity of	
system)	231–3, 235–7	England, (RASE)	179
complaints and	241	National Institute for the Blind	262
contractual relationships in	240	Mail	103
corrective actions and	242	ROSPA	197
establishing a	236–7	RSA examinations	59
financial affairs and	241	RSI (repetitive strain	
handling and storage and	241	injury)	108, 195, 199, 252, 256
kinds of	235–6	Rural	
production and process control and	241	Area Training and Information	
record-keeping and	241	Opportunities (RATIO)	183

Areas Videotelephone Access Network (RAVAN)	168
Community Councils	189
Development Commission	25, 188
rural urban divide	25–6
safe and legal, staying	195–230
safety,	
fire	225–6
health and	60–1, 195–9
sales-force support	162
Savill, Ted	225
scanners	300–1
scanning	158–9, 255
Scottish	
Professional Development Award in teleworking	329
Widows	160
security	222–6
computer	307–12
data	63–4, 225, 308–12
physical	222–4
telecentres and	223
selecting teleworkers	45–9, 56–7, 244–5
self-employed	
contractors	67
advantages	9–11
and the introduction of teleworking	16
and labour legislation	23
and taxation	24
disadvantages	15–6
financial implications	205–11, 214
selling	142–3
serious health problems	215
Shaw, Jeffery	255
Shell UK	60, 65, 69
Sheridan, Nicola	10
Shetland Enterprise	130
Single Regeneration Budget (SRB)	188
sites for teleworkers	141
Skandia Life	70–1
skills registers	130, 159
Slevin, Joanna	51
Small Claims Court	206
Small World Connections	
surveys	4–5, 12, 18, 20, 43, 49, 56, 65, 70, 90, 79, 113, 165, 171, 180–1
smoke detectors	225
social factors in teleworking	20–6
Society of	
Freelance Editors and Proofreaders	71
Telecoms Executives	73
software support	

for PCs	100–2
for quality management	238–9
services	149
software	303–7
anti-virus	307–8
graphics	305
Somerset Computer Services	245–7
Sonnet, Keith	198
Southern Marches Area	
Rural Telematics (SMART) project	179
spam (junk email)	271
Speakman, David	153
SPIC (Standon Parish Information Centre)	177–8
Spektra Systems	239
sponsorship	184, 187
spreadsheet software	304
SRM (Systems ReMarketing)	201
staff selection	45–9, 244–5
Standon Parish Information Centre (SPIC)	177–8
Stanford Institute for the Quantitative Study of Society in CA	89
Stanworth, Celia and John	5
start–up costs	123
Starting	
a Business in Ireland	119
on a Shoestring	124
state support	188–9
Steele, Sonia	81
Stepping Stones	155
Stoke City Council	60
Stroud District Council	200
Suffell, Helen	251
suitability for teleworking	80–3
Sulzer survey	195
Surrey	
County Council	21, 199
University headset survey	199
survival guide	80–116
Suzy Lamplugh Trust	224
Svensson, Lindsey	183
Sweden	210
Syal prison telecentre	171
Systems ReMarketing (SRM)	201
tacit teleworking	39
Tallington UK	151
tape recorders	313
tax,	
and benefit-in-kind	211–2
capital gains	201, 211
income	205–11
TCA (Telework,	79, 110–1, 114,

Telecentre	117, 136–7, 189,	success factors	180, 182
and Telecottage	196, 213, 223	telecottages,	
Association)		Swedish	165, 181
TCA/IES/MITEL survey	17, 29, 251–2	types of	165
TCA Online	114, 137	Telecottages Wales (TCW)	114
technical		telecroft, Isles (Shetland)	173–6
aids for the disabled	253–6	Telefutures study	119
technology and telework	29–32	telemarketing and telesales	151
TECs	111, 159, 188, 329	telephone	
telebureau Antur Tanat Cain	258	answering machines	94–5, 313
telebusiness centre, Eccles House	172	standard greeting	131
telebusinesses, ideas for	148–163	as communications means	93–6
Telecentre Models	181–2	audioconferencing	96, 291–3
telecentres (see also telecottages)		communication skills	84, 94–7
business opportunities for	162	enhancements	290–3
global perspective of	180–4	equipment	93–4, 290–1
location	119, 190–1	headsets	199
premises	69	recording devices	313
problems with	182	repairs	224
RATIO project	183	Telephone Preference Service	88, 220
security	223	telephones,	
setting up	184–9	ISDN	205, 290
statistics	165–7, 184	mobile	197, 274–5
Styal prison	171	skill in using	84, 94–7
Telecom Éireann (eircom)	27	telephony	291–3
telecommuting	28	Internet	293
Telecommuting Review	28	Telergos	158
teleconferencing	291–3	telesales and telemarketing	151
telecottages,		Telework	
Antur Teifi	242–4	America Association	7
Barnham	168–9	Ireland (TWI)	27, 113, 331
Cape Clear	169	Telecottage and Telecentre	79, 110–1,
cashflow	192	Association (TCA)	114, 117, 136–7, 189,
Daily Information	161, 165, 170		196, 213, 223
East Clare	170–1	Teleworker magazine	80, 97, 111, 113–4,
KITE	9, 151, 175–6, 168, 185, 326		126, 137, 159–60,
Moorlands	176–7, 165, 185		165, 190–1
Project Cosmic (Ottery St Mary)	178	teleworkers,	
RNIB (Royal National Institute		career development of	63
for the Blind)	262	categories of	80
setting up a	184–9	culture changes for	69
SPIC (Standon Parish Information		family life of	15, 59–60
Centre)	177–8	financial implications	201–17
Styal prison	171	home-based	17, 106–8
training	326	howeworker	17
visiting	185	isolation and	14, 55, 110–2
WREN	168, 179–80, 185	labour rights of	22–4
telecottages	164–80	maintaining	108–10
and centres for teleworking	164–94	monitoring and evaluation of	54–5, 58
in the UK and Ireland	190–1	motivation of	13, 55, 80–3, 87
statistics	165–7, 184	numbers of	16–20
services	162, 167	occasional	17

organisations using	46–7	implementation of	39–56
personal security of	17	in Britain	6, 22
quality for	231–50	jobs suitable for	14–6, 44
selecting	45–9, 244–5	monitoring	13
support for	31–2, 55, 112–4	pilot project	44–9
training for	50–3, 63, 317–40	planned introduction of	39
reducing overheads of	32	raising awareness of	189

teleworking
- advantages for
  - employee or self-employed   9–11
  - employer   6–9
- agreements   56–68
- and careers   15
- and communication   62–3
- and disability   251–65
- and employers   6–9, 12–5
- and globalisation   26
- and rural urban divide   25–6
- and self-employment   22, 39
- costs   41–3

teleworking companies (table of)   46–47
- disadvantages for
  - employee or self–employed   15–6
  - employer   12–5
- equipment   29–32, 287–316
- feasibility/pilot studies   39–41
- furniture   195–6
- gender issues   20–2
- jobs suitable for   4–6
- laws, EU   210
- networks for the disabled   261–3
- NVQ   332–8
- policies, agreements and unions   49
- quality management   231–50
- security risks   14–5
- work, getting   117–47
- workplaces   196–7

teleworking,
- advantages of   6–11
- carers of disabled children and   261
- background and history of   2–4
- centres for, and telecottages   164–94
- cost/benefit estimates of   41–3
- company   39–79
- definition of   1
- disability and   251–65
- disadvantages of   11–16
- gadget wish-list   97
- and Gender   20, 22, 107
- and Globalisation   17
- endemic   39
- environmental considerations of   26–9
- Handbook   113–4

- reasons for   4–6
- and Rural Development   25–6
- should you be,?   80–2
- social and economic factors in   20–6
- staff suitability for   45–9
- tacit   39
- technological trends and   29–32
- trade union guidelines on   71–4
- what is it?   1–2

Telnet code of conduct (quality)   239–40
Templeton, Brad   221
Thomas, Siân   156
Thurlow, Jane   252
time
- management   86–8
- managers (databases)   87, 306

Tolson Messenger
- insurance services   226

Touche Ross   65, 212
tourist information   155–6
trade union guidelines on
- teleworking   71–4

trade unions and consultation   68–74
Trade Union Congress (TUC)   70
training
- and delegation of learning   318
- and distance-learning   332–3, 331
- and enterprise councils (TECs)   159, 259
- and learning opportunities   318–27
- by telecottages   159, 170–1, 177, 326
- certification of   327–9
- costs   45, 158
- course types   318–23
- for managers   50–3, 320
- for teleworkers   50–3, 158, 317–40
- needs analysis   317–8
- needs, basic   319
- overheads, reducing   32, 45
- plans   50–3
- structure   330–3
- VQs (vocational qualifications)   332–8

training,
- company teleworking   320
- funds for   159, 329–30
- IT skills   319
- prioritisation of   318

translation services	59–60
Transport Research Laboratory	197
travel	
agency services	153
allowances	65–7
Treadwell, Steve	71
Trodd, Eric	27
TUC (Trade Union Congress)	70
Údarás na Gaeltachta	169
UNISON trade union	73, 198
University of Westminster	71
University for Industry project	179, 188
Usenet News	280–1
utilities, business charges by public	204
value-added tax (VAT)	217, 223
Verity, Judith	117
VHI (Voluntary Health Insurance), Ireland	217
videoconferencing	102–3, 292–3
VIP Global Consultants	78
virtual	
office	71, 160, 206–7
private networking (VPN)	310–1
Virtual Office, the	155, 206
viruses	307–8
visually-impaired, employment for the	264
Vocational Qualifications National (NVQs)	332–8
voice	
mail	93
over IP (VOIP)	31
recognition	255
Voluntary Health Insurance (VHI), Ireland	10
VQs (vocational qualifications)	332–8
Walker, Amanda	206
Walsh, Bill	22, 71
WAP	96, 274–5, 295
Web	
browsers	273–4
online commerce on the	277–8
pages	127, 275–8
creating	275–6
designing	161
publicising business on the	127, 275–8
purchasing equipment on the	287–9
reaching your audience on the	277
searching the	275
space on the Internet	269
website	
authoring	306

Welsh Development Agency	189
Western Provident Association	217
White, Stuart	27
Williams, Geoff	49
Willow CSN	152
wireless application protocol (WAP)	96, 274–5, 295
Woodhams, Anne	183
word processing	161, 303–4
word processor software	303–4
Wordwrights	7
Work Global	130
Workability	262–3
Workright Consultants	197
World	
Bank	40
Wide Fund for Nature (WWF)	27
Wide Web (see Web)	127
WREN telecottage	154, 179–80, 185
Wright, Andrew	28
Wustemann, Louis	79
Yellow Pages	120, 127
YEP Ltd	251
Yortel project	189